Strength and Honor
The Life of
Dolley Madison

Other books by Richard N. Côté

Mary's World
Love, War, and Family Ties in Nineteenth-century Charleston

Born to affluence and opportunity in the South's Golden Age, Mary Motte Alston Pringle (1803-1884) represented the epitome of Southern white womanhood. This powerful true story explores the lives of Mary; her wealthy rice planter husband, William; their thirteen children; and 337 slaves before, during, and after the Civil War. Biography. 480 pp., 86 illustrations and maps, bibliography, and full index. Available in hardcover, quality paperback, and as an audio CD set.

"This elegant saga of the Pringle family before and after the Civil War is a must read for anyone interested in Southern and American history." —Walter B. Edgar, Ph.D., author of *South Carolina: A History*.

Theodosia Burr Alston
Portrait of a Prodigy

From her birth until her marriage in 1802, Vice President Aaron Burr's daughter, Theodosia, was groomed to take her intended station in life: president, queen, or empress. From her own letters emerges the portrait of an amazing woman, a true American prodigy, and—for the twenty-one days before she vanished at sea—the First Lady of South Carolina. Biography. 416 pp., 56 illustrations and maps, bibliography, and full index. Available in hardcover and quality paperback.

"This exciting biography, fast-paced and carefully researched, reads more like a novel than the carefully researched non-fiction book it is." —Ray Swick, Ph.D., Historian, Blennerhassett Island State Park.

Strength and Honor
The Life of
Dolley Madison

Richard N. Côté

CORINTHIAN
BOOKS

Mount Pleasant, S. C.

Publishers Cataloging-in-Publication Data
(Provided by Quality Books, Inc.)

Côté, Richard N.
   Strength and Honor: The Life of Dolley Madison
by Richard N. Côté.--1st ed.
   p. cm.
   Includes bibliographical references and index.
   LCCN: 2004092710
   ISBN: 1-929175-09-4 (hc)
   ISBN: 1-929175-20-5 (pb)

   1. Madison, Dolley, 1768-1849. 2. Presidents' spouses--United States--Biography I. Title.

E342.1.M18C68 2004   973.5'1'092
                                      QBI33-2083

First Edition:
   First printing, September 2004; second printing, January 2005.

   This book is printed on archival-quality paper that meets the guidelines for performance and durability of the Committee on Production Guidelines for Book Longevity for the Council on Library Resources.

Corinthian Books
P.O. Box 1898
Mt. Pleasant SC 29465-1898
(843) 881-6080
http://www.corinthianbooks.com

Contents

Chronology

Date	Event

Date   **Event**

1751   James Madison, Jr., was born on March 16 to James Sr., and Nelly Conway Madison at Port Conway, Virginia.

1765   Dolley's parents, John and Mary Payne, moved from Hanover Co., Virginia, to the New Garden Quaker settlement in present-day Guilford Co., North Carolina.

1768   Dolley Payne was born May 20 at the New Garden settlement.

1769   The Payne family returned to Hanover Co., Virginia.

1783   John Payne manumitted his slaves and moved his family to Philadelphia.

1790   Dolley Payne married John Todd., Jr., in a Quaker ceremony in Philadelphia.

1792   Their first son, John Payne Todd, was born in Philadelphia.

1793   Their second son, William Temple Todd, was born in Philadelphia.

1793   Between September and October, a yellow fever epidemic took the life of Dolley's son, William Temple; her husband, John; and both of John's parents.

1794   Congressman James Madison, Jr., was introduced to Dolley Payne Todd by Senator Aaron Burr.

1794   Dolley Payne Todd married James Madison, Jr., on September 15 at Harewood plantation, the western Virginia home of her sister, Lucy Washington.

1794   Dolley Payne Todd Madison was disowned by the Quakers for marrying a non-Quaker.

1797- Madison retired from Congress and the Madisons
1801   spent four years at their Orange Co., Virginia, plantation, Montpellier.

1801   James Madison, Sr., Dolley's father-in-law, died at Montpellier.

Date	Event
1801–1809	Madison served as Thomas Jefferson's secretary of state. Dolley assumed the role of Jefferson's official hostess at the President's House.
1809–1813	Madison succeeded Jefferson as president. Dolley became First Lady and took on the task of decorating the unfinished President's House.
1812	The United States declared war on Great Britain.
1813	Madison was inaugurated for his second term on March 4.
1814	British troops landed and marched on Washington.
1814	On August 24, Dolley saved the portrait of George Washington and official state papers and fled only hours before British troops burned the White House.
1814	The Madisons moved into the Octagon House and lived there until the end of Madison's second term.
1814	The War of 1812 ended with the signing of the Treaty of Ghent on December 24.
1817	The Madisons retired to Montpellier.
1817–1836	Dolley helped her husband prepare his professional papers for publication. She also played hostess to legions of relatives and guests.
1817–1849	John Payne Todd's gambling losses and dissolute behavior plagued the Madisons both financially and emotionally.
1829	Nelly Conway Madison, Dolley's mother-in-law, died at Montpellier.
1832	Anna Payne Cutts, Dolley's beloved younger "daughter-sister," died.
1836	James Madison died on June 28 and was interred in the family cemetery at Montpellier.
1837	Dolley moved from Montpellier into a house on Lafayette Square, Washington, which had been willed to her by her husband. She lived there the rest of her life with her niece, Anna Payne Causten, her companion and successor to her namesake, Anna Payne Cutts.

Date	Event
1842	In dire financial straits, Dolley sold part of Montpellier to Henry W. Moncure.
1844	The House of Representatives honored Dolley with a lifetime seat in the gallery.
1844	In financial distress, Dolley sold the rest of Montpellier and its enslaved workers to Moncure.
1844	Samuel F.B. Morse invited Dolley to dictate the first personal message sent by telegraph.
1845	Dolley became a member of St. John's Episcopal Church in Washington.
1848	Congress purchased the remainder of Madison's papers from Dolley for $25,000.
1849	Dolley Madison died on July 12 after a rapid decline in her health. She was eighty-one years old. Her body was interred in the Congressional Cemetery, Washington.
1852	Dolley's remains were moved to the private vault of James H. Causten, Sr., in Washington.
1852	John Payne Todd died unmarried and was buried in the Congressional Cemetery.
1858	Dolley's remains were reinterred next to those of her husband at Montpellier.

The Payne Family

John Payne was a son of Josias Payne (1705-1792) and Anna Fleming, both Anglicans. He was born on February 9, 1740, in Hanover County, Virginia, and married Mary Coles in 1761 in Hanover County, Virginia. He and his wife applied for membership in the Quakers in 1764 and were admitted in 1765. John manumitted his slaves from 1782-1783 and then moved his family to Philadelphia in 1783. He went bankrupt and was disowned by the Quakers for insolvency in 1789. John died on October 24, 1792, in Philadelphia and is buried there in the Free Quaker Cemetery.

Mary Coles was a daughter of William Coles, an Irish immigrant, and his second wife, Lucy Winston, both Quakers. She was born on October 14, 1745, in Virginia and grew up on Coles Hill plantation, Hanover County, Virginia. Mary died of a palsy (paralysis) on October 21, 1807, at the home of her son-in-law, John G. Jackson, in Clarksburg [West] Virginia.

Their children (all birthright Quakers):

1. Walter Payne, born November 15, 1762, Hanover Co., Virginia. Died after December 26, 1784. Believed lost at sea enroute to England in early 1785.

2. William Temple Payne, born June 17, 1766, New Garden settlement, Rowan (now Guilford) Co., North Carolina. Died before January 5, 1795. Believed lost at sea.

3. Dolley Payne, born May 20, 1768, New Garden settlement, Rowan (now Guilford) Co., North Carolina. Married first John Todd, Jr. (1763-1793), a Quaker, on January 7, 1790, at Philadelphia. He died of yellow fever October 24, 1793.

Two children:

a. John Payne Todd, born February 29, 1792, in Philadelphia. Died January 16, 1852, unmarried and without issue.

b. William Temple Todd, born September 1793 in Philadelphia; died October 24, 1793, of yellow fever at Gray's Ferry, near Philadelphia.

Dolley married second James Madison, Jr. (1751-1836), an Anglican, at Harewood plantation, Jefferson Co., [West] Virginia, September 15, 1794. Disowned by Quakers for marrying out, 1794. No children. Died July 12, 1849, in Washington, D.C. Buried at Montpellier plantation.

4. Isaac Payne, born c. 1769, Hanover Co., Virginia. Disowned by Quakers for dissolute behavior, 1789. Shot dead before January 5, 1795, at Norfolk, Virginia.

5. Lucy Payne, born c. 1777, Hanover Co., Virginia. Married first, George Steptoe Washington (1771-1809), an Anglican, on May 20, 1793, in Philadelphia. Disowned by Quakers for marrying out, August 13, 1793. Four children. Married second Supreme Court Justice Thomas Todd (1765-1826), March 29, 1812, in the President's House. Three children. Died February 19, 1848. Buried Zion Episcopal Churchyard, Charles Town, West Virginia.

6. Anna Payne, born November 11, 1779, Hanover Co., Virginia. Dolley's "sister-child" who lived with Dolley until she married Richard Cutts (1771-1845), U.S. representative from Maine, on March 30, 1804. Seven children, including Mary Estelle Elizabeth Cutts (1814-1856), Dolley's niece, who wrote a two-part unpublished memoir of her aunt Dolley. Anna Payne Cutts died December 4, 1832.

7. Mary ("Polly," "Molly") Coles Payne, born 1781 in Hanover Co., Virginia. Married between October 1800 and

January 1801 U.S. Representative John George Jackson (1777-1825) of western Virginia. Died February 13, 1808. Had issue, including Dolley, Lucy, and Mary Elizabeth Payne Jackson.

8. John Coles Payne, born 1782 in Hanover Co., Virginia. Married Clara ("Clary") Wilcox (d. after 1829) in 1814. Lived at Montpellier and helped edit the James Madison papers until he moved to Kentucky and, in 1837, Illinois. Died 1841? Eight known children, including Anna C. Payne (1819-1852), who was Dolley Madison's companion after James Madison died. Anna married Dr. James H. Causten in 1850.

9. Philadelphia Payne, born July 9, 1783, and known to be living in Philadelphia in 1786.

According to Ella Kent Barnard, in *Dorothy Payne, Quakeress*, 33, "three children who were probably theirs were buried at [the burial ground of the] South River [Meeting], 'Mary, William, and Ruth Paine.'"

The Madison Family

James Madison, Sr., was a son of Ambrose Madison (c. 1700-1732) and Frances Taylor (1700-1761), both Anglicans. His parents married in 1721. James Sr. was born on March 27, 1723, in Orange County, Virginia. He married Nelly Conway, of Caroline County, Virginia, on September 15, 1749. He died on February 27, 1801, at his home, Montpellier plantation, Orange County, Virginia, and is buried there.

Nelly Conway, a daughter of Francis Conway (1696-1733) and Rebecca Catlett (1702-1760), was born on January 9, 1731, in Caroline County, Virginia. Her parents were also Anglicans. She died on February 11, 1829, at Montpellier plantation and is buried there.

Their children (all birthright Anglicans):

1. James Madison, Jr., born March 5, 1751 (o.s.) / March 16, 1751 (n.s.) at Port Conway, King George Co., Virginia. Married Dolley Payne Todd (1768-1849), widow of John Todd, Jr., on September 15, 1794, at Harewood plantation, Jefferson Co., [West] Virginia. Died June 28, 1836. No issue.

2. Francis Madison, born June 18, 1753. Married Susannah Bell, 1772. Died April 5, 1800. Issue: at least nine children.

3. Ambrose Madison, born January 27, 1755. Married Mary Willis Lee (d. 1798). Died October 3, 1793. Issue: one daughter.

4. Catlett Madison, born February 10, 1758. Died March 18, 1758, aged 36 days.

5. Nelly Conway Madison, born February 14, 1760. Married Maj. Isaac Hite, Jr. Lived at Belle Grove plantation, Belle Grove, Virginia. Died 1802. Issue: four children.

6. William Madison, born May 1, 1762. Married first Frances Throckmorton (1765-1832), ten children. Married second Nancy Jarrell in 1834. Died July 20, 1843.

7. Sarah Catlett Madison, born August 17, 1764. Married Thomas Macon (c. 1765-1838) in January 1790. Died c. 1843. Issue: eight children.

8. A Madison male child, born and died the same day in 1766.

9. Elizabeth Madison, born February 19, 1768. Died May 17, 1775, age seven years, three months.

10. A Madison child, born and died July 12, 1770.

11. Reuben Madison, born September 19, 1771. Died June 5, 1775, age three years, nine months.

12. Frances Taylor ("Fanny") Madison, born October 4, 1774. Married Dr. Robert Henry Rose II in 1800. Died November 15, 1823, Huntsville, Alabama. Issue: eleven children.

Note: This Payne and Madison genealogical information was assembled from the work of many researchers, but their information, in many cases, was not systematically documented or based on primary sources. For that reason, the genealogical details presented here are tentative, not definitive. The author welcomes documented additions and corrections, which will be incorporated into the next edition.

Introduction

In 1923, Gamaliel Bradford, one of America's earliest psychobiographers, produced a collection of sketches with the short but pointed title, *Wives*. In it he portrayed the lives of seven prominent women, including Dolley Madison, who came of age in the late eighteenth and early nineteenth centuries and married men who rose to national prominence. Bradford wrote that the seven women "would probably have lived quiet, utterly unknown lives except for their masculine connections." Given this assumption, he should have left Dolley out of his book.

When applied to Dolley, Bradford's premise is fundamentally flawed, for he asserted that her marriage to James Madison alone, rather than her heritage, natural talents, education, upbringing, free will, and choice, defined her capability for achievement. She became a national heroine, the most important and best-loved First Lady of the nineteenth century, and an unquestioned leader of society in the nation's capital through her own skills and talents, not her husband's.

Dolley did not become a woman of gracious manners, good will, high integrity, dignity, sound judgment, and extreme heroism by way of either of her two marriages. Those were her own accomplishments. Dolley seldom made waves. She generally acted in private rather than in public and never sought the limelight. Yet she effectively helped an endless list of friends, and even total strangers, and aided her brilliant, but often frail, husband. She deftly influenced and advanced many political and social causes and facilitated the healing of political differences by creating a warm, neutral social space where even the most bitter political opponents could gather and interact in peace and dignity.

She also played a myriad of other roles, including private secretary and affectionate nurse to an ailing husband; mother to a wayward son; doting sister and aunt; hostess to a huge flock of relatives; mistress of Montpellier; interior designer *par excellence* for the President's House; and the Federal City's chief fashion tastemaker and social lodestar for four decades.

Her achievements flowed from her personal qualities. Dolley was highly principled, hard-working, ebullient, and vivacious (a friend described her as "a foe to dullness in every form"), and extraordinarily adaptive. Indeed, she was the personification of the concept "bloom where you are planted."

Fate paired her with her first husband and then stole him away three years after their marriage. Fate again, this time wearing the mask of Senator Aaron Burr, brought Congressman James Madison to her doorstep. It was a good match, but it was not her "fine little husband" who led her to become one of the most-acclaimed women in American history. Were it not for Dolley's inherent good sense and upbringing, the future president's wife might have become little more than a frivolous social butterfly, as did many other wealthy Washington women. Instead, she was transformed into a gracious hostess, a consummate facilitator, and the national heroine of the War of 1812 through her own choices and actions.

Dolley's own character, not her husband's name, impelled her to take the hard, high road and put the interests of the nation over her own. Gamaliel Bradford got it all wrong. Whenever she was put to the test, Dolley proved herself to be

D. P. Madison

a woman of strength and honor. She earned her own place in history.

Biographers who have tried to find the "real" Dolley Madison have often been frustrated, for two reasons. The first was Dolley herself. Her public face—the skilled hostess, the devoted wife and mother, and the heroine of the war of 1812—has often been described. Her private side has always been masked: the woman who perpetually feared for the health of her loved ones, the facilitator of careers and finder of jobs for far-flung friends and relatives, and the politician's wife who constantly juggled the heavy responsibilities of her position as First Lady and was besieged daily by the pleas of the poor, the stricken, the incarcerated, and the greedy.

Having been steeped in the Quaker tradition of modesty, Dolley shunned public acclaim. To ensure her privacy, she built a nearly impregnable wall between her personal life and her public world. In the mid-1830s, she told a confidante that she would not give even her close friend, Margaret Bayard Smith, who was then writing a biographical sketch of her, "anything of importance in my own Eyes," which is to say, anything private from deep within her own heart. Dolley also urged her friends to burn her letters. Consequently, contemporary writers, as well as those in the century after her death, had little of substance to work with. So few of her original papers were available to journalists, novelists, historians, and biographers that every writer prior to 1958 (except for Irving Brant, a James Madison biographer), including a niece and a grandniece, spelled her name wrong, using "Dolly" instead of "Dolley." The error lingered on in publications for a century after her death and still appears on commercial products bearing her name.

The Papers of James Madison publication project at the University of Virginia changed everything. Beginning in 1956 and continuing to this day, the project's editors collected, deciphered, transcribed, and edited more than twenty-five thousand documents relating to James Madison, as well as more than two thousand letters to or from Dolley. There at

Charlottesville, I delved into her papers with the invaluable guidance of the two people who know Dolley best. The first is Dr. Holly Cowan Shulman, Research Associate Professor in the Studies in Women and Gender program at the University of Virginia, as well as Director of The Dolley Madison Project. The second is Dr. David B. Mattern, Research Associate Professor and Senior Associate Editor of The Papers of James Madison. As a result of their help, I was granted full access to the world's most complete collection of Dolley's correspondence. My goal was to find and use previously unavailable information that would cast light on this complex, private, and enigmatic woman whose accomplishments set a high and enduring standard for innovation, integrity, and heroism.

My data-gathering efforts also included research trips to read manuscripts and photograph artifacts preserved at James Madison's Montpelier, in Orange County, Virginia, and at the Greensboro Historical Museum and the Friends Historical Collection at Guilford College, both in Greensboro, North Carolina. I also drew information from twenty other archives and manuscript collections.

My chief printed resources were the twenty-six (to date) volumes of *The Papers of James Madison* and *The Selected Letters of Dolley Payne Madison*. I supplemented this material with background information and details from Ralph Ketcham's *James Madison: A Biography* and with data from approximately one hundred twenty other secondary sources and several dozen online sources.

Most Americans under the age of fifty know little about Dolley. Today, she is usually recognized as the woman whose name appears on millions of boxes of snack cakes and containers of ice cream. As David Mattern and Holly Shulman stated in the preface of their book, *The Selected Letters of Dolley Payne Madison*, "There has yet to be a good biography of Dolley Madison.... None of the biographies captures her inner life or discusses the range of her emotions or thoughts." To that I can only add, "and her many concerns," which included an endless deluge of requests for aid, assistance, and political patronage;

the reckless actions of her financially profligate son, Payne; the illnesses of her husband of forty-two years; the cruel necessity of selling Montpellier; and the grinding poverty that pervaded her last thirteen years.

Dolley's earliest surviving letter was written in 1783, when she was a fifteen-year-old Quaker farm girl preparing for her family's move from rural Virginia to Philadelphia. The first known biographical sketch of Dolley was written in June 1809, just three months after she became First Lady. The unpublished manuscript was one of a series penned by an unknown Englishwoman for Sir George Hammond, who had served as the British Minister Plenipotentiary in Philadelphia between 1791 and 1795 during George Washington's administration.

The first published biographical sketch of her was written by Dolley's friend, Margaret Bayard Smith. It appeared in 1838 in volume three of *The National Portrait Gallery of Distinguished Americans*. The most recent book-length biography of her was an admiring volume titled *Mrs. James Madison: The Incomparable Dolley*, written in 1972 by Ethel Stephens Arnett of Greensboro, North Carolina, who lived just a few miles from where Dolley was born. Other published biographies are interesting and readable, but each has its own limitations. Virtually all of them seek to glorify Dolley, something wholly unnecessary, for she earned her own place in history and needs only competent biographers, not publicists.

I began my fascination with Dolley as a result of writing my first biography, *Mary's World: Love, War, and Family Ties in Nineteenth-century Charleston* (Corinthian Books, 2000). It explores the lives of Mary Motte Alston Pringle (1803-1884); her husband, high-born Charleston rice planter William Pringle; their thirteen children; and their 337 slaves during a forty-year period before, during, and after the Civil War.

During that research, I was introduced to Mary Pringle's mysterious sister-in-law, Aaron Burr's daughter, Theodosia (1783-1813), who almost became the first empress of Mexico. Theodosia did become First Lady of South Carolina in 1812, but she vanished at sea without a trace three weeks after her husband, Joseph Alston, became governor. The biography that resulted was *Theodosia Burr Alston: Portrait of a Prodigy* (Corinthian Books, 2002).

While I was gathering data for her biography, Theodosia introduced me to her friend, Dolley Madison, much in the same way that her father, Aaron Burr, had introduced James Madison to Dolley when she was a grieving young widow in Philadelphia.

I have sought to make this presentation of Dolley's life comprehensive, accurate, and enjoyable to read, especially for those with no extensive prior knowledge of this elegant woman or her times. However, this is not an encyclopedic biography, which would be too ponderous for what I had in mind. I designed this volume with the same goal as my previous two biographies: to open up, survey, and create interest in a talented and complex woman, rather than to try to define her life in every detail. I hope this work will provide a doorway through which new generations of general readers and scholars alike will pass to meet Dolley and start their explorations of her rich and colorful life.

Mt. Pleasant, South Carolina
July 4, 2004

Richard M. Coté

CHAPTER ONE

In Harm's Way

Pennsylvania Avenue, Washington City
Wednesday morning, August 24, 1814

Since sunrise, from an upper window in the President's House, Dolley Madison had peered in vain through the highly polished brass tube of her spyglass, desperate for a glimpse of her returning husband and friends—or for any other sign of hope. By noon, watching with intense and growing anxiety, all she could make out through the trees was an occasional glimpse of the gallant but untried American militiamen and volunteers in civilian clothes. There, under the scorching sun, they worked feverishly alongside the regular soldiers from the District, Georgetown, Baltimore, and Prince George's County to mount cannons behind the bridge over the Eastern Branch River at Bladensburg, Maryland, six miles northeast of Washington City. The bridge itself was supposed to have been destroyed to delay the attacking British forces, but for reasons unknown, the order had never been carried out. The entire American defense consisted of about 7,000 men.[1]

D. P. Madison

Through the shimmering heat waves, Dolley strained her eyes to make out signs of red-coated British infantry, Royal Marines, and their artillery on Lowndes Hill, to the far side of the bridge, but all she could see was an occasional puff of smoke that accompanied the rumbling of distant guns. The swirling clouds of dust made any fine distinctions impossible. It was the end of the hottest, driest summer in anyone's memory. The parched city had felt no rain in three weeks.

As she had done countless times on that sweltering day, Dolley steadied the telescope on its tripod base and slowly panned across the horizon with intense concentration, searching yet one more time for some sign that the advancing British troops had been stopped at the bridge. Beyond the view of her lens, about 1,400 British soldiers, panting in the heat trapped by their thick, red wool uniforms and parched from hours of marching and a serious lack of drinking water, headed toward their confrontation with the Americans. These men of the 85th Regiment of the King's Light Infantry were the lead unit of the 3,000-man attacking force. The rest consisted of blue-jacketed seamen from the fleet, Royal Marines, the Twenty-first Regiment of Foot, four cannons, and a supply of a terrifying (if wildly erratic) new artillery weapon: explosive Congreve rockets. Dolley had been born a British subject herself, she mused briefly, but that was many years ago, and now, her former countrymen were, for the second time, her nation's battlefield enemies.

A telescope similar to Dolley's, made c. 1800 in Glasgow

The British troops were led by Rear Admiral Sir George Cockburn, then forty-two years old and at the pinnacle of his military career. A handsome and respected officer with eighteen months of amphibious warfare experience under his belt, he led his spearhead division from the saddle of a magnificent white Arabian stallion. A British sailor since he was nine years old, he wore a highly conspicuous all-black full-dress uniform, which included a gold-laced black hat and gold epaulettes — a tempting target for every American marksman, but an inspiration to his own troops.[2] James and Dolley Madison would never meet Lord Cockburn in person, but they would have ample time to contemplate his handiwork.

Her Irish blue eyes blazing with fierce concentration, the First Lady, now forty-six years old, tucked wayward wisps of her curly black hair into her bonnet as sweat dripped down her brow from the ninety-eight-degree heat. In her plain gray morning dress, she could easily have been mistaken for any typical Quaker woman of the city, but she was a Quaker no longer, and far from typical. Twenty years earlier, she had been severed from the embrace of the Society of Friends for taking an Anglican—the wealthy Virginia planter, James Madison—as her second husband. Furthermore, in the eighteen years between that marriage and the onset of the War of 1812, she had risen far above the role of the typical woman of her time. No person in his or her right mind would ever have called Dolley ordinary.

A few days earlier, Madison had received a note from Brigadier General William Henry Winder, commanding general of the Tenth Military District, expressing Winder's uncertainty about what the British were planning. Although the note had been addressed to Secretary of War General John Armstrong, it was delivered to the president by mistake. Madison reacted immediately. In a show of personal bravery, he rode directly into the path of the oncoming enemy. Madison, then sixty-three, took his constitutional responsibility as commander-in-chief literally and arrived just behind the front lines, which were immediately to the rear of the Bladensburg bridge.

President James Madison

D. P. Madison

Although he was there chiefly to gather intelligence on the intentions of the British troops, Madison—to the great annoyance of the battlefield commander—personally gave advice on how Winder's soldiers should conduct their last-ditch defense of the capital city. The city's population then consisted of about 6,700 free white persons, 1,300 enslaved workers, and an unknown number of free persons of color.[3]

Madison wrote to his disquieted wife on August 23, "We reached our quarters last evening at the Camp between 8 & 9 o'c. and made out very well. I have passed the forenoon among the troops, who are in high spirits & make a good appearance. The reports as to the enemy have varied every hour. The last & probably truest information is that they are not very strong, and are without cavalry and artillery, and of course that they are not in a condition to strike at Washington."[4]

The Washington newspapers had downplayed the likelihood of any attack on the capital city. The nation's military leaders and elected officials had made little preparation for war on America's home soil. They, as well as the president, would soon find their optimism fatally mistaken.

On the morning of the twenty-third, Dolley wrote to her sister, Lucy Payne Washington:

My husband left me yesterday morning to join Gen. Winder. He enquired anxiously whether I had the courage, or firmness to remain in the President's house until his return, on the morrow, or succeeding day, and on my assurance that I had no fear but for him and the success of our army, he left me, beseeching me to take care of myself, and of the cabinet papers, public and private. I have since received two despatches from him, written with a pencil; the last is alarming, because he desires I should be ready at a moment's warning to enter my carriage and leave the city; that the enemy seemed stronger than had been reported and that it might happen that they would reach the city, with intention to destroy it. I am, accordingly ready; I have pressed as many cabinet papers into trunks as to fill one carriage; our private property must be sacrificed, as it is impossible to procure wagons for its transportation. I am determined not to go myself until I see Mr Madison safe, and he can accompany me, as I hear of much hostility towards him.... My friends and acquaintances are all gone.[5]

The day that Madison took to the field, his secretary of war, General John Armstrong, a "stubborn, arrogant" New York Democrat, wrote to Major General John Van Ness, chief of militia in the District of Columbia, about the British. "They would not come with such a fleet without meaning to strike somewhere. But they certainly will not come here! What the devil will they do here? No! No! Baltimore is the place, Sir. That is of so much more consequence."[6]

While her husband was gone, Dolley maintained a brave front. To keep up the morale of the city and minimize the fear of a British invasion, the Madisons had not cancelled any scheduled social events at the President's House for the twenty-third. Nevertheless, Eleanor Young Jones, wife of the secretary of the navy, sent the First Lady a polite letter, laced with fear, expressing her apologies and her plight.

In the present state of alarm and bustle of preparation, for the worst that may happen, I imagine it will be mutually convenient, to dispense with the enjoyment of your hospitality today — and therefore pray you to admit this as an excuse for Mr. Jones, Lucy and myself. Mr. Jones is deeply engaged in dispatching Marines and attending to other public duties. Lucy and myself are busy packing up ready for flight, but in the event of necessity we know not where to go, nor have we any means yet prepared for the conveyance of our effects. I sincerely hope the necessity may be averted, but there appears to be serious cause of apprehension. Our carriage horse is sick, and our

D. P. Madison

coachman has left us, or I should have called last evening to know what Mrs. Cutts had determined upon—I feel great solicitude on her account.[7]

Madison returned from the front to spend a few hours with his wife that night. It was the last time they would spend together in their house on Pennsylvania Avenue. Wednesday morning, August 24, Madison received a distraught letter from General Winder, stating that he had received "very threatening" news and required "the speediest counsel." Madison immediately mounted his horse and set out again for Winder's camp, then near the Navy yard.[8] He was accompanied by Secretary of War John Armstrong, Secretary of State Colonel James Monroe, other government officials, and several friends. Almost all the residents of the capital city were in full flight, having already decided how the battle would go.

At the President's House, Dolley hurriedly read the morning newspapers but probably put little stock in what they said. Washington's *National Intelligencer*, published by her close friend, Samuel Harrison Smith, and edited by Irishman Joseph Gales, Jr., was the unofficial voice of the government.

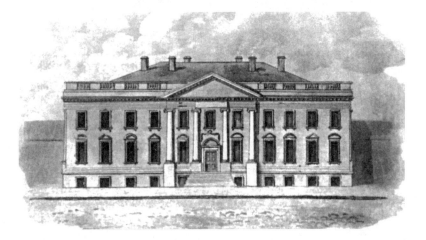

The President's House in 1807

It stated with confidence, "We feel assured that the number and bravery of our men will afford complete protection to the city. The Baltimore troops, about 2,500 [6,000 had been requested], completely equipped, have arrived in our vicinity; and last night 700 men [2,000 had been ordered] reached the city from Virginia. These and reinforcements every moment expected, added to our other forces, will secure the safety of the metropolis."[9]

The Georgetown *Federal Republican* was equally optimistic. It claimed, "It is highly improbable that. . . the enemy would advance nearer to the capital," blithely ignoring the fact that the British had been advancing steadily into the Chesapeake Bay, up the Patuxent River, and then overland towards Washington for two weeks.[10]

By noon, all Dolley could see through her glass was an occasional puff of blue-gray smoke on the horizon. Indeed, the very morning of the attack, none other than the secretary of war himself assured her that there was no danger.[11] Dolley evidently did not share the secretary's confidence, for she started preparing for the worst, while still maintaining a public appearance of calm.

Twice already that day, the silence of the nearly deserted President's House had been broken by visits from Washington's mayor, Dr. James H. Blake, who warned the First Lady of the increasing peril and urged her in the strongest terms to flee immediately. Blake was in a position to know the danger level, as he had posted an urgent notice in the *National Intelligencer* that morning, urging all able-bodied white citizens and all free men of color residing in the city to form up the next morning at six o'clock to proceed to Bladensburg and create earthwork defenses for the troops.[12] Despite the mayor's strong exhortations, Dolley remained, awaiting word from her husband.

With a finely woven handkerchief, she dabbed perspiration from her brow and swatted at the mosquitoes that swarmed up mercilessly from the hot, humid swamps that surrounded the thinly populated new city and had given it a dubious reputation as a place of residence. Her sharp mind

D. P. Madison

raced through a review of her limited options. The first was to remain and stand watch over her home and the priceless national treasures it sheltered — and risk almost certain capture by the enemy. The second was to abandon the mansion, taking with her to safety what few things of the greatest public value she could arrange to be transported. The third option, to surrender, never entered her mind. She took a deep breath, pulled herself up to her full five feet, six inches, and waited.

Fifteen months before the British threatened Washington, Dolley had written her first cousin, Edward Coles, who served as her husband's private secretary, a spirited letter about the possibility of danger. She stated boldly, "I have allways been an advocate for fighting when *assailed*, tho a *Quaker* — I therefore keep the old Tunesian Sabre within my reach."[13] Now, two years into the war with Britain, which was called the "Second War of Independence" by some and "Mr. Madison's War" by his detractors, Dolley was standing guard over the nearly deserted president's mansion and all its public treasures. Her pacifistic Quaker upbringing notwithstanding, she came within minutes of being forced to put the Tunisian sabre to its intended use.

Although British newspapers had openly discussed the possibility of an invasion of Washington City on many occasions, most of the American lawmakers had not seriously considered the magnitude of the threat to the nation's capital until shortly before the battle. That proved to be a disastrous mistake. Dolley was more sensitive to the threat than most of her contemporaries. Four weeks before the British invaded Washington, she wrote with tepid optimism to her friend, Hannah Nicholson Gallatin, the wife of Swiss-born Albert Gallatin, Madison's secretary of the treasury, then in Europe negotiating what would become the Treaty of Ghent:

> We have been in a state of purturbation here, for a long time — The depredations of the Enemy approaching within 20 miles of the City & the disaffected, makeing incessant difficulties for the Government.

Such a place as this has become I cannot discribe it—
I wish (for my own part) *we ware* at Philadelphia. The
people here, do not deserve that *I* should prefer it—
among other exclamations & threats they say, if Mr.
Madison attempts to move from *this House*, in case of
an attack, they will *stop him* & that he shall *fall with
it*—I am not the least alarmed at these things, but entirely disgusted, & determined to stay with him. Our
preperations for defence by some means or other, is
constantly retarded but the small force the British have
on the Bay will never venture nearer than at present
23 miles.[14]

She was wrong. The British had not forgotten their humiliating defeat at Yorktown thirty-one years earlier. They
also wanted revenge for the burning of the Parliament buildings
in York (now Toronto, Ontario) Canada by the Americans in
1813. That rash, unprofessional, and completely unnecessary
act alone was sufficient to doom Washington City. United
States diplomats in Europe had warned the Madison administration that Napoleon's defeat in April 1814 would free
thousands of British soldiers to take on the Americans. With
the French war behind them, the soldier-filled British ships
wasted little time in sailing for the United States.

On August 6, Dolley wrote to her son, John Payne Todd,
then in London, that she was still optimistic. "Nothing has
occured either publick or private, worth writeing, since my
last—The British on our shore's are stealing & destroying private property, rarely comeing to battle, but when they do, are
allways beaten."[15]

Although Washington offered little of strategic importance
to the British, the invasion and destruction of the young
nation's capital would be a symbolic defeat of immense pro-
portions, if for no other reason than its humiliation value.
The haughty British commander-in-chief of the North American expedition, Vice Admiral Sir Alexander Cochrane, a man
with "good organizing ability, good connections, and a strong

D. P. Madison

distaste for Americans," was prepared to "chastise Jonathan" and give the former colonists "a complete drubbing."[16] Although the city had adequate time to prepare for an attack—the war was, after all, nearly two years old—the necessary preparations had not been made. Almost to a resident, everyone had vastly underrated the willpower and vindictive intent of the British troops who loomed close to the city.

The field commander of the British fighting forces, Rear Admiral Cockburn, was the second-ranking naval officer of the expedition. He was totally committed to his orders, which were explicit: destroy the seat and emblems of power of the former colony that had had the effrontery to declare war on Great Britain. Cockburn's objective was equally unequivocal: the unconditional submission of the United States.[17]

Two years of sporadic fighting along the Canadian border had brought no decisive victory for His Majesty and his vast military machine, and London was impatient. When the British invasion fleet arrived off the Atlantic coast late in the summer of 1814, the size of their armada was immense: more than seventy warships. On August 18, a squadron entered the Chesapeake Bay and sailed up the Patuxent River. As the troops landed and proceeded inland, they encountered little resistance. Less than a week after setting foot on American soil, they attacked Bladensburg, Maryland, a two-hour march from Washington City.

While Dolley was extremely concerned about the safety of her husband, the residents of Washington were equally concerned about their city. Dolley knew that there was increasing hostility toward the president. The American people blamed him for economically debilitating trade sanctions brought about by the war, and the sense of sacrificial patriotism so evident during the Revolution was lacking. Now, Washingtonians gathered outside the President's House, concerned that the Madisons would "sneak off to save themselves," but James and Dolley Madison had no such thing in mind.[18]

Even in the hours of greatest terror, Dolley did not ask her younger sister, Anna Payne Cutts, to keep her company in the President's House while their fate was being decided. Although Anna lived nearby, and the two sisters shared the most intimate details of their lives with each other, Dolley felt that her every movement would be scrutinized, and she did not want to do anything to suggest that she was frightened or lacked confidence in the troops.

Instead, the strong-willed First Lady firmly held her ground, waiting to receive further word from her husband about the battle, which her spyglass clearly indicated was underway. None arrived. By early afternoon on the twenty-fourth, everyone who was still in the city could hear the sound of cannon fire. At Bladensburg, the battle started between noon and one o'clock and raged for several hours. In the afternoon, the guns fell silent.

Forty-one-year-old Dr. James Ewell, the city's most respected physician, peered out of a third-floor window of his fine brick house across the road from the east front of the Capitol and saw a cloud of dust on the horizon. The dirt rose from the feet of the American soldiers and their horses fleeing the battlefield. Ewell first saw only a few men, then small knots of them, then a frightened horde, gripped by terror. When he saw Secretary of War Armstrong among the stampeding soldiers, he knew that all was lost. Unnerved by the exploding Congreve rockets and the polished precision of the British regulars with bayonets fixed, the American defenders had lost their nerve. Their formations dissolved into a headlong tidal wave of retreat; the men running pell-mell for the city. Inside their home, Dr. Ewell's daughters ran in terror to their mother, who was sobbing, "What shall we do? What shall we do? Yonder they are coming."[19]

Across the city at his home on F Street, Superintendent of Patents William Thornton saw a mounted courier riding for his life towards the President's House. The news, he thought, could only be grave.[20] His fears were confirmed. The rider was Madison's free black servant, James Smith, who had raced from Bladensburg to the president's mansion, waving his hat and shouting, "Clear out, clear out! General Armstrong has ordered a retreat."[21] He delivered a penciled note in Madison's handwriting to Dolley. It was short and clear: the British had broken through their lines. She should run for her life.[22]

Dolley did not have to look far for confirmation that the worst had come to pass. On Pennsylvania Avenue, all was in chaos. As she peered out the window, she saw that the terrified populace of Washington had already formed a mob, using every horse, cart, and wagon available to drag their valuables out of the path of the advancing enemy. Colonel Henry Carberry, whose detachment of 100 troops had been charged with guarding the President's House, had already fled with his men. Madison's valet and butler, Paul Jennings, the fifteen-year-old mulatto son of an Englishman and a Madison slave woman, later recalled that "people were running in every direction" in the final hours before the British overwhelmed Washington's defenders.[23] Ninety percent of Washington's population had already abandoned the city.

Dolley remained resolute. She later wrote to Mrs. Benjamin Latrobe, "I confess that I was so unfeminine as to be free from fear, and willing to remain in the *Castle*. If I could have had a cannon through every window, but alas! those who should have placed them there, fled before me, and my whole heart mourned for my country!"[24]

Jean Pierre Sioussat, known as "French John," the Madisons' sophisticated *major domo*, offered to spike the remaining twelve-pounder cannons, which stood at the gate of the President's House, and to "lay a train of gunpowder which would blow up the British, should they enter the house."[25] Dolley declined his impassioned offer, stating, "I positively objected, without being able, however, to make him understand why all advantages in war may not be taken." [26]

By mid-afternoon of the twenty-fourth, it was clear that the inevitable would come to pass. Dolley continued her letter, "Three O'clock. Will you believe it, my Sister? We have had a battle or skirmish near Bladensburg, and I am still here within sound of the cannon! Mr. Madison comes not; may God protect him! Two messengers covered with dust, come to bid me fly; but I wait for him."[27]

As the enemy bore down on the young republic's capital, Paul Jennings was setting the table for dinner, which, according to the Madison custom, was customarily served at four o'clock. Madison had earlier directed that his entire cabinet, some military officers, and friends would be dining with them that afternoon, and until he cancelled the order, preparations for the president's dinner would continue.

At Dolley's direction, their renowned French chef, Pierre Roux, and his staff had prepared a sumptuous meal, but the hearty smells of meat cooking on the kitchen's spits and the rich aroma of brimming saucepans were now mingled with the acrid odor of gunpowder that wafted in through the windows from the conflict just a few miles away.

Nevertheless, just before four o'clock on the afternoon of August 24, Paul Jennings finished setting the table with a damask tablecloth, matching napkins, and enough fine china, silver, engraved wineglasses, and chilled ale, cider, and Madeira wine to accommodate forty guests. Neither he nor his mistress could have conceived that the diners who sat at the table five hours later would all be British soldiers.

DIEU ET MON DROIT

GEORGE III.

London Published as the Act directs by January 1. 1803. by J. Stratford Holborn Hill.

R. Corbould del.

C. Warren sculp.

CHAPTER TWO

A Child Among Friends

New Garden Monthly Meeting
Rowan County, North Carolina
Ye 20 of ye 5 mo. 1768

On May 20, 1768, an ordinary spring day in the American colonies, His Royal Highness, George III, King of Great Britain, France and Ireland, Duke of Brunswick-Luneburg, Elector of Hanover, and Defender of the Faith, acquired by birth, as he did every day, a number of new subjects. Although he was quite unaware of it, one of them was Dolley Payne, the third child of John and Mary Payne. She made her inconspicuous debut onto the world's stage in a small, isolated Quaker frontier settlement known as New Garden, in the central part of His Majesty's Province of North Carolina.

George III was to play a substantial role in her life. It was during his reign that the Americans revolted against British rule, and the king's troops and ships—the mightiest war machine in the world at that time—were defeated. George III never forgot the humiliation, but by the time British troops

$\mathcal{D}.\mathcal{T}.$ Madison

invaded the United States in 1814 during what was then called "the second war of American independence," he was in the advanced stages of dementia, and his young female subject never got to meet him.

In 1811, his son, the Prince Regent, later George IV, assumed rule of the kingdom. Three years later, he received the news that his troops had burned Washington, sending the American government into temporary flight, along with its president, James Madison, and his wife. It wasn't until 1814 that a British monarch finally heard of the woman named Dolley Payne Madison.

The outcome of the War of 1812 resolved little and ended with the signing of the Treaty of Ghent on December 24, 1814, four months after Dolley and her husband, James Madison, had been burned out of their house. They learned of the treaty seven weeks later, and celebrated it with champagne. The British had been chased out of the United States and that was a sweet victory, but in order to keep them as a trading partner, so necessary to the survival of the still-young nation, concessions to that victory had to be made, and they included the end of the dream of an American Canada.

Dolley outlived not only George III and IV but also William IV. She never met any of these British rulers, but as hostess for President Thomas Jefferson during his two terms as president and as First Lady during James Madison's own two terms, she entertained their ambassadors. During her life, she became one of the best-known and best-loved women in America. Indeed, she is better remembered than some of the kings under whose rule she lived and many of the presidents who succeeded her husband in office.

At the time of Dolley's auspicious, if unheralded, birth at the edge of white civilization in the near-wilderness of central North Carolina, a person's place in society was determined by gender, religion, and the character of the family into which he or she was born. Most people lived in small, closely knit settlements and knew everyone else's business — as well as their secrets.

By the outbreak of the Revolution, when Dolley was eight years old, all thirteen British colonies in North America together had a population of only about 1.6 million people — about the same as present-day Nebraska. The vast majority of them were of English or Scottish descent and lived east of the Allegheny Mountains; south of Boston, Massachusetts; and north of Charleston, South Carolina.

In such a group of colonies, where people lived chiefly in small clusters widely separated from each other, good relations with one's family, relatives, friends, and neighbors were paramount in importance. Any relative of Dolley's, no matter how distant, was always welcomed as if he or she were a member of the family's inner circle. Dolley's belief in the importance of kinship is reflected in the delighted comments of Elbridge Gerry, Jr., son of Vice President Elbridge Gerry. After a visit to the First Lady in 1813, the younger Gerry recalled, "I was soon informed by her, that I was second cousin to her, and felt highly honored, and peculiarly favored in being related to a lady, who is not rivaled in excellence and worth."[1] Throughout her life, Dolley's focus on nurturing close-knit and cordial relationships with her vast cousinage demonstrated the importance of ancestry, parentage, and family in her life and the life of the young nation.[2]

In both pre- and post-Revolutionary America, the personal impact of institutions, such as legislatures, local governments, and churches, was limited chiefly to issues of taxation, record-keeping, lawbreaking, and regulation of only the most flagrant examples of public immorality. During the colonial period, with no national government or political parties and only weak provincial governments, it was the interrelationship between family members, relatives, friends, and business colleagues, bolstered by the church, that provided the social glue which held society together. The parishes of the Anglican Church were the basic units of government in the South, where Dolley spent most of her life. Each parish church had a minister in its pulpit, but his duties were strictly ecclesiastical. The vestrymen and wardens of the parish served both

D. P. Madison

church and state. As officers of the church, they oversaw the construction, maintenance, and financial operations of the church. They were also responsible for ensuring that the Sabbath was respected and that all citizens, regardless of denomination, registered their births and marriages in the parish register. As civilian officers of the parish, they served as the equivalent of present-day county commissioners. They supervised the maintenance of the roads, bridges, and canals; regulated public markets; cared for the poor; tried, punished, and sometimes executed slaves; adjudicated grievances; and punished whites who broke local ordinances. White colonists accused of major crimes were tried by the courts.

Governments, both provincial and local, were administered by male relatives: grandfathers, fathers, sons, uncles, and cousins. Many public offices and church pulpits were virtually hereditary. Nepotism was the standard. Indeed, it was viewed as the best way to maintain public order and stability and to facilitate communication in a thinly populated society. Public and church offices were closed to women, save for one exception: the Quaker church. There, women could, and did, speak freely and hold the same offices as men.

Communication was chiefly a person-to-person affair. Although newspapers existed, they were relatively few in number, were published only in major population centers, and were chiefly devoted to disseminating information about shipping and commerce. Virtually all community news was communicated by word of mouth and personal letter. Because of the high cost of postage, the relatively few post offices, and the lack of privacy (postmasters, who were political appointees, routinely opened and read private mail), the written word traveled chiefly in the pocket or purse of a trusted friend or family member.

Families frequently changed their residence as they sought ever better opportunities. Dolley's family was a good example. In their first twenty-two years of life together, which lasted from 1761 to 1783, John and Mary Payne married in Virginia and had one son, Walter. Next they moved to North Carolina for just over three years and had two more children, William Temple and Dolley. Then they moved back to Virginia for fourteen years and there had five more children. Finally, they moved to Philadelphia, where they had their final child for a total of nine.

When people moved from one place to another, or traveled to distant places, they took with them formal letters of introduction from relatives, business colleagues, and the religious congregations from which they were departing. If the newcomers came from a distant family known to be of good character and had proper letters of introduction, they would quickly be welcomed into their new community. Without references, newcomers would be viewed with suspicion until it was known where they had come from and, more important, which family they belonged to.

This protocol was not an act of snobbery but a commonsense method of protection; a way to determine the nature of the stranger's character and whether or not he or she could be trusted. Those without verifiable family references were likely to be excluded from the companionship of their neighbors until they could personally demonstrate their character—a time-consuming process. For all these reasons, one's family reputation was one's passport through life. Each time the Paynes moved from one place to another, they carried a letter of reference from their former Quaker meeting. Upon arrival at their destination, the presentation of this credential guaranteed them a warm and immediate welcome.

No images of Dolley's grandparents, Josias and Anna Fleming Payne, have survived, but they could have afforded to have portraits painted, as they were wealthy. Josias and Anna settled in Goochland County, which lies along the northern shore of the James River above Richmond, and lived in the top echelon of the early Virginia plantation aristocracy.

Dolley's grandmother was known as "the beautiful Anna Fleming," the granddaughter of Sir Thomas Fleming, second son of the Earl of Wigdon of Scotland. He married a Miss Tarleton, of Wales, emigrated to America in 1616, landed at

James Town and settled soon thereafter in the county of New Kent, where he lived and died.[3] This claim has been challenged, however, and one biographer wryly noted that "Virginians of that day were wont to trace their ancestry to the aristocracy of Great Britain as naïvely as the Roman emperors derived theirs from the gods."[4]

Anna, who was an Anglican, not a Quaker, was referred to as Dolley's "worldly grandmother" and allegedly spoiled young Dolley with gifts of jewelry not allowed by her religion.[5] In addition, her elegance, good looks, and fine clothing may well have influenced Dolley's flair for fashion later in life. According to a late nineteenth-century descendant, Anna inherited part of her good looks from her ancestor, Pocahontas, the legendary Native American princess from Virginia.[6] The accuracy of her noble connections notwithstanding, her good character and wealth qualified her for membership in the first tier of Virginia's tobacco-planting gentry.

Josias Payne, a wealthy planter of English ancestry, was, like Anna, a fine catch. He was the grandson of George Payne, and served as justice of the peace and high sheriff of Goochland County.[7] Like his grandfather and father before him, Josias was a public-spirited man. He shouldered the burden of service to his community through service as a vestryman of his parish and also as a member of the Virginia House of Burgesses from 1761 to 1769. Josias owned six plantations encompassing more than 3,200 acres of prime plantation land along the James and Anna Rivers, as well as a large enslaved labor force to work them.[8] The great planters of the Tidewater region, whose wealth was built through a combination of inheritance, intelligence, good business choices, and the work of thousands of African-American slaves, were the ruling class of eighteenth- and early nineteenth-century Virginia. Upon his death in 1785, Josias Payne's material legacy was divided among seven children (including his fourth son, John Payne, who would marry Mary Coles and become Dolley's father), and two grandchildren.[9]

An English traveler painted a colorful portrait of the wealthiest of the Anglican planters, which is to say, the class to which all the other planters aspired to belong. "These in general have had a liberal education, possess enlightened understanding and a thorough knowledge of the world, that furnishes them with an ease and freedom of manners and conversation highly to their advantage in exterior, which no vicissitudes of fortune or place can divest them of, they being actually, according to my ideas, the most agreeable and best companions, friends and neighbors that need be desired. The greater number of them kept their carriages and have handsome services of [silver] plate; but they all, without exception, have studs (horse breeding facilities), as well as sets of elegant and beautiful horses."[10]

Their gentility, conviviality, and love of fine horses aside, the gentlemen who founded the first and second generations of the great Virginia plantation dynasties often did not have the educations they provided to their sons and grandsons. Alexander Spotswood, a Scot who served as Virginia's lieutenant governor from 1710 to 1722, complained to the members of the House of Burgesses that "the grand ruling party in your house has not furnished chairmen of two of your standing committees who can spell English or write commonsense, as the grievances under their own handwriting will manifest."[11]

Dolley took great pride in the maternal side of her ancestry, the Coles and Winston families of Virginia. Both families were Quakers and, by the 1760s, had become quite prosperous. This made them the social and economic equals of their "worldly" neighbors, but their Quaker beliefs and practices set them apart from the Anglicans who surrounded them.

The immigrant ancestors of the Coles branch consisted of two brothers, William and John Coles, who lived in Enniscorthy, a town on the west bank of the river Slaney, in County Wexford, about four miles from the port city of Wexford, Ireland. Of these two, Dolley's grandfather was William Coles, who married Lucy Winston Dabney, the widow of William Dabney.[12] They settled in Hanover County, Virginia, on a plantation they named Coles Hill and had three

D. P. Madison

known children: Mary Coles, who married John Payne and became Dolley's mother; Walter Coles, who married Sally A. Stevenson; and Lucy Coles, who became the second wife of her cousin, Isaac Winston. Whatever his profession of faith in Ireland, a 1757 Quaker document stated that William Cole[s] made an open confession of truth.[13]

John Coles, Sr., had settled in America shortly before his brother, William. William, Dolley's maternal grandfather, was probably the second husband of Lucy Winston, who married first William Dabney. John Coles made his fortune as a merchant in Richmond and married Lucy's sister, Mary Winston. Lucy, Mary, and their sister, Sarah, were the daughters of Isaac Winston, an early Virginia Quaker. After the 1731 death of Sarah Winston's first husband, Colonel John Syme, she married John Henry. This marriage produced a son who became one of America's best-known patriots. He was Patrick Henry, and his plantation home, "Scotchtown," briefly sheltered Dolley and her family during her girlhood. Henry, thirty-two years her senior, was one of Dolley's legion of cousins. In 1775 when she was just seven years old, it was he who stood before the House of Burgesses and proclaimed in a strong, clear voice for all to hear, "I know not what course others may take; but as for me, give me liberty or give me death."

Isaac Winston's son, William, the brother of Lucy, Mary, and Sarah, was said to have "wild blood in his veins."[14] William was a great hunter, admired by the Indians, and gained distinction as a soldier during the Revolution. William's son, Judge Edmund Winston, read and practiced law with his cousin, Patrick Henry. When his law partner died in 1799, Judge Winston married his cousin's widow, Dorothy "Dolly" Dandridge Henry, another one of the many relatives close and dear to her cousin, Dolley Madison.[15]

Isaac Winston died in 1760, long before his grandson, Patrick Henry, who later became a fire-breathing revolutionary. According to one biographer, Isaac allegedly thought of Patrick as his "wayward grandson" and "unworthy even of mention in his will." His granddaughters, Lucy and Mary Coles, fared better, each receiving £45 to be paid to them when they came of age or married.[16]

Dolley's paternal great uncle, John Coles, a Quaker, erected an impressive country home in Albermarle County, Virginia. He named it Enniscorthy, after the place of his birth in Ireland.[17] John and Mary Winston Coles had five children, one of whom, Colonel John Coles, Jr., had eight children of his own. One was Edward Coles, a cousin of Dolley's own generation, although eighteen years her junior. Edward was a close friend and later served as the private secretary to her second husband, James Madison, from 1809 until 1815. Another was Edward's brother, Isaac A. Coles, who served in the same capacity to presidents Jefferson and Madison.

Their sister, Rebecca Coles, married Richard Singleton of South Carolina, and their daughter, Angelica Singleton, was the beneficiary of Dolley's matchmaking talents. She introduced Angelica to Abraham Van Buren, son of President Martin Van Buren, with the hope, as legend has it, that the two would marry and Angelica would serve her father-in-law as hostess at the President's House. To Dolley's delight, the romantic plot succeeded.[18] Dolley loved all the Coles cousins—and all her other cousins, for that matter—as much as her own brothers and sisters. Thus, Dolley Payne was a typical child of the American colonial period: the product of a complex intermarriage of English, Welsh, Scottish, and Irish ancestors.

If we assume that the fruit falls close to the tree, then we must conclude that Dolley's parents, John and Mary Coles Payne, were indeed people of good character, as both were deeply respected and made indelible marks on their community. Few people who met them during their brief sojourn in New Garden, the visionary Quaker community in the North Carolina Piedmont; at the Cedar Creek Meeting in Hanover County, Virginia; or at the Pine Street Meeting or the Free Quaker Meeting in Philadelphia ever forgot them. They passed on their ethic of hard work, personal responsibility, devotion to God, idealism, and respect for their fellow men and women to all their children. Dolley, in particular, proved herself a worthy fruit of her deeply rooted family tree.

Dolley's father, John Payne, was born on the plantation of his father, Josias Payne, in Goochland County, Virginia, on February 9, 1740 (o.s.).[19] Like his father and grandfather before him, he was an Anglican. John, a planter of moderate but not considerable means, is said to have received "the upbringing of a cultured Virginia gentleman. He had gracious manners, polished speech, and a notable talent for keeping records."[20]

John's father, Josias Payne, gentleman, a planter and slave owner, served as a justice of the peace, high sheriff, vestryman in the Anglican Church, and member of the House of Burgesses from Goochland County from 1761 to 1769. He acquired thousands of acres of Virginia's richest land on the James River, in Goochland County, southeast of Charlottesville.[21]

Dolley's mother, Mary Coles, was born October 14, 1745 (o.s.), at her parents' plantation, Coles Hill, in nearby Hanover County.[22] John and Mary were married there in 1761, when he was twenty years old and she was scarcely sixteen. There the newlyweds set up housekeeping on a 200-acre farm, which belonged to his uncle, Colonel John Payne, and lay adjacent to Little Bird Creek. On May 13, 1763, [Colonel] John Payne conveyed to John Payne, minor, the son of Josias Payne, 200 acres of land on Little Bird Creek, where the younger John Payne, the newlywed, was already living.[23] Josias Payne reiterated the transaction in his will: "I confirm the gift made to my son John of Two hundred acres of land on the little Bird Creek as also Four hundred acres in the fork of James River with the following Negroes, Peter, Ned and Bob."[24] John's father died in 1785. Thanks to his generosity, the newlyweds got off to a solid start.

At the time of their marriage in 1761, John Payne, the son of Anglican parents, was not a Quaker; Mary was.[25] It wasn't until after their marriage that he converted, and they both applied for membership in the Cedar Creek (sometimes called

Cedar Creek Monthly Meeting

New Garden Monthly Meeting

Quaker settlements in Virginia and North Carolina

the Caroline) Monthly Meeting in Virginia. They were not immediately accepted, and patiently waited through an unusually long period of investigation before being taken into fellowship.

The Society of Friends was one of several religious groups that emerged in seventeenth-century England attempting to purify the Anglican Church. Most of these groups rejected ecclesiastical and royal authority and called for more democratic forms of governance. About 1650, George Fox began preaching that all people have an "inner light" and that no one is greater or lesser than another. His designation of "Friends" implied equality. In refusing to kowtow to the British hierarchy, he was repeatedly jailed and members of his Society were constantly harassed. The British public derisively dubbed them "Quakers." At first, Friends resented the nickname, but gradually it became accepted as a matter of course.[26]

The Quakers constituted a small minority of the English population but stood out because of their practices. They refused to pay tithes or register births and marriages with the Church of England. The resulting harassment and persecution by Anglicans gave the Quakers yet one more reason to band together, put distance between themselves and their antagonists, and take care of their own.

Fox's doctrine of equality eventually led to radical political stands: equality for women, the abolition of slavery, compassion for the mentally ill, and the refusal to bear arms. But at the same time, the Society became ever more narrow in focus. Fox felt that since all promptings to action should come from within, one's outer life should be simplified so that the inner voice could be more easily heard. In his mind, worldliness got in the way of godliness. Quaker simplicity took many forms. As William Penn admonished them, "Let thy garments be plain and simple.... If thou art clean and warm, thy end is accomplished; to do more is to rob the poor."[27] Friends were warned against wearing costly attire, new fashions, "striped or flowered stuffs," and wigs or jewelry. They were strongly urged to forgo such "vain and viveous Prosceedings as Frolicking Fiddling and Dancing." They did permit drinking alcoholic beverages, but only sparingly, and forbade members from keeping taverns and selling liquor.[28]

Simplicity in speech meant strict truthfulness, without an oath.[29] Quakers refused to pay homage to anyone. Men did not tip their hats to any person, nor did Friends bow, curtsey, or stoop to flattery. Quaker lips used no titles or formal salutations such as "Sir," "Madam," "My Lord," or "Reverend." All persons were addressed as "Friend," and were referred to as "thee" or "thou" to avoid using titles of honor. Dolley Madison maintained this manner of speech throughout much of her life. Months and days were designated by numbers instead of using the familiar names of the months because those names had pagan origins. Thus, while a person belonging to the Church of England might write "November 4th," a Friend would write, "4th day eleventh month."

Quaker meetings were times for spiritual reflection and meditation, and were filled with long periods of silence. This was a radical departure from Anglican liturgy, where the priest conducted the service according to the prescribed rituals of written liturgy in the *Book of Common Prayer*. Friends observed no such forms of sacramental observances: no hymn singing, Scripture readings, or formal prayer. Communion with the Living Christ was a personal experience, not an orchestrated one. While Friends' meetinghouses were similar in their simplicity to Puritan churches, Friends' meetings contrasted with the Puritan practice of a two-hour, closely reasoned sermon delivered by an ordained minister standing above a silent congregation. Any Friend was free to speak spontaneously during the meeting if he or she felt led by the Holy Spirit do so. Quakers of both genders could also serve as "Public Friends," that is, as preachers of the Gospel to the unconverted and as emissaries to other meetings.

Quakers began arriving in the southern colonies in 1665. Their emigration to North Carolina was a direct outgrowth of the guarantee of religious freedom embodied in the charter granted to the Lords Proprietors of Carolina by King Charles

II in 1663. It stated, "No person...shall be in any ways mo-
lested, punished, disquieted, or called into question for any
differences in opinion or practice in matters of religious
concernment, but every person shall have and enjoy his conscience in matters of religion throughout all the province."[30] As
a result, dissenters from the Anglican Church, such as Quakers
and Baptists, as well as Huguenot (Protestant) refugees from
Catholic persecution in France, flocked to present-day North
and South Carolina beginning in the 1670s. As the tide of
immigrants from England, Ireland, Wales, Holland, and Ger-
many increased, many settlers followed what was beginning
to be known as the "Great Wagon Road" south into Virginia
and North Carolina.

The Quaker way was well-suited to life on the frontier.
Since there was no need for paid, "hireling priests" or sancti-
fied places of worship, Quaker services could be held in any
place, indoors or out, at any time where two or more Friends
came together. The first meetings were held in homes, though
meetinghouses were eventually established.

As the Quaker population of North Carolina and Virginia
grew, irregular local meetings developed into more formal
monthly meetings, and these, when in sufficient number,
affiliated with the larger Friends organizations and sent delegates to quarterly and annual meetings. In the first decades
of North Carolina's history, Quakers were in virtual control
of the colony, and by 1703, half of the members of the House
of Burgesses were Quakers.[31] As the Church of England,
through its missionary arm, the Society for the Propagation
of the Gospel in Foreign Parts, began to send ministers to the
colony in the first years of the eighteenth century, the Quakers
came under pressure to conform. They were soon ejected from
the Council and Assembly because their religion forbade them
to swear oaths to any power other than God. By 1710, all
Friends had been removed from high office in the North Carolina colonial government.[32] Throughout the last half of the
eighteenth century, American Quakers rarely held public office
because of their unwillingness to swear or administer oaths.

Membership in the Society required shouldering the duties of the meeting's administration and attending to the needs of other members when they were in distress. Meetings regulated themselves, and enforced strict rules of moral and ethical conduct upon their members. Those who violated the Quaker rules of conduct could be—and often were—disowned by the meeting. The pages of the record books of Dolley's own Cedar Creek Meeting in Hanover County, where her father and mother were both elders, are filled with records of members being disowned for actions forbidden by the Quaker discipline.

Between 1767 and 1799, Cedar Creek members were disowned for neglecting to attend meeting, joining the Masonic society, attending a Baptist church, fighting, using ill words, uttering profane expressions, drunkenness, adultery, moving out of state without endeavoring to settle with creditors, taking solemn oaths, engaging in military service, attending muster, marching in procession with music and weapons of war, following in the corrupt ways of the world, partaking of the "vain fashions and customs of the world, such as horse racing and frequenting places of diversion," frequenting places of sport and gaming, and laying a wager. Any act in support of slavery also made a member liable to swift disownment, including hiring a slave, purchasing or receiving manumitted Negroes, abuse of slaves, "selling one of his fellow men or women into bondage," or working as an overseer of slaves.[33]

Marriage rules were strict. Marrying at home instead of at meeting was a punishable offense, as was marrying a first cousin. Marrying a partner who was not a Friend or being married by a hireling priest was cause for automatic disownment. Second marriages were also a possible source of trouble, should the surviving spouse choose to remarry too quickly. These marriage rules played a dark, divisive role in the life of Dolley and her family.

Because Quaker meetings were dependent on voluntary membership, marriage within the Society was supremely important for family stability, the proper rearing of children, and the preservation of the Quaker faith. John and Mary Coles Payne faced two barriers to membership. Mary had automatically become subject to disownment by the Friends for having married outside of her faith, for at the time of their wedding, John was not a Quaker. Indeed, although no record has so far come to light, she may already have been disowned by her meeting. In the eyes of the Cedar Creek Meeting, the two people who were applying for membership consisted of an apostate Quaker woman married to a libertine worldly man. Such a weighty matter required formal letters of application and confession from the outcasts, repenting for their transgressions, and solemn deliberation by the meeting as to whether the supplicants were worthy of being admitted.[34]

The meeting's records state that on September 8, 1764, "John Payne and his wife requested to be taken under the care of the Friends of [the Cedar Creek Monthly] Meeting, and John Harriss and James Crow are appointed to enquire into their lives and conversation and report to the next monthly meeting." The phrase "and his wife" suggests that Mary Payne had, indeed, already been disowned by her former meeting.

The procedure for investigating the correctness of the application was rigorously prescribed. The women's meeting appointed a committee to see if the intended bride was clear from other marriage entanglements. The men's committee did the same.[35]

Because of the complexity of the Paynes' application, the process dragged on. Month after month, the meeting's records noted, "The matter concerning John and Mary Payne is referred for further consideration under the same Friends care until next monthly meeting." During the same period, other people were accepted into the meeting without delay, indicating the gravity and complexity of the matter under consideration. It is obvious that the extended inquiry was to determine John Payne's fitness for being taken into the Quaker fold, as well as to find good reason to excuse Mary Coles for having married out.

On May 10, 1765, a full eight months after their request, John and Mary were finally admitted. The recorder of the meeting made the following entry into their minutes: "John and Mary Payne request some time ago to be reserved [accepted] as members of this meeting and after the necessary cear being taken to enquier into theire lives and conversation, the friends appointed for that purpus report they know nothing to hinder there being reserved, therefore they are reserved as members of this meeting."[36] The meeting had spoken. Both John and Mary were acceptable.

Once they had been approved for membership, the Paynes quickly became active in shouldering the duties of their congregation. Within a month, John was appointed to a committee to help straighten out the meeting's records, and after two months, he was appointed as a delegate to the Quarterly Meeting.[37] Despite this, John and Mary Payne remained with the Cedar Creek Meeting for only six months after their acceptance.

In the late fall of 1765, John, then twenty-five; Mary, who had just turned twenty and was pregnant; their three-year-old son, Walter; and their slaves left their Virginia home. John and Mary joined the great Quaker influx into the fertile wilderness of the North Carolina Piedmont, where John planned to earn a living as a farmer and merchant. The migration was fueled by several factors. First, the exploding population in the northern colonies was leading to overcrowding, forcing Quakers into closer proximity with non-Quakers. This escalated the threat of losing members to the less-demanding, pleasure-loving worldly community. Opposition from their Anglican neighbors to their views and practices accelerated the emigration. Although Anglicans of colonial Virginia were frequently lax practitioners of their faith, they jealously protected their status as the official state church. During John Payne's time, the feeling was still prevalent which inspired a remark made to James Madison: "A man may be a Christian in any church, but a gentleman must belong to the Church of England."[38]

In addition, the influx of new immigrants from Europe was forcing existing land prices up. The weather was also an inducement: the Carolina Piedmont had four full seasons, none of them extreme, and the countryside was very attractive. Delegates to the Yearly Meetings reported favorably of the rich soil, swift-flowing streams, and modest land prices available in the North Carolina Piedmont. By 1750, "bands of Friends from New Jersey, Pennsylvania, Maryland, Virginia, eastern North Carolina, and—after 1765—from Nantucket [Island], Massachusetts, had moved 'like bees in regular or connected swarms' into the area."[39]

The settlement of central North Carolina had been underway since the 1730s. The New Garden Monthly Meeting was established in 1754, during the reign of King George II, in a section of Rowan County, North Carolina that was later united with a piece of Orange County in 1771 to form Guilford County. The Quaker settlement was located in the north central part of North Carolina, not far from its border with Virginia. Hence, when John Payne and his family arrived, they were living in what was then Rowan County, but two years after they departed, that same place was part of present-day Guilford County. By the time the Payne family arrived in the New Garden settlement in 1765, the meeting there had already been in existence for over ten years.

In his *Letters from an American Farmer*, published in 1782, J. Hector St. John DeCrèvecoeur, wrote a glowing report of the New Garden settlement: "No spot on earth can be more beautiful; it is composed of gentle hills, of easy declivities, excellent low lands, accompanied by different brooks which traverse this settlement. I never saw soil that rewards men so early for their labours and disbursements.... It is perhaps the most pleasing, the most bewitching country which the continent affords."[40]

Quakers, for whom good standing in their meeting was of paramount importance, did not casually move from one place to another without the blessing of their congregation. Consequently, John and Mary Payne obtained a certificate of good standing from the Cedar Creek Monthly Meeting on October 12, 1765, before they set off for North Carolina.[41] The records of the New Garden Monthly Meeting show that the Paynes were accepted into meeting on November 30, 1765, the same day they presented their certificate of good standing from the Cedar Creek Meeting. Many of the Paynes' North Carolina friends soon joined them. Within a few years, the New Garden Meeting had welcomed twenty more certificates of transfer from the Cedar Creek Meeting.[42] Through their hard work in support of their fellow Quakers and their diligence as members of their meeting, the Paynes quickly earned the respect of their neighbors.

For the Paynes and the other Quaker families who moved there in the middle of the eighteenth century, New Garden offered economic opportunity, the freedom to practice their religion, and, because of its isolated location and the weakness of the colonial government, the promise of living their lives relatively undisturbed.

Within six months after arriving at New Garden, John Payne acquired title to three parcels of land: one of 81.75 acres, one acre on which his store was probably located, and 198 acres of farm land that included the site of his log house. Two of the deeds were recorded in the Register of Deeds' Office of Rowan County in July 1766, and the other, for an August 1766 purchase, in April 1767. The land totaled 280.75 acres and cost a total of £500 proclamation money, that is, the local currency of the North Carolina royal colony. The land lay on the east side of Horsepen Creek in the neighborhood of what is now Guilford College.[43] John Payne was the fourth owner of the land. The first had been the Keyauwee (Kiawah) tribe, Native Americans whose nearby village was first visited by Europeans in 1701 by John Lawson, surveyor general of the province, and five traveling companions.[44] Lawson visited their palisaded village, which was situated about thirty miles northeast of the Yadkin River near the present High Point, in Guilford County.[45] He was impressed with their hospitality, and wrote that their chief, whom he called Keyauwee Jack, had prepared "very good entertainment of Venison, Turkies and Bears" to welcome him and his traveling companions.[46]

John Payne's land had been part of 640 acres granted in 1753 to Henry Ballinger II, who received the grant from the Right Honourable John Carteret, Earl of Granville. The latter was one of the original eight Lords Proprietors of the Carolina Colony who had helped restore Charles II to his throne in 1660 and who, in return, obtained enormous land grants in the unexplored wilderness called America.[47]

William Temple Payne, named after William Temple Coles, Mary's cousin, of Salisbury, North Carolina, was the first of the Payne children to be born in the New Garden community. Dolley Payne was the second and last. Like her older brother, William, Dolley was born in a notched-log house on land that is now within the city limits of Greensboro.[48] As a girl, Myrtle Armfield, who served for thirty years as curator of the Greensboro Historical Museum, saw the house in which Dolley Payne was born. "It was built of logs," she said, "had two large rooms, one a little larger than the other, with a huge rock chimney between them, with a fireplace in each room, with a front door into each section, with two big flat rocks for doorsteps, and with a stairway leading to one big attic room for extra sleeping space and storage." She added that the spaces between the logs were filled with mud and

Drawing by Anna Belle Bonds

An artist's conception of the Paynes' house
at the New Garden settlement, c. 1765

that the roof was covered with hand-split shingles.[49] Another visitor, Mrs. Martha Russell Hodgin, visited the log house in the late nineteenth century, and was "impressed with the massive corner cupboards on either side of the fireplace in the sitting room." She felt that the house "appeared roomy and reflected comfortable living."[50] The house stood in the way of development in the late 1800s and was dismantled. The logs were moved across Friendly Road onto the grounds of property belonging to Samuel F. Taylor. There he reused them to construct a smokehouse. In 1968, the smokehouse was deeded to the Greensboro Historical Museum.[51]

The many rules that regulated Quaker meetings necessitated meticulous record-keeping. The responsibility was sufficiently important that the recorder was often the only member of the meeting who was paid for his or her services. At New Garden, the recorder was paid "eighteen pence for recording marriages, four pence for births, burials gratis."[52] There, in 1768, the Paynes' fellow Friend, Thomas Thornbrough, Sr., was recorder of the meeting. Known for his crisp, clear hand, he sharpened his quill with a carefully honed pen knife, dipped it into an inkwell, and carefully recorded the Payne family's births on page twenty-nine of the New Garden Monthly Meeting's first book of records: Walter Payne, named for his mother's only brother, Walter Coles, had been born in Virginia and was six years old when his little sister was born; William was a toddler.[53]

> John Payne was born ye 9 of ye 2 mo 1740 old Stile
> Mary his wife was born ye 14 of ye 10 mo 1745
> Walter their Son was born ye 15 of ye 11 mo 1762
> Wm. Temple their son was born ye 17 of ye 6 mo 1766
> Dolley their daughter was born ye 20 of ye 5 mo 1768[54]

Dolley's arrival was greeted by her father, her two young brothers, the Payne family slaves, including her enslaved nursemaid, "Mother Amy," and the loving members of their Quaker meeting.[55]

In her later life, when she was answering the questions of Margaret Bayard Smith, Dolley indicated that she had been born in 1771 or 1772, thereby clipping three or four years off her age.[56] This confused her biographers for nearly a century. Her vanity or forgetfulness notwithstanding, the New Garden Meeting records are the definitive source for her birth date and place, and, even more important, for the spelling of her given name. It was officially Dolley.

In the two and a half centuries since her birth, Dolley's name has frequently been misspelled and its origins mistakenly attributed. Legions of journalists, biographers, and historians—and even two descendants who wrote about her—spelled her name "Dolly" or stated that her real name was Dorothea or Dorothy and that "Dolley" was a nickname. After her death, commercial firms that used her name to sell their wares inadvertently spelled her name wrong. They included Dolly Madison Wine Fruit Industries, Dolly Madison Popcorn, The Dolly Madison Bakery, The Dolly Madison Dairy, Dolly Madison Ice Cream, manufacturers of several Dolly Madison dinnerware patterns, numerous "Dolly Madison" historical dolls, and even the makers of Dolly Madison cigars.

In fact, Dolley Payne's given name has always been spelled Dolley, never Dolly, and she never used Dorothea or Dorothy in any public or private record. Her parents named her Dolley and her name was recorded as such in the official Quaker minutes of the New Garden Monthly Meeting in 1768. Her family and both of her husbands referred to her and addressed letters to her only as Dolley. Further, she herself invariably spelled her name Dolley on every piece of personal and professional correspondence in which she spelled out her given name. Dolley never omitted the "e" so often edited out by others. In short, she never used the spelling "Dolly." Her biographers were the ones who introduced the confusion over her name, and subsequent writers, including the editors of the nation's finest encyclopedias, perpetuated the error.

Dolley's own personal confirmation of the correct spelling came in 1845, just four years before her death, when she joined St. John's Episcopal Church in Washington. The rector, the Reverend Smith Pyne, wrote to her, asking her to state her full name. In a cordial letter, Dolley promptly replied: "According to your intimation of this morning, dear Friend, I send you my name in full and hope if there is aught else for me to do, that I shall know it from you, who I am proud to greet in the fine character of our good and kind Pastor. [signed] Dolley Payne Madison."[57]

Yet the origin and meaning of Dolley's given name may never be learned. One speculation is that it derives from "doly," a narrow meadow with a stream. This type of landscape was abundant at the site of the New Garden settlement where she was born. However, the true story behind the choice of her name seems to have gone to the grave with her parents, as there is no known record of why John and Mary Coles Payne chose this distinctive and delightfully interesting name for their daughter.

John Payne was about twenty-five years old and still relatively new to the faith when he arrived in New Garden, a fact supported by the lack of references to him in the minutes in the first months after the family's arrival. After Dolley's birth, however, he was given numerous responsibilities to serve the needs of the meeting. Eight days after Dolley was born, John Payne, along with two Quaker women, accompanied Ann Jessop, a Quaker minister, to hold a service for a nearby group of Friends. He accompanied other members on a similar trip a few months later. On October 29, 1768, John was named one of four delegates from the New Garden Monthly Meeting to the Quarterly Meeting, an indicator that he was respected by and stood in the good graces of his fellow New Garden Friends.[58]

John Payne acquired three substantial tracts of land near the meetinghouse, one of which was sold to Thomas Jessop, a recent arrival to the community, on March 26, 1768. That deed describes the land as "one certain tract or parcel of land whereon I the said John Payne now lives."[59] When John Payne left Virginia, he was a planter but had no known experience as a merchant. Weeks later, in North Carolina, Payne identified himself as a merchant, though we do not know what kinds of goods he bought and sold or where he got them. His land purchases indicated that he had the funds one might expect of a successful young man, but those were undoubtedly funds he brought with him from the sale of his Virginia property, not money earned from his new occupation.

Something problematic happened to the Paynes at New Garden shortly after Dolley's birth, but we may never know what it was. On November 11, 1768, John Payne requested a letter of transfer back to Virginia. As was usual, two members of the meeting were chosen to "enquire into his life, and conversation, and affairs" and if they found nothing out of order, would prepare a certificate of good standing and produce it at the next meeting.[60] The enquirers, Richard Williams and Boeler Beals, evidently found something amiss or incomplete; an unresolved problem of some sort, or perhaps the still-unexplained event that triggered their return to Virginia. Was his business failing, or was there another cause? The isolation of the New Garden community and its monolithic Quaker orthodoxy may have been too much for the couple, or it may have been simple loneliness for their parents, relatives, and friends back in Hanover County.

Another influence must be considered. During the time of the Paynes' residence in New Garden, unscrupulous, unsupervised local officials were overcharging for fees and taxes, creating havoc in the court system, and causing problems with registering land claims.[61] Those who opposed the oppression of the country people became known as the Regulators. The conflict came to a head in 1771, when North Carolina Governor William Tryon called out the provincial militia to march against the Regulators. On May 16, 1771, on the banks of Alamance Creek, located in Alamance County, just east of the New Garden settlement, Tryon's troops prevailed over the Regulators, who lost the battle to secure reform in local government. Many of the Regulators left North Carolina, and "those who stayed were offered pardons by the governor in exchange for pledging an oath of allegiance to the royal government."[62]

Since the swearing of oaths was also a violation of conscience for the Friends, many more Friends left North Carolina in the years following the Battle of Alamance Creek.

Three months dragged by until the Paynes' certificate was granted. The reason is not recorded, but before a transfer was approved, a member's financial accounts had to be investigated, and a certificate of transfer would not be issued until all debts were settled.[63] John's certificate was finally issued on February 25, 1769, when the New Garden Friends "continued last meeting, to Correct the certificate of John Payne; having complied there-with: and produced it to this: which was read and signed."[64]

With his removal certificate in hand, the Paynes started selling off their land. It appeared that John wanted to leave the area as soon as possible because he sought satisfaction in court from several people who owed him money—a decidedly un-Quaker practice—and then sold his land for less than he had paid for it. He received £340 for two lots for which he had paid £450, and on March 6, 1769, he sold for 40 shillings 8 pence the one-acre lot for which he had paid £50. In just thirty-nine months, he had lost approximately £120, or twenty-four percent of his £500 investment. His financial losses in 1768-1769 notwithstanding, John continued to serve his meeting and also shouldered civic duties, including designing and developing public roads and witnessing deeds, in North Carolina until his departure.

For a century after her death, the duration of Dolley's residence in North Carolina was somewhat of a mystery, and Dolley herself complicated the story. When she was sixty-six years old and still in the prime of life (she was eighty-one when she died), she provided a limited amount of information to her friend, Margaret Bayard Smith, wife of the editor of the *National Intelligencer*. In a letter to Smith, Dolley stated, "My family are all Virginians except myself, who was born in N. Carolina, whilst my Parents were there on a visit of one year, to an Uncle. Their families on both sides, were among the most respectable."[65] The latter was indeed true, but in her effort to tie herself more closely with the finest of Virginia's bluebloods, Dolley altered some facts in the process.

When referring to 1783, the year the Paynes moved from Virginia to Philadelphia, Dolley told Smith "I believe my age at that time was 11 or 12 years." This would have made her birth year 1771 or 1772, thereby cutting three to four years off her actual age. The confusion was not necessarily the product of feminine vanity. As one of her admirers explained, "Dolley had a way of getting dates confused."

The discrepancy between Dolley's statement and the Quaker records led most of her biographers to perpetuate the error for nearly a century, for they had no access to the Quaker records. The 1772 birth date also led most to believe that Dolley was a native-born daughter of the Old Dominion.[66] Some authors have suggested that in later life, Dolley suppressed mention of her North Carolina nativity for snobbish ancestral reasons, but to be fair, one must consider that few people remember much of what they experienced during the first year of life and that they tend to identify most closely with the friends, relatives, and places they have known for the longest periods of time. For Dolley, that would have been the Paynes, the Coles, the Winstons, and their home, Virginia.

The records are clear that her parents and her eldest brother moved from their plantation in Hanover County, Virginia, to the New Garden Quaker settlement in November 1765, and that both she and her younger brother, William Temple Payne, were born in North Carolina. The New Garden Meeting records state clearly that she was born May 20, 1768, and that her parents lived in New Garden for forty-one months. No record of the unnamed uncle in North Carolina has yet been identified. In 1838, Margaret Smith's biographical sketch of Dolley appeared in volume III of *The National Portrait Gallery of Distinguished Americans.*[67]

The Payne family's departure from North Carolina took place in the early spring of 1769, as witnessed by the records of the Cedar Creek Monthly Meeting in Hanover County, Virginia. The clerk wrote in their minutes, "8th day, 4 mo, 1769:

On the removal of John Payne, his wife, and three children, to wit: Walter, William Temple, and Dolley Payne into this colony, a certificate was produced to this Meeting from the Monthly Meeting at New Garden in North Carolina, bearing date of 25 of 2 month 1769, which was read in this Meeting and approved of and they reserved into membership."[68] Dolley was barely ten months old at the time she returned to Virginia.

In later life, Dolley consistently identified herself as a Virginian, but this was not done to slight the place of her birth. Rather, it was a matter of the timing of her birth, the brief duration of her stay at New Garden, and her deep and ancient ties to the Old Dominion. Although born in the Tarheel State, she lived there for only ten months and spent all of her formative years through the age of fifteen in Hanover County, Virginia. That, plus the fact that both her parents and their American-born ancestors were all Virginians, and their immigrant ancestors had all come directly to Virginia, gave Dolley the logical perspective she held throughout her life: that she was a Virginian who, through a fluke of fate, had been born in North Carolina.

When they returned to Virginia, John and Mary Payne were back in the bosom of their large and sprawling extended family. There in Hanover County, John Payne must have felt greatly relieved to have the New Garden experience behind him. From a financial standpoint, it had been a major blow. For a young ex-merchant, and head of a growing farming family, it was a bad start.

For Dolley, her childhood years in Virginia were to be full of growth, learning, and frivolity—despite the strictures against it—as she progressed from infant to child to mischievous teenager. For her parents, danger lurked ahead, as John Payne's enlightened conscience forced his family down a perilous path paved with difficult challenges.

CHAPTER THREE

The Flower of Youth

Cedar Creek Monthly Meeting
Hanover County, Virginia
Ye 8 of ye 4 mo. 1769

The pain of John and Mary Payne's misfortune in North Carolina was softened by the warmth of their reunion with family and friends when they returned to Virginia. With hearty greetings and fond embraces, they were immediately accepted back into membership of the Cedar Creek Monthly Meeting. The event was duly noted in the congregation's records on April 8, 1769. It has often been stated that the Paynes purchased Scotchtown plantation in Hanover County shortly after their return, lived there for a period of time, and then sold the property to their cousin, Patrick Henry, in late 1770 or early 1771. However, an examination of the Paynes' financial condition and a close reading of the court and estate records of the period and suggests otherwise.

The Paynes had just returned from North Carolina after having suffered a substantial financial loss. Scotchtown consisted of an enormous house, 960 acres of farmland, and a

43

substantial enslaved labor force, all of which was sold to Patrick Henry for over £600. The Paynes returned from North Carolina with, at best, £380. On that basis alone, it is unlikely that the Paynes could have bought an estate of Scotchtown's

size. Furthermore, with such a relatively small family, they didn't need a house or plantation anywhere near that big. The exact whereabouts of the Paynes in the two years after their return from North Carolina has never been documented,

Scotchtown plantation in Hanover County, Virginia

but later in life, Dolley fondly recalled living at Scotchtown as a child.[1] However, living there and owning the property are separate issues.

The first record of the property appears in 1717, when Charles Chiswell, Gentleman, a Scot, and a "sensible, well-bred man" to boot, paid Virginia Lieutenant Governor Alexander Spotswood £50, in return for which Chiswell received a 9,976-acre royal grant from King Charles I on the land that would later be known as Scotchtown. Chiswell may have started work on his house as early as 1719. He had improved the land and had established a residence—probably modest in size—and an iron works on the property by 1732, when William Byrd of Westover stopped by while prospecting for minerals on the nearby New Found River."[2]

Charles died in 1737 and the property passed to his son, Colonel John Chiswell, who expanded the house to its present eighty-foot length and lived on the property until 1752. On October 4, 1757, he advertised household goods, 26,000 acres of land, and "all the buildings thereon," at "Scotch Town in Hanover County," thereby creating the first record of the plantation's name. On October 4, 1760, Colonel Chiswell sold the property to his new son-in-law, John Robinson, Speaker of the House and Treasurer of the Colony, to whom Chiswell was deeply in debt. Robinson had married Chiswell's daughter, Sukey (Susannah) Chiswell, on December 21, 1759. John Chiswell's final connection to Scotchtown was the stuff of legends. On June 3, 1766, he killed his friend, Robert Routledge, in a drunken brawl at Ben Mosby's Tavern, near Cumberland Courthouse. Chiswell died that November, while awaiting trial for the crime. Because of his dastardly deed, his body was denied burial in Williamsburg and was removed to Scotchtown.

In May of that same year, John Robinson died virtually penniless in his home in King & Queen County, Virginia. The executors of his estate tried to sell Scotchtown several times, but failed. In 1769 they again advertised the property for sale, to no avail. In September 1770 they advertised again and were successful. The property then consisted of 3,866 acres of land, fifty-six slaves, one hundred forty head of cattle, one hundred eighty hogs, fifty-four sheep, and seven horses.[3] The name of the buyer is not stated in their records, but Patrick Henry's own account book lists four payments to the executors of the Robinson estate: two in November 1771, one in May 1772, and another in November 1772, for a total of over £600. According to his grandson, William Wirt Henry, this paid for the house and 960 acres, which was a considerable bargain. The account book of a nearby store lists transactions with Patrick Henry at Scotchtown as early as April 1, 1771. Hence, the property passed directly from the estate of John Robinson to Patrick Henry, leaving no possibility that Dolley's parents, John and Mary Payne, ever purchased it.

The ladies' parlor at Scotchtown

About 1771, Col. Samuel Meredith wrote that Henry was "uncommonly hospitable," and that hospitality was probably extended to the Paynes in their time of need. Both the Scotchtown house and grounds were large by any standard and could easily have embraced two families.[4] The immense, story-and-a-half wooden residence stood on a 960-acre tract. The house was eighty-five feet long and thirty-six wide, with a half-hipped, jerkin roof. The top floor was undivided and formed a high-roofed attic, which would have provided ample space for drying tobacco and peas and storing the corn and apples from which Henry made whiskey and cider.

The first floor was divided into eight rooms, separated by a great hall, with brick fireplaces boasting black marble mantels serving each room.[5] At the back of the hall was a stairway. A visitor wrote, "Climbing the rough stairs, one is surprised to find an enormous attic covering the entire floor. Without any fireplaces or even partitions, it could house a swarm of merry and none too finicky guests, congregated for one of the numerous colonial dances or house-parties."[6] Henry, who loved music, played the fiddle, and owned a fine pianoforte, hosted many a cheerful time in the house. In addition to the huge attic, where he would also have stored his heat-loving Madeira wine, he had a full-height brick basement, which consisted of eight rooms, including a large wine cellar for his heat-sensitive wines.[7]

The house stood at one end of a courtyard, which also contained an office, a schoolhouse, a kitchen, an ice house, a laundry, a warehouse, a washhouse, an ashhouse, and a blacksmith shop. A brick-lined, twenty-five-foot-deep dry well was dug for the storage of foods. It maintained a temperature of forty-seven degrees year-round. The plantation's enslaved African-American field hands lived in thirty cabins down the hill, on the New Found River, where a mill was also located. Slave cabins typically housed an extended family of four to six persons, which suggests a large agricultural workforce. The house was surrounded by a white picket fence and a wide variety of carefully chosen boxwood, oak, and locust trees, shrubs, and perennial flowers. An orange clay road skirted the plantation.

The Henry family was Anglican, not Quaker, and Patrick was given careful religious training. His father, Colonel John Henry, was a resolute Anglican, though his mother, Sarah Winston Syme Henry, belonged to a group of Scots-Irish Presbyterians and often took Patrick to listen to Dissenting ministers.[8] Consequently, the Henry family's bonds to the Paynes were familial, rather than religious.

Dolley's stay at Scotchtown provided her with her first contact with mental illness. The Quakers viewed this condition with exceptional compassion, whereas most of their fellow Christians considered the problem to be a frightening manifestation of demonic possession. Patrick Henry and his first wife, Sarah Shelton, had six known children: Martha ("Patsy"), Anne, Elizabeth ("Betsy"), John, William, and Edmund ("Neddy") who lived with them at Scotchtown. Henry shared the first twenty-one years of his married life with Sarah, whom he dearly loved.

In the early 1770s, just after he bought Scotchtown, Sarah started to manifest disturbing behaviors which could not at that time be diagnosed or treated. The disorders could have been induced by post-partum depression; lead poisoning from the pewter plates, mugs, and flatware the family used; manic depression from a lithium imbalance; or any number of other now-treatable problems. Whatever the reason, her mental condition deteriorated rapidly, and when she became dangerous to herself and others, she was clothed in a "Quaker shirt," an early form of strait jacket.[9]

Henry's friends and his physician, Dr. Thomas Hinde, suggested that she be moved to the public hospital in Williamsburg. When Henry inspected the institution, he saw that if he agreed, his wife would be locked into a windowless brick cell containing only a filthy mattress on the floor and a chamber pot. There she would be chained to the wall with a leg iron. Appalled by what he saw, he instead prepared a private, two-room apartment for her in the basement of Scotchtown.

D. P. Madison

Each room had a window, providing light, air circulation, and a pleasant view of the grounds. The apartment also had a fireplace, which provided good heat in the winter, and a comfortable bed to sleep in. It was certainly not a "dungeon," as it has sometimes been described.

Whenever Henry was not away on business, he personally cared for Sarah, and when he was gone, an enslaved servant watched over her, fed her, bathed her, and prevented her from harming herself. Sarah Henry died in the spring of 1775 when Dolley was only seven years old.[10] Because of her illness — then thought to have been caused by being "possessed by the devil" — she was denied a religious funeral service or a Christian burial. Her grieving husband, "bowed down and bleeding under the heaviest sorrows and personal distresses," buried her thirty feet from the home they shared and planted a lilac tree next to her grave to remember her.[11] The tree still stands there, a few steps from the door to her basement apartment.

Patrick Henry, then a widower with six children, was living at Scotchtown when he was elected as the new state's first governor in 1776. That same year he married Dorothea Dandridge, who assumed charge of his flock. The emotional pain from the loss of his first wife led him to abandon everything that would remind him of her. As a result, he left Scotchtown behind and took his second wife to live in the Governor's Palace in Williamsburg. Henry sold Scotchtown to Wilson Miles Cary in 1778, and Cary owned it and its 960-acre plantation until he sold it in 1787.

In retrospect, it is likely that when the Paynes returned to Hanover County from North Carolina, Patrick Henry and his family offered the Paynes the hospitality of their house for a year or two until John and Mary Payne moved onto their own land. If they did spend time at Scotchtown, the Paynes would probably have moved out some time shortly after September 5, 1771, when they purchased 176 acres on a part of the Coles Hill plantation from William Coles.[12] There, about nine or ten miles from Scotchtown, is where Dolley and the Paynes lived until they moved to Philadelphia in 1783.[13]

The Paynes' modest house at Coles Hill, which disappeared more than one hundred years ago, was described as being "one of those low story-and-a-half Virginia houses, built of frame.... Two rooms, one on either side the wide hall, sufficed, with the broad porch, for summer living, and the quaint bedrooms peered out through dormer windows from the roof above. There were outbuildings, too, on the north and east sides, and a few cabins for the negroes."[14] It was here at Coles Hill that Dolley spent the years from about 1771 to 1783 and grew from a three-year-old little girl into a vigorous young woman of fourteen.

What is important about Dolley's formative years is not how many months or years she spent at Scotchtown but rather the style of life and the experiences she had during her childhood. Whether at Scotchtown, Coles Hill, or her parents' own plantation on part of Coles Hill, her life would have been much the same. Dolley grew up on a working farm in east central Virginia, not on a luxurious plantation. She was a farm girl, not a pampered plantation mistress, and the horses she knew best pulled plows, not elegant carriages. She got up early, worked hard at her chores, helped cook food, sew clothes, mind younger children, and shouldered the responsibilities of the eldest daughter in a farm family. During her farm girl days, she learned the solid, practical, virtuous things that became the core of her character. In later years, her high-fashion clothes and sophisticated social life attracted great attention, but it was her unpretentious, unaffected country values, not her elegant dresses, that saw her through the hard times, inspired her to great courage, and endeared her to the nation.

The childhood of Dolley and the other Payne children was probably typical of most Quakers of their status and place of residence. Quaker infants, unlike their Puritan counterparts, were thought to be born innocent, without the taint of original sin. Therefore it was not necessary to baptize them to save their souls from damnation or to punish them to root out the devil. Quakers felt there was a sweetness to infancy, and "infancy" then lasted to the age of reason—ten or twelve years—when it was expected that the Inner Light would make itself known. On the other hand, unlike Anglican children, they missed hearing lullabies, nursery rhymes, and fairy tales. They had no frilly infant clothes, no lace petticoats or ribbons, and few toys to play with. As children grew, they were encouraged to exercise their muscles in healthy ways. Swings, kites, hobby horses, and wagons were allowed, but there could be no dancing, racing, or competitive games. Girls had dolls and doll houses to play with. For amusement, they might cut out paper dolls, draw on slates, or read edifying poetry.

Quaker parents were expected to "govern, counsel, and correct" their children, but not bully them. Punishments were meted out to fit the offense, and the usual order was first a rebuke, second a "timely restraint." If all else failed, physical punishment was used, but without anger. Anger was never acceptable in a Quaker household. An even temperament, without the extremes of grief or exhilaration, was the ideal.

It is clear that as a child, Dolley chafed considerably under the rigid discipline. Many years later, after a particularly irritating visit from former Quaker neighbors, she commented to her sister, Anna Cutts, that their lecture "made me recollect the times when *our Society* used to controle me entirely & debar me from so many advantages & pleasures—& tho so entirely from their clutches, I really felt my ancient terror of them revive to disiagreeable degree."[15]

All American children at that time were taught the virtues of duty and obedience, along with their ABCs, and were encouraged to give substantial help with housework, indoors and out, from an early age. Quaker children were not allowed to give instructions to servants or slaves because they were taught to serve rather than to be served.

Children born to Quaker parents were "birthright" Quakers, and as such they had slightly more leeway in following the rules than converts, such as John Payne, who were closely monitored for infringements. All Quaker children were isolated from the world as much as possible in order to preserve the faith and keep them separated from the temptations of worldliness. The Quaker goal was to create an individual who had the courage to stand against the world but who cheerfully submitted to the regulations of the Society of Friends. Children began attending meetings at age four or five. The two hours of silence were a test of patience for both children and parents. Boys and girls were segregated in the loft of the meeting house and several adults were assigned to sit with them to keep them quiet, a chore that was not often successful. Family devotions at home were no substitute for meetings, but supplemented them.[16]

Girls often resented their drab clothing, and Dolley evidently did as well, although she may not have complained. Margaret Fell Fox, the mother of Quakerism, thought it "a silly poor gospel" that Quakers were instructed to be all in one dress and one color. The changing—and often brilliant—colors of nature were on her side, but she was overruled by those who thought plain clothes opened the way to the Inner Light.[17] One of Dolley's biographers credited Dolley's mother for her daughter's "laughing Irish eyes, her heavy eyebrows and long lashes, her black curling hair, [and] the brilliancy of her skin." She also suggested that Dolley, despite her conservative Quaker upbringing, was naturally loquacious and "not unacquainted with the groves and the magic stone of Blarney."[18]

During her childhood, Dolley had at least one infatuation with worldly goods. There is a long-standing family tradition that Dolley had some decidedly un-Quaker jewelry, supposedly

"A child ought to have pretty trinkets to wear."

D. P. Madison

given to her by her affluent grandmother, Anna Fleming Payne. As the story goes, "Her grandmother testified her affection by constant presents of her old fashioned jewelry, for which it must be confessed her grand child had ever a woman's fondness—tho' child as she was, she dared not offend her parents by wearing them in full sight, they were however put in a bag and tied around her neck—and we have heard her say that the first grief of her childhood was when in her country school that the string had become unfastened in her ramble through the woods and her treasures were gone!"[19] But even after she put this childhood tragedy behind her, Dolley never gave up her love for finery.

As did the proper Boston merchants and the aristocratic Charleston rice planters, the landed tobacco gentry of Virginia considered themselves the elite members of colonial American society. Although she had been born in the heart of North Carolina and held a special fondness for that state, Dolley consistently identified herself as a Virginian. This is not all that surprising, considering that that she spent only the first ten months of her life in North Carolina and the next fifteen years in Virginia. Then, after eleven years in Philadelphia,

The Cedar Creek Meeting House, Hanover County, Virginia

she again returned to Virginia, the home of her ancestors, and spent the rest of her life there, save for her time in adjacent Washington City.

Little is known of Dolley's parents and siblings during their fourteen-year residence in Hanover County from 1769, when they returned from North Carolina, and their removal to Philadelphia in 1783. None of their letters have survived from this period, and virtually all we know of John and Mary Payne comes from the records of the Cedar Creek (sometimes known as the Caroline) Meeting and of the South River Meeting, in Campbell County, Virginia, seventy miles to the southwest of Hanover Court House. John and Mary's names regularly appear in the records as clerks of these two closely affiliated meetings from May 1775 to July 1782.[20] At the time the Payne family returned to Virginia in April 1769, it consisted of John Payne, age twenty-nine; his wife, Mary, age twenty-three; and their three children: Walter, age seven; William Temple, almost three, and Dolley, a month shy of turning two years old, and an unknown number of slaves. In the years following the Paynes' return to Virginia, children named Mary, William, and Ruth Paine were buried at South River, the site of another Quaker meeting.[21] Given the infant mortality rates of the time, it is not illogical to speculate that John and Mary Payne may have had children born in the 1770s who did not survive. These three may well have been Dolley's siblings or relatives.

Save for Quaker church records and two letters in her own hand, there is virtually no surviving documentary evidence to tell us about Dolley's first twenty-five years prior to 1793. Anecdotes and family tales abound, however, and from them it appears that Dolley enjoyed an extremely happy childhood in Virginia. There she was surrounded by dozens of family members and cousins, a large and loving extended family who enjoyed the fellowship of the other Quakers at their monthly and quarterly meetings. One observer noted that "on the Meeting days, good will and sociability flowed unchecked; Friend greeted Friend after a long separation, and a festival atmosphere hung over the company regardless of restraining principles."[22]

In Dolley's era, a woman's education was not valued highly. The standard for female education had the "merit of being quite comprehensible and comparatively easy of attainment. Two questions only were to be answered. 'First, what would make her most sought as a wife? Second, what would make her the best help-meet, wife and mother? From beginning to end, her intellectual development was regarded from the point of view of its pleasingness or usefulness to a man.'"[23] This viewpoint reflected the view of the eminent lexicographer, Noah Webster, who wrote, "In all nations, a good education is that which renders the ladies correct in their manners, respectable in their families, and agreeable in society."[24]

Dolley's parents were not highly educated, but neither were they uneducated. In 1775, John Payne became the clerk of the Cedar Creek Meeting, and the next year, his wife, Mary, was named an elder.[25]

The extent and nature of Dolley's formal education has always been sketchy. In true Quaker fashion, education for the sake of personal embellishment or satisfaction would have been discouraged. Her first lessons were in the domestic arts, as was true for all girls, and were learned at her mother's knee in Hanover County. There she was taught basic seamstress skills, the carding of wool, the use of the spinning wheel, and fancy needlework. Lovely examples of the intricate needlepoint she created can be found in the collection at James Madison's Montpelier and the Greensboro Historical Museum. Dolley apparently was fond of creating remembrances of her Quaker friends' weddings, as she gave both Hannah Foster and Rachel Woolman pincushions made from snippets of their wedding dresses, which date from about 1789 to 1791.[26] Another fine piece of sewing is an underskirt, twenty-four inches at the waist and two yards around at the bottom. It was described as having "four sections of nine or ten pin tucks each, alternating with three sections of delicate embroidery, every stitch done by hand."[27] However, as early as 1794, when she was only twenty-six, Dolley was already complaining about the "excessive weakness" in her eyes, a problem that would plague her on and off for life.[28] Years later, a grandniece wrote that vision problems were attributed to the excruciating eyestrain brought about by endless hours of tedious needlework as a young girl, but most girls of Dolley's acquaintance received this type of instruction, and it did not necessarily lead to later eye problems for them.[29]

As the eldest daughter in a planter's family, Dolley had to learn the basic elements of cooking and plantation housewifery. These included making soap; storing fruit and vegetables under deep layers of sand so that rats could not get to them; curing meat; supervising cooks, maids, and other household slaves; and overseeing the medical care and provisioning of the slaves on her family's plantation. Following her mother's example, she would have learned to supervise workers with gentleness and compassion, something she became noted for as a Washington hostess. As children were added to the family, Dolley would also have been given more childcare responsibilities.

Dolley would have been taught basic reading and penmanship at home, as well as the rudiments of arithmetic. Family tradition states that Dolley received her earliest school education in an "old field" log schoolhouse in Hanover County, about three miles from her home.[30] Tradition also states that as she grew older, Dolley attended the subscription-based Quaker school held at the Cedar Creek Meeting house, a substantial, sixty-foot-by-forty-foot two-story brick building.[31] In 1791, Benjamin Bates, Jr., a Quaker, was teaching his charges reading, writing, and English grammar for 30 shillings per year at the Cedar Creek school. He charged £3 extra for instruction in mathematics.[32] Most assuredly he did not allow creative writing or the reading of imaginative literature. The only text available for the children to read was the Quaker's own *Book of Discipline*, for worldly books were considered dangerous.

The names of John and Mary Payne were on the subscribers' list for the school in 1791, although they had previously turned over their share to C. Moorman, probably a neighbor, when they moved to Philadelphia in 1783. Hence, it is unlikely that Dolley received much, if any, formal schooling in Hanover County. Later in life, Dolley stated that she had been educated in Philadelphia, and she may well have attended school there. "If so," wrote Conover Hunt-Jones, "then she arrived in Philadelphia near the end of the usual course of study prescribed for young women, who normally attended school between the ages of eight and sixteen. The subjects offered probably reading, mathematics, history, geography, religion, fancy sewing, French, and sometimes the classics."[33]

Dolley's earliest surviving letter was written in late June 1783, when she had just turned fifteen. It was addressed to Judith Richardson, a friend five years Dolley's elder, who lived near Rocky Hills, Virginia.[34] Dolley lamented, "I cannot think I am never more to see thee my Dear Judath But still hope there will be some way for us to enjoy each other Company — to visit you now is impracticable as we Embark for Philadelphia In a few days I have a great deal to do." Dolley was sad that she could not first visit Judith and Nancy Morris, as she had planned, and urged Judith to give Nancy and her other friends her "affectionate Love." Dolley noted that there had been several "farewell frolics," noting that if Judith could visit her, there would be another. Dolley closed by saying, "Adieu my Dear. May the smiles of Fortune be equal to thy Merit."[35] Seventeen years later, Dolley was still in touch with Judith, who had married Charles Kent and was living at Wakefield plantation in Hanover County. Dolley closed her letter with a typical expression of hospitality: "Farewell, my dear Judea. I look forward to the pleasing moment when I shall salute you at my House."[36]

Dolley's earliest letters reflect a strong, legible, but ragged and unpolished hand. Her letters display the random capitalization and phonetic spelling common to middle-class citizens of her time. Soon after she married James Madison, she Anglicized her use of dates and began to use worldly titles of address such as "Sir." However, as a tender-hearted daughter, she still used "thee" and "thou" in her letters to her Quaker mother.[37]

Her later handwriting became more regular, practiced, and disciplined, but her letters still contained run-on sentences, frequent use of terminal dashes to the near-exclusion of periods, and sentences that frequently ran very much downhill. Even by 1823, when she was fifty-five, her letters showed some of these idiosyncrasies, although the drooping lines were now level and even.[38] Dolley was an expressive and colorful correspondent and possessed a good vocabulary, but until she reached the age of forty, her handwriting lacked precision and uniform layout of lines on the page, and her spelling improved only slowly over the years. Nevertheless, her letters were as lucid and her handwriting as good as most other upper-class Americans of her time.

While Dolley probably received no more than a basic education, and that highly colored by Quaker objectives, she quickly learned what she needed along the way. Whatever formal intellectual education she may have lacked, Dolley more than made up for by the depth of her character. Throughout her life, her consistent demonstration of honesty, bravery, hope, love, and charity impressed all who met her.

In her later childhood, some of Dolley's fondest memories revolved around outings at the Creighton Tavern, now the Indian King Tavern Museum, in Haddonfield, New Jersey.

The Indian King Tavern Museum, Haddonfield, New Jersey

The historic tavern was built in 1750, when the village was a major Quaker settlement. At the onset of the American Revolution, members of the New Jersey Council of Safety met in one of its substantial rooms and, in 1777, convened in the tavern to officially create the independent state of New Jersey and adopt its Great Seal.

When Dolley Payne was a teenager in the 1780s, Hugh and Mary Creighton, both liberal Quakers, were her hosts at the tavern for weeks at a time. They were affectionately known as "Aunt" and "Uncle" Creighton, despite the lack of any known direct blood ties to the Paynes. "Hugh Creighton was not a strict Friend, and his wife, Mary French, was a woman of most loveable character, with a heart large enough to take in all the world's people who chanced to cross her quiet pathway," wrote W. Jay Mills.[39] As a result, Dolley was exposed to a much more worldly lifestyle than she experienced on her father's plantation. Taverns were then family restaurants, and this one boasted a second-story assembly room that was the largest non-religious meeting place in the countryside. It hosted meetings of the New Jersey legislature, sectarian schools, and music and dancing fests. Hoag Levins, the official historian of the tavern, wrote that "the dancing—similar to what is today known as clogging or step dancing—literally shook the tavern as up to forty men and women stomped up and down in unison across groaning floor boards as fiddlers flailed away." Although Dolley was prohibited from dancing, she delighted in the social excitement and pageantry of the affairs.[40]

Mills also recorded that in those early Haddonfield days, Dolley often took "frolicsome rides with her cousins in the mail-coaches that stopped twice a day at the tavern, driving a mile or two out on the highway and then walking home."[41] The mail coaches brought with them the most important documents of the day and the most important people of the country. Although the Quakers disapproved of tavern-keeping for their members, someone had to provide food, drink, and lodging for the travelers, and the Creightons were not expelled from their sect because of their occupation. Dolley never forgot her old friends at Haddonfield. In later days, when she was mistress of the President's House, old friends would call, some making social visits and others seeking patronage positions from her husband. All would be greeted warmly, and Dolley gladly reminisced about her early days among them and asked fondly about the old Haddonfield families.[42]

Dolley and her young Quaker friends made excursions to Gray's Ferry, on the western bank of the Schuylkill River, "a veritable garden of delight to the youth of old Philadelphia and Southern New Jersey."[43] Mrs. Creighton often took a coach to Trenton to visit her friends and generally took a small flock of young people with her. Dolley delighted in these trips. Wandering through the Green Street and Pinkerton Alley shops, she must have reveled in the chance to see the "world's goods," such as bright silk dresses, ribbons, lace, and jewelry.

On their Virginia plantation, Dolley's parents spent their time supervising the field and housework, educating their eight children, and assisting their fellow Friends. As soon as they returned to the Cedar Creek Meeting, both John and Mary Payne took up the duties of clerks of the meeting. Because the Quakers were such meticulous custodians of the daily lives of their members, the clerks of a meeting were kept busy recording the minutes, registers, and other records of the congregation. The Paynes' clear and precise handwriting is a testament to their own literacy and that of the entire congregation.

Both were equals in the eyes of the meeting, and they each co-signed the documents they registered in the same manner: "John Payne, Clerk" and "Mary Payne, Clerk." Both were elected elders in the congregation, and John progressed to the status of "Public Friend," which permitted him to preach. For reasons of her own, Mary did not choose this step, although other women did. Both were strong pillars of their meeting and "looked forward with confidence to the ultimate reward of those who walk by the Inner Light and the rules of the Book of Discipline."[44] One entry into the Cedar Creek Meeting records must have inspired special pride in the hearts of John and Mary Payne. It was on December 20, 1780, when Dolley was twelve-and-a-half years old, that she performed what may have been her first recorded public act: signing, with her mother, the marriage certificate of Thomas Stanley, son of John Stanley, and Unity Crew, daughter of James Crew, all members of the Cedar Creek Monthly Meeting.[45]

D. P. Madison

Their plantation was prosperous, and their family was growing. Life seemed good for the Paynes, but for two profoundly troubling issues: the imminent threat of a war with England and the moral dilemma they faced as slaveowning Quakers.

In a landmark assembly in the fall of 1776, the Philadelphia Yearly Meeting invited the other five American Yearly Meetings to send delegates to Philadelphia to consider "the conduct that ought to be observed by our Society throughout the Continent in these times of probation and difficulties."[46] The Declaration of Independence from Great Britain had been signed only months earlier, and war fever was engulfing the new nation. The Quakers' deliberations resulted in directions to all Friends to perform no military service and pay no fine in lieu of military service; to avoid any trade or business likely to promote the war; to help all war victims, Quaker or non-Quaker; and to withdraw from all political activity, even voting in elections, since they perceived that the Revolutionary government "was founded and supported the spirit of wars and fighting."[47]

The Virginia Quakers had made their position clear: they would not fight for either side. Because of their refusal to bear arms, their loyalty to the patriot cause was under suspicion— even by close relatives. On September 15, 1777, when Dolley's first cousin, Virginia Governor Patrick Henry, met with his council, it was resolved that the governor should write to the magistrates of several counties, including Hanover, directing them to seize the records of the Quaker meetings there and arrest any Quaker found guilty of treason. The Cedar Creek Meeting's records were "seized, kept for a month or two, and returned to John Payne of Scotchtown, the Meeting's clerk. No treason was discovered."[48]

Could John Payne remain at his plow with the Revolution going on all around him? The answer is yes. The Quakers, with few exceptions, were conscientious objectors to the Revolutionary War—and all wars. As one of their historians noted, they would "endure persecution rather than go forth and slay their fellow man."[49] The Friends had foreseen the events to come and had taken steps to distance themselves from them. This included declining to join the Continental association, which rallied opposition to the British. James Madison, then a twenty-four-year-old patriot from Orange County, Virginia, wrote to an acquaintance in Philadelphia about the Quakers' absolute neutrality.

> I suppose the inhabitants of your province are more reserved in their behavior, if not more easy in their apprehensions, from the prevalence of Quaker prin- ciples and politics. The Quakers are the only people with us who refuse to accede to the continental asso- ciation. I cannot forbear suspecting them to be under the control and direction of the leaders of the party in your quarter; for I take those of them that we have to be too honest and simple to have any sinister or secret views, and I do not observe anything in the associa- tion inconsistent with their religious principles. When I say that they refuse to accede to the association, my meaning is, that they refuse to sign it, — that being the method used among us to distinguish friends from foes, and to oblige the common people to a more strict ob- servance of it.[50]

Did John Payne support his countrymens' fervent desire for justice and peace? Undoubtedly so. Did he bear arms and fight the British? Undoubtedly not. Nevertheless, three of Dolley's early biographers let their patriotic enthusiasm overrule the clear realities of the Payne family's life. All three writers, none of whom were Quakers, assumed that the ven- erable Mrs. Madison, a child of the Revolution, must have had a father who picked up his musket, jumped on his horse, joined the army, and fought the British. All three were wrong.

The first of these was Dolley's own niece, Mary Estelle Elizabeth Cutts, who wrote of John Payne in her unpublished 1850s memoir, "He was a Capt. in the Revolutionary War."[51]

D. P. Madison

The first to publish the unfounded allegation was Elizabeth Lummis Ellet, an enthusiastic chronicler of the patriots and their victory over the British. She wrote to Dolley, then a very old lady, to inquire about her family's background. Dolley, who was eight years old when the fighting started and fifteen-and-a-half years old when the last British troops sailed out of New York harbor in November 1783, was both deft and self-deprecating in her response. Knowing what she did about her family's pacifistic Quaker principles, and aware of Ellet's burning zeal to immortalize Revolutionary War patriots, Dolley's reply to her would-be biographer is as interesting for what it does not say as for what it does:

> I have received, my dear Madam, your letter of the 18th ult. informing me of your design to publish a volume of sketches of the patriotic ladies of the Revolution — and of your wish to include my life among the number. Having been but a child at the close of that glorious struggle which resulted in our Independence, I can lay no claim to be included among that distinguished class whose exploits and sacrifices well deserve to be commemorated. Thanking you for your kindness and assuring you that I shall look forward with much interest to your promised volume.[52]

One of Dolley's later biographers wrote of this letter that the reason Dolley's letter was vague and even evasive "may be attributed to her unwillingness to revive a long-past and outlived period for which Mrs. Ellet would presumably have little sympathy or understanding."[53] Undaunted, Ellet, who was not willing to let one of the most socially prominent women in American history slip through her biographical fingers, did not allow historical fact to stand in the way of a good story. She either invented or, perhaps, retold Mary E. E. Cutts' story of John Payne's alleged service as a captain in the Revolution, thus establishing Dolley's father in print as a uniformed, gun-carrying soldier and enabling Dolley's life to become Chapter XI in her 1867 book, *Queens of American Society*.[54] In the process of creating a Revolutionary War hero, these two writers cast John Payne in the role of traitor to his Quaker principles.

Similarly undaunted, patriotic zealot Maud Wilder Goodwin took Ellet's creative writing to a yet higher level of conjecture by attributing a set of motives of her own creation to John Payne's already fabricated military service history. In 1896, Goodwin wrote that "John Payne, forgetful of his Quaker peace principles, or believing them overruled by the necessity of his country, had buckled on his sword and ridden away to become a captain in the Continental Army." By perpetrating and expanding the fiction, Goodwin portrayed John Payne as a man capable of forgetting a fundamental principle of his faith or abandoning his deeply held beliefs in the passion of the moment.

Later writers never claimed that John served under arms, and no record of his Revolutionary War service has yet been located. In the context of John Payne's life, his lack of military service makes perfect sense. Given the length and depth of John Payne's commitment to his faith, it is almost inconceivable that he would forsake his Quaker pacifism and join the Continental Army.[55]

The question of slavery was an early dilemma for the Paynes. Slaveholding among Quakers, including Dolley's parents, was most prevalent in the South, where the "peculiar institution" had its deepest roots. Abuse of slaves was severely admonished, and the Quakers were among the first to press for their emancipation. Eventually, they became founding operators of the Underground Railway. The New Garden settlement in North Carolina became a major transfer point in the journey north for the runaway slaves. Quakers also championed humane treatment of other oppressed or neglected classes, including Native Americans, prisoners, and the mentally ill.[56]

Friends came to this country not to seek gold or conquer, but to live a life in accordance with their religious convictions. Unlike the Puritans of the Massachusetts Bay Colony,

who fled England to obtain religious freedom and then denied it to all other sects, the Quakers never persecuted those who did not believe as they did.

John and Mary Payne, as well as their ancestral families, the Winstons and the Coles, were all slaveowners. No record of the number of John and Mary's slaves has yet been found, but we do know about the holdings of some of his relatives. John's father, Josias Payne, an Anglican, left more than thirty slaves to his heirs. John's brother, George Payne, left over forty to his, and another brother, Colonel John Payne, devised over one hundred slaves to his heirs.[57] One estimate of John and Mary Payne's holdings puts the tally at about fifty slaves.[58] If that number is accurate, the family would have ranked as a major slaveholder for the time.

In 1760, it was illegal to emancipate a slave in Virginia except by special government act. Virginia Quakers and their meetings could oppose slaveholding and support emancipation, but they were prohibited by law from freeing their slaves. If a slave was freed, by a Quaker or anyone else, he or she could be captured and sold as a runaway.[59]

Virginia was a bastion of slaveholding. In 1765, the Quaker minister John Griffith wrote that "the life of religion is almost lost where slaves are numerous... the practice being as contrary to the spirit of Christianity as light is to darkness."[60] By 1769, when the Paynes returned to Virginia from North Carolina, they had come to believe that slaveholding was morally indefensible. John wrote, "I am persuaded that liberty is the natural condition of all mankind."[61] In 1769, the Yearly Meeting recommended that each Monthly Meeting "discourage the iniquitous trade" of selling and holding slaves.[62]

In an act which demonstrated that Dolley's father was a leader and not a mere follower in the anti-slavery movement, John Payne freed one of his slaves within six months after the Declaration of Independence was signed. His record leaves no doubt of his motives or intent. It stated:

I, John Payne of Hanover County, Virginia, from mature, deliberate Consideration, and the Conviction of my Own mind, being fully persuaded that Freedom is the Natural Condition of all mankind, and that no law, moral or Divine, has given me a right Or property in the persons of my fellow Creatures; and being desirous to fulfil the Injunction of our Lord and Saviour Jesus Christ, by doing unto Others as I would be done by; do therefore declare that having Under my care a Negro man Named Cuffe, aged about Twenty-four years, I do, for myself, my heirs, Executors and Administrators, hereby release Unto him the said Cuffe all my right, Interest and Claim Or pretension of Claim whatsoever, as to his person, or to any Estate he may hereafter Acquire, without any Interruption from me, or any person Claiming for, by, or under me. In Witness whereof I have Hereunto set my hand and Seal this third day of the Twelfth month in the year of our Lord One thousand Seven Hundred and Seventy Six.[63]

The emancipation of Cuffe was followed by the emancipation of all of John's slaves. The act was dramatic and noble, but fraught with problems. Emancipation deprived the Paynes of the guaranteed availability of their workforce. In addition, it gained them the immediate hostility of their neighbors. Nevertheless, John persevered. In 1778, the Cedar Creek Meeting showed that they were freely defying the law, for they spent 30 shillings for a well-bound book in which to record manumissions. With their strong anti-slavery views a matter of record, both John and Mary were put in charge of maintaining the manumission records, a task they performed between 1778 and 1782.

The legal tide against emancipation in Virginia began to turn shortly after John Payne's act, but manumission did not become legally permissible in Virginia until 1782. By that time, John Payne had freed all his slaves, as had most of his Quaker neighbors. Many of them chose to move to the West, but John had already experienced the isolation of rural North Carolina and found it wanting. Now he prepared to leave his comfortable Virginia home and strike out for the place that was the stronghold of his religion: Philadelphia.

During the Revolution, anti-Quaker sentiment in Virginia increased steadily over two key issues: their refusal to bear arms, which was viewed by many patriots to be passive assistance to the Crown, and the open—though illegal—manumission of their slaves. After years of scorn from many of his neighbors, it was natural that John Payne would look longingly to Pennsylvania, the epicenter of the American Quaker world, as a new home for his family. Before long, the dream evolved into a bold plan based on conscience: break their ties with family and friends, pull up stakes, and move to Philadelphia.

The Paynes continued to operate their plantation between 1776 and their emigration to Philadelphia in 1783 without slaves, but it must have been very difficult for both the Paynes and their former enslaved workers. Without their guarantee of food and shelter, and with neighboring slaveowners hostile to them, the former Payne slaves may have become early sharecroppers, remaining in their cabins and farming the Payne plantation in return for a share of the crops. Although this is only speculation, this model quickly evolved in the South after the end of the Civil War. The planters, who did not have cash to hire farm labor, provided the Freedmen a place to live, furnished seed and farming implements, and gave them a share of the crops. The rest of the crop went to the planter.

According to an early biographer, not every one of the freed slaves wanted to leave the Payne family. Dolley's nurse, known as Mother Amy, remained with them, moved to Philadelphia, and worked for the family until her death. It is said that she saved most of her wages and "at her death bequeathed five hundred dollars to Mrs. Payne."[64]

In the summer of 1779, when their son, Walter, was seventeen, the Paynes asked the Cedar Creek Monthly Meeting for a certificate for him because they had sent him to Philadelphia as the family's pathfinder.[65] Walter was indeed the best person to investigate employment opportunities for the family and pave the way for their emigration, but there could well have been another motive. Walter was of age and eligible to shoulder arms and serve in the Continental Army. As the eldest son in the family, he would have been dearly missed on the farm, but in Philadelphia, he stood a lesser risk of being inducted into military service, even though Philadelphia had been occupied by the British just two years earlier.

On August 11, 1779, the clerk of the Cedar Creek Meeting recorded the following: "By a report from Cedar Creek Preparative Meeting, it appears that Walter Payne has moved to Philadelphia. Micajah Terrell, James Hunnicutt, Moses Harris and Micajah Davis are appointed to prepare a certificate for him, and assign the same in behalf of the Monthly Meeting, if nothing obstructs."[66] The fact that Walter asked for a letter of transfer from his meeting only after he arrived in Philadelphia suggests the precipitous nature of his departure. Back at home, his younger brother, William Temple Payne, thirteen years old, took his place as eldest son on the family's plantation.

Eighteen months later, in January 1781, Mary informed the meeting that she planned a visit to Philadelphia. As she was a respected elder of her meeting, her letter of introduction was authorized the same day.[67] For an unaccompanied woman, the two-hundred-mile journey was not only wearying, it was fearsome. The Revolutionary War was winding down, but was not over, and British troops were moving into Virginia from North Carolina at that time. The long trip by carriage or stagecoach, over rough, muddy, half-frozen roads, was bone-jarring. Twenty-five miles a day would have been considered good progress. The inns and taverns were often crude and uncomfortable, and the eight- or nine-day trip would have been exhausting for anyone.

Upon her arrival, Mary was greeted and welcomed by Elizabeth Sandwith Drinker, a well-known Quaker hostess whose intimate journal chronicled the joys of birth, courtship, and marriage, as well as the miseries of pestilence, war, and death, in the city for forty-nine years.[68] Elizabeth's husband, Henry, was a prosperous partner in James and Drinker, a Philadelphia shipping and importing firm, and the family maintained their hospitable house at the corner of Front Street and Drinker's Alley.[69] John and Mary Payne had first visited the Drinkers on April 20, 1779, when Elizabeth recorded in her diary that they had dined with her family.[70] Two years later, on March 5, 1781, Elizabeth, then forty-six and a semi-invalid, noted that, "Molly [Mary] Payne spent the day, and lodg'd with us. she and Son Walter Breakfasted the 6th."[71] The two women shared a bond beyond being conscientious members of the Society of Friends: both their fathers had emigrated from County Wexford, Ireland. After surveying the city with her own eyes, Mary knew all she needed to know. She left for Virginia soon thereafter; Walter remained until June 4 and followed her.[72] It was time to move the family.

The courage of early abolitionists like John Payne bore fruit more quickly than he might have thought possible. The legal authority to manumit slaves in Virginia became a reality in 1782, when the Virginia legislature passed a law that gave all slaveowners the power to emancipate their slaves by will after death, "or by acknowledging the will while still alive, in open court, provided they agreed to support all the aged, infirm, and young persons thus set at liberty."[73]

Philadelphia Quakers

The Quakers finally had the legal authority to act on their beliefs. A clear-cut choice now faced them: grant their slaves freedom and remain in the Society, or keep their slaves and be disowned by their fellow Friends. The majority followed their consciences, but those who chose to keep their slaves were lost from the fold. Even more significant, the Virginia Quakers who freed their slaves were forced to brave the wrath of their neighboring non-Quaker slaveholders. Like the Paynes, many of the abolitionist Friends chose to leave the state for more congenial surroundings.

John Payne's act of manumission cost him not only most of his capital investment — perhaps as much as $25,000 — but also his entire workforce.[74] Manumission of his slaves rendered it impossible for him to continue the profitable farming of his land in Hanover County. John and Mary Payne had served the Cedar Creek Meeting with diligence and honor. Nevertheless, John's request for a certificate of good standing from the meeting was not immediately granted, though that same body had speedily approved the certificates for his wife and son. For the third time, John was required to wait as the elders pondered his fate.

Given his standing in the meeting, the delay might solely have been the necessity to formally review and approve all the actions he had taken while member, elder, Public Friend, and clerk. The final record of the Paynes in the Cedar Creek Meeting is as straightforward and pragmatic as any John had himself made while clerk. The minute book stated, "And as John Payne is about to remove without [outside of] the verge of this Meeting, James Hunnicutt is appointed Clerk thereof in his stead."[75]

Whatever the reason for the delay, six weeks later, on April 12, 1783, the Cedar Creek Meeting finally approved and signed John's certificate of transfer to the Northern District Monthly Meeting in Pennsylvania for the family: John and Mary Payne and their children, William Temple, Dolley, Isaac, Lucy, Anne, Mary, and John.[76] Sometime during the next three months, the Paynes uprooted their family for the third and final time. From their rural, agricultural home in Hanover County, Virginia, they set off for Philadelphia, one of the largest and most sophisticated cities in colonial America, where their children "could be educated in their religion" and where John Payne could make the transition from slaveowning farmer to urban manufacturing merchant.[77]

Pennsylvania had been granted to the Quaker William Penn in 1681, about fifty years after the first Dutch settlers arrived in the area. The City of Philadelphia, still known as the "City of Brotherly Love" from Penn's influence for tolerance, was founded in 1682. Penn induced settlers to come to the colony with offers of cheap land—40 shillings per 100 acres and tracts of 5,000 acres for £100—and thousands responded.

The Paynes' trip of two hundred miles to Philadelphia was extremely arduous, whether the family traveled by water or by land. Travel by packet sloop would have been the most comfortable option, but would have been slow and filled with tedious delays and would have required considerable advance planning. The route would have taken the family by land to Richmond, then down the James River, up the length of Chesapeake Bay, and then up the Delaware River to Philadelphia.

If they chose the overland route by coach and wagon, the likely route would have taken them through Alexandria and Baltimore. That ride would have been lengthy and rough. "Outside Philadelphia lay black and treacherous quagmires in which the horses floundered and struggled for hours, making no progress towards getting out, while some of the hills were so steep that wagons must pause till other teams came to their assistance," wrote one observer. "These wagons had no springs, and the unlucky passengers were jolted from side to side as the wheels of the vehicle rolled over rocks or sank to the hubs in mud."[78] The trip was especially hazardous for Mary Payne. She was now thirty-nine years old, and in the final months of her ninth pregnancy.

Despite the hazards and hardships, the Paynes persevered. The tiled roofs and lofty church steeples of Philadelphia must have been an inspiring sight when they came into view. The city welcomed the Paynes. John Payne immediately entered into the duties of a lay preacher, or "Public Friend," and on the first day in the Free Quaker Meeting House at the south-west corner of Fifth and Mulberry Streets, he "removed his broad-brim [hat] and with his eloquence moved his hearers."[79]

Dolley immediately fell in love with the City of Brotherly Love, and quickly learned her way around the large, bustling Quaker metropolis. The beautiful, light-hearted girl was then just one month shy of her fifteenth birthday.

CHAPTER FOUR

Love, Marriage, and Yellow Fever

T he Payne family's move from unpretentious, rural Virginia to sophisticated, urban Philadelphia in the summer of 1783 may have been a thrilling opportunity for fifteen-year-old Dolley, but it was much more problematic for her father. With his noble but costly decision to manumit his slaves, move to the city, and take up the trade of a laundry starch maker, John Payne had cast the die of his fate. It would not roll in his favor.

Philadelphia had grown rapidly since its founding as a refuge for Quakers in 1682. In 1701, it had 4,400 residents. When Dolley's family arrived in 1783, they had about 22,000 neighbors. By the time the first federal census takers canvassed the city in 1790, when Dolley was twenty-two, the population of the city proper had swelled to 28,522. Inclusion of nearby settlements raised the count closer to 42,000.

Thus, Dolley found herself living in the second-largest city in the nation, edged out only by the nation's former capital, New York. Only three other American cities had even 10,000 inhabitants at the time: Boston, Massachusetts; Charleston, South Carolina; and Baltimore, Maryland. A decade later,

D. P. Madison

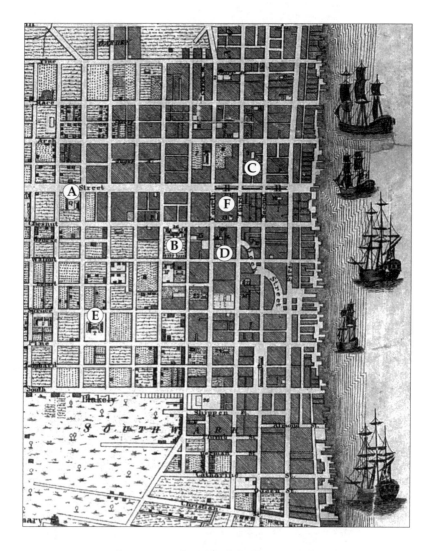

The City of Philadelphia in 1776

A: President's House
B: State House & Congress Hall
C: Christ Church
D: John Todd Home
E: Hospital
F: Bank of the United States

Philadelphia had edged out New York as the country's premier metropolis.

Dolley, a country girl who had rarely been in a town with more than 500 residents, must have found Philadelphia astonishing. The city's 4,000 houses provided homes for its affluent residents. Rows of willow, poplar, and buttonwood trees provided shade for the homes of the city's elite, whose elegant mansions, modeled after those of London, were as fine and stately as any in Charleston, Boston, or New York. Many of the city's colonial buildings were handsome examples of Georgian architecture, but the décor lacked ornamentation because the Friends strongly preferred simplicity. The central part of the city boasted paved streets and sidewalks made of raised brick.

Dolley must have marveled the first time she viewed Christ Church on Second Street, an imposing four-storied, hipped-roof edifice with a towering white steeple that housed a magnificent ring of bells imported from England—a far cry from the unpretentious meetinghouses of her own denomination. She would have undoubtedly been as impressed by the city's other public buildings: the grand courthouse; Carpenter's Hall; and the Pennsylvania statehouse, erected in 1735 and soon to become known as Independence Hall. Now, instead of the rolling hills of Virginia, Dolley was surrounded by masses of sophisticated people and elaborate architecture. John Payne had probably never considered that in the Quaker epicenter of America, his family would face the ubiquitous presence of the profane world and would be barraged by its worldly enticements. In addition, the city had a darker side. It was described as:

> A low, level town, hottest and dampest of all the American seacoast, hotter even than Charleston, Savannah, or the West India cities. Wharves jutted out into the river and cut off the current; high tide deposited rotting stuff on the banks and in the mud. Below the city were swamps, marshes, pools in clay pits, stagnant

water. Most of the streets were unpaved. There was no water system, and only one sewer, under the serpentine Dock Street. Elsewhere holes were dug, as at Market and Fourth streets, to receive water from the gutters. These 'sinks' exhaled a noxious effluvia, for dead animals and all kinds of nauseous matters were hurled into them to putrefy. All the wells were shallow; citizens continually pronounced them polluted.[1]

In a word, Philadelphia stank. It could also be brutal. At the west end of Market Street, a platform raised eight or ten feet above the ground provided a good view of the public whipping post and the pillory. "Here on Saturday, which was

Independence Hall, Philadelphia

high market-day, between ten and eleven in the morning, the miserable victims of the law stood with head and arms ignominiously pinioned, or, still worse, with clothes stripped to the waist and backs bleeding from the strokes of the lash, while school-children looked on with eager curiosity as at a spectacle."[2]

From an economic perspective, Philadelphia in the late 1780s was in disarray. Although it was the richest city in the nation, its economy had been on a roller-coaster ride during the Revolution. Life in Philadelphia centered on the numerous wharves along the Delaware River, and the city was heavily involved in maritime trade. During the Revolution, all economic efforts focused on war-related goods. Following the Revolution, with the ports of the British-controlled West Indies closed to American traders, the re-conversion to overseas trade was stymied. Continental paper currency, which John Payne had probably received in payment for his plantation, was now nearly worthless, and prices for staple goods were high. Worse yet, Payne's laundry starch was considered a luxury commodity, and few could afford it.[3]

Elizabeth and Henry Drinkers' house on the corner of Front Street and Drinker's Alley was the Paynes' first home in Philadelphia. Mary Payne gave birth just weeks after her family arrived in the city. The Paynes were so enthralled with their new home that they named their ninth and final child Philadelphia Payne. Evidently the little girl's life was brief, as the only record of her existence shows her alive in 1786.[4]

Tragic news arrived soon after the Paynes started to enjoy their new surroundings. In a journal entry on December 26, 1784, Elizabeth Drinker noted that Dolley's eldest brother, Walter Payne, then twenty-three, "took leave of us, intending to set of early to morrow for Virginia, and in a few weeks to embark there for Great Britain."[5] He was never heard from again and was apparently lost at sea.

By 1785, the Paynes had moved into a home of their own at 57 North Third Street.[6] The row houses favored by Philadelphia Quaker families consisted of individual three-story family dwellings with small front porches facing the street. The porch served as the place where the family could sit, interact with the neighbors, and watch the world go by—including Philadelphia's flocks of wealthy, well-dressed, worldly people. It may have been here that Dolley's taste for high fashion was whetted, a trait for which she would later acquire an international reputation.

John Payne probably conducted his business from the two front rooms on the ground floor of his house. The rear room would have been reserved for family use. The second floor probably contained a parlor for entertaining friends or holding family meetings and a master bedroom or guest room. The third floor contained additional family bedrooms.[7] There was a separate kitchen building to the rear of the main house, kept apart to minimize the spread of cooking fires.

Payne's large family was both a source of joy and a heavy financial responsibility. In 1783, his children included four boys, four girls, and another daughter on the way. Walter, the eldest, was an able young working man of twenty-one. Next came William Temple, seventeen; Dolley, the eldest daughter, fifteen; Isaac, fourteen; Lucy, six; Anna, four; Mary, two; and John Coles, one. Their last child, daughter Philadelphia, was born in the summer of 1783.[8]

With the exception of Quaker meeting records and the journal of Elizabeth Drinker, there are few authoritative sources that describe Dolley's early years in Philadelphia. Nevertheless, all the traditional accounts paint a picture of a sprightly, enthusiastic young girl, who came into full bloom in her teenage years. Many years later, Anthony Morris, a Philadelphia Quaker merchant, long-time family friend, and best man at her wedding, wrote in rapture bordering on worship of young Dolley:

> She came upon our comparatively cold hearts in Philadelphia, suddenly and unexpectedly with all the delightful influences of a summer sun, from the Sweet South, in the season of May and at the age of sixteen,

bringing with her all the warm feelings, & glowing fancies of her Native State. She was the first and fairest representative of Virginia in the female Society of Philadelphia, and she soon raised the mercury there in the thermometers of the Heart to fever heat. But she was not altogether in appearance a Virginian, her complexion seemed from Scotland and her soft blue eyes from Saxony.[9]

Almost immediately upon her arrival in the Quaker capital, the outgoing girl flourished. One writer noted that Dolley was "exceptionally pretty by the standards of her time, with a natural vivacity. Even at fifteen she had a magnetic quality that drew people to her, an attraction that a later age would call charisma. People were always aware of her proximity. Men stared at her when she walked down the streets and at social gatherings she became the center of attention."[10]

Strolling along the riverside or watching well-dressed upper-class belles and beaux promenading on Chestnut Street in the afternoons were two of Dolley's favorite pastimes. "Here the young fashionables congregated in great numbers and always attired as for a dress parade. The men were arrayed in very tight small-clothes and silk stockings, with pointed shoes ornamented with shining buckles" noted an observer. "Their waistcoats were often bright colors, and the outer coats with several little capes were adorned with silver buttons, from whose size and number the owner's wealth might be guessed. Old men carried gold-headed canes, which, being a badge of gentility, were always very much in evidence."[11]

Dolley's worldly female counterparts took equal pride in their appearance. "The women were attired even more gorgeously than the cavaliers who bowed and flourished and scraped before them. Their gowns of brocade were of a prodigious fullness as needs must be when the hoop spreads out like a balloon. The musk-melon and calash bonnets were of correspondingly wide dimensions, and altogether a woman prepared for the promenade resembled a ship under full sail."[12] The streets of Philadelphia were Dolley's fashion college. In later years, it would become apparent that she had learned her lessons well.

The Quakers, on the other hand, were under strong pressure to dress simply, especially when attending meeting or appearing in public, for looking worldly went against their religious principles. However, not every Philadelphia Quaker dressed conservatively. One writer noted that the Quaker philosophy notwithstanding, "human nature is not to be regulated by creed or formula, and, in spite of all the prayers and exhortations of the Friends, their women-folk continued to love fine apparel, yes, and to buy and wear it, too, under the very shadow of the broad brims which shook with disapprobation. Men as well as women sometimes donned gay apparel, but they were much condemned, and the limpness of their principles won them the appellation of 'Wet Quakers.'"

Indulging in Philadelphia's finery was both financially impossible and morally impermissible in the conservative, financially strapped Payne family. As a proper mother and elder of the Pine Street Meeting, Mary Payne saw to it that Dolley was clothed in a long, plain, shoe-length, gray dress, devoid of buttons, tucks, or gathers; a simple, high-necked, white blouse; a shawl (if weather required); and a large, close-fitting, white sunbonnet into which her black curls were tucked. The ensemble was completed with gloves to cover her arms and hands and a white linen facemask to protect her fair skin from the sun, and her face from undue attention by male strangers.[13] Despite the care that her mother took to keep her appearance from seeming worldly, Dolley's stern Quaker neighbors still clucked and frowned about the cut of her clothing and restricted her with so many formal rules of behavior that she felt her natural personality stifled.

By the age of sixteen, brimming over with warmth and enthusiasm, Dolley had made an active, if demure, place for herself in the social circles of the City of Brotherly Love.

Elizabeth Drinker recorded one of Dolley's early social events in her journal on July 10, 1784: "Sally Drinker and Walter Payne, Billy Sanson and Polly Wells, Jacob Downing and Dolly Payne, went to our place at Frankford—Dolly and Josey Sansom and Nancy Drinker (from Par La Ville) mett them there. A Squable—Nancy returned home in the evening with her sister &c."[14] The origin of the "squabble" soon became clear: Jacob Downing asked for Sally Drinker's hand in marriage fifteen months later.[15]

By 1786, Dolley was being described as one of the fairest of the fair, and "it was easy to imagine that many a good Quaker lad's love was laid at her shrine."[16] As a girl of eighteen, she was described as "of slight figure, possessing a delicately oval face, a nose tilted like a flower, jet black hair, and blue eyes of wondrous sweetness." The author added that "those beautiful eyes, with their power to scintillate with playfulness or mellow with sympathy, wrought great havoc with the hearts of the Quaker lads of Haddonfield."[17]

As a teenager, Dolley was not isolated from contact with others of her own age, but the Quakers had strict rules about what constituted appropriate behavior. Dolley once made a trip with three other girls and four boys to nearby Gray's Ferry, a respectable natural resort for Quakers just across Schuylkill River from Philadelphia. When word reached her mother that the group had been unchaperoned, her mother consulted with Elizabeth Drinker and both agreed that "it was quite improper for youthful Quakers to go even in groups to public entertainment places of any kind."[18]

One of Dolley's chief attributes in later life was her ability to make anyone, regardless of rank or social status, feel at ease. This was an outgrowth of her Quaker training. The Friends did not acknowledge any claim of rank or wealth. Her standing within her Quaker meeting was determined solely by her own personal conduct. Consequently, not even her father's eventual bankruptcy marred Dolley's standing among her religious peers. The classless structure of Quaker society permitted her to gain the social self-confidence that

would become a cornerstone of her personality. Nevertheless, Dolley's upper-class, first-family connections through her
Winston and Coles ancestors would also prove to be solid
social assets.

While Dolley was enjoying the sights and sensations of
her newly adopted city, major political decisions were being
made that would have a profound effect on her future. Philadelphia had hosted the Continental Congress in 1776, when
the Declaration of Independence was written. In the summer
of 1787, it hosted the Constitutional Convention. During a
few months of intense debate, the Constitution was forged,
primarily under the leadership of James Madison, a "tiny,
sickly-looking little man who weighed little more than a hundred pounds and always dressed in black," but who possessed
enormous intellectual capacity.[19] In the year before this remarkable document was ratified, its authors attempted to
explain its rationale to the citizenry.

The *Federalist Papers*, a series of eighty-five brilliant essays
written by John Jay, Alexander Hamilton, and James Madison,
were published anonymously under the pen name *Publius* in
several influential New York newspapers. At the time, the
United States was still operating under the Articles of Confederation, which had produced a weak, unsatisfactory
government that allowed states to compete with each other.
The *Federalist Papers* were written as part of the debate about
the best way to govern the new nation. Federalists argued
that if the United States was truly to be a single nation, its
leaders would have to agree on federally binding rules of governance: a strong Constitution. They wanted a strong central
government, rather than a coalition of unequal state governments, and made a strong case for power-sharing between
state and federal authorities. The essays explored in great detail
the implications of establishing a kind of rule that would be
based on the inherent rights of man, would engage as many
citizens as possible, and would include a system of checks
and balances. The Federalists ultimately prevailed, and the
Constitution took effect in 1789.

Having settled the matter of governance, the nation's leaders next struggled over the question of where the nation's capital city should be located. On this issue, Hamilton and Madison clashed along regional lines. New Yorkers, such as Hamilton, and New Englanders were eager to keep the capital in New York and had already started to build President Washington a handsome executive mansion by the Battery, with a majestic view of the Hudson River. Pennsylvanians argued for Philadelphia. Virginians, including Madison, wanted the capital on the Potomac River.

The issue was resolved in June 1790, when Thomas Jefferson invited Madison and Hamilton to his house in New York. There, a deal was struck. Hamilton, President Washington's secretary of the treasury, had earlier proposed that the new federal government should pay off the federal debt and also assume the debts incurred by the separate states during the Revolution, as the latter had been incurred for the common good. Madison opposed the debt assumption legislation.

Jefferson proposed that in order to get the debt issue resolved, Hamilton should press the Pennsylvanians to vote for a permanent capital on the Potomac River in exchange for locating it in Philadelphia for a decade. He also proposed that his friend, Madison, should agree not to object too strongly to the debt assumption bill.[20] In a hotly debated historic compromise which was resolved on July 12, 1790, both houses of Congress voted to pass the Residence Act, which directed that the nation's capital would be relocated from New York to Philadelphia for a period of ten years, after which it would move it to its permanent site, Washington City, on the Potomac.

When Congress adjourned in the summer of 1790, the government started packing its bags for the move to the Quaker city. From there it would govern the nation's 3.9 million people for the next decade while the new capital was being laid out and constructed in the wilderness. In the golden years of the 1790s, Philadelphia would become even more worldly, and as it did, the influence of the Quakers would diminish.

Dolley Payne's attention was focused on love, not politics, during the debate over the Constitution. The strong possibility that she might marry was evident as early as December 1788, when Dolley, then twenty years old, wrote to her friend, Elizabeth Brooke of Montgomery County, Maryland. After apologizing for a delay in her correspondence, she assured Elizabeth that any change in Dolley's marital status would not disrupt their friendship. "I should most gladly have offered <u>you</u> the tribute of my tender remembrance long before this by the Performances of my promis of wrighting, but my ignorance of a <u>single</u> conveyance was the only preventative. To this however my Dear Betsy obliterate the Idea of my neglect occation'd by my <u>prospects</u> of <u>Happiness</u> for be assur'd that no sublimary bliss Whatever should have a tendency to make me forgetful of friends I so highly value."[21] Dolley's reference to her "ignorance of a single conveyance" referred to the fact that post offices were often located far from the residence of the recipient. As a result, most letters were transported by family members or friends who were traveling in the neighborhood, rather than being sent by post. Her "prospects of happiness" referred to her possible marriage to John Todd, Jr., a young Quaker lawyer.

The rest of her letter, devoted to gossip about who was marrying whom in Philadelphia, reflects a troubling trend within the Society of Friends: the Quaker girls Dolley wrote about were all marrying out of her denomination. "A charming little girl of my acquanture & a Quaker two, ran off & was married to a Roman Catholic the other evening—Thee may have seen Her, Sally Bartram was her name Betsy Wistar & Kitty Morris too plain girls [Quakers] Have Eloped to effect a union with the Choice of their hearts—so thee sees Love Is no respectar of persons," Dolley wrote.[22]

John Todd, Jr., was a good match for Dolley, whom he first met in 1786, when her family transferred to her religious home, the Pine Street Meeting. Born November 17, 1763, he was an up-and-coming young lawyer; an educated man with a solid future.[23] The rest of his family was similarly respectable.

His brother, James, was a bank clerk. His father, John Todd, Sr., a Quaker from New London, Chester County, Pennsylvania, was a schoolmaster, teaching at Robert Proud's Quaker school for boys at the corner of Fourth Street and Chestnut. [24] The Todd family also resided there. John Sr. was characterized as a strict disciplinarian who "taught the r's, and while doing so, to appease his brutal nature, applied on pretexts constant castigations."[25] In other words, he frequently whipped his students.

John Jr., a slender, twenty-seven-year-old man with reddish-brown hair and blue eyes, lacked nothing a suitable suitor might need.[26] As Dolley's social life expanded, potential suitors came and went, but John Todd's affections never wavered. There also may have been pressure from Dolley's father to marry young Todd, for John Payne's unprofitable starch-making business was driving him towards ruin. Indeed, John Todd, Jr., had been brought in as a business partner, undoubtedly to provide some financial stability to the family business. In addition, Dolley's father may have wanted to see his daughter safely married before he died. As one story goes, "when Dolly was sent for, to the bedside of her father, and told that he wished her much to become the wife of John Todd...there was nothing for it but to obey."[27] However, based on their letters soon after their marriage, it is clear that Dolley and John married for love, not just duty, and nothing changed until tragedy destroyed their warm and tender union.

In 1789, disaster struck the family. John Payne's starch-manufacturing business went bankrupt. The failure left Payne a ruined man with his family in desperate financial straits. For any businessman, financial distress was a grave threat, but for a Quaker, financial solvency was literally considered a part of godliness.[28] In accordance with the strict rules concerning financial responsibility, the Pine Street Meeting quickly disowned Payne for insolvency.[29] The harsh blow delivered by his fellow Friends stunned Payne, a man who had dedicated his entire adult life to Quaker principles and the welfare of his meeting. Nevertheless, he did not question the act because of his familiarity with the discipline of his church, which he himself had often been called upon to enforce.

After his expulsion from the Pine Street Meeting, Payne joined the Free Quakers, a society of independent-thinking Friends whose meetinghouse still stands at the corner of Fifth and Arch Streets.[30] These Free Quakers had supported the Revolutionary War. Some had even fought in the Continental Army. Along with the aged Benjamin Franklin, Payne signed a memorial to Congress urging emancipation of the slaves.

Formerly a vibrant man, Dolley's father was now unable to support his family. The financial tragedy, along with his

Mary Payne's boardinghouse at 96 North Third Street

expulsion from the Pine Street Meeting, sent him slipping into a deep depression. By 1791, to keep food on the table and a roof over their heads, Mary Payne turned her home at 96 North Third Street (later renumbered 150 North Third Street) into a boardinghouse for federal officials who were transferring into the new national capital.

As her father was becoming progressively more demoralized, love was blooming for Dolley. Delicious rumors of the impending marriage spread through Philadelphia's close-knit Quaker community. Sarah Parker wrote to her friend, Elizabeth Brooke:

Dolly Payne is likely to unite herself to a young man named J. Todd, who has been so solicitous to gain her favor many years, but disappointment for some time seem'd to assault his most sanguine expectations, however things have terminated agreeable to his desires & she now offers her hand to a person whose heart she had long been near and dear to—he has proved a constant Lover indeed & deserves the highest commendation for his generous behavior as he plainly shows to the world no mercenary motives bias'd his judgment (on the contrary) a sincere attachment to her person was his first consideration else her Father's misfortunes might have been an excuse for his leaving her.[31]

Love and romance notwithstanding, Quaker marriage was an act that transcended personal choice. Not only did the Friends view the marital union as a solemn contract between a woman, a man, and God, they also regarded it as a compact with their fellow Friends. Every proposed marriage between a Friend and another person had to be thoroughly investigated and sanctioned by the monthly meeting before a marriage could take place.

The first step in the solemn, complicated matrimonial procedure required the engaged couple to officially notify their meeting of their intention to marry. The protocol went as follows: "On the occasion of this announcement, the groom-to-be, accompanied by a Friend from the men's division, entered the women's side of the church, took his intended bride on his arm, and announced to both the men and women, who were separated by a low partition inside the church, that 'We propose taking each other in marriage.'"[32]

The meeting would then carefully consider whether the two individuals were living lives acceptable to the tenets of their faith. The "passing of meeting" was a formidable proceeding. The bride-elect was then obliged to pass yet another meeting, declaring to her congregation that her intention to marry was still firm.[33]

If no good reason was found to deny the union, the couple received the approval of the meeting and were said to have

The Pine Street Meeting House

"passed meeting." Permission would then be granted to perform the marriage at the next monthly meeting.[34]

A thorough examination of Dolley's and John's characters produced no objections to the union, and on January 7, 1790, the couple declared their wedding vows at the Pine Street Meeting House. Dolley was four months shy of her twenty-second birthday. Her intended, John Todd, Jr., had celebrated his twenty-sixth birthday six weeks earlier. It was a solemn affair. "Friends were appointed to attend marriages 'as governors of the marriage feast, and see that things were managed in good order, and bring report to the next monthly Meeting,'" wrote Quaker historian, Stephen Weeks.[35]

At the head of the meeting sat the elders, all of whom were among Philadelphia's most respected Quaker leaders. They included James Pemberton, a prominent Philadelphia merchant, who also served as an overseer of the public schools. He sat "erect and immovable, with his crossed hands residing on his gold-headed cane." At his side sat attorney Nicholas Waln, "with his smile of sunshine. He was a leading member of the meeting and one of the shrewdest and wittiest members of the Philadelphia bar...." The rest of the meeting was comprised of the "solid Quaker element of the city, while the gay folks again crowded the galleries to their utmost capacity."[36]

The meetinghouse was filled to capacity with Quakers and other well-wishers. After the meeting was called to order and the house fell silent, Dolley and John arose, turned to face each other, and repeated their vows. John took Dolley's hand and "did in a solemn manner declare that he took her the said Dolly Payne to be his wife, promising with Divine assistance to be unto her a loving and faithful husband until death should separate them." In return, Dolley pledged the same. The marriage ceremony having been concluded, John Todd signed the marriage certificate, followed by Dolley, using her new name, Dolley Todd. Elizabeth ("Eliza") Collins, who later married Virginia Congressman Richard Bland Lee, served as the bridesmaid, and Anthony Morris was John's groomsman.[37] Eighty-two of Philadelphia's foremost citizens signed the wedding certificate as witnesses.

Although the premarital examinations and marriage ceremony were formal and solemn, Quaker weddings could become boisterous. Weddings at the Pine Street Meeting often produced a noisy crowd of well-wishers who filled the gallery. In 1789, Sarah Parker wrote that for one couple, the "Pine Street meeting house was amazingly crowded, a number of gay folks—I heard a young man say that he was surprised on viewing the galleries, as they had more the appearance of a play house than of a Friends' meeting."[38] Parker wrote that there were "great affronts" given when Dolley was in the process of passing meeting. Nicholas Waln tried to hold back the wedding crowd, saying that "it was not customary for those who do not belong, unless near

Elizabeth ("Eliza") Collins Lee

connections, to go into the meeting of business." Nevertheless, some visitors at that ceremony were "so rude as to press in without any kind of ceremony, very indecent behavior [which] was too obvious to be unobserved, even by children."[39]

Dolley was probably married with snow on the ground, but little else is known about the day. No eyewitness description of her wedding has survived. Her gown was probably much like that of another Quaker bride, who lamented, "My wedding gown was ashen silk, too simple for my taste; I wanted lace around the neck, and a ribbon at the waist."[40] Although no record survives of the details of the Todds' wedding reception, a contemporary account describes what was expected of Philadelphia Quaker newlyweds:

> Marriage entertainments at this time were very extensive, and harassing to the wedded. For two days afterward punch was dealt out in profusion, and, with cakes and other sweetmeats, were set out on the lower floor, and were also sent out generally throughout the neighborhood, the bride received the visitors, and was kissed by all comers, often as many as a hundred a day. The richer families also had as many as one hundred and twenty to dine and stay to supper the day of the marriage. All who signed the marriage certificate were also invited to tea or supper. At the time of the 'passing of meeting' for two days all the male friends of the bride were privileged to call, drink punch, eat cake and kiss the bride. Even the plain Friends submitted to these things.[41]

John Todd's wedding gift to Dolley was a miniature watercolor portrait of himself, painted on ivory and meant to be used as part of a bracelet, following the English fashion. It was painted c. 1790 by Charles Willson Peale, one of the leading painters in America in the late eighteenth century.[42] The newlyweds may first have lived at Dolley's mother's boardinghouse on North Third Street. On January 23, 1791,

John Todd, Jr.

barely a year after their marriage, John Todd's law practice was evidently flourishing, for he purchased a "genteel and convenient" house on the corner of Fourth and Walnut Streets, built in 1775 by Jonathan Dilworth and sold to Todd by his widow, Ann Dilworth.[43] Built of English red-and-black brick, the handsome and substantial house had an adjacent two-story brick kitchen and a wooden stable. Every wall was filled with costly windows. The three-story west wall alone had eighteen, and two west-facing attic dormers contributed even more light and ventilation to the comfortable house. Todd used a front room on the first floor as his law office, and the adjacent room was used by several of his law clerks and his hard-working young apprentice, Isaac Heston.[44]

John and Dolley Todd's house at Fourth and Walnut Streets

A contemporary description said that "the lower story is finished as Customary, Chamber, washboards and windows cased, winding stairs, Yellow pine floors, two chimnies have marble, no Dormer Window, nor Battlement to the East."[45] A 1793 inventory showed that the Todds' home was extensively furnished with conservative, tasteful furniture and high-quality accessories, including a large sideboard, a settee, eleven mahogany and pine tables, thirty-six mahogany and Windsor chairs, three looking glasses

D. P. Madison

The Todd family's kitchen

(mirrors), china, carpets, six pictures, and other goods valued at just over £191. Transportation was provided by a horse and riding chair, for which John Todd was taxed. The rich intellectual environment in which the Todds lived was reflected in the size of the family library, which was valued at £187 — enough for at least one hundred fifty books — and was worth almost as much as all of the furnishings combined.[46]

When John bought their new brick home, the young Todd family was headed for a prosperous and comfortable urban life. Their first child, John Payne Todd, named after Dolley's husband and her father, was born in the Fourth Street house on February 29, 1792, when Dolley was almost twenty-four.[47] The following summer, their second son, William Temple Todd, named for Dolley's brother, was also born in the house. Dolley's birthing pattern was normal for her time. Her first child was conceived within sixteen months after her marriage, and her second child was delivered about fifteen months after the first.

The warmth of John's love for Dolley and their children was expressed in a letter he wrote to her while he followed the judges who traveled from courthouse to courthouse on their legal circuit. On July 30, 1793, just before catastrophe struck him and his family, John's letter expressed both the depth of his love for Dolley and the degree of trust he had in her: "I hope my dear Dolley is well and my sweet little Payne can lisp *Mama* in a stronger Voice than when his Papa left him — I wish he was here to run after Mrs. Withy's Ducks he would have fine sport — Let the Boys be attentive to the office and Business. I have no doubt of my Dear Dolleys Assistance when necessary. Thine forever, John Todd Junr."[48] With a good start on a comfortable station in life, and with Dolley's heritage of ancestors who had produced large families, John and Dolley Todd surely looked forward to years of raising many happy, healthy children.

Shortly after Dolley's wedding, her sister, Lucy, then only fifteen, eloped with George Steptoe Washington, seventeen, "a good, kind young man" who had studied at the Philadelphia College for two years. He was also heir to Harewood House, a substantial western Virginia plantation in Jefferson County, three miles northwest of Charlestown, near Harper's Ferry. The groom, who was President George Washington's ward, namesake, and nephew, was the son of the president's brother, Samuel, and his wife, Ann Steptoe Washington. Samuel, a jolly, cosmopolitan fellow, was described as "a gay, fox-hunting squire, who thought much of his wives [he eventually had five], and his horses and dogs."[49]

Lucy's 1793 wedding brought heartbreak rather than joy to her mother, and became the next increment in Dolley's estrangement from the Quaker community. Unlike more liberal Christian denominations, such as the Anglicans and Presbyterians, who invoked excommunication only in the most extreme cases of blasphemy and other grievous acts against God, the pious Quakers had a lengthy list of actions and behaviors they would not tolerate. An Anglican who married a Presbyterian, for example, might, at worst, face a few clucks of the tongue, raised eyebrows, and whispers, but little else, and neither person would be excommunicated from the Anglican or Presbyterian Church for his or her act. But if a Quaker was married by a "hireling priest" or to someone not enrolled as a member in good standing with the Quaker community, the monthly meeting was duty-bound to disown the member and formally remove him or her from the rolls of the society. In Lucy's case, her meeting was quick to take notice and act. The minutes of the Philadelphia Monthly Meeting left nothing in doubt:

> Friends are appointed to assist women Friends in preparing a testimony against the misconduct of Lucy Washington, late Payne, who had by birth a right of membership among us, having disregarded the wholesome order of our discipline, in the accomplishment of her marriage with a person not in membership with us, before an hireling priest, and without the consent of her mother, after being precautioned against such outgoing. We therefore testify that the said Lucy Washington is no longer a member of our religious Society, nevertheless desiring she may be favored with a due sense of her deviation and seek to be rightly restored.[50]

Like many other former Quakers, Lucy Payne Washington never sought to return to the fold and was lost forever to the world of plaincloth. Her marriage to a worldly man, coming as it did after the disownment of her father, further strained the family's relations with their fellow Friends. This trend would accelerate in the next few years, pushing Dolley progressively further away from the people who had surrounded her, educated her, and guided her life since childhood.

John Payne's life continued to deteriorate. He made out his will on September 2, 1792, naming his wife, Mary, executrix. John and Dolley Todd were among the witnesses. While the red and golden leaves of autumn were falling on the streets of Philadelphia, John Payne died on October 24, 1792.[51] His body was laid out for viewing so that the spectators could reflect upon their own mortality and the need to live their remaining days in harmony with God's teachings. His funeral service was read at the Free Quaker Meeting House, where he had served with honor as a speaker of that congregation. The mourners did not wear black armbands, veils, or any mourning costumes, for such dress would have been considered heathenish and out of harmony with the teachings of Scripture.[52] His body was interred in the Free Quaker cemetery on Fifth Street, near Locust.[53] His estate was so small that Mary Payne did not bother to bring it to probate until 1796.[54]

One of the most gruesome events in all of American medical history played itself out in Philadelphia in the summer and fall of 1793. On August 5, noted physician Dr. Benjamin Rush recorded in his diary that he had seen his first case of "malignant fever" for that year. Before the summer was over, about 5,000 Philadelphians had died of yellow fever. Dolley's loved ones, and the families of her friends and neighbors, were not spared.

Yellow fever epidemics were well known to American cities long before 1793. This one began about the same time that several thousand refugees arrived from Haiti, where rampaging blacks were killing whites, causing white settlers to flee.

D. P. Madison

Many came to America, some already infected with the non-contagious yellow fever virus. The villain was in the casks of drinking water they brought with them, for it was the *Aedes aegypti* mosquitoes, and not human-to-human contact, that spread the disease. The imported mosquitoes only added to the ample supply of disease-laden insects that already infested the city.

On August 4 and 6, respectively, Mr. Moore, an Englishman, and Mrs. Parkinson, an Irish woman, died at Dennie's boardinghouse on North Water Street in Philadelphia. Moore died so quickly that the physician attending him thought he might have been poisoned, but an autopsy found nothing suspicious. Dr. Isaac Cathrall, the physician attending Mrs. Parkinson, found an appallingly different progression of disease with his patient. "Cathrall marveled at the long morbid dance the fever put on the Irish woman, Mrs. Parkinson, though: severe head and back pains, great thirst, offensive stools, much vomiting, delirium, red spots on the face and breast, blindness, sore throat, hiccupping, and death." She died a slow and tortured death just one room away from a man whose symptoms and quick death were quite different from her own. Oddly, her family remained healthy. The disease, it seemed, was often lethal, but not contagious.[55]

Abruptly, the death toll from the "summer fever" in Philadelphia started to rocket. Dolley's friend, Elizabeth Drinker, who chronicled the minute details of the Quaker city for six decades, recorded on August 16, 1793, "John Gillenham was bury'd on second day last—'tis a sickly time now in Phila[delphia] and there have been an unusual number of funerals lately here."[56] Two days later, she noted the funeral of George Thomas, who died of "a lax and vomiting." Then she wrote of calling on "the Widdow Rigers, a poor woman with three Children, who lost her Husband a week or 10 days ago." On August 23, Elizabeth noted that "a fever prevails in the city…. 'Tis really an alarming and serious time."[57] Congress was nearing its scheduled recess, and its members hurriedly fled the capital. Philadelphians had good reason to wonder if they would ever return. Still, no one could imagine the extent of the catastrophe that would rapidly envelop the city.

By August 23, Alexander Hamilton was feeling the effects of the "putrid fever." On September 8, Thomas Jefferson, who was still in his Philadelphia residence, wrote Madison, "The yellow fever increases. The week before last 3 a day died. This last week about 11 a day have died, consequently, from known data about 33 a day are taken and there are about 330 patients under it."[58] A committee of Friends came together to raise money to help provide medical care for the poor who were stricken. On September 14, Dolley's generous husband contributed twenty dollars.[59] The epidemic spiraled out of control so quickly that the committee never had the opportunity to thank him.

At the time, the fever was thought to be caused by "bad air" produced by a lack of sanitation in the poorer parts of town, especially the streets closest to the waterfront and its wharves. The role of insects in the transmission of disease was unknown, and doctors sought cures for symptoms, such as fever and the telltale jaundice, rather than treating the cause of the disease that produced the symptoms. Because fever epidemics routinely broke out in cities throughout America, there was no obvious link between the influx of refugees and mosquitoes from tropical Haiti and the fevers that were killing Philadelphians.

One clue surfaced. As the death toll rose, it was noted that incidences of the disease appeared to be clustered in the Water Street area, one block from the wharves that lined the Delaware River. Nearby, a load of water-soaked coffee had been left to rot. The "foul air" from the rotting coffee was soon blamed for the fever outbreak.

Dr. Benjamin Rush warned his fellow physicians that the city faced an epidemic of the "highly contagious, as well as mortal...bilious remitting yellow fever."[60] Rush was a brilliant physician, prominent from his extraordinary service during the Revolutionary War and for being a signer of the Declaration of Independence. As a doctor, his powers of observation were both systematic and intense, but his deductions were based on the commonly accepted, inaccurate assumptions about the nature of disease. Indeed, yellow fever can easily become an epidemic if the mosquito-breeding conditions are right, but the disease is not contagious because it cannot be communicated from human to human, only from mosquito to human. Ultimately, Rush's conclusions as to the origin and methods of treatment of yellow fever made him "the right man at the right time in the right place with precisely the wrong ideas to be able, better than any contemporary, to assess and react to the situation correctly."[61]

Rush's theories on yellow fever and the regimen for its treatment were supported and endorsed by a large segment of Philadelphia's medical community, and he was considered a genius by many of his colleagues. Sadly, Rush and his fellow physicians were grasping at straws and relying on guesswork. Because of the state of medical knowledge at that time, patients often died as quickly and surely from the treatments as they did from the diseases themselves.

As they watched their friends and neighbors become afflicted and die, fear crept into the hearts of the Todd family. The death toll steadily increased, despite the best efforts of residents to stave off the disease or cure it once it struck. Tar was supposed to ward off yellow fever, and many people carried tarred ropes with them. Others lit bonfires in front of their houses to purify the air. On August 28, Elizabeth Drinker wrote that her son, Henry, left home that morning and that "I gave him a small spoonful of Duffy's Ellixr and Vinager in a spunge, and a sprig of wormwood."[62] Duffy's Elixir, a popular patent medicine, consisted of a tincture of senna leaves, jalap root, coriander seeds, and alcohol. Wormwood is the dark-green, bitter-tasting oil of a strong-smelling flowering plant. Although it is poisonous at full strength, and is sometimes used as an herbal remedy, in that era, wormwood was chiefly used in the production of absinthe, a liquor with a high alcoholic content that has the capacity to induce mild euphoria.[63] Sadly, none of these concoctions had any curative effect on yellow fever.

All around the Drinkers' house, the neighbors fell like dominoes. "There is a man next door but one to us, who Doctor Kuhn says will quickly die of this terriable disorder—Caty Prusia over against us is very ill, and a man at the Shoemakers next door to Neighbor Waln's, some sick in our ally, we do not know what ails them.... The inhabitance are leaving the City in great numbers, poor John Lamsback died yesterday," Elizabeth Drinker wrote.[64]

Dolley's second son, William Temple Todd, was born in the midst of the epidemic in September 1793. The birth left both mother and child weak. The death rate from yellow fever was increasing at an alarming rate. On September 1, nineteen died; by September 8, the number was forty-two; and entire families were wiped out within the course of a few days.[65]

Intensely alarmed, John Todd carried the ailing Dolley and infant William out of the city on a litter to Gray's Ferry, across the Schuylkill River, a good distance beyond the city's limits. Dolley's firstborn son, John Payne Todd, and her mother traveled with them. In all likelihood, her sisters, Anna and Mary, and her brother, John, also accompanied them.[66]

John Todd's faithful law clerk, Isaac Heston, stayed behind at the house and office at Fourth and Walnut to take care of legal work, which consisted chiefly of drawing up wills for the dying.[67] On September 19, he wrote to his brother, describing the almost unbelievable devastation the fever was causing: "You can not imagin the situation of this city. How deplorable. it continues to be more and more depopulated. both by the removal of its inhabitants into the Country, and by the destructive Fever which now prevails. They are Dieing on our right hand and on our left... in fact, all around us. great are the numbers that are called to the grave, and numbered with the silent Dead." Heston closed his letter by writing, "Through all the danger, thanks be to God, we have yet been preserved, but how long It may continue so, it is impossible to say, for this hour we may be well, and next find ourselves past recovery."[68]

D. P. Madison

Undaunted by the threat, John Todd returned to the plague-infested city to make provisions for his parents and his business. When he arrived at Walnut Street, he found the shadow of death darkening his own doorstep. On September 27, Dolley's father-in-law showed the deadly symptoms himself. John's valiant clerk, Isaac Heston, was also dangerously ill and died on September 29. John Todd's brother, James, had already moved his family into the country about eight miles out of town. On October 4, 1793, a desperate and distraught Dolley wrote to James:

> Oh my dear Brother what a dread prospect has thy last Letter presented to me! A reveared Father in the Jaws of Death, & a Love'd Husband in perpetual danger — I have long wished for an oppertunity of writeing to thee & enquireing what we could do? I am almost destracted with distress & apprihension — is it two late for their removal? or can no interfearance of their Earthly friends rescue them from the two general fate? I have repeatedly Entreated John to leave home from which we are unavoidably Banished — but alass he cannot leave his Father. I did not receive thy first Letter & am in ignorence of the particulars thee Mentions — pray write me soon again — I wish much to see you, but my Child is sick, & I have no way of getting to you.[69]

John Todd's parents would not leave the city while John was attending to his clerk, and all three paid the ultimate price for their moral support. John Todd, Sr., died on October 2, 1793, about 5:00 p.m. His wife followed him to the grave on October 12, but the Grim Reaper was not yet finished with the Todd family. The next two victims were Dolley's husband and then, only hours later, her son.

The details of the death of young William Temple Todd at Gray's Ferry on October 24, 1793, have not survived. The child was described as "very weakly from birth" and may have died from the fever or other natural causes. The medical treatments given to children with the fever would have been of little use to Dolley's infant son. We have no record of Dolley's observations of yellow fever treatment, but years later, another distraught mother wrote her husband about the onset and progress of the disease in their two-year-old boy. At the outset, he was "acting like a skylark," she wrote. When the boy became feverish and his head drooped, the woman sent for a nearby physician. He concluded the boy had "a great deal of fever" and treated him with calomel pills, powders, and blisters, but all to no avail. Two days later the boy complained of nausea, and the doctor ordered that a blister be placed on his stomach. Although the doctor was confident, the fever soon returned, and after the doctor's last visit, "that ominous brown-coffee coloured fluid came up, staining the pure lips of our little one." The doctor pronounced it "black vomit." The boy died that afternoon.[70]

Dolley may well have watched the same horrific scenario unfold with her son, William, and with her husband. Both of them died — or in the language of the Quakers, "settled in the land of fixedness" — on October 24, 1793. One account states that John Todd, Jr., consumed with the fever for six days, struggled back to Gray's Ferry, where he died as his young wife watched, helpless to do anything except comfort him.[71]

The onslaught of yellow fever ultimately claimed the life of four members of Dolley's immediate family: her husband, her son, her father-in-law, and her mother-in-law. Two years later, she lost her two remaining elder brothers, William Temple and Isaac, to other causes. Dolley never fully recovered from these crushing emotional blows. For the rest of her life, October was a dark and solemn month on Dolley's calendar, and she remained fearful of the disease, which continued to be a threat to her family and neighbors in the years ahead. Despite the efforts of physicians and scientists for more than two centuries after the great Philadelphia yellow fever plague of 1793, there is still no cure for the disease, and only the symptoms can be treated.[72]

Fear kept Dolley; her surviving son, John; her mother; and other kin from re-entering the city until the death toll slackened after the November frosts killed off the mosquitoes. Dolley's desolation and desperation were described in an October 25 letter from her mother, Mary, presumably still at Gray's Ferry, to a Todd family nurse in Philadelphia:

> How shall I express my feelings O it seems to me as if my heart would brake my Poor Dear Dolley what dose she and will she suffer. how distressing is her situation the day she consined her Dear husband and her little babe to the silent grave she has no friend in town Nurse but thee to depend on she is here among strangers and frenless she is in debt for the buriel of her babe and nearly moneyless having only nineteen Dollars Left and a number of other Debts to pay before she can move and we must go from this in a few days pray consider her Condition and if her poor Dear husband has left any money with thee contrive to send it to her also if it is possible for thee to appoint a time and place we will try to meet thee Dolley is very unwell and wishes the [riding] Chair and horse sent Imeadately to her that she may get from this place.[73]

After the crushing loss of her husband and infant son, Dolley sought the consolation of her mother. Sometime in the late stages of her husband's financial distress, probably 1792, Mary had turned the family home at 96 North Third Street into a boardinghouse for government officials.[74] Because the nation's transitional capital, Philadelphia, had become crowded to its utmost capacity, Mary Payne's establishment became the residence of several prominent men, including Colonel Aaron Burr, a hero of the Revolution, an able attorney, and at that time, a U.S. senator from New York.

When Dolley met Burr at her mother's boardinghouse, she was twenty-four years old, he was thirty-six, and his wife, Theodosia Bartow Prevost Burr, was in the terminal stage of stomach cancer. Burr's only child, Theodosia, was almost eleven years old and nursed her failing mother in New York City. Burr was a slender, handsome, charismatic man with impeccable taste in clothing and female companionship. He also had an extremely generous nature and often gave emotional and financial support to friends and relatives in need. Women responded readily to his charm and attentions. Indeed, as one writer aptly observed, "Burr was catnip to women."[75] One of Dolley's biographers suggested that the "beautiful young widow might have been a tempting morsel for Burr's universal rapacity."[76] Politically inspired rumors later implied that their relationship included illicit behavior, but Burr appears to have kept his libido in check, and Dolley her virtue intact.

Now, when Dolley and her mother returned to the boardinghouse in Philadelphia, Congress was in recess. Potential visitors were acutely aware of the unhealthiness of the city and stayed away in droves. Soon, Lucy and George Steptoe Washington, now sixteen and eighteen, the young couple who had caused Mary Payne so much heartbreak, came to her aid. They took Mary, forty-nine years old, and Lucy's siblings, Mary and John, to live with them in comfort at Harewood plantation. Dolley's mother sold the Philadelphia house, which held so many memories of hardship and grief. Dolley, her son, and her sister Anna Payne, then fourteen, regrouped at Dolley's house on Fourth and Walnut Streets in December 1793. Bound by family ties and tragedy, Dolley and Anna had become virtually inseparable.

Dolley faced an immediate financial crisis when she and her mother returned to Philadelphia after burying their dead. John Todd had been on the path to future success but had not yet accumulated substantial assets. Three months prior to his death, he had made his will. Much more than a dry legal document, the testament is a tender reflection of the great love that bound him and Dolley together. On July 2, 1793, with his wife six months pregnant, John wrote:

D. P. Madison

I give and devise all my estate, real and personal to the Dear Wife of my Bosom, and first and only Woman upon whom my all and only affections were placed, Dolley Payne Todd, her heirs and assigns forever, trusting that as she has proved an amiable and affectionate wife to her John, she may prove an affectionate mother to my little Payne and the sweet Babe with which she is now *enciente* [pregnant]. My last Prayer is may she educate him in ways of Honesty, tho' he may be obliged to beg his Bread, remembering that will be better to him than a name and riches. Having a great opinion of the integrity and honourable conduct of Edward Burd and Edward Tilghman, Esquires, my dying request is that they will give such advice and assistance to my dear Wife as they shall think prudent with respect to the management and disposal of my very small Estate, and the settling of my unfinished legal business. I appoint my dear Wife executrix of this my will.[77]

In a calm display of the resolution, strength, and common sense that would be hallmarks of her character, Dolley took charge of her family's shattered life just four days after John's death. She wrote to her brother-in-law, James Todd, to obtain copies of her late husband's business accounts and a copy of his father's will. James had evidently already been forced to think of how to liquidate his brother's estate, and Dolley's response to his suggestions showed her deep devotion to education. She wrote to James, "I was hurt my dear Jamy that the Idea of [John's] library should occur as a proper source for raising money—Books from which he wishes his child improved, shall remain sacred, and I would feel the pinching hand of Poverty before I disposed of them."[78]

After four days, Dolley had no response, so she again wrote to James, expressing her strong disappointment and growing irritation over the delay in receiving the papers of her father-in-law and her husband: "I wrote thee some days ago requesting a copy of will & the papers contain'd in the Trunk. I hope friend West may be the bearer of them as it is highly improper that I should be without them."[79] Dolley's polite but forceful requests were ignored. James Todd provided little assistance. John Todd's will was ultimately probated on November 1793, and his estate was inventoried on November 21 of that year.[80]

As the weeks and months passed, Dolley became progressively more distressed, for her brother-in-law appeared to be contesting her claim to her husband's estate. On February 7, 1794, four months after her first request, she sent James a written demand which was hand-delivered by a messenger. "As I have already suffered the most serious Inconvenience from the unnecessary Detention of my part of my mother in law's property and of the Receipt Books and papers of my late Husband," she wrote, "I am constrained once more to request—and if a request is not sufficient—to demand that they be delivered this day—as I cannot wait thy return from this proposed Excursion without any material Injury to my affairs. The bearer waits for thy answer."[81] In March, James finally provided her with an account of his mother's estate, and Dolley gave him a receipt for a watch that John Todd, Sr., had bequeathed to his son, John Todd, Jr., in trust for his grandson, John Payne Todd.[82]

Then there was the matter of her father-in-law's estate. In his last days, while he lay dying of the fever, John Todd, Sr., had bequeathed to his son, John Jr., £500, and to his grandsons, John Payne Todd and William Temple Todd, £50 each, with the rest of his estate, save for a silver watch, to be divided equally among his five grandchildren. He named his two sons, John and James, and his friend, Samuel Jones, as his executors. George Walker, Dolley P. Todd, and John Todd, Jr., witnessed the will. The senior Todd's estate was not settled until January 11, 1796. Since both father and son John were now dead, Dolley stood to inherit £600 plus two-fifths of her father-in-law's considerable estate.[83]

Dolley's careful reasoning, arithmetic skills, and willpower are evident in her correspondence about the estate settlements.

Her difficulties in obtaining her share of her father-in-law's estate were eased through the friendly intervention of her mother's former boarder, Aaron Burr. Acting as a trusted friend and legal advisor, he helped with the arrangements that enabled Dolley to take possession of her inheritance.[84]

Aaron Burr

Separated from his dying wife and the daughter he loved to the extreme, Burr was a lonely man in Philadelphia, and Dolley's quintessential charm made her attractive company. Dolley, whose family had been decimated, was probably happy to have the brilliant, articulate man as a conversational companion. Her pleasing appearance undoubtedly appealed to his manly nature, and her plight certainly appealed to his generous heart. As a result, Burr quickly took the widow Todd and her surviving son, Payne, under his protective wing.

With the recent death of so many of her friends and family members, with yellow fever still raging through the cities of the new nation, and with the prudent preparations her husband had made for his family still fresh in her mind, Dolley Todd made out her own will. She appointed her mother, Mary; her favored brother-in-law, George Steptoe Washington; and William W. Wilkins, her Philadelphia lawyer friend, to be the executors of her estate.

Inspired by Burr's friendship, legal advice, and intense devotion to education, Dolley named him sole guardian of her son, then just over two years old. Like her late husband, Dolley demonstrated how much she valued learning over prosperity when she wrote: "As the education of my son is to him and to me the most interesting of all earthly concerns, and far more important to his happiness and eminence in

Life than the increase of his estate, I direct that no expense be spared to give him every advantage and improvement of which his Talents may be susceptible."[85] Dolley signed the document on May 13, 1794.

Five days later, Aaron Burr's wife died, the sad end to years of suffering from stomach cancer, which Burr had done everything in his power to alleviate. After her death, the Colonel, as Burr was addressed, then thirty-eight, could easily have taken a romantic interest in the attractive twenty-six-year-old Quaker widow. It would have been a logical and appropriate match. They were both widowed parents with a young child apiece, and of appropriate ages for a marriage to each other. However, if Burr had any such inclinations, he preserved a gentlemanly silence, and Dolley's surviving papers make no mention of a romantic interest in her helpful friend.[86] Nevertheless, Dolley's provision for the education of her son demonstrated that she esteemed Burr as a respected and highly responsible man.

The cold, emotionally desolate winter months of 1793 were a heavy burden for Dolley. Yet, when Philadelphia was warmed by the sun the next spring, Dolley's irrepressible warmth and good humor began to resurface. Dolley was seen more often in public, and her attractive personality, scarcely hidden by her Quaker bonnet, became progressively more apparent to her fellow Philadelphians. At that time, young, attractive widows — especially those with property — usually did not remain unmarried for long. Unknown to the grieving widow, but not to her friends, a rapid metamorphosis was in progress.

By the time the daffodils and crocuses of the city were again in bloom, Dolley, with her quick smile, curly locks, bright eyes, and handsome bosom, had become one of the city's most eligible women. Her close friend, Eliza Collins, noticed the attention being paid to her on the streets and said only halffacetiously, "Really, Dolly, thou must hide thy face, there are so many staring at thee."[87]

One of the men doing the staring was James Madison, then a prosperous and well-known forty-three-year-old planter and a U.S. representative from Virginia. It was Madison's congressional colleague, Senator Aaron Burr, who played Cupid and facilitated Dolley's rapid, unplanned transition from grieving young widow to blushing second-time bride. Madison and Burr had come to know each other well as classmates at the College of New Jersey (now Princeton University) from 1769 through 1771. Both were brilliant, accomplished men and omnivorous readers, but in the social arena, they were radically different. Burr was a gregarious man of the world with an intense interest in women. Madison was socially naïve and uneasy in the arena of interpersonal relationships and had never courted a woman until the winter of 1782-1783, when he was thirty-one years old.[88]

The first object of his affections was a girl half his age. Catherine, known as Kitty, was the vibrant fifteen-year-old daughter of William Floyd of New York. A Republican, Floyd was a friend of Thomas Jefferson and an admirer of Madison. Given the matrimonial standards of the time, the match, while lopsided as to age, was nothing that would have raised many eyebrows. Madison's heart swelled at the prospect of marriage and starting a family with his betrothed.

Miss Floyd, however, developed reservations about the match in the spring of 1783. After a relatively brief engagement, she broke off with Madison and turned her attention to William Clarkson, a nineteen-year-old medical student who shared her musical interests.[89] Her letter announcing the end of the relationship was written in July 1783.

On August 11, 1784, a broken-hearted Madison wrote to Thomas Jefferson of his shattered romance. His friend at Monticello responded, "I sincerely lament the misadventure which has happened from whatever cause it may have happened. Should it be final, however, the world presents the same and many other resources of happiness, and you possess many with yourself. Firmness of mind and unintermitting occupations will not long leave you in pain."[90] Kitty Floyd married William Clarkson in 1785, thereby forfeiting (although she could not have known it then) her opportunity to become

First Lady of the United States. Madison was crushed. His pain over the loss of Kitty's heart never subsided. For the rest of his life, Madison systematically obliterated all references to her in his correspondence from earlier years.

His poor luck with romance sent Madison scurrying into his emotional shell. His friends lamented that he might remain a lifelong bachelor, but Dolley's personal magnetism ultimately lured him back out. Inhibited by the lingering fear of rejection, he asked his cosmopolitan friend, Burr, to introduce him to her.

In the spring of 1794, Dolley rented out her house and furniture at Fourth and Walnut. She planned to spend the summer at Harewood plantation with her sister, Lucy Washington, and their mother, Mary. In May, when Dolley was turning twenty-six and still grieving the loss of her husband, son, and in-laws, she received a note by messenger that was to transform her life. She quickly recognized the handwriting of her old friend, Colonel Burr. He asked her permission to make a social call that evening to introduce James Madison. With breathless excitement, Dolley immediately dashed off a note to her intimate friend and former wedding attendant, Eliza Collins. "Dear friend," Dolley wrote. "Thou must come to me. Aaron Burr says that 'the great little Madison' has asked to be brought to see me this evening."[91]

Extreme good fortune was on the way for both the middle-aged Virginia planter and the young Quaker widow. As the fragrant willows blossomed in Philadelphia that spring, James Madison again found himself smitten. Dolley was delighted with the prospect of his attentions, and the unmistakable scent of love was in the air.

CHAPTER FIVE

In Second Blush

Dear Friend, thou must come to me. Aaron Burr
says that the great little Madison has asked to be
brought to see me this evening.
　　　　　—Dolley Payne Todd to Eliza Collins

Philadelphia
Spring 1794

Great of mind, conservative of dress, short in stature, seventeen years and two months her senior, and a brilliant conversationalist in intimate groups (though he greatly disliked large ones), Virginia Congressman James Madison set out to win the heart and hand of the widow Todd. On a warm, spring evening, escorted by his slender, elegantly dressed friend and colleague, Aaron Burr, Madison left his lodgings at Mrs. House's boardinghouse. Madison probably wore the new round beaver hat (size 7¼) he had purchased that spring.[1]

The two men were a study in contrasts. "Burr," wrote one chronicler, "was full of grace, of charm, of vivacity, with mobile expressive features, and an eye potent to sway men against their will, and women to their undoing." Madison was "slow, unimpassioned, and unmagnetic, yet with a twinkle in his mild eye which bespoke a dry humor."[2] The two men, each with a mind sharper than any razor, walked to the widow Todd's candle-lit brick house at Fourth and Walnut Streets, three-and-a-half blocks from the docks on the Delaware River.[3] There they were greeted by Dolley and her Quaker friend, Eliza Collins, her chaperone for the evening.

No doubt Madison wore his habitual costume: a black suit with vest; a white, ruffled shirt; white knee britches ornamented with silver buckles; and powdered hair, pulled back into a queue and tied with a black ribbon. Dolley wore a mulberry-colored satin dress, with a thin, finely woven silk tulle kerchief over her "fair white neck," and "an exquisitely dainty little cap, from which an occasional uncropped curl would escape."[4] The fact that Dolley was wearing a colored satin dress and hosting a man with romantic intentions only six months after her husband's death shows that she had already set some of her strict Quaker ways aside and was open to being courted.

Known to his friends as "little Jemmy," Madison had long since earned the right to be called great. Known throughout the nation as brilliant, he was a framer of the Constitution and the Bill of Rights and had served in the Virginia legislature and held other state offices. While Madison was serving in the first U.S. Congress, President Washington chose him to draft his inaugural address and often consulted him on a wide array of topics. When he started courting Dolley, Madison was the leader of what would soon become known as the Republican party. In 1794, political parties *per se* were still undeveloped, and his party was known simply as "Madison's." He was a man wealthy in slaves (just over 100) and fertile land (about 5,000 acres). It is possible that he first met Dolley through her uncle, Congressman Isaac Coles, as early as 1789 because, much later in life, he said he "was indebted for his matrimonial success to the friendly aid" of Coles.[5]

James Madison

Few public men have suffered more than Madison at the hands of their observers. He was variously characterized as small, sickly, wizened, awkward in manners, and sallow of complexion. In 1789, Jacques Pierre Brissot de Warville, a

French revolutionary, political writer, and traveler, met Madison. "He had, when I saw him, an air of fatigue," wrote the sympathetic Frenchman. "Perhaps it was the effect of the immense labors to which he has devoted himself for some time past. His look announces a censor, his conversation discovers a man of learning, and his reserve is that of a man conscious of his talents and of his duties."[6] A Federalist political opponent reviled him as "the little Pygmy."[7] One of Madison's harshest critics likened him to "a country schoolmaster in mourning for one of his pupils whom he has whipped to death."[8]

Madison suffered from thinning, prematurely white hair, which formed a pronounced widow's peak at the crown of his head. No matter what his age was at the time his various portraits were painted, the three characteristic expressions he presented to the artist—aloof, dour, or disapproving, with no hint of warmth or trace of a smile—inevitably added an extra decade or more to his appearance.

Much has been said of Madison's short, slender stature, which his close friend, private secretary, and cousin by marriage, Edward Coles, measured and recorded as between five feet six inches and five feet six-and-a-half inches.[9] This would have made him the same height as his colleague, Burr, who stood five feet six. Other accounts describe him as shorter, closer to five feet two inches, with a weight of about 100 pounds.

Dolley was said to be five feet six inches tall, but it is almost universally acknowledged that she stood substantially taller than Madison. With her erect carriage, rouged cheeks, Reubenesque figure, prominent (and much-noticed) bosom, coupled with her stylish high-waisted, low-cut Empire gowns and her exotic turbans, with their lavish use of bright colors, patterns, textures, and bird plumage, Dolley dwarfed him visually.

Nevertheless, when Madison's blue eyes met Dolley's, the resulting warm smiles held great promise for both. The evening was evidently a major romantic success. Dolley's niece, Mary

Cutts, wrote, "in this first interview, at her own house, she conquered the recluse bookworm Madison, who was considered an old bachelor."[10] They were an interesting pair. He was the oldest son of a family of twelve children; Dolley the oldest daughter of at least nine (and perhaps as many as twelve) children. Both had assumed the responsibilities of the first-born of their gender in large families early in their lives.

The rumors of a possible match did not take long to reach the Philadelphia home of President and Mrs. Washington at Market Street near Sixth. Martha Dandridge Custis Washington, then sixty-three, knew the Payne family well, as her husband's favorite nephew, George Steptoe Washington, was married to Dolley's sister. Based on their close kinship, the first First Lady invited Dolley to the President's House, just a few blocks away, where she inquired of the widow Todd's intentions.

Martha Washington offered Dolley valuable insights acquired through years of life in Virginia society. She was in a

good position to provide sound advice. A well-bred, warm-hearted, gentle, uncomplicated woman with little formal education, she had married at the age of eighteen and lost two of her four babies and her first husband, Daniel Park Custis, by the time she was twenty-six. A gentleman who visited Mount Vernon in 1801 described Martha Washington's normal attire as a black dress and a plain white cap with a black ribbon. He found her

Martha Washington

"affable and polite," and she made him and his party welcome in a "hospitable though unceremonious manner."[11]

According to Dolley's niece, Mary Cutts, Martha Washington addressed Dolley using the Quaker manner of speech to put her at ease. Mrs. Washington asked:

"Dolley, is it true thou art engaged to James Madison?"

The conscience-stricken widow hung her head and answered stammeringly, "No, Madam."

Mrs. Washington said, "If it is so, do not be ashamed to confess it, rather be proud. He will make thee a good husband, all the better for being so much older. We both advocate it."[12]

In her willingness to give matrimonial advice, Martha Washington differed from her husband. When placed in a similar situation, the father of the nation wrote with his customary good sense, and more than his customary sense of humor:

> For my own part, I never did nor do I believe I ever shall give advice to a woman who is setting out on a matrimonial voyage. First, because I never could advise one to marry without her own consent; and, secondly, because I know it is to no purpose to advise her to refrain when she has obtained it. A woman very rarely asks an opinion, or requires advice on such an occasion, till her resolution is formed, and then it is with the hope and expectation of obtaining a sanction, not that she means to be governed by your disapprobation, that she applies.[13]

Because Dolley's mother was saddled with heavy family responsibilities, and Dolley had no other close relatives in Philadelphia, Martha Washington's forthrightness in offering Dolley her opinion was both appropriate and welcome. Their families were closely related by marriage, and the Washingtons were a highly influential couple. George Washington held a keen appreciation for James Madison (although, at the time, the two were not close). Martha Washington, the *grande dame* of the nation, was known to take a particular delight in matchmaking. Having received official permission from the former President and First Lady to marry and be happy, Dolley allowed herself to seriously consider Madison as her suitor.

Few details of their whirlwind courtship have survived, but in June 1794, when Congress adjourned, Madison left for Montpellier to care for his sick mother, Nelly. Madison's marital hopes were high, but as his romantic track record had been severely disappointing, he had evidently not told his close friends, Jefferson and Monroe, that a serious romance was brewing. At the same time, Dolley, her son, and her sister Anna had left Philadelphia to visit her relatives in Hanover County and to be closer to Madison, if he chose to make a formal proposal of marriage. Her friends thought that prospect quite certain.

That summer, Dolley's mother, Mary Payne, wrote that she had accompanied Dolley on her trip from Philadelphia to Hanover. "We have been favored to preform our jurney without any disagreable accedent & have injoyed our helthy Dolley excepted she has been indesposed with sore eyes for six weeks but they are now almost well She has spent some time at the Sulphir spring about seven miles from this [place] the water we think has been of grate use to her eyes." Mary went on to say, "I cannot say at present when I shall return to Philadelphia as Lucy will not consent I should leave her in her present condition but Dolley talks of returning the last of next month [i.e., September] as she thinks it will be necessary for her to look after Business."[14]

Dolley did not lack for other suitors. William W. Wilkins, Dolley's Philadelphia legal counsel and friend who had helped her settle the estates of her husband, was also her admirer. In June, Catharine Thompson Coles, wife of Dolley's cousin, Congressman Isaac A. Coles, wrote that a "Mr Grove is in the Pouts about you."[15]

Mindful that Dolley had other suitors, Madison had enlisted Catharine to facilitate his path into Dolley's heart, and

𝒟. 𝒫. 𝑀𝑎𝑑𝑖𝑠𝑜𝑛

she was enthusiastic about the intended match. Acting as Cupid's co-conspirator on June 1, 1794, she sent Dolley a letter that spared nothing in its attempt to inspire her to accept Madison's attentions.

"Now for Madison," Catharine wrote, "he told me I might say what I pleas'd to you about him to begin, he thinks so much of you in the day that he has Lost his Tongue, at Night he Dreames of you & Starts in his Sleep a Calling on you to relieve his Flame for he Burns to such an excess that he will be shortly consumed & he hopes your Heart will be calous to every other swain but himself he has Consented to everything that I have wrote about him with Sparkling Eyes, Monroe goes to France as Minister Plenipotentiary—Madison has taken his House do you like it?"[16]

Madison did not leave all the work of courting to his friends. In a letter that has not survived, he proposed marriage. Dolley's letter, containing news of a bout of illness, as well as her acceptance of his proposal, reached him later that summer. Jubilant to hear the wonderful news, Madison replied from his Orange County estate on August 18:

> I received some days ago your precious favor from Fredericksburg. I cannot express, but hope you will conceive the joy it gave me: The delay in hearing of your leaving Hanover which I regarded as the only satisfactory proof of your recovery, had filled me with extreme...disquietude, and the communication of the welcome event was endeared to me by the *stile* in which it was conveyed. I hope you will never have another deliberation on that subject. If the sentiments of my heart can guarantee those of yours, they assure me there can never be a cause for it.[17]

While waiting for his mother to recover, Madison made a quick trip to Monticello, where Jefferson was delighted to hear the news of his engagement but was appalled to realize that the newly affianced Madison apparently desired to retire from

Congress if he married.[18] In the first days of September, when he knew that his mother's health was no longer in danger, Madison and his twenty-year-old sister, Fanny, departed Montpellier for Harewood House, where Dolley had been spending the summer with her sister and brother-in-law, her mother, and her younger siblings, John and Mary. He would return as a married man.

Dolley must have felt that William Wilkins was more a devoted friend and counselor than a potential lifemate, for she wrote him a letter asking his opinion of James Madison as a marriage partner. Whether her request preceded or followed an undated, babbling, self-loathing, and borderline incoherent love letter from Wilkins (in which he addressed Dolley as "Julia") is not known.[19] On August 22, 1794, by which time Dolley had made her choice to marry Madison, Wilkins penned a manly, though undoubtedly painful letter, in which he placed his duty as a friend above his personal interest as a suitor. Wilkins wrote to her from Philadelphia in care of George Steptoe Washington:

> I will not delay a Moment my ever dear and valued friend to reply to your last interesting Epistle. Flattered as I am by your Condescension in consulting me on this important Occasion and disinterestedly solicitous for your Welfare—the Task I undertake is far from being a painful one. As your friend I feel not the least Hesitation in forming my Opinion—ought I then to feel any Reluctance in communicating it? Mr. Madison is a Man whom I admire. I knew his Attachment to you and did not therefore content myself with taking his Character from the Breath of popular Applause—but consulted those who knew him intimately in private Life. His personal Character therefore I have every reason to believe is good and amiable. He unites to the great Talents which have secured him public Approbation those engaging Qualities that contribute so highly to domestic Felicity. To such a man therefore

I do most freely consent that my beloved Sister be united and happy.[20]

Wilkins went on to advise Dolley about the disposition of funds she had or was about to receive from the estates of her late father and husband. Then, in a thinly veiled reference to the Quaker community, he wrote, "You are placed in a critical Situation in this Affair — the Eyes of the World are upon you and your Enemies have already opened their Mouths to censure and Condemn you." He continued, "Mr. Madison is as I am informed a Man of genteel tho not of large property. He has every right to expect some part but does not want the whole of your Estate. I would suggest therefore that your House and Stables situate in Fourth Street be previously to your marriage conveyed to Trustees in Trust to receive the Rents Issues and profits during the Minority of your Son."[21]

Dolley took his advice. She also accepted a handsome engagement ring from Madison. Unfortunately, the date for this momentous event is not recorded. The ring was made of rose gold, with a central diamond surrounded by seven others in a circular pattern. It was very similar to one given by Madison's friend, James Monroe, to Elizabeth Kortright of New York City, whom Monroe married in 1786. Madison may well have sought his friend's advice in mak-

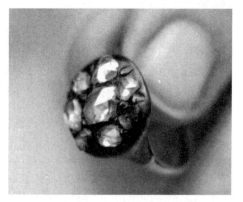

Dolley's engagement ring from James Madison

ing the selection. Dolley found it completely to her liking, and her great-niece, Mary Causten Kunkel, wrote, "this ring Mrs. Madison wore always and died with it on her hand."[22]

Quick remarriage was common in eighteenth-century America. As historian Robert Meade wrote, "Widows, by virtue of their proven charms and inherited estates, rarely lacked suitors; there were instances of remarriage when the grass had scarcely grown over the deceased spouse's grave."[23] Everyone seemed happy about Dolley's imminent wedding. Everyone, that is, except the Quakers.

Because of the relocation of the federal government from New York to Philadelphia, a great influx of male newcomers to the city was wreaking havoc on the supply of eligible single women, a large percentage of whom were Quakers. The number of out-marriages quickly outweighed the number of Quaker births, and the Friends began to see their membership diminish. In response, they kept their remaining members on very short doctrinal leashes and imposed quick, harsh penalties on those who strayed.

A formal mourning period of at least a year was required for a Quaker widow of good moral character. Dolley's fellow Friends, she could be certain, would never countenance any marriage before the first anniversary of her late husband's death.[24] The relative haste of her marriage to Madison certainly did not arise from Dolley's lack of funds, for the final settlement of her late husband's estate left her comfortably fixed. Nor did it stem from any impropriety. Dolley's choice to marry James Madison was a perfectly logical and harmonious match — for everyone but the Quakers.

A conflict with the Friends loomed large. Dolley's decision to marry the respected Anglican planter, who was both a non-Quaker and a major slaveholder, brought with it the swift and certain consequence of disownment. It would be the same fate that had been suffered by Dolley's mother, Mary, thirty-three years earlier, when she had married Dolley's father, an Anglican; by her sister, Lucy, when she married George Steptoe Washington; and by her close friend, Eliza Collins, who had recently married U.S. Representative Richard Bland Lee. All three women had been quickly stricken from the rolls of Quaker membership when they married out.

D. P. Madison

As a proper and godly woman who had spent her entire life within Quaker society, the prospect of being cut off from the community of people who once formed her closest circle of friends must have weighed heavily on Dolley's mind. In balance, the anticipation of marriage to a good, worthy man who would love and support her and her infant son was a powerful impetus for her to break ranks with the Friends. Although disownment would surely follow, she could look to Lucy and Eliza and see that married life outside the Quaker circle had not harmed either of them to any appreciable extent.

Late that summer, Dolley, her son, her sister Anna, and a maid stepped into a barouche—a large carriage—in Philadelphia and headed off for Harewood, the home of her sister and brother-in-law, Lucy and George Steptoe Washington, who had begged Dolley to celebrate her wedding at their home. The reason was obvious to both sisters. Two years earlier, Lucy had invited the scorn of the Quaker community by marrying out, and now her older sister was about to do the same. She needed a supportive place to marry.

The drawing room of Harewood House

The carriage ride, which would take nearly a week, was undertaken in a more festive mood than the departure from Philadelphia just eight months earlier, when Dolley and the others were fleeing for their lives from yellow fever. Along the way, the party paid a visit to Dolley's uncle, Isaac Winston, who had married her aunt, Lucy Coles. On the way to Harewood, the party stopped at Fredericksburg, where Dolley wrote and posted the letter to Madison that announced her acceptance of him as her intended husband.[25]

Madison and his youngest sister, Fanny, then almost twenty years old, proceeded to Harewood from Montpellier, stopping along the way at Winchester to briefly visit their aunt, Frances Madison Hite.[26]

On Monday, September 15, 1794, the large, Palladian drawing room of Harewood House was filled with festivity and good cheer. Inside the handsome house, built between 1756 and 1758 by Colonel Samuel Washington under the supervision of his brother, George, sunlight reflected off the richly carved, green marble mantle. The walls, which were paneled from floor to ceiling, were festooned with finely framed family portraits.

The wedding party consisted of Madison, forty-three; Dolley's mother, Mary Payne, forty-nine; and a group of seven vivacious, festive young men and women, all well under thirty: Dolley; her unmarried younger siblings, Anna and John Coles Payne; George Steptoe Washington and his wife, Lucy Payne Washington; Madison's sister, Fanny; and Harriot[27] Washington, George Steptoe Washington's sister. James and Dolley had auspiciously chosen the same wedding date that his parents, James Sr. and Nelly Conway Madison, had selected forty-five years earlier.[28] Prior to the ceremony that day, Dolley began a letter to her friend, Eliza Collins Lee:

> I receav'd your precious favour from Bath & should have indulged myself in writing an answer but for the excessive weakness in my Eyes—And as a proof my dearest Eliza of that confidence & friendship which

has never been interrupted between us I have stolen from the family to commune with you—to tell you in short, that the cource of this day I give my Hand to the Man who of all other's I most admire—You will not be at a loss to know who this is as I have been long ago gratify'd In having your approbation—In this Union I have every thing that is soothing and greatful in prospect—& my little Payne will have a generous & tender protector. A Settlement of all my real property with a considerable Addition of Money is made upon him with Mr. Madison's full approbation—This I know you feel an Interrest in or I should not have troubled you with it—you also are acquainted with the unmerited sensure of my Enimys on the subject. Mr. & Mrs. Ludwell Lee[29] have left the neighbourhood to our great regret as we wished much their presence to day, they being the only Family invited except *his* sister & Brother Washington—but how shall I express the anxiety I feel to see you? That friends whose goodness, at many interesting periods I have greatfully experienced would now rejoice us by a sight of her—tell your dear Lee that he must not supplant D P T in your Affections but suffer her whilst she deserves it to share with him your ever valuable Esteem—Adieu! Adieu! It is yet uncertain whether we shall see you before the meeting in Philadelphia. mama, Madison, Lucy, George Anna and Hariot joine in best love to you & yours.

Dolley Payne Todd

Evening——————

Dolley Madison! alas!—

Before sending the letter, Dolley crossed out the date 15th and changed it to 16th. At the bottom, she appended the enigmatic words, "Dolley Madison! Alass!"[30] We may never know the significance of that word, as the rest of the letter is torn off. The wedding ceremony was performed by the Reverend Dr. Alexander Balmain of Winchester, who was the husband of Madison's cousin, Lucy Taylor Balmain. The Anglican priest received a handsome fee for his professional services: five pounds, four shillings, ten pence, his second largest for the year.[31] The wedding was a joy to both bride and groom. Dolley and James Madison remained devoted to each other for forty-two years of marriage, which was terminated only by Madison's death.

The groom was probably married in his traditional dark suit, and it is said that "the girls vowed they would have a remembrance of the evening and cut the Mechlin lace from Mr. Madison's shirt ruffles."[32] Dolley's stunning wedding gown has survived — and a Quaker dress it was not. The stylish, elaborately designed, multi-paneled, silk dress was accented with panels of lace. The V-neck was cut moderately low, and the whole bodice was tightly fitted to Dolley's twenty-three-inch waist. A wreath of orange blossoms crowned her black hair, and she thoughtfully wore matching low-heeled white satin slippers so that she would not appear taller than her husband.[33] In one account of the wedding, Madison's wedding present to his bride was said to have been

James Madison's white silk wedding vest, embroidered with white flowers

a "wondrous necklace of Byzantine mosaic work, of temples and tombs and bridges, eleven pictures in all joined by delicate chains."[34] These worldly pagan Greco-Roman symbols would certainly never have been sanctioned by the Quakers.

A fluting iron, used to produce shirt ruffles

The change from plain-cloth Quaker to affluent Anglican planter's wife is also clear in a beautiful miniature portrait painted of Dolley in the last weeks of 1794 by James Peale, using watercolors on ivory.[35] Gone are the drab gray dress, the plain shawl, and the simple cap worn by James Todd's wife. In their place, Mrs. James Madison's black curls extend out from a fancy lace cap with a wide lace band and narrow lace ribbon tie. Around her neck are four thin, dainty, gold necklaces, which she was now free to wear. The same is true of the relatively low cut of the bodice, with no scarf to cover the bosom, an immodest fashion option not permitted by Quakers.

In the portrait, Dolley's dress features an elaborate lace collar that sweeps across her chest, is anchored by a fancy lace fan, and is held in place with a hand-painted brooch. The overall fashion statement is one of elegance coupled with exquisite restraint. The portrait makes it clear that only weeks after her second marriage, Dolley was already discarding her Quaker ways and reinventing herself as the wife of a wealthy Virginia planter. In addition to wearing an elegant and costly wedding dress, she dated her first letter as Mrs. James Madison in the worldly style, writing "September the 15th," rather than the traditional Quaker form, which would have been "ye 15th day of ye 9th month."

The newlyweds lingered for four days at Harewood before starting out on their bridal tour, which was undertaken to introduce the bride to relatives and friends who could not attend the wedding ceremony. The bridal tour party consisted of James and Dolley; her son, Payne Todd; Anna Payne; and Harriot Washington. Their first stop was Winchester, where they stayed overnight with Reverend Balmain's family. From there, they continued on to Belle Grove, the home of Madison's sister and brother-in-law, Nelly and Isaac Hite. There Dolley was afflicted with a relapse of the malarial fever and chills she had experienced shortly before the wedding. A doctor administered cinchona, the bark of a cascarilla bush, which is native to South America. It contains quinine, an effective medicine used to combat the symptoms of malaria, and the patient recovered

Dolley Madison,
by James Peale, about 1794

after two weeks' treatment. The Madisons then returned to Harewood, where Dolley rested and made visits in the neighborhood.

Unfortunately, the illness and recovery had consumed the time they had planned to use visiting the elder Madisons at Montpellier. Upon their return to Harewood, Madison wrote an apology to his aged father, then seventy-one, "Your daughter-in-law begs you and my mother to accept her best and most respectful affections, which she means to express herself by an early opportunity. She wishes Fanny also to be sensible of the pleasure with which a correspondence with her would be carried on."[36]

In the weeks following the wedding announcement, letters of congratulation flooded in from all quarters. One of the first came from the Reverend Mr. James Madison, a second cousin, who was president of William and Mary College and had become the first bishop of the Protestant Episcopal Church in Virginia in 1785.[37] "I cannot refrain sending you my sincere Congratulations, upon an Event, which promises you so much Happiness," the bishop wrote on November 12. "It was my Intention to have paid you a short Visit, in September, upon my Return from the Mountains, but heard, when in your Neighbourhood, that you were [away] from Home, & engaged in the Pursuit, which terminated so agreeably to yourself, & I trust also, to the amiable Partner whom you have selected. Present her too, if you please, with my Congratulations & ardent Wishes for your mutual Happiness."[38]

His letter echoes similar greetings from Thomas Jefferson, who had just left service as George Washington's secretary of state; Philip Freneau, publisher of Philadelphia's *National Gazetteer*; Revolutionary War General Horatio Gates; and other close friends. Congressman Dr. Samuel L. Mitchill wrote of Madison's new bride, "She has a fine person and most engaging countenance, which pleases not so much from mere symmetry or complexion as from expression. Her smile, her conversation, and her manners are so engaging that it is no wonder that such a young widow, with her fine blue eyes and a large share of animation, should indeed be a *queen of hearts*. By this second marriage she has become the wife of one of the first men of the nation, and enjoys all the respectability and *eclat* of such a position."[39]

At the Pine Street Meeting, the news of the wedding did not get the same reception as it had from Dr. Mitchill or Bishop Madison. The Todd-Madison union had taken place outside the Quaker faith. Worse yet, it was celebrated only three hundred twenty-seven days after the death of Dolley's first husband. The congregation's reaction was predictable. On December 20, 1794, ninety-six days after the wedding, Dolley was declared an apostate member of the faith and was disowned by her meeting. Now she was churchless—and free to explore worldly pleasures she had only dreamed of during her youth.

Although Dolley would never abandon the principles of moral integrity she had learned as a Quaker, she had burned her formal ties to her former church and would never look back. She was now a Virginia planter's wife with a husband to care for her and her son and a new family and social circle to adjust to. Joys and challenges lay in wait for her in Philadelphia, but many of the most precious days in her life lay ahead at her new husband's magnificent ancestral plantation home, Montpellier.

CHAPTER SIX

Mrs. Madison's Debut

Whuen Dolley Payne Todd Madison stepped from her carriage onto the streets of Philadelphia in the last days of October 1794, she was a different person from the one who had left the city only a few weeks earlier. Her arrival after her whirlwind wedding trip did not return her to the quiet, understated world of her Quaker past but rather to the exciting world of fashion, politics, government, and international intrigue. Her previous ten years had been filled with change, discovery, anguish, and sorrow. Her future seemed to offer joy and hope. One thing was certain: her marriage to a respected planter, scholar, and statesman placed her squarely in the national limelight. She would quickly have to adapt to her new position in society, and the accompanying acclaim and attention.

When Dolley married James Madison, the wedding linked the bride and groom with a widespread and influential network that included a significant percentage of Virginia's leading families. Within Orange County, Madison's connections touched virtually every family. Within Virginia, he could travel to almost any town and find friends or relatives.

Before her first wedding, Dolley had received marital advice from friends and family. This time, she had been counseled by the First Lady of the United States. Previously, she socialized with other farm children in Hanover County and was surrounded by pious Quakers, all of whom were called "Friend" and who spoke, dressed, dined, and lived simply. Now, as the wife of a socially prominent, highly respected landed gentleman who was rising rapidly in the ranks of the national government, Dolley found herself in a sink-or-swim social environment filled with rich, famous, and powerful people from all over the world.

Dolley quickly began to demonstrate the abilities that would become hallmarks of her personality: observation and adaptation. With few precedents and no rulebooks to teach her how to manage the challenges of her social role, she responded by developing a new set of worldly friends, keenly observing their behavior, and quickly adapting her actions to the needs of the occasion. Dolley's common sense, personal warmth, and ability to adapt enabled her to evolve quickly and successfully into the role of congressman's wife, then hostess for President Jefferson, and, ultimately, First Lady of the nation. The speed of her metamorphosis was breathtaking. In two years, the former farm girl and Quaker lawyer's wife made the transition to high-society matron and political helpmate to a rising national star.

Although to some, she probably appeared to be little more than a country girl who had married well, Dolley soon showed the stuff of which she was made. Everything she had learned during her childhood was solid preparation for the challenges she would face as a matron in political high society. As a small mountain stream gathers strength as it winds its way through the countryside and evolves into a broad, robust river, so Dolley's life flowed quickly and naturally from her rural origins and Quaker roots into her new position as the leading woman in her husband's family.

Unlike those who forget their roots as they rise from one level of fortune to another, Dolley never lost touch with her basic values. Her church may have cast her out, but she never forgot the fundamental moral and ethical principles she had been taught as a Quaker. Nothing about her new life among the worldly people she had been forbidden to emulate ever led her to abandon what one early biographer described as "that softness of manner and gentle dignity, that sympathizing kindness of heart and universal charity, which she inherited from her parents as part of her nature."[1] She quickly came to enjoy her new opportunities and proved to be a highly talented lifelong helpmate to her husband. She did, indeed, bloom where she was planted.

Unfortunately, Dolley's marriage split her friends and acquaintances into two distinct groups. The first consisted of the Quakers, who, except for her stalwart friends Anthony Morris and Betsy Pemberton (Eliza Lee having already married out), now averted their eyes when they saw her on the street and ceased making social calls to her home. Dolley, who had already watched this happen to a number of her friends and family members, was now largely anesthetized to its inevitable consequences. In fact, she was part of a strong trend. So many Quakers were marrying out of the faith that Moreau de Saint-Méry, a French intellectual and royalist exile bookseller, whose shop was on First Street, wrote in the mid-1790s that the number of Quakers in Philadelphia was in serious decline.[2] It helped her none at all that in 1789, her younger brother, Isaac Payne, was disowned by the Philadelphia Monthly Meeting for "resorting to houses of ill fame and gaming."[3] By January 5, 1795, Elizabeth Drinker recorded in her journal that he was dead, having "offended a man in Virginia, who some time afterward shot him with a pistol, of which wound he dyed."[4]

The second group, much larger and faster growing, consisted of James Madison's enormous family and cousinage, his friends and their families, and the many other men with whom Madison worked as a congressman, along with their wives and *their* connections. Although Dolley was generally acquainted with Madison's family before their marriage, it

D. P. Madison

took her a lifetime to learn all the branches of his family tree and meet the majority of his relatives.

James Madison, Jr., made his entry into the world at the home of his maternal grandmother, Mrs. John Moore, formerly Mrs. Rebecca Catlett Conway, on the Rappahannock River opposite Port Royal, Virginia. The event was meticulously recorded in the family Bible by his father, James Sr. The elder Madison wrote that his young namesake was born on midnight of the evening of March 5-6, 1750/1, and that he was baptized on March 31 of that year by the Reverend Mr. William Davis, the Anglican rector of the Hanover parish church.[5] Because of the British change from the Julian (old style) to the Gregorian (new style) calendars in 1752, James Madison has two birthdays. As his biographer, Ralph Ketcham, pointed out, an old style (o.s.) calendar on the wall on the night of his birth would have read March 5, 1750, but after the change, his birthday according to the new style (n.s.) calendar would have been March 16, 1751. Unless otherwise noted, all dates in this book are stated in the new style.

Nowhere was the elaborate intermarriage of Virginia families better displayed than in James Madison's ancestry. He often spoke of his "connections," the term he used to describe the enormous network produced by his family's kinship by blood and marriage with scores of other prominent Virginia families.[6] Despite the fact that he could have rightfully boasted of his European bloodlines, which were said to run all the way back to Charlemagne in the eighth century, Madison never claimed anything beyond his native shores. When pressed on the subject, he modestly and correctly stated that in both his paternal and maternal lines, his ancestors were, for five generations, Virginia planters of "the respectable though not the most opulent class."[7]

James Madison's forebears had settled in his native state by the end of the seventeenth century. His immigrant ancestor in the Madison line was John Maddison, a ship's carpenter. John arrived in Virginia in 1653 and acquired his land by head right, that is, by land grants based on fifty acres for every immigrant (family member, relative, or indentured servant) for whom he paid passage to the under-populated new colony. In all, John Maddison acquired 1,900 acres by head rights before his death, which occurred about 1683. Most of his land was situated on the York and Mattaponi Rivers in King and Queen and King William counties in the tidewater section of Virginia.[8] John's descendants included his son, John Maddison, a respected planter, sheriff, and justice of the peace in King and Queen County.

The next generation included the second John's three sons, John, Henry, and Ambrose, who spelled their surname "Madison," as did their descendants. Each generation of Madisons enlarged the family's land holdings, and by 1728, Ambrose, the grandfather of the future president, had assembled more than 5,000 acres under his name. Most of this land was located on the Appalachian frontier, in the rolling hills and small mountains of the Virginia Piedmont.

In 1721, Ambrose married Frances Taylor, the eldest daughter of James Taylor II and his wife, Martha Thompson, who lived on a huge estate of about 13,500 acres on the Rapidan River. His wife's family was extensive. Frances had four brothers and four sisters, most of whom produced large families for several generations. Among other notables in Frances' extended family were James Taylor III, a quartermaster general in the War of 1812; George Taylor, who saw ten of his sons serve in the Revolutionary War; and Zachary Taylor, President of the United States from 1849 to 1850. Frances' niece, Lucy, married an Anglican priest, the Reverend Mr. Alexander Balmain, who later would marry James Madison and Dolley Payne Todd.

Frances and Ambrose Madison moved to the western edge of the American frontier in what would later be known as Orange County, Virginia. There, in 1723, Ambrose and his brother-in-law, Thomas Chew, the husband of his wife's sister, Martha Taylor, had patented 4,675 acres of uncleared land, where they planned to plant tobacco. Chew took the eastern part of the land; Madison took the section to the west.

Ambrose named his plantation "Mt. Pleasant." It was all that and more.

The land and the location of the original Mt. Pleasant house and its successor, Montpellier, were dear to every generation of Madisons that lived or visited there. Both houses sat on fertile, orange-colored, clay soil on high ground looking to the west, facing the American future. The site commanded a sweeping vista of the Blue Ridge Mountains, thirty miles distant. Because the land was far from the swamps and humidity of the coast, the invigorating fresh air of the mountains was a tonic to all who breathed it. The spot was a permanent magnet for three generations of Madisons and remained in the family for 121 years, from 1723 until financial distress forced Dolley Madison to sell it and her slaves in 1844.

The land patent process required the owner to make specific improvements to the property, notably clearing the land for use and erecting a dwelling, within three years. If this was done, and the neighbors inspected the land and certified that the conditions had been met, the property deed could be finalized. Ambrose visited the land after acquiring it, taking with him an overseer and a gang of slaves. The clearing of the land for farming and the construction of the basic necessities, including a residence, barns, fences, a cookhouse, storage buildings, and slave quarters, took the better part of a decade. During that time, Ambrose returned to his family on the coast, leaving his overseer and slaves behind to carry out the work. He probably made periodic visits to check on the progress, which was rapid. By the time his neighbors inspected his property in 1726, the records show him to have been one of the wealthiest men in the Virginia Piedmont—even though he did not yet reside there. Ambrose moved Frances and their three children (including James Madison, Sr., father of the future president) to Mt. Pleasant in the spring of 1732.

The Mt. Pleasant house stood near the present family graveyard, where James and Dolley Madison were ultimately buried. The site of the first house was about three hundred yards from its replacement, that mansion of great taste and refinement which Dolley and James named Montpellier.[9] Their nearby neighbors included their kinfolk, Thomas and Martha Taylor Chew and Frances Madison's younger brother, James Taylor III.

In his earliest adult days, Ambrose was a tobacco planter of moderate means. He owned twenty-nine slaves, of whom only ten were adult males capable of working the fields. His first home at Mt. Pleasant was a single-story wooden frame house that measured thirty-two by twenty feet, with an eighteen-by-ten-foot stone-lined cellar under part of the house. It was utilitarian and comfortable, but it stood very close to its working buildings — the cookhouse, sheds, barns, and slave cabins — and bore little resemblance to the mansion that re-placed it thirty years later.

In the middle of the nineteenth century, when slave own-ership in the South reached its peak, those who owned one hundred or more slaves were ranked in the socioeconomic class known as the "great planters," whose wealth, exempli-fied by elaborate carriages, impressive mansions, liveried house servants, and opulent lifestyles, was later glorified in works of fiction such as *Gone With The Wind*. Such was not the lifestyle of Ambrose Madison, who died forty-four years before the American Revolution.

Although he was the master of all he surveyed from the knoll overlooking his Piedmont paradise, Ambrose Madison probably spent six days a week in the fields, working the typical farmer's day from "can see to can't see," riding from field to field on horseback to supervise his field hands. Nevertheless, at the time of his death, he was noted as being the richest man in the county.

Ambrose did not live to enjoy his plantation for long. He was poisoned by three slaves: two from Mt. Pleasant and one from a neighboring plantation. As historian Ann L. Miller wrote, the poison "did not kill him outright but rather caused sufficient damage to his system to condemn him to a slow death over several months." Ambrose's death — apparently the region's first by murder — came on August 27, 1732. He was probably the first to be buried in the new family cemetery at Mt. Pleasant. The three slaves were arrested and tried, and Pompey, owed by Joseph Hawkins, was executed for having conspired to kill Ambrose. Madison's slaves, Turk and Dido, were sentenced to be whipped rather than hung when it was determined that they had less involvement in the plot to kill their master. After their sentence was carried out, Turk and Dido were returned to Madison's widow, Frances.[10]

At the time of Ambrose's death, his widow was thirty-two and had three young children. The eldest, James Sr., father of the future president, was only nine years old; his sister, Elizabeth, was seven; and his other sister, Frances, was six. In his will, written shortly before his death, Ambrose left the management of his property to his wife until his eldest son, James Sr., turned eighteen in 1741.[11] Because the lad was only nine years old at the time of his father's death, the immediate burden of managing the plantation fell to Frances, who took charge of the 2,500-acre property and its slaves and successfully raised tobacco and food crops. Five years after her husband's death, she settled the original patent division and inserted a clause that put her in full control of the land until she died.[12] She was so successful in running the plantation that she ultimately maintained effective control over the tobacco operations until her death in 1761. In her time, female management of a plantation where an able male was available was highly unusual, and the profitability of Mt. Pleasant's operation from 1732 to 1761 is high testament to Frances' business and management skills.[13]

James Madison, Sr.

Tobacco prices and crop yields could rise or fall drastically in any given year, so as he grew older, James Sr. wisely invested his time in diversifying Mt. Pleasant's income base, encouraging his mother to plant corn, wheat, and rye in addition to tobacco. He worked for a time as a merchant factor and then established a peach brandy distillery and a sawmill,

Nelly Conway Madison

jobbed out slaves as a construction contractor, and erected barns and tobacco houses for his neighbors. In the late 1750s he started what soon became a large and profitable blacksmithing operation. The smithy stood at the present-day site of a beautiful neoclassical temple, which covers an underground icehouse.

James Sr.'s two younger sisters, Frances and Elizabeth, married into substantial families. Frances Madison wed first Taverner Beale and second Jacob Hite; Elizabeth Madison wed first John Willis and second Richard Beale. Upon their first marriages, both young women moved away from home. Their departure left James Sr. as the head of a large property, an enslaved workforce of more than one hundred souls, and a small household.

The love of the elder James Madison's life came in the shapely and pleasing form of Nelly Conway, who was born in 1731.[14] Like those of her husband, Nelly's roots stretched deep into the early history of the central counties of Tidewater Virginia. Nelly's father, Francis Conway, who was born in 1696, was the son of Edwin Conway, Jr., and his wife, Elizabeth Thornton. Francis became a prosperous merchant and planter of Caroline County, Virginia.

In 1718, Francis Conway married Rebecca Catlett, the daughter of John Catlett and his wife, whose name has been lost. Rebecca Catlett Conway was born in 1702 in Essex County, Virginia. Francis and Rebecca lived on the Rappahannock River, where they owned a tobacco warehouse, known as a "rolling house," nine miles southeast of Fredericksburg and thirty-five miles east, as the crow flies, from Montpellier. After Francis' death in 1733, Rebecca achieved the respect of her community when she successfully took over the management of her late husband's warehouse, worked it profitably, and passed it along to her descendants, again proving that a woman could successfully manage a substantial and intricate business.[15] Rebecca married second John Moore, who lived at Port Conway, Virginia.

Nelly Conway, the mother of the future president, was born in 1731, the youngest of six known children. Her home was filled with the hustle, bustle, and voices of her brothers Francis II, Catlett, and Reuben, and sisters Elizabeth and Sarah, both of whom married men of the Taylor family from Orange County, thereby extending the vast cousinage across another generation. She was only one year old when her father died, and she grew up with her mother, who died in 1760; her stepfather; her previously mentioned full brothers and sisters, and two half-brothers, William and James.

Nelly wed James Madison, Sr., on September 15, 1749, and moved into the Mt. Pleasant house built by Ambrose Madison near the site of the present-day Montpellier mansion. She returned to the plantation of her mother and stepfather at Port Conway to give birth to her first child, James Jr., on March 16, 1751. Her marriage ultimately increased the population of pre-Revolutionary Orange County by twelve known children, seven of whom lived to adulthood and married. They included the first-born, James Jr., the future president, who married the widowed Dolley Payne Todd; Francis Madison, who married Susannah Bell and had nine children; Ambrose Madison, who married Mary Willis Lee; Catlett Madison, who died in 1758 at the age of one month; Nelly Conway Madison, who married Major Isaac Hite, Jr.; William Madison, who married first Frances Throckmorton, who bore him ten children, and after her death, Nancy Jarrell. Then came Sarah Catlett Madison, who married Thomas Macon; a Madison child born in 1766; Elizabeth Madison, who died in 1775 at the age of seven; another child who died at birth in 1770; Reuben Madison, who died in 1775 at the age of three years, nine months; and the youngest known child, Frances "Fanny" Madison, who married Dr. Robert Henry Rose II and accompanied her oldest brother, James, to Harewood House plantation, where he married Dolley Payne Todd in 1794.

Dolley Madison spent the rest of her life meeting her husband's relatives. She had the pleasure of knowing her new father-in-law for seven years after her marriage to James, and she knew her mother-in-law, Nelly, of whom she was very fond, for thirty-five years.

Members of dissenting denominations, such as Quakers, Presbyterians, and Baptists, were fairly rare in early eighteenth-century Virginia. Therefore, as were most of his neighbors, James Madison, Sr., was an Anglican. He attended and served on the vestry of the Brick Church, located on the road between Orange Court House and Fredericksburg. There, after a two-hour ride, he and his fast-growing family could listen to the priest's sermon, take communion, and share political, local, business, and personal news with their legions of friends, neighbors, and relatives.

By the middle of the eighteenth century, most of Mt. Pleasant's income was derived from serving the local economy and exporting tobacco. When James Jr. was born in 1751, Mt. Pleasant was at its diversified zenith: a large and prosperous operation run by his grandmother, Frances, and father, James Sr., which permitted the newest James the luxury of attaining a superior education and following a political career. After his mother's death, James Sr., maintained a "rock hold" on the direct operation of the plantation until his last years.[16] James Jr. lived at Mt. Pleasant until he was nine years old, when he helped carry smaller items from the old house up the hill to the newly built brick house that soon came to be known as Montpellier. As James Jr. grew up, he studied his father's business methods but did not become actively involved in managing the plantation until the 1790s, when his father's health began to decline. An account book kept by James Sr. between 1755 and 1765 tells us that a man named John Connor and his wife acted as overseer and midwife, respectively, on Madison's plantation. John issued "Negro shoes" and probably other basic slave provisions, such as cloth, needles, and thread, on an annual basis.[17] Over a five-year period, his wife was paid ten shillings each for delivering the babies of "15 Negro wenches."[18]

Madison's dealings with merchants in London and with Virginia shopkeepers, lawyers, doctors, and neighbors were typical of the buying, investing, trading, and selling that was part of every planter's life. In addition, the plantation records contain entries for the purchase of silver shoe buckles and expensive women's clothing, which indicates that James Sr. had worked efficiently and had increased the production and profitability of his father's plantation. By the 1750s, before the construction of the Montpellier house, he already had a wine cellar, filled with custom-made wine bottles bearing his name, an unmistakable testimony to his wealth and prestige.

Dolley Madison never saw the original Mt. Pleasant house, which burned sometime in the 1770s and collapsed into the cellar. The old house seems to have been

One of James Madison, Sr.'s, custom-made wine bottles, c. 1770

stripped of all reusable items, such as door latches, hinges, and window parts, prior to the fire, which may have been the simplest way to dispose of a structure that was no longer useful.

By 1782, through a combination of purchase and "natural increase," at least 118 enslaved workers labored on the plantation, which was now known as Montpellier. This was a fourfold increase from the days of Ambrose. James Sr.'s references to his slaves as "of the family" and President James Madison's lifelong distaste for the peculiar institution suggests that the Madison slaves were generally treated well by the standards of the day and not overtly abused.[19] On the other hand, although James Madison often wrote about and voiced his objections to slavery, he never emancipated any of his slaves, and he left them all to Dolley in his will.

The slaves did not often enjoy the fruit of their labors. Although slaves were granted small plots of land, usually near their cabins, where they could grow non-competitive plants (such as vegetables) and raise small animals (such as chickens and hogs) for their personal use, they lived a life of service. Their role was to fell trees; clear land; produce crops; run lumber mills and liquor stills; make bricks and build buildings; slaughter farm animals; cook and serve food; care for livestock; tend the gardens; clean the mansion; mind the younger children; and provide transportation and musical entertainment. They worked from sunup to sundown, in all kinds of weather. Sundays and the Christmas holiday period were the exceptions. As on most southern plantations, slaves did not have to work on those days. An Englishman visiting Montpellier in the early 1830s reported that "The Ex-President said very calmly, that in an afternoon, it was Sunday, he could not have the servants to wait on him, as they made it a holiday."[20]

When James and Dolley entertained at Montpellier on a large scale, as they often did, the male field hands donned fancy blue wool livery jackets with shiny brass buttons and served food to as many as one hundred guests at banquets and outdoor barbecues. Female field hands donned clean aprons and aided overnight visitors, building fires in the bedroom fireplaces, warming the beds with iron bed-warmers in the winter, washing and ironing clothes, and emptying the chamber pots. In some cases, a slave slept on a pallet in the same room, ready to attend the guest if needed during the night.

Usually, the enslaved servants were trained to be "invisible," and visitors rarely acknowledged their presence. However, there are written references to several house slaves at Montpellier who had lively discussions with guests, usually about their masters or their own families. One was "Old Sawney," who served as James Jr.'s body servant when he attended college. Old Sawney later became one of Montpellier's overseers—a highly responsible position, one generally reserved for whites. In his later years, he served as Mother Madison's personal servant in her (and his) old age. "Granny Mill" was another of the family's favorites, and the Madisons and many guests often visited her cabin at the slave village, "Walnut Grove," which was situated a short walk from the big house.[21]

Even at its best, chattel slavery was brutal. As the property of their owners, slaves were valued in accordance with their skill level, childbearing capacity, labor productivity, and the extent of their remaining productive life. A field hand in his or her prime might be valued at $500 or more, but an infirm old slave might be declared "worthless." In 1850, an enslaved family, consisting of "Raph, wife, children, and old women," that formerly belonged to Dolley Madison was appraised at $2,200.[22]

Not all local slaveowners were as enlightened as Madison, and slaves who broke the strict regulations that governed them were liable for punishments unheard of for whites. The elder James Madison's uncle, Thomas Chew, was sheriff of Orange County for many years. In 1738, Chew executed a female slave convicted of poisoning her master by burning her at the stake. In another case, a cannibalistic slave accused of killing and partially eating a white child was tied up and dragged by a horse until dead. Then his body was dismembered, and pieces of it were nailed up in different parts of the county as a warning to others.[23] Nearby Negrohead Run, a small stream, was named after an Orange County slave who was beheaded. The court ordered that his head be displayed on a stick, a practice well known in England at the time.[24] Thus, the place names Negrofoot and Negrohead became familiar terms in Hanover County.

This was the setting in which Dolley found herself as the wife of James Madison. James was a devoted homebody. He never traveled abroad, and even when called to congressional duty in Philadelphia (about two hundred fifty miles away) or Washington (ninety miles), he returned to Montpellier as quickly as possible after each session. When he and Dolley made their frequent visits to Montpellier, guests flocked in to join them. Dolley once reported in amazement that on at least one occasion, their country estate was filled with over one hundred friends and relatives.[25] Because of his broad acquaintanceship, James already had the ear, and usually the support, of his far-flung connections when it came time to take up a discussion, carry on a debate, or lead a cause. As soon as the Madisons leased their first house in Philadelphia, prudent, plantation-trained Dolley directed that the cellar be fully stocked with firewood. When Congress was in session, she had to be ready at the drop of a hat to entertain the multitudes of Madison's friends, family, colleagues, and patronage seekers who flocked to their house.

Philadelphia gave a warm welcome to the newlyweds. The capital city's social season was well underway. Christmas was near, and Congress would soon adjourn. The Madisons ultimately spent three seasons in Philadelphia, the first in quarters recently vacated by James Monroe, who had just sailed after his appointment as minister to France. Monroe had leased a house at 4 North Eighth Street for one year starting in June 1793. Madison lived there with the Monroes during the first session of the Third Congress, and, after his marriage, he

James Monroe

and Dolley returned there in October 1794 for the second session.[26]

The positive effects of Madison's marriage were quickly apparent to his colleagues. Jonathan Trumbull, a congressman from Connecticut, predicted that "the present campaign of politics will be carried on with much more mildness & good humor, than the last. Mr. Madison's late connection it is said has drawn off much of his atrabilious Gall—& indeed he appears with much more complacency & sociability than I have ever yet seen in him."[27]

When Monroe left to become U.S. minister to France, the Madisons had the house to themselves. Monroe soon notified them of the great bargains to be had from the sale of former noblemen's furnishings in Paris, and the Madisons placed a large order for draperies, carpets, and china. Monroe scurried all over the city to find what they wanted, and wrote in September 1795 that the packing was complete. The two crates he shipped contained furniture in the Louis XVI style, including an iron French bedstead, mattresses, and large quantities of silk, for a total price of £2,500. "The price will I fear exceed what you expected, for by Dr. Edwards account the reports in America were very erroneous in this respect. It is however in my opinion comparatively with what in America is very cheap. In the bed are about 80 French ells of Damask besides the Mattrasses which we added. The window curtains are rich and good. The carpets are not entirely new, but almost so, and are good."[28]

The furniture, waterlogged, arrived in the winter of 1795-96, just before Madison finished his term as congressman and left the city.[29] This was the first French furniture Dolley had ever owned, but Madison had formed a bond with French tastes years before. Monroe was eager to see Madison adopt the latest French decorating styles, and offered to outfit the Madisons' drawing room. He proposed to obtain a set of twelve to eighteen chairs, two or three tables "after the taste which we prefer," one or two sofas, a clock to stand on the chimneypiece, and even the chimneypiece itself.[30] He did not think that the ornate gilt furniture then in fashion was proper in a republic (though Monroe would change his mind by the time he was elected president), so the furniture he bought for the Madisons would have been painted beech or mahogany with simple ormolu trim.[31]

French furniture had been arriving in America since the 1780s, and both Washington and Jefferson had homes filled with Louis XVI furnishings. Madison, and especially his new wife, evolved into solid, if slightly conservative, Francophiles, relishing not only French furniture but also china, draperies, and food. His slight figure notwithstanding, Dolley noted that her husband generally had a hearty appetite; was fond of a wide variety of foods and beverages, including tea and coffee; and kept a substantial cellar of fine wines.[32]

Like his friends Jefferson and Monroe, Madison developed a connoisseur's taste for French wines and had friends and wine agents scour the land for the finest varieties and vintages. Like most of the southern planters, Madison bought his Madeira wine by the pipe (pine barrels holding about 110-120 gallons) and, as had his father, transferred the wine to his own bottles when it arrived.[33] Madeira was the most-favored wine of all the southern planters because, unlike most other wines, it improved when stored hot. Madison also bought other wines in great quantity, often two hundred bottles at a time.[34] Guests at Montpellier raved about the elegant dinners and the exquisite quality and diversity of Madison's wines.[35]

Dolley and James spent their second and third years in Philadelphia in a "Neat & good Brick three Story House...not far distant from Congress Hall" at 429 Spruce Street, between Fourth and Fifth, which they rented for £200 per year. The house had two rooms on each floor plus a kitchen, a coach house, and a stable behind it, and it was close to the hall where Congress met.[36] During the Fourth Congress, to fill their immediate needs, the Madisons brought over furnishings from Dolley's house on Walnut Street. Other furniture and some household slaves were transported from Montpellier. When Congress was in session, Dolley and James lived in Philadelphia; when it was in recess, they immediately returned to Orange County to join his parents.

The house that Dolley had shared with her late husband, John Todd, was put up for rent. From May 1796 until 1807, it was occupied by Stephen Moylan, a general in the Revolution and aide-de-camp to General George Washington. During his occupancy of the house, Moylan was commissioner of loans for the City of Philadelphia and kept his office there. The property was managed for the Madisons by Dolley's long-time Philadelphia Quaker friend Dr. Thomas Parke, who solicited tenants and collected the rent for the Madisons.[37] Parke probably also supervised repairs to the house, for in 1797 Moylan complained to the Madisons that the north wall of the house was so poorly built that water soaked through every time it rained, and he was worried the wall might collapse.[38]

During their residence in Philadelphia, Dolley's renewed status as a married woman permitted her to sue in court. In a surprising move, and for reasons no longer known, she (with husband James) brought suit against Edward Heston, father of Isaac Heston, John Todd's late legal clerk. The suit was brought to recover the costs of nursing and burying the young law clerk during the 1793 yellow fever epidemic that took his life. The Madisons dropped the suit when Heston agreed to settle out of court.[39]

If Dolley was unaware that her life was now inextricably intertwined with the future of the new nation, she had only to read the letter from Thomas Jefferson to her husband, dated December 28, 1794. Fearing that domestic bliss might rob the country of one of its ablest leaders, the red-headed sage from Monticello wrote:

> Hold on then, my dear friend, that we may not ship-wreck in the meanwhile. I do not see, in the minds of those with whom I converse, a greater affliction than the fear of your retirement; but this must not be, un-less to a more splendid and more efficacious post. There I should rejoice to see you. I hope I may say, I shall rejoice to see you. I have long had much in my mind to say to you on that subject. But double delica-cies have kept me silent.... Present me respectfully to Mrs. Madison, and pray her to keep you where you are for her own satisfaction and the public good, and accept the cordial affections of us all. Adieu.[40]

The decade of the 1790s was a golden age for Philadel-phia. When Congress was in session, the city was the intellec-tual and social center of the American universe, hosting the best minds, fashions, and entertainments to be found in the country. It would be difficult to overestimate the effect of the French Revolution on the minds of Americans in the de-cade when Philadelphia was the national capital. The city hosted some of the best minds from France, including both highly educated royalist expatriates and representatives of the new Republican government. The combined effects of the success of the American Revolution in 1783 and the fall of the Bastille in 1789 created an ideal climate for the growth of new ideas.

During the 1790s, the politics of the French Revolution preoccupied American society. One profound and lasting result was the polarization of American political thought into two national parties: the conservative, pro-English Federalists and the liberal, pro-French Democratic Republicans. During the administrations of George Washington and John Adams, the

Federalists initially held sway, but soon the democratic ideals of the "French tide" took hold. This ultimately resulted in the election of the Democratic-Republican ticket of Thomas Jefferson, president, and Aaron Burr, vice president, in 1801. Jefferson (sans Burr, whom Jefferson replaced with George Clinton) was re-elected in 1805, bringing his colleagues James Madison and James Monroe under his wing. Each of the two friends eventually succeeded the man from Monticello in the nation's highest office.

The women of America, inspired by the revolution that freed their country from despotic rule, began to seek freedoms of their own. As historian Susan Branson noted, an American woman of the 1790s was bound to her father or husband. A single or married woman could not sign a contract, make a will, or sue in a court of law. "Women were put into the same category as children, idiots, Indians, and slaves: they were judged to be dependents, lacking a free will, and consequently disqualified from voting."[41]

Their second-class legal status automatically excluded them from entering a formal institution of higher learning; practicing a learned profession, such as medicine or law; or being elected to public office. Even the Quakers, who were among the first to provide women with the same leadership opportunities as men within their meetings, did not offer girls the same educational opportunities or training as boys.

When Dolley returned to Philadelphia in 1794, upper- and middle-class women were reading books and magazines that could not have existed or been published a decade earlier. American women were starting to voice the long-held opinion that they should no longer submit to the total domination of men any more than their new country should submit to the domination of a British monarch. Two prominent female intellectuals fueled the fire for women's rights: Judith Sargent Murray of Gloucester, Massachusetts, and Mary Wollstonecraft, a zealous reformer from England.

Murray was a prolific essayist who had steadily built a national audience for her ideas. Prior to the 1780s, virtually everything written or published about or for women was written by men. Murray's first article appeared in 1784, and by 1792, she was writing monthly essays for the *Massachusetts Magazine*. Her themes included the need for social change, specifically in the areas of equal legal and educational rights for women, arguing that lack of education, not nature, "made women seem inferior to men."[42]

Mary Wollstonecraft, about 1797

Wollstonecraft also became a prominent reformer through the print media. Her incendiary book, *A Vindication of the Rights of Woman*, was published in London in 1792 and was immediately reprinted in Boston and Philadelphia. It called for "justice for one-half of the human race," and catalogued the long, and to Wollstonecraft, irrational and counter-productive list of restrictions women faced in private and public life.

The book provoked immediate controversy and brought an instantaneous reaction from women and men on both sides of the Atlantic. Senator, later vice president, Aaron Burr not only adopted it as the model for the education of his daughter, Theodosia, but also had Wollstonecraft's portrait copied and hung over her bed. Elizabeth Drinker, Dolley's ubiquitous, conservative Philadelphia Quaker friend who chronicled all things great and small, wrote in 1796 that some of the Englishwoman's thoughts mirrored her own. "In very many of her sentiments she, as some of our Friends say, *speaks my mind*, in some others I do not, altogether coincide with her—I am not for quite so much independence."[43]

While many women were extolling Wollstonecraft's philosophies and urging other women to "overthrow the oppression
by man, your tyrant lord," the men the author was referring
to generally viewed her as a smoldering menace. In addition
to denouncing her views as directly contrary to the natural,
Biblical order of the family and likely to cause chaos in society,
the men attacked her character.

In 1798, William Goodwin, her common-law husband,
wrote a memoir of Wollstonecraft, who had borne him a
daughter, Mary. The girl eventually married Percy Bysshe
Shelley and authored the famous novel, *Frankenstein*.
Goodwin's memoir revealed that Wollstonecraft had also
borne a child out of wedlock with an American, Captain
Gilbert Imlay. Prior to her common-law marriage to Goodwin,
he wrote, she had attempted suicide several times. Wollstonecraft's detractors quickly used this ammunition to argue
that the consequences of her philosophies were immorality,
illicit sexual practices, mental instability, and self-destructive
tendencies. Nevertheless, her message reached a wide audience and fueled the fire of women's rights. A century later,
Wollstonecraft was being heralded as one of the founding
mothers of feminism.

Both Murray and Wollstonecraft agreed that women,
given the same education as men, had every right to hold
political opinions — and public office. While the notion was
openly derided by virtually all men of the time, women nevertheless started to openly voice their political views. In return,
some progressive men started discussing matters of politics
and government with them. It wasn't liberation, but it was a
mark of progress.

Within months after Dolley's wedding, it was clear that
men found her to be a woman worthy of such weighty discussions. In January 1795, Dr. Robert Honyman, a forty-eight-
year-old Scottish immigrant to Hanover County and a friend
of Dolley's aunt and uncle, Isaac and Lucy Winston, wrote
her a letter that probably would never have been written a
decade earlier. Honyman was a well-read man who often

borrowed books from the Madisons' library, and they often bought books on his behalf.[44] He thanked Dolley for the judicious selections of books she had recently sent to him and asked her to procure others that he could not find in Richmond. His first request was a four-volume set by François LeVaillent (available in French, Dutch, and German, but not yet English) describing his explorations of the interior of Africa. The second was a book by Dr. Jean Devèze, director of Philadelphia's besieged Bush Hill hospital during the yellow fever epidemic that had claimed so many of Dolley's neighbors and loved ones. Then Honyman launched into the mainstream of his communication, sharing with Dolley the local reaction to Thomas Paine's radical new book, the 1794 Boston edition of *The Age of Reason*. Paine had expanded upon George Fox's concept that God dwells within each individual and argued against any claim, royal or priestly, of divine partiality.

Honyman noted that although many Hanover residents were appalled by Paine's notions of a "natural theology," Dolley's aunt, Lucy Coles Winston, had let her curiosity get the better of her and was reading Paine's book. From philosophy, Honyman then dove into the mechanics of grass-roots politics. He gave Dolley a briefing on the four congressional candidates vying for election in their Virginia districts and concluded by sharing in detail his views on a land bill being debated in the Virginia legislature and a national bankruptcy law then under consideration in Congress.[45] Unwittingly, Honyman had paid Dolley a great compliment: He had written her the same kind of letter he would have composed for her husband.

From this letter, and others like it, it is clear that Dolley was interested in far more than society gossip and fashion trends. From the start of her new marriage, she became a strong political ally of her husband and often communicated important details to him.

During Philadelphia's era as the nation's capital, it was not only ideas, books, and magazines that flourished. The once-staid Quaker city had also become an elegant fashion

D. P. Madison

paradise and a center for sophisticated entertainment, both public and private. One of the most fascinating and elegant places in the city was Oeller's Tavern on Chestnut Street. It was the site of many festive public events and dances, of which the grandest of all were the weekly "assemblies" held there during the social season, when Congress was in session and the city was full.

Oeller's boasted a fine ballroom, sixty feet square, with a musicians' gallery at one end and walls "papered after the French taste with Pantheon figures on the panels." The dances performed included the quadrille, a West Indian country dance that became popular in France in the 1760s and in America in the following decades, and variations of square ("contra") dances, which were much livelier than the stately minuet they eventually replaced.[46] Each quadrille dance "set" consisted of four couples, who performed five "figures," the dance equivalent of an act in a play. Cotillions were larger versions of the quadrille, with eight couples. In the early 1800s, the popularity of the quadrille was challenged by the waltz, which shocked some members of polite society because it encouraged couples to dance face to face. The quadrille remained popular well into the 1840s. Lamentably, though she greatly enjoyed music, Dolley had been raised a Quaker girl, and Quaker girls were not taught dancing.

The city was filled with wealthy men whose beautifully furnished homes hosted an endless array of formal, European-style receptions, intimate private dinners, evening parties, and balls, which proliferated during the Washington and Adams administrations. During her previous marriage, Dolley had never been invited to such events, but now things were different. Her Quaker upbringing had equipped her with the grace, equanimity, and dignity suited to her new stature in society. Her quick mind easily adapted to the complex rules of etiquette demanded of a congressman's wife, surrounded as she was by American luminaries, foreign dignitaries, titled members of the European nobility, their wives, and, occasionally, their mistresses.

Now, as the wife of a Virginia gentleman and respected statesman, Dolley was immediately welcomed into the innermost circles of Philadelphia's high society. A year earlier, she was wearing simple white caps and plaincloth. Now she was surrounded by silk dresses, powdered wigs, lace handkerchiefs, penciled eyebrows, rouged cheeks, perfumes, diamond and gold jewelry, ivory fans, and snuffboxes.

James Madison was accustomed to Philadelphia's gaiety and luxury, but Dolley must have been at least temporarily overwhelmed. In her Quaker days, she had seen President Washington's

Dolley's calling card case

imposing, globe-shaped, white coach with its scarlet panels, driven by a white coachman wearing the imposing scarlet-and-white livery of the Washington family.[47] On state occasions, the coach was pulled by a matched set of six white horses, and on ordinary days, by four. Now, only weeks after returning to Philadelphia, the former Quaker farmer's daughter from New Garden, North Carolina, was the honored guest at elaborate dinners and dances hosted by legendary people she had only read about in newspapers or glimpsed briefly through the windows of their elegant carriages as they passed by.

Dolley quickly became aware of the reality of her new status. Only a few months after the Madisons returned to Philadelphia, the Washingtons invited the younger couple to dine with them in a *family way*, that is, at a private dinner as friends, rather than at the president's official dinner, which was held on Thursday afternoon each week.[48] This was despite the fact that Madison, then the head of the Democratic Republicans, was leading the opposition to President Washington's

Federalist policies. As a token of her continuing affection, Martha Washington later gave Dolley a cream pitcher, which was part of a large service given to the Washingtons by the Comte de Custine during the American Revolution.[49]

Her new high-level social connections notwithstanding, Dolley's friends from childhood remained close. Eliza Collins Lee, Dolley's longest-standing woman friend, had met her in Philadelphia when Dolley was a young woman; served as her bridesmaid at her wedding to John Todd, Jr.; remained close to her always; and was with her in 1849 on the day she died.

A 1794 letter, written shortly after Eliza married (with Dolley's warm blessing) Virginia planter and U.S. congressman Richard Bland Lee, provides a warm, humorous insight into Dolley's relationship with Madison. Dolley wrote Eliza a brief note of thanks for some shopping she had done to obtain socks for Madison. Eliza evidently thought him to be even smaller than he was and misjudged the size. Dolley wrote, "I regret the trouble I have given you.... the Hose will not fit even my darling little Husband. If the merchant has them of large size, black & White I will take 6 pair of each—but do not trouble yourself further."[50]

Dolley's social circle soon expanded into more exotic realms. The French Revolution had forced numerous titled noblemen to flee their country. Many flocked to the American capital to call upon President Washington, who was almost as great a hero in France as in America. Forced to abandon their mansions and country estates, they soon found themselves living in boardinghouses and tavern rooms in housing-deprived Philadelphia. The second wave of Frenchmen consisted of the newly appointed diplomatic emissaries of the French Republic.

Within months of her return to the capital, Dolley had been introduced to such French notables as Jérôme Bonaparte, the teenaged youngest brother of Emperor Napoléon Bonaparte, who quickly fell in love with and married Elizabeth Patterson of Baltimore in 1803, when he was nineteen and she was eighteen. Elizabeth (whom Dolley referred to as

Betsy) and Dolley soon became close friends. She also met Louis Philippe, the "Citizen King," who was elected to succeed Louis XVIII. He visited America from 1796 to 1800, followed by his brothers, the Duc de Montpensier and the Bourbon prince, the Comte de Beaujolais, who packed himself into a tiny room over a barber's shop. An observer noted that "when the count extended royal hospitality in this apartment, he was compelled to seat half of his guests on the bed, but with the happy grace of his nation, he remarked that he had himself occupied less comfortable places without the consolation of an agreeable company."

The royal exile—and half of the single men in Philadelphia—was said to have been infatuated with Maria Bingham, whose extravagant displays of charm and figure were legendary in the city. Unimpressed, her father, William Bingham, scotched the alliance, replying to the Comte de Beaujolais, now a nobleman in exile, "Should you ever be restored to your hereditary position, you will be too great a match for her; if not, she is too great a match for you."[51]

Other notables in Dolley's new sphere of influence included Constantin François de Chassebœuf, Comte de Volne, a French author, intellectual, historian, and senator under Napoléon, who was invited to consider the Madison house his second home. Charles Maurice de Talleyrand-Périgord, a "first-rate genius," consummate politician, and close friend of Aaron Burr, found a room to rent at Oeller's Tavern. The Madisons met François-Alexandre-Frédéric, Duc de la Rochefoucauld-Liancourt, France's "Benjamin Franklin of the Revolution," who visited Philadelphia in 1795. He spent a great deal of time in Virginia, including a week with Jefferson at Monticello in the summer of 1796. The duke visited all the major cities and estates of the new nation while conducting research and making notes for his landmark two-volume description of America, *Travels Throughout the United States of North America*, published in 1799.

Attending assembly dances and formal dinners required the city's women to seek out the latest hairstyles and clothing fashions. By the time the government had been in Philadelphia for four years, the city had attracted a bevy of sophisticated dressmakers, milliners, and cosmetologists. A 1794 newspaper advertisement stated that a Monsieur Lacave "has the honor of informing the ladies of Philadelphia that he cuts and dresses hair in the most approved and late fashion. He also ornaments the head-dress according to the wish of his employers, with the handkerchief, ribbon, feather, flower, gauze, perle, etc. All in the newest taste. He lives at number fourteen Cherry Alley, between Third and Fourth Streets."[52]

The mesmerizing new French neoclassical clothing styles, which were the rage of Philadelphia in the 1790s, were described to Dolley's sister, Anna Payne, by her friend, Sally McKean, soon to become the wife of a Spanish nobleman and diplomat. Sally was the daughter of Thomas McKean, a conservative Pennsylvania-born governor, statesman, and signer of the Declaration of Independence. The new, flowing, short-sleeved, Empire-style dresses, with their flowing lines, elevated waists, and plunging necklines, were a radical departure from the long, heavy, full skirts; whalebone corsets; tight bodices; high collars; and long sleeves that had been popular before and just after the American Revolution. Sally wrote:

> And now, my dear Anna, we will have done with judges and juries, courts, both martial and partial, and we will speak a little about Philadelphia and the fashions, the beaux, Congress, and the weather.... Philadelphia never was known to be so lively at this season as at present; for an accurate account of the amusements, I refer you to my letter to your sister Mary. I went yesterday to see a doll, which has come from England, dressed to show us the fashions, and I saw besides a great quantity of millinery. Very long trains are worn, and they are festooned up with loops of bobbin, and small covered buttons, the same as the dress: you are not confined to any number of festoons, but put them according to your fancy, and you cannot

conceive what a beautiful effect it has. There is also a robe which is plaited very far back, open and ruffled down the sides, without a train, being even with the petticoat. The hats are quite a different shape from what they used to be: they have no slope in the crown, scarce any rim, and are turned up at each side, and worn very much on the side of the head. Several of them are made of chipped wood, commonly known as cane hats; they are all lined: one that has come for Mrs. Bingham[53] is lined with white, and trimmed with broad purple ribbon, put round in large puffs, with a bow on the left side. The bonnets are all open on the top, through which the hair is passed, either up or down as you fancy, but latterly they wear it more up than down; it is quite out of fashion to frizz or curl the hair, as it is worn perfectly straight. Earrings, too, are very fashionable. The waists are worn two inches longer than they used to be, and there is no such thing as long sleeves. They are worn half way above the elbow, either drawn or plaited in various ways, according to fancy; they do not wear ruffles at all, and as for elbows, Anna, ours would be alabaster, compared to some of the ladies who follow the fashion; black or a colored ribbon is pinned round the bare arm, between the elbow and the sleeve. There have come some new-fashioned slippers for ladies, made of various colored kid or morocco, with small silver clasps sewed on; they are very handsome, and make the feet look remarkably small and neat. Everybody thinks the millinery last received the most tasty seen for a long time.[54]

Dolley most likely met Sally McKean through her sister, Anna Payne. She then met Sally's ardent suitor, Carlos Fernando Martínez, Marquis de Casa Yrujo y Tacón. A "short, full man," Don Carlos de Yrujo was Spain's first ambassador to the United States, and presented his credentials to President Washington on August 25, 1796.[55] Sally's dashing, talented,

Sarah (Sally) McKean Martínez,
Marchioness de Casa Yrujo

and well-educated beau spoke Spanish, Italian, Portuguese, French, and English; sang; and played the guitar and the forte piano "divinely."[56] At a dinner party hosted by Martha Washington, the dashing Spaniard wore his hair "powdered like a snowball, [a] dark striped silk coat lined with satin, black silk breeches, white stockings, buckled shoes." An observer also noted that he wore "a jeweled small-sword at his side and a hat tipped with white feathers and borne under his arm completed this miracle of Spanish grandeur."[57] During his courtship, the "charming Chevalier" entertained Sally with "fine riding parties and musical frolics," sent to Spain for a proper guitar for her, and serenaded her every night with divine music."[58]

Sally was delightful company for the light-hearted Mrs. Madison. One chronicler wrote of Sally as "that merry, mischievous, altogether charming young woman, who looks out at us from Stuart's portrait with lips that can scarcely refrain from smiling long enough to be painted, with neck and arms of snowy whiteness, and a general air of innocent and high-bred coquetry."[59] She was born for the role of an international socialite and reveled in the attention she provoked. Open-minded, discreet Dolley Madison, nine years her elder, was the perfect confidante. The two had become fast friends by the summer of 1796. At that time, Dolley was twenty-eight, and Sally was nineteen, single, and had formed a strong romantic attachment to Yrujo.

In 1798, Sally amazed the city when she converted to Roman Catholicism, married the Spanish diplomat, and became the Marchioness de Yrujo, thereby becoming the first titled member — and Roman Catholic, for that matter — of Dolley's inner circle of personal friends. The union between the American Protestant and the Spanish Papist ignited a firestorm of gossip in the cosmopolitan capital city —

Carlos Fernando Martínez, Marquis de Casa Yrujo

to the delight of the city's worldly upper crust, who were voracious consumers and discriminating connoisseurs of risqué stories.

Another of Dolley's new friends, Betsy Patterson Bonaparte, "the pretty little Duchess of Baltimore," had her own legion of admirers. When she visited the Federal District, swarms of men followed her everywhere. They came, one commentator observed, "to see a naked woman." She dressed to please her young husband, Jérôme, who had "a boyish nostalgia for the way women dressed (or undressed) in the early frenzy of the French Revolution." Betsy had no use for petticoats, so the outline of her shapely form was only nominally covered by what little she wore. At her wedding on December 24, 1803, performed by the Archbishop of Baltimore, a guest said, "Whatever clothes were worn by the bride could have been put in my pocket."[60] Soon thereafter, some of the most socially prominent women in Philadelphia made it clear that if Mrs. Bonaparte wished to be invited to their parties, she would have to wear more clothing.

The elder generation, typified by First Lady Abigail Adams, was aghast at the new dress styles and use of rouge, both of

D. P. Madison

which Abigail thought to be thoroughly immodest. She wrote to her sister, Mary Smith Cranch:

> The stile of dress...is really an outrage upon all decency. I will describe it as has appeared even at the drawing Room—A sattin petticoat certainly not more than three breadths gored at the top, nothing beneath but a chemise. Over this thin coat, a Muslin sometimes, sometimes a crape made so strait before as perfectly to show the whole form. The arm naked almost to the shoulder and without [corset] stays or Bodice. A tight girdle around the waist, and the 'rich Luxurience of natur's Charms' without a handkerchief fully displayd. The face, a la mode de Paris, Red as a Brick hearth. When this Lady has been led up to make her curtzey, which she does most gracefully, it is true, every eye in the Room has been fixed upon her, and you might literally see through her.... To do justice to the other Ladies, I cannot accuse them of such departures from female decorum, but they most of them wear their Cloaths too scant upon the body and too full upon the Bosom for my fancy. Not content to *show which* nature bestows, they borrow from art, and litterally look like Nursing Mothers.... They show more of the [bosom] than the decent Matron, or the modest woman.[61]

Abigail Adams

While his wife disapproved of the new French fashions, John Adams, a devout Massachusetts Federalist, disapproved of James Madison's abandonment of Alexander Hamilton's ideals to follow the "false Republican gods of Thomas Jefferson." Nevertheless, Adams was charmed by Dolley upon their first meeting. He wrote to his beloved Abigail, "My Dearest Friend. —I dined Yesterday with Mr. Madison. Mrs. Madison is a fine Woman and her two sisters are equally so: one of them is married to George [Steptoe] Washington one of the two Nephews of the President who were sometimes at our House. Mr. Washington came and civilly enquired after your Health. These Ladies, whose Names were Pain [Payne], are of a Quaker Family once of North Carolina."[62]

With her radiant smile, narrow waist, and full bosom, there was never a woman so perfectly sculpted for the new French Empire fashions as Dolley Madison in her late twenties and thirties. Dolley, in her high-waisted, low-cut dress, wholeheartedly embraced the glamorous new styles. Within two years after her marriage, Dolley, who was once astounded by the parades of women wearing fancy dresses of silk, satin, and brocades trimmed with lace, was now one of them. In public, Dolley and her sister, Anna, both dressed like worldly society women, such as Betsy Patterson and Sally McKean, and could pass unnoticed among their friends. James Madison, the former life-long bachelor, certainly must also have enjoyed the splendid displays of the feminine form, or he would have discouraged his wife from emulating them. In private, in Philadelphia, and for many years later in Washington, however, Dolley continued to adhere to Quaker tradition. At home, she wore "a dark greystuff dress with snowy cap and apron and modest kerchief" in the mornings, before the start of her official duties, and when alone with her husband.[63]

The international political scene in Philadelphia in the late 1790s was charged with danger and intrigue. Personal choices were viewed as political statements. Both Sally McKean and Dolley found themselves dealing with these realities. Sally's father, Thomas McKean, was a rising star in the Democratic-Republican Party, of which Jefferson and

Madison were leaders. McKean, like many other American men, loathed the 1795 ratification of the treaty that John Jay had negotiated with the British, which was supposed to have resolved outstanding issues between the United States and Great Britain after the end of the Revolutionary War in 1783. The British continued to occupy some military posts in the northwestern U.S. territory that they were supposed to evacuate in 1783, and they hindered American trade and shipping. Jay was a Federalist and considered to be pro-British, and Jefferson's friends, Madison among them, were not amused when the U.S. emissary kissed the Queen's hand when presented in court. Jay had little to offer the British, who were at war with France and seeking to isolate the French Republic.

While the Jay Treaty resolved the issue of the British forts, an agenda item the British had previously agreed to, and then ignored, it granted "favored nation" status to the British, while seriously restricting U.S. trade with the West Indies, a major market. To add insult to injury (from a Republican perspective), the treaty also made major concessions to the British relating to the seizure of U.S. goods bound for France and French goods bound for the U.S., and it left unresolved a legion of other contentious issues.

Jay was all but universally damned for caving in to the British, but the treaty passed the Senate by a vote of twenty to ten in 1795. Despite popular disapproval, President Washington implemented it because he knew it was the price America had to pay for peace, temporary though it proved to be.

Madison was concerned. In 1797, from his viewpoint as a statesman and businessman, he wrote to James Maury, an old Virginia friend and schoolmate, who was the U.S. consul in Liverpool at the time, that the country was suffering from financial and trade problems and that the treaty, which was supposed to resolve so much distress, was instead causing new problems with several foreign countries.[64]

For Dolley, the Jay Treaty was more than a piece of diplomatic paper. It permitted the British to seize cargoes of French merchandise on American ships without compensation for the owners of the goods. That made the treaty personal, since the Madisons had recently ordered a large quantity of furniture from France. If the ship were seized by the British, Dolley and James would never see their furniture and would lose the considerable sum of money they had spent for it.

The Federalists were delighted with the treaty; the Democratic-Republicans, including Madison, were aghast. The Marquis de Yrujo, whose government opposed any rapprochement with the British, sided with Jefferson and Madison. George Washington's reluctant acceptance of the treaty made it a political hot potato and turned Sally McKean's engagement to the Spanish minister into political cannon fodder in a city that reveled in controversy.

Against the background of this international arm-twisting, the women of the nation's capital played out their traditional roles while creating others. Parlor politics was nothing new. Because they were denied direct access to power and could not vote, obtain a college education, practice a profession, or hold public office, women had to exercise power in subtle ways, by nurturing relationships, pulling strings, and orchestrating affairs of state from behind the throne.

In addition to friendship and companionship, the fashionable women of Dolley's new world provided her with something of extreme value in her new role: information. The same women who bantered about hemlines and bonnet styles also exchanged first-hand information about what was going on in the homes of the men in Congress and the courts of Europe. In an age when family connections and inter-family relationships had a persuasive and sometimes deciding effect on political decision-making, intimate knowledge of the inner workings of the ruling families at home and abroad was a considerable asset. In the arena some have dismissed as "women's gossip," Dolley and her female contemporaries shared valuable information, formed personal alliances, and learned the intimate details of the lives of families who ran the world.

Dolley never sought personal glory or public admiration. Indeed, she was one of the most modest and self-effacing women ever to live in the President's House. Neither did she seek power for its own sake. But when she saw how power could be influenced through nuanced relationship building, she chose to master that art for the benefit of her husband and the causes he served. Her ability to build bridges and create a neutral social space where hostile opponents could speak frankly and in privacy, along with the depth of her personal bravery, would be the benchmarks of her fame for the rest of history.

The fine art of political relationship building — and the consequences of not doing so — was a skill that had to be learned. Sally McKean (now the Marchioness de Yrujo) was one of Dolley's first teachers. Like many men and women in the capital, Sally was fiercely partisan, showering praise on her friends and openly attacking those she did not favor. She had a sharp tongue, a wicked wit, and a keen eye for scandal — the more salacious, the better. Sally wrote the following letter to Dolley in the summer of 1797, in response to Dolley's request for Philadelphia gossip about the new administration of President John Adams. After lambasting Abigail Adams for her "hawks eyes," during a public open house, or "drawing room," she painted a shabby picture of the rustic New Englander, John Adams, whom she believed to be ignorant of even the basic rules of protocol. Next she took on Timothy Pickering, Adams' secretary of state, and finished with a ribald exposé of her future husband's colleague, José Ignacio de Viar.

I hasten to thank you my Dearest Sister (for so hereafter I intend to stile you, as I cannot bear the dry, affected stile of — Dear Madam,) as you really are my sister in affection — for your charming letter dated the 23d of June — which was handed me by our friend [Richard] Brent, in the first place you ask me for a description of the Drawing room, I now hasten to give it you — that we have none at all — for that old what shall I call her — with her hawks eyes [Abigail Adams], gave out that the weather was too warm, and it would affect her

nerves, they must be very delicate of course, but I suppose we shall have it in full splendor in the fall: her,
and her Caro sposa [beloved spouse], accompanied
by Miss Smith—a niece of hers, and who I suppose
will sett up for the Miss Custis of the place—but there
I defy her—for she is not young, and confounded ugly,
have sett of a few days ago, for Boston, where I suppose they want to have a little fuss made with them
for dear knows they have had none made here. But I
must give you an anecdote about the elegance of his
[John Adams'] manners, and very great attention on
the fourth of july, the *foreign Ministers*, the members
of the Cincinata,[65] and some few Members of Congress, waited on him in the morning, and he was so
polite as to put his hat on—before them, but after a
little while he recollected himself and took it off—and
appeared quite frightened at his absence, some of the
Gentlemen were going to put theirs on also; in order
to keep him company—only they thought it too
warm—Pray tell me now—was ever our former *President* known to behave in that manner—no you will
say—because he was a Gentleman: the conclusion I
have drawn from it is—that he meant to introduce a
new custom and for its elegance and politeness—it
exceeds any thing I ever saw, or have even heard of
happening in any of the Courts of Europe, the only
Ladies who visited *his Right Honorable* Lady—was
Madame Freire,[66] and forlorn Mrs Wolcott.... The Man
[Timothy Pickering] has been behaving in a very devlish
manner—but our amiable friend the Chevalier [the
Marquis de Yrujo] has written a very excellent letter,
address'd to him and which gives Tim a very good
dose. It is allow'd by every body to be exceedingly well
written, and to contain the naked truth—Oh! you cannot have any idea what a noise it has made some of
the Timothy gang says he is worse than Genett,
Fauchett, or Adete[67]—but on the other hand all the

clever fellows say that nothing can be better than it is, and that the Minister deserves well of his Country for it....we are going to lose Nancy Emlen—she is to be married very shortly to a Mr Russel from Boston. I beleive you saw him last winter, he is very rich, but ugly as the Devil. Our friend Molly Wharton[68] is still very much enamour'd of Fatio, but I beleive his heart is made of something harder than ice ore it would melt... I shall write to morrow to the girls—my paper warns me that It is time to conclude—I therefore take its advice by signing myself your sincere and affectionate friend, Signora Catoni

I dont venture to put any other name as there is something of the nature of treason contain'd in my letter.... 4th. August. I cannot seal this without giving you a little anecdote of [José] Viar, which I have just heard and which accounts for my not seeing him these two, or three days, he has been making love to the wife of a servant who formerly lived with Mr Jaudenes, and he afterward lived with the Chevalier—The wife is a remarkable pretty woman, but no great things in point of character, the husband lives at service.[69] He came home a few days ago to see her—it was at twelve oclock at noon—and behold—verily, he caught the old goat, with his wife, and in not the most decent situation—so the fellow very politely took him by the nose and saluted him with kiks till the corner of the next Street. He is going to make him pay a devlish large sum of money, or else he says he will prosecute him, it has made a confounded noise, the Emlens, and Moll Wharton—all the shoemakers and in fact all the town knows it.[70]

Sally McKean may have known her husband's colleague and deputy, Don José Ignacio de Viar, the amorous Spanish consul general, as a philandering cad, but she also liked him personally and referred to him as the "jolly Viar."[71] Dolley knew him, too, but in a different light: as a thoughtful man who had sent her a toothache remedy in 1796.[72]

When John Adams defeated Thomas Jefferson and was elected president in late 1796, Washington's administration came to an end. At the same time, Madison's term as representative from Virginia ended, and he gladly set aside his political career, or so he thought, to retire to Montpellier. He signaled his intentions in an April 7, 1796, letter in which he told his friend Monroe, who was still shopping for goods for him in Paris, that "whatever articles you may be good enough to provide for me after the receipt of this, I wish you to address to Virginia, not to this place [Philadelphia], unless it may be such as will be wanted particularly here & in the course of next winter—which I mean to *be my last here*."[73] To a friend in England, Madison wrote a cordial, formal letter, which outlined his plans:

> After a warm contest for the succession to General Washington, the vacancy will be filled by Mr. Adams. He has seventy-one votes, and Mr. Jefferson only sixty-eight.... Mr. Jefferson, it is now well known, will serve in the secondary place allotted to him. This being the last session of Congress of which I shall be a member, I must, at the same time that I return you thanks for all your past favors, request that your future ones be addressed to Orange County, Virginia, and that they may not be sent on the calculation that I shall get them free of postage.[74]

Just after Adams was inaugurated in March 1797, and the nation bade farewell to its founder, James and Dolley moved out of their Philadelphia quarters and went back to Orange County. There, they were greeted by James Sr., now seventy-four and in declining health, and Nelly Madison, sixty-six, and robust for her age. In August, the Madisons hosted James and Elizabeth Kortright Monroe, after which both families visited their friend Jefferson in the first week of September. Next James and Dolley returned to Montpellier, where they welcomed Mary Payne, her sisters, and the Count de Volney.[75] He was a French academician of the highest esteem in European circles and epitomized rationalist and political thought in eighteenth-century Europe. Madison, who held strong views on the moral impropriety of slavery, must have relished Volney's company and had probably read his most famous work, *Ruins of Empire*, published in France in 1791 and translated into English in 1792. In it, Volney had written, "There [in Africa] a people now forgotten discovered while other were yet barbarians, the elements of the arts and sciences. A race of men, now rejected for their black skin and wooly hair, founded on the study of the laws of nature those civil and religious systems which still govern the universe."[76] It was a view not often expressed in the South in Madison's time.

James Madison's dream of becoming one again with the land had come true, but many felt it would not, indeed could not, last. The newly elected president, John Adams, wrote to his wife, Abigail, "Madison I suppose after a Retirement of a few Years is to become President or V.P. It is marvelous how political Plants grow in the shade."[77]

The last quarter of the eighteenth century, during which Dolley grew up and ripened into full womanhood, proved to be radically different from previous eras. The American and French Revolutions, coming as they did in rapid succession, had opened the floodgates to new ideas. In 1776, the American patriots challenged the mightiest empire in the world and won. In 1789, ordinary French citizens stormed the Bastille and toppled the monarchy of Louis XVI, who was guillotined in 1793. In England in the early 1790s, the revolutionary feminist, Mary Wollstonecraft, had begun to infuse her countrywomen with the radical notions that women, like men, had souls and that girls deserved the same educational opportunities as boys. In America, the Quakers, through the emancipation of their slaves, had driven a moral wedge between godliness and the ancient practice of slave owning.

The Western world was experiencing a period of radical change, and a new generation of smart, perceptive, innovative women was going to play a fundamentally different role than that of their mothers. Dolley's simple Quaker upbringing had never prepared her for such a contingency, but she was nothing if not adaptable. When challenges and opportunities appeared, she proved to be ready, willing, and able to take full advantage of them.

CHAPTER SEVEN

Within a Squirrel's Jump of Heaven

*I wish you had just such a country home as this,
as I truly believe it is the happiest and most independent life, and would be so for your children.*
— Dolley to Anna Payne Cutts[1]

Montpellier Plantation
Orange County, Virginia
March 1797

With the hustle, bustle, and heartaches of Philadelphia now behind her — or so she thought — Dolley
must have looked forward with great anticipation
to moving to the Madisons' spacious Orange County estate,
Montpellier. James had planned to take here there to meet his
parents just after the wedding, but that proved impossible.
Now, three years later, Dolley would meet them for the first
time. There, surrounded by birds, flowers, and a magnificent
vista of the Blue Ridge Mountains, she could rebuild the inner
peace and tranquility that had been eroded by a decade of
stressful changes. Her recent past, though often thrilling, had
also been grueling. In the previous decade, she had experienced

the Quakers' disownment of her destitute father, his depression and death; her first marriage and two childbirths; and the terror of the yellow fever epidemic, which cost her the lives of a son, her first husband, his parents, and numerous friends and relatives. She was forced to fight with her brother-in-law over her husband's estate. She lost two brothers to violent death. She and her sister, Lucy, were both disowned by the Quakers for marrying outside the faith. The welcoming arms of her elderly in-laws, James Sr. and Nelly Madison, and the beauty of their spacious estate must certainly have been comforting to Dolley, who was about to turn twenty-nine.

James Jr. eagerly anticipated his retirement from Congress and relief from the incessant Federalist-Republican conflict. The presidential election of 1796 had split the nation into two clear-cut political parties: the liberal, French-leaning Republicans, headed by Thomas Jefferson, and the conservative, pro-English Federalists, headed by John Adams. Both Washington and Madison had desired an earlier retirement but had yielded to the knowledge that their services were essential to the new nation. When Adams ascended to the presidency in March 1797, Washington gratefully withdrew from public life and returned to his beloved Mount Vernon. The timing was also perfect for Madison, who found it the opportune time to retire, leave behind the rented houses of Philadelphia, and return to his highly enjoyable life as a Virginia country gentleman.

Despite his strenuous opposition to the ratification of the Jay Treaty, Madison had lost that fight. That was just one of the countless causes he had championed; one of the numerous skirmishes he had fought in his zeal to build a strong new republic. But all of the political conflicts had taken their toll, and no one more than Dolley understood her husband's desire to get out of politics. Madison took no joy in contemplating the triumph of Alexander Hamilton's pro-British ideas in John Adams' Federalist administration, but being a practical man, as well as an idealist, he knew that he could not win every battle. Furthermore, from atop the hill facing the Blue Ridge Mountains, Montpellier called to him. How beautiful, he thought, to retire to his agrarian utopia, let his political bruises heal, and spend his days farming. For the rest of his life, except when he was required to be in Washington on public business, and one visit to Philadelphia required by Dolley's health, Madison lived at Montpellier. He had become "the complete Virginian."[2]

Madison, who was forty-six when he left Congress, did not have to apologize to anyone for retiring from political life, for he had dedicated himself to community service since he was twenty-three. He had first entered public office on December 22, 1774. Madison, his father, and nine neighbors formed the Committee of Safety for Orange County, an act authorized by the First Continental Congress to enforce the ban on trade with England. Although commissioned a colonel in the Orange County militia, he did not see active military service in the

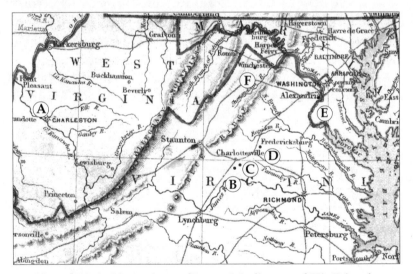

The Virginia Plantations of James Madison and His Friends.

A: George Steptoe Washington's Harewood House **B:** James Monroe's Highland **C:** Thomas Jefferson's Monticello **D:** James Madison's Montpellier **E:** George Washington's Mount Vernon **F:** Isaac Hite's Belle Grove

Revolutionary War because of his fragile health. Instead, he served the patriots' cause as an intellectual. As his biographer, Ralph Ketcham, wrote, "He had henceforth his vocation: he was a nation builder.... By the time of the battles of Lexington and Concord, Madison had found the purpose and adopted the ideals that were to motivate and guide him for years in public life and twenty years as his country's authentic sage."[3]

Madison had been a diligent student at the College of New Jersey at Princeton, which he entered in the summer of 1769 after a ten-day journey from Montpellier. He found his quarters at the college's imposing central building, Nassau Hall. There he lived and studied for three years, having successfully by-passed the freshman year by examination. At Princeton, Madison formed some of his longest lasting friendships. They included the future poet and Philadelphia newspaper publisher Philip Freneau, future novelist Hugh Henry Brackenridge, future president of the college Samuel Stanhope Smith, future U.S. attorney general William Bradford, and Thomas Jefferson's future vice president, Aaron Burr. Madison reveled in learning and studied for such long hours that his study regimen often threatened his health. Nevertheless, he found time to be an enthusiastic member of the American Whig Society and was active in their "paper wars" and typical undergraduate pranks.

Though in later life Madison was revered chiefly for his abilities as an intellectual and statesman, his classmate, Philip Freneau, recalled a demonstration of his personal bravery. While at school, one of Madison's young friends had run up a considerable tab at a local cake and Beer shop. The owner, unable to collect the money, seized the boy, locked him in his cellar, and let it be known that he would not free him until someone paid his debt. The boy's classmates assembled at the grog shop to attempt a rescue, but the owner stood firm in the door, an axe in hand, and threatened to split the skull of anyone who would try to free him without paying the bill. Young Madison, then quite small, slipped through the group of boys and confronted the man face-to-face. "You villain, would you dare strike any of us with that axe?" The man was so astounded that the little fellow would act with such conviction that he put up only a token resistance. Madison took the axe from him, threw it down, set the boy free, and the crowd dispersed.[4] Greatly respected by his professors and classmates, Madison graduated in 1771, "a paragon of the well-educated scholar."[5]

In April 1775, Madison and his uncle, William Moore, represented Orange County at the Williamsburg convention. There, the delegates chose Madison's trusted friend, Edmund Pendleton, over Dolley's second cousin, the fire-breathing patriot, Patrick Henry, as their presiding officer. In 1776, Madison served as a member of the Virginia constitutional convention, which drafted the state's first constitution and a bill of rights that later became a model for the Bill of Rights amended to the U.S. Constitution. Madison's active support for religious freedom and advocacy for the separation of church and state helped forge a life-long bond with his legislative partner and friend, Thomas Jefferson. From March 1780 to December 1783, he was a representative from Virginia to the Second Continental Congress, establishing himself as a tireless advocate for a strong federal structure, while watching in frustration as the loose confederation of states dwindled in power and effectiveness after the war's end.

A 1785 convention on interstate trade led to a call for a general convention to revise the Articles of Confederation. Madison was a driving force in organizing this general convention, setting its scope and tone and negotiating every obstacle that threatened adoption of the Constitution, which superseded the Articles of Confederation. In the summer of 1787, he drafted a comprehensive plan for a more powerful federal government. His role as chief architect of the Constitution enabled him to help create a new form of government and ultimately gained him a larger place in history than did his later presidential terms. His personal notes on the deliberations, which are virtually the only record of the momentous events because of the rule of secrecy adopted in the first days

James Madison about 1797

of the convention, provide an invaluable window into the minds of the framers of the Constitution.

Madison also made a major contribution to the ratification of the Constitution by writing, with Alexander Hamilton and John Jay, *The Federalist* essays, which were published in the nation's newspapers in 1788. Uncomfortable with the personal acclaim his work generated — he was now called the "Father of the Constitution" — Madison protested that the document was not the product of a single mind, but the collaboration of many dedicated men. After he returned home to Virginia, he was elected to its ratifying convention, ensuring that Virginia became the tenth state to ratify the Constitution.

Madison was reelected to the second, third, and fourth U.S. Congresses. While serving in Congress, he helped frame the Bill of Rights and enacted the first revenue legislation. From his opposition to Hamilton's financial proposals, which Madison felt would unduly bestow wealth and power upon northern financiers, came the development of the Democratic-Republican, or Jeffersonian, Party. However, he declined an appointment to be the nation's minister to France and turned down Washington's invitation to become secretary of state.

By 1797, Madison was ready to lay down the heavy mantle of public service and return to the soil. His retirement was also spurred on by the practical needs of his family. Although his mother, Nelly, was sixty-six and very fit, James Sr. was now seventy-four, unwell, and slipping away, and he needed his eldest son to relieve him of his remaining plantation duties. These duties had increased when his third son, Ambrose, who served as the dependable on-site caretaker of the plantation, died in 1793.

In the early spring of 1797, with the help of James and her sister, eighteen-year-old Anna, Dolley closed their Philadelphia townhouse. They packed their belongings and left with her five-year-old son, John Payne Todd, for the welcome, but wearying, week-long journey to Orange County, Virginia. They probably proceeded down the Delaware River to Wilmington. From there, they would have traveled overland or by ship to Havre de Grace, and then by stage or ship to Baltimore. Next they continued

Dolley Madison about 1797

on by stagecoach to the village of George Towne, from which they could see the embryonic shapes of the future hall of Congress and the President's House rising from the middle of a swamp. After a probable stop at Mount Vernon to see their friends, George and Martha Washington, they had another bumpy ride over rutted roads thick with mud to Fredericksburg and a final thirty-nine-mile push to Montpellier.

When their weary bodies arrived at the door, they were welcomed by Nelly and James Madison, Sr.; Dolley's sister-in-law, Fanny, twenty-three; and a great sea of black faces. James and Dolley quickly settled into their new life with hopes of enjoying their first permanent home.

The renewal of friendships and family ties was a special pleasure. Madison's closest friends were also his neighbors. They included Thomas Jefferson, at Monticello, and James Monroe, who returned from France in 1797 and moved to Highland plantation, adjacent to Monticello, in December 1799. Both were within a day's ride. Jefferson was always attentive to Dolley, and frequently closed his letters with a salutation to her. One written just after the end of his service in the Adams administration read, "Present me affectionately to Mrs. Madison, and convey to her my entreaties to interpose her good offices and persuasions with you to bring her here and before we uncover our house, which will yet be some weeks."[6] His sentiments for Dolley were undoubtedly an extension of the high regard he held for her husband, but soon he and his entire family developed a fondness for Dolley that sprang directly from her own gifts and graces. Jefferson set aside one special guest room for the Madisons when they made the all-day, thirty-mile trip to Monticello. Dolley, in particular, was a favorite guest of Jefferson's daughters, and the "Madison Room" became a part of Monticello's historical traditions.

The level of neighborly cooperation between Madison and his fellow farmers is expressed in a letter he wrote to James Monroe in February 1798, after a particularly difficult farming season:

> Calling to mind the difficulty you may experience from the general failure of the potato crop last year, I beg you to accept by the bearer a couple of bushels, which may furnish the seed for your garden, if nothing more. Mrs. Madison insists on adding for Mrs. Monroe a few pickles and preserves, with half a dozen bottles of gooseberries and a bag of dried cherries, which will not be wanted by us until another season will afford a supply, and which the time of your return home must have deprived her of, as the fruit of the last season. We both wish we could substitute something more worthy of acceptance.[7]

The plantation house to which Madison and Dolley returned was built about 1760 by his father, James Sr., who named it Montpellier. Located about fifty miles northwest of Richmond, it sits on a knoll about one-third of a mile southeast of Ambrose Madison's house, Mt. Pleasant. Montpellier faces slightly north of west, towards the Blue Ridge. A broad lawn, perhaps better called a well-kept field, sloped gently downward. At the rear of the house was a smaller porch, level with the ground, which gave a view of the Southwest Mountains. Paths led to the barns, storehouses, sheds, kitchens, and slave cabins. Those outbuildings were built over a period of about ten years after the main house was finished and were constructed to replace those of the original house, Mt. Pleasant, which gradually passed out of use and were dismantled or abandoned.

From the front portico, where Madison exercised in stormy weather, a walk down a graveled path led to the first gate, near which he had placed a large cup to catch the rain. After each rainfall, a slave measured the amount and reported it to his master so that he could adjust his planting and harvesting schedules accordingly. Two extremely tall poplars, which Madison called "the twins," stood just north of the building.

Behind the house was another, smaller colonnade, which led to an extensive back lawn and large formal gardens, where the Madisons raised a wide variety of ornamental trees, shrubs, and exotic flowers, as well as vegetables. The lawn and gardens were bounded by a ha-ha, or small moat, which kept the farm animals from intruding into the formal spaces.

The original building plan called for a two-story, eight-room brick house eighty-three feet wide and thirty-three feet deep. The house was designed in the neoclassical Georgian style, and when it was built, its owner was the richest man in Orange County and his home was the most elaborate (and second largest structure) in the county.[8] James Sr., an experienced building contractor, probably designed the house himself, and the construction crew was probably drawn from his own pool of enslaved mechanics, two of whom, named George and

Peter, are known to have been excellent carpenters. First a cellar was dug, and then the brick foundation and walls, laid in Flemish bond, were constructed.

The first floor consisted of four rooms, two on each side of a central passage, each with its own fireplace and separate chimney. On the right, at the rear of the hallway, a stairwell led to the second floor, which contained four living spaces and a large closet. The handsome house featured a wood-shingled, hipped roof with two chimney stacks at each end, and it served James Sr. and Nelly's family well for more than thirty-five years.

When James Jr., Dolley, Payne Todd, and Anna Payne took up residence at Montpellier in 1797, the first order of business was to expand the house, for now it had become a two-family dwelling. Soon there was yet another new face in the house. James's brother, Ambrose, had died in 1793, leaving behind his widow, Mary Willis Lee Madison, and a young daughter, Nelly Conway Madison. Mary died in March 1798, and Nelly came to Montpellier to become James' ward.[9]

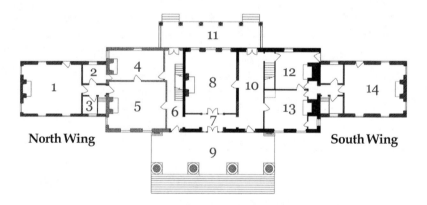

Montpellier in the Retirement Years

1: Dolley's bed chamber. **2:** Dolley's "elegant little chamber" / dressing room. **3:** Scullery. **4:** James Madison's bed chamber and sitting room. **5:** Dining room. **6:** North passage. **7:** Front passage. **8:** Drawing room. **9:** Front portico. **10:** South passage. **11:** Rear colonnade. **12 & 13:** Mother Madison's apartments. **14:** Mother Madison's chamber.

Madison built a thirty-foot addition to the north end, with two new rooms per floor. This provided a dining room and an additional chamber downstairs and two living chambers upstairs. He also added a second front door and new halls and staircases. To unify the overall appearance of the now divided house, Madison built a large Tuscan portico two stories high, eighteen feet deep, and forty-seven feet wide, supported by four brick columns. The entire addition, which was constructed over a three-year period between 1797 and 1800, was erected using a combination of local white and enslaved craftsmen.

For a time, the house was literally a duplex. There was no provision for entering one section from the other, save for walking out one front door and then in through the other. This provided a formal separation between the sedate lifestyle of the two elderly Madisons and that of the younger, more socially active family of five who now lived next door. The separate living arrangements did not indicate any degree of dissention or discord between the elder and younger Madisons, who spent their lives expressing their love and greatly enjoying each others' company.

Between 1809 and 1812, during James Madison's presidency, he again expanded the house. This renovation added symmetrical wings to each end and a new two-story portico, which was supported by four massive white Tuscan columns and two pilasters. A Palladian eyelid fanlight was added sometime later during Madison's lifetime. Except for the columns of the front portico, none of the house's 1760, 1797, or 1809 brickwork was stuccoed.

The carriage road skirting the expansive front lawn led the visitor past a replica of a Greek temple, built about 1809. A practical and innovative man, Madison designed the beautiful structure as an outdoor place to study—and to cover an otherwise undistinguished utility building: an underground icehouse. Peaceful as it was, the temple ultimately served only as an aesthetic contribution to the landscape and as a place to keep food cold.

The Temple

Madison also made major changes to the interior floorplan. The basement of each wing had its own kitchen, and the cooking ceased to be done in an exterior kitchen house. The first floor rooms served as chambers for the widowed Mother Madison, on the south end, and for Dolley and James, on the north. At this time, the wall dividing the original building from its first addition was torn down. The north rooms of the original house were given a new entryway featuring a single, Federal-style door opening into a formal entry hall and leading to a large drawing room used for entertaining. The two separate front doors were converted into windows. Off the right and left sides of the entry hall were arched doorways, which provided access to both sides of the house. A colonnade (rear porch) was added to the back of the house. The final result was an elegant country mansion in the neoclassical Federal style. The original eight-room house, valued at $5,000 to $6,000 before 1797, had increased to twenty-two rooms and was valued at $15,000 by 1813.[10] No further major structural changes were made during James' and Dolley's lifetimes.

Prior to James' marriage and their move to Montpellier, the estate chiefly reflected the conservative tastes of his parents. The construction of the new wing in 1797 enabled the younger Madisons to furnish their quarters to their own tastes. Soon, another of Dolley's newly emergent skills surfaced: a strong talent in the decorative arts. Her newly acquired taste for the latest French fashions began to enliven the mansion.

Although Madison's wallet was adequate, his tastes were somewhat more subdued and traditional than those of his Frenchified neighbor-friend, James Monroe. Consequently, Montpellier's interior décor reflected more the earlier, less ornamental styles than did Monroe's Highland, where rococo gold table ornaments and brightly colored French tableware made the interior look more like a wing of Versailles than a Virginia plantation house.[11] In 1798, Monroe sent the Madisons some basic equipment for their expanded family's housekeeping: two mattresses, four dozen napkins, four tablecloths (two suitable for a room of eighteen feet, plus two more), but lamented that he had no more kitchen furniture to offer. Montpellier, though more conservatively furnished than Highland, was nonetheless grand in every feature.[12]

In its 1820s configuration, after Madison retired from his two terms as president, visitors would walk up a wide flight of steps to the pillared portico, through the front door, and into a foyer, which opened into the stunning drawing room. An 1827 visitor wrote, "much of the furniture of the room had the appearance of Presidential splendour…. every thing displayed in its arrangement great order, neatness & taste, for which I fancy Mrs. Madison is remarkable."[13] Madison's favorite seat was a comfortable campeachy [campeche] chair, with its graceful, downswept frame, similar to one owned by his friend, Jefferson. The sofas were covered with damask in crimson, one of Dolley's favorite colors. To the rear of the drawing room were three triple-hung windows. They could be raised so that people could walk out onto the back porch, which provided a handsome view of the back lawn and gardens.

Off the drawing room to the left was the formal dining room, whose décor, furnishings, and fine food reflected Dolley's hospitality and love of rich, vibrant colors. The walls were painted or papered in a bright, sunflower yellow, and the floor was covered with a Venetian carpet of raspberry red, chrome yellow, and bright apple green. The walls of the room displayed more than thirty engravings, prints, and paintings, including portraits of Madison's personal friends, George Washington, John Adams, Thomas Jefferson, James Monroe, and Benjamin Franklin, as well as those of Louis XVIII of France, Napoléon, an African king, and the Chinese philosopher, Confucius.[14] The overall theme of the house celebrated American history and the outstanding leaders who created it.

Dolley and James occupied the left, or north, wing of the house. The last room to the north was Dolley's bedchamber, featuring crimson walls, crimson bedcovers, and a large four-post tester [canopy] bed. Dolley's friend Margaret Bayard Smith wrote in 1828 that this room was "very large and commodious and furnished with every convenience and much elegance. Before a large sopha, lay her work. Couches, easy-chairs, &c. invited us to ease and comfortable indulgence.... I reclined at my ease while we talked—and oh, how we did talk."[15]

Madison's bed chamber and sitting room was a small room at the back of the north wing, just off the dining room. It was furnished with chairs, a high-posted iron day bed (*a la Polonaise*) with a canopy of crimson damask, china that had belonged to the ill-fated Marie Antoinette, and a desk. The walls were filled with souvenirs from the George Towne Ball, held to honor Madison after he finished his second term as president; mirrors; and pictures.[16]

The elder Madisons occupied the south wing of the house. James Sr. died in 1801, but Nelly survived him and kept her own quarters until her death in 1829. Like the rest of the house, the walls of her chambers were filled with ancient oil paintings and fine engravings. The Madison library was located on the second floor of her wing. Madison's niece wrote that the room held not only plain bookcases all around the room, "but in the middle with just sufficient room to pass between, these cases were filled with books, pamphlets, papers, all, of every thing of interest to our country before and since the Revolution."[17]

Nelly's old servants aged with her, and Old Sawney was still waiting upon his elderly mistress until he was ninety, although by that time, his only real duty was to fetch her a glass of water. He had his own house and patch of garden, where he raised cabbage, sweet potatoes, and other vegetables, as well as the chickens and eggs he regularly sold to Dolley.[18]

"The Old Lady," as Nelly was reverently called, admitted visitors to her wainscoted and closeted chambers at two o'clock and dined at three, an hour before the younger generation. "She was a lady of excellent education, strong mind and good judgment, action, and will to her last moments," wrote Mary Cutts. "She took an interest in modern events as well as the many friends by whom she was surrounded.... She lived to be ninety-eight; her usual seat was on a couch in the centre of a large room, a table in front, on which was her Bible, prayer book and knitting; these divided her time. The gloves and stockings, with the name knit in by her were precious gifts to her grandchildren."[19]

At Orange Courthouse, on the well-traveled road to the famed Virginia healing springs, strangers were often informed that they were only a short distance from the Madisons' home. Many made unplanned stops to pay their respects and found themselves invited to stay and enjoy the legendary hospitality of their hosts for several days or even weeks.[20] To ensure that visitors would receive a warm welcome, Madison kept a telescope mounted on the portico so that his household staff could watch the approach road and notify him of arriving guests.[21]

Those who visited Montpellier quickly came to understand the splendid, peaceful perfection of country life it provided, set as it was far from the noise and bustle of any city. One day, a visitor from Portland, Maine, found himself at Orange Courthouse and wrote:

> As Mr. Madison's plantation is only five miles distant from this [place], I resolved to stop, and to visit almost the last of the Romans.[22] I took a horse, raining though it was, and after going over a Virginia road, about three miles, which you probably know is one of the

D. P. Madison

worst in the world; for here it is 'unconstitutional'
to have good roads, I came to a bye-path, a sort of a
carriage road that led into the woods, when I kept
on riding and riding for nearly two miles, or one
and a half, passing one gate that led to a plantation,
till I came to another where I met an old negro, who
told me the way, and added that his 'old master would
be glad to see the young genman.... I rode on then
through a well-built gate—on the road-way—leading
to an immense field of rye—by yet another gate—
and came at last to a large and elegant brick-house,
built in the Virginia fashion, with wings, a projecting
portico, a walk in front, &c. &c. What on earth could
send a man here, I said to myself—here, so far from
the road, so far from neighbors, so far from the village, the post office—in this hide-and-go-seek place in
the woods, where it is difficult to find a dwelling, no
matter how conspicuous it may be. But such is the
Virginia fashion. The Virginians get off from the road
with the same zeal that we crowd on—and here you
may travel where there are no signs of life, but where,
if you were to sound a trumpet to call men together,
they would jump up as from the earth. Truly this is
retirement, this habitation in such a field—in such a
valley—with the morning music of the whippoorwill
and the evening song of the nightingale—undisturbed
by the little bustle in the neighboring negro camps, or
the solitary traveller who, perchance, strays here, as I
have done, to pay homage to character, to patriotism,
to an upright and well-done political career.[23]

As usual, Dolley adapted quickly to the requirements of
entertaining guests at Montpellier, and by the time the
Madisons' four-year sojourn there ended, her home was a
model of gracious Southern hospitality. Quoting an unnamed
visitor, her devoted niece, Mary Cutts, wrote, "There are few
houses in Virginia that gave a larger welcome, or made it

more agreeable, than over which Queen Dolley — the most gracious and beloved of all our female sovereigns — reigned." The visitor went on to say that everything under her personal supervision, including the care and entertainment of visitors and the management of the enslaved staff, "was admirably managed with an equal grace and efficiency."[24]

Visitors arriving at Montpellier were first struck by the stunning natural beauty of the location. In Madison's time, the view from the front portico took in a wide panorama of forests, meadows, and fields of grain and tobacco, with the Blue Ridge Mountains of the Appalachian chain forming a magnificent backdrop. Wild birds of every description flocked to the place, and deer, foxes, rabbits, chipmunks, and squirrels abounded. Montpellier became the physical center of Madison's universe. He was so inspired by the beauty of the place and the warm memories it furnished him with that he fondly described it as being "within a squirrel's jump of heaven."[25]

Both Dolley and James invariably spelled the name of their plantation Montpellier, with two *l*'s. It is said to have derived its name from Montpellier ("Mount of the Pilgrim"), a medieval town in the south of France, noted as being a center of learning and for having a salubrious climate. The first surviving record of the plantation's name is found in a 1781 letter written to Madison by his cousin, Edmund Pendleton: "I have enjoyed some pleasant hours with my friends, Amongst others a few happy days at your fathers, who I was glad to find enjoying fine health, after being many years without seeing him, Tho' I was the less surprised at it, after experiencing the Salubrious Air of his fine Seat, not to be exceeded by any Montpelier in the Universe."[26]

The 1797 move to Montpellier offered Dolley the opportunity to evolve into the Virginia plantation mistress she might have become if her father had not emancipated his slaves and moved to Philadelphia. The differences would have been matters of scale, wealth, and slaveholding. By accepting Madison as her husband, Dolley married several rungs up the socioeconomic ladder. Had her family remained in Hanover County, Virginia, instead of moving to Philadelphia, her husband would likely have been a stalwart, young Quaker planter of modest to moderate means like her father, not a mature member of the wealthy, worldly Anglican gentry.

Yet her marriage to Madison also introduced a moral dilemma: Dolley's ethics were grounded in Quaker principles, and Quakers had declared slaveholding morally impermissible. Her parents' strong abolitionist views had led them to free their slaves, forfeit their monetary value, and risk the family's economic future; a risk that failed and brought the family financial disaster. Now Dolley had married the owner of more than a hundred slaves. Did her family's experiences with emancipation affect her perspective on slaveowning? As an Anglican planter's wife, she would have had little to say about the matter. Powerless to reconcile the dilemma during her husband's lifetime, Dolley knew she would nevertheless have to face it if James died before she did.

Despite the dilemma over slaveholding, Dolley rapidly took to her new role as the mistress of a plantation and wife of a prominent man. No sooner did the Madisons reach home in 1797 than the word spread throughout the region. The social season was in full swing, and Dolley quickly found out what it was like to be part of Madison's vast cousinage. She and "Colonel Madison Jr.," as her husband was called while his father was still alive, were deluged with invitations to visit his relatives.

Madison's brothers and sisters had settled into their own families. His younger brother, Francis, lived nearby with his wife, Susannah Bell, and their nine known children until his death in 1800. His next youngest brother, Ambrose, had married Mary Willis Lee. He died in 1793, five years before his wife. His youngest brother, William, married first Frances Throckmorton, and they had ten children on their Orange County plantation. After her death in 1832, he married Nancy Jarrell. William survived his oldest brother by seven years. Madison's sister Nelly married Major Isaac Hite, Jr., and moved to Belle Grove plantation, near Middletown, Virginia, where she lived until her death in 1802. His sister Sarah ("Sally") Catlett Madison married Thomas Macon in 1790, and they lived at Somerset plantation, adjacent to Montpellier. She survived her oldest brother by seven years. The baby of the family, Fanny, married Dr. Robert Henry Rose II, a local physician, in 1800 and reared a large family. They later moved to Huntsville, Alabama, where she died in 1823.

During this retirement period, Madison began what would become twice-annual pilgrimages to visit Jefferson at Monticello. The Madisons were guests at James Monroe's Highland plantation on many occasions. Towards the end of August 1797, the Monroes visited the Madisons at Montpellier, and then accompanied them to Monticello. The Madisons enjoyed Jefferson's company the first week of September, and then returned to Montpellier to prepare for a visit by Dolley's mother, sisters, and the Count de Volney.[27] Dolley also made extended visits to her mother, Mary; sisters, Mary Payne and Lucy Payne Washington; and brother, John Coles Payne, at the George Steptoe Washington estate, Harewood. In 1799, the younger Madisons also visited Dolley's uncle and aunt, Colonel Isaac and Lucy Coles Winston, who lived in Hanover County. Colonel Winston, six years Madison's elder, was a close and respected friend, and James often took his sage counsel to heart.[28]

An event in the spring of 1800 reflected Madison's social openness towards African-Americans. In April 1800, Jefferson wrote Madison to say that Christopher McPherson, a mulatto freedman, would be bringing some books and a letter from Monticello to Madison. McPherson was the son of a slave woman named Clarinda and Charles McPherson, a Scots merchant in Louisa County, Virginia. When he reached Montpellier, he was treated with a degree of hospitality rarely accorded a Free Person of Color in the South: he was invited to dine with the master and mistress of the plantation. McPherson wrote, "Mr. Jefferson by letter introduced me to Mr. Maddison—I sat at Table Evening & morning with Mr. M his Lady & Company & enjoyed a full share of Conversation."[29]

After his 1797 retirement, Madison made the complete transition from a plantation-born boy to the master of Montpellier. Madison loved the land. The role of plantation master came naturally to him, and he excelled in it. The transition he was never able to achieve was that from husband to father, a sorrow that troubled the Madisons throughout their long and happy married life. Dolley and James both came from large healthy families. Madison was one of twelve children and Dolley one of nine. In the last months of 1800, Dolley's younger sister, Mary Payne, married Virginia congressman John George Jackson, and soon started bearing children.[30] After their first year of marriage and no resulting pregnancy, Dolley and her husband and friends were all attuned to the subject. When the marriage had attained the eighteenth month, Aaron Burr wrote to James Monroe "Madison still childless—and I fear like to continue so."[31] In 1801, Jefferson commented to an old friend that Madison was "not yet a father," and given that three of his close friends were discussing the matter with each other, Madison may also have expressed his concern to them.

Because of the births of her two sons by John Todd, we know that Dolley was fertile prior to the yellow fever epidemic of 1793, but we also know that her second son was "sickly," dying within weeks of his birth, and that Dolley herself was laid low by the birth. Whether she was suffering from birth-related problems—which could have affected her future ability to bear children—or from the effects of a nonlethal yellow fever infection is not known.

On May 15, 1809, when Dolley was a few days short of turning forty-one, an enigmatic reference to a possible pregnancy appeared in a letter from Joseph Dougherty to Thomas Jefferson. "Mr. Barry is painting in the President's House," Dougherty wrote, "but Mrs. Madison cannot abide the smell of the paint: that may be on account of her pregnancy, but I think she will bring forth nothing more than dignity." Nothing else about any pregnancy survives in the historical record.[32]

In the past, fingers have pointed at Madison as being the cause of the couple's childlessness, for Dolley had already produced two children. Given the enormous number of possible causes for infertility, there is no way to ascertain the reason for their childlessness. Marital strife or emotional coolness certainly did not seem to stand in the way. A study of the Madisons' letters, as well as descriptions of the couple by close friends, paints a portrait of two warm, loving people who were totally devoted to each other and rarely apart.

Whatever the cause of their misfortune, both Madisons deeply lamented their inability to have children. That may well account for the great enjoyment Dolley took in spoiling her son, Payne, and in entertaining the hordes of children belonging to their friends and relatives. Visitors definitely did not have to be past the age of majority to be welcome at Montpellier. As a child, Payne reveled in the country life on the Madison plantation and was a frequent visitor to the Madison slave settlement, Walnut Grove. There he played with the slave children and listened to their tales and the music their elders provided.[33] The Madisons' childless state may have encouraged Dolley's over-indulgence of Payne, who in later life caused them considerable anguish.

Dolley rapidly adapted to country life, relishing Montpellier's enchanting natural beauty. She found a special friend in their French gardener, Monsieur Bizet (whom Dolley spelled Beazée). Bizet was paid the handsome sum of $400 per year to train and supervise enslaved gardeners and maintain the plantation's magnificent flowerbeds and walkways and the fruit and vegetable gardens that provided the family with their daily staples. He also taught some of the slaves the rudiments of French.[34] His wife was noted for protecting her complexion with "a mighty shade," which Dolley also wore and referred to as her "Beazée bonnet."[35] The Bizets came to Montpellier just after the French Revolution and returned to France shortly before Madison's death.

Despite their apparent hopes for relief from the public eye, the period from 1797 to 1801 was not the beginning of a permanent retirement for the Madisons. Instead, it was a series of endings and beginnings that ultimately led to a total renaissance for both of them. The family donned mourning clothes after the death of Dolley's cousin, the ardent patriot and former Virginia governor, Patrick Henry, who died on June 6, 1799. A pall fell over the entire nation when, on December 4 of that same year, George Washington died of a throat infection. The Madisons, now in mourning for the former president, made a condolence visit to his widow, Martha, who had given such supportive advice to Dolley when she was contemplating the momentous decision to marry Madison.

The year 1799 also brought James back into public service, but at a comfortable level, as a member of the Virginia Assembly from Orange County. The Madisons took lodging in two rooms of George Watson's boardinghouse in Richmond so that James could attend the assembly in December 1799 and January 1800. Madison warned Dolley that the accommodations were "in a style much inferior to what I had hoped. You must consequently lower your expectations on this subject as much as possible before you join me."[36] The lack of luxury was not an issue for Dolley. She dearly loved her husband and would have slept on bare floorboards to be with him.

In January 1800, Dolley wrote to Eliza Collins Lee, whom she hoped would be in Richmond with her husband, who was also an assemblyman:

> A prospect of meeting thee which is now clouded with disappointment, was my first inducement to visit Richmond — having heard that Mr. Lee's family would certainly be with him. I have found the place, however, to my surprise, a most agreeable one — many ladys joine in my regret that you are not with us.... Mr. L. tells me you have 2 little ones — I would give the world to see them — why will you not come to Orange? Make an Effort my dear Girl to visit us — & if your heart is unaltered towards me you will Immagin the happiness such

a favour would occasion—My time is so short that I can only add our affectionate salutations. Pray write me and kiss the children.[37]

Shortly after the turn of the century, Madison became the patriarch of his family. In February 1801, James Madison, Sr., died. He had named his eldest son, age fifty, executor of his estate and bequeathed to him his beloved Montpellier, its 5,000 acres, and about a hundred slaves. By that time, the Madisons had turned their attention to national politics again.

Both major Republican candidates in the presidential election of 1800 were friends of the Madison family: Thomas Jefferson and Aaron Burr. In the general election, the Republicans won—but the popular vote was not the deciding factor for the presidency. The ultimate decision of who would become president appeared to lie in the hands of the Electoral College.

On January 2, 1801, the votes were counted in the Electoral College. For the Democratic-Republicans, Jefferson and Burr tied at seventy-three votes each. The Federalists' candidate, John Adams, got sixty-five votes; South Carolina's Charles Cotesworth Pinckney received sixty-four; and John Jay, one. The top two candidates would become president and vice president, but which man would take which office? That would be determined by the House of Representatives.

In the House, both Jefferson and Burr had their supporters. The Federalists had only one poor choice to make: to support either Jefferson or Burr, and thereby to promote whichever man they thought might best destabilize the Republican administration.

Burr had accepted the vice president's role in advance. Jefferson was in a good mood and was already picking out his cabinet. Because the office of the vice president was not considered part of the president's cabinet, Burr had not even planned to be present for the inauguration.

Burr remained in New York while the debate raged, although his enemies charged him with politicking to have himself chosen over Jefferson. A letter he wrote to Joseph Alston on January 15, after nearly two weeks of balloting had taken place, clearly shows that Burr had no such notion. "I believe that all will be well, and that Jefferson will be our next president," he wrote.[38]

After an agonizing seven-day struggle and thirty-six rounds of voting, which ended on February 17, 1801, Jefferson was elected president and Burr, vice president. Had Burr muscled the political effort of which he was known to be capable, he might well have influenced the one crucial vote he needed to best Jefferson for the presidency. Instead, he stayed out of the fray and let history take its course. Burr's forbearance cost him the presidency and sealed his fate. His decision ultimately led to the opening of a Pandora's box that would see the proud Burr disgraced, destitute, starving, and in desperate need of Madison's mercy a decade later.

The Madisons could not attend the Jefferson-Burr inauguration in March 1801 because of the death of James Sr., and the necessity for arranging the financial affairs of his estate. In May 1801, a request arrived from Monticello. Jefferson wanted his friend Madison to be his secretary of state. The call to duty came from the man whose character and vision Madison respected more than any other. With his acceptance, the world of James and Dolley Madison was again turned on its ear. The "young Colonel" no longer, Madison took office on May 2 for what was to be an eight-year role at Jefferson's side. On May 20, Dolley's Spanish diplomatic friend, José Ignacio de Viar, whom Sally McKean had once lampooned for his philandering and who had earlier sent Dolley a toothache remedy, wrote to congratulate Dolley on her husband's important new position.[39]

For Dolley, who turned thirty-three the month her husband embraced his new role, the appointment meant abandoning the peace and quiet of her comfortable rural retreat and moving to the nation's capital. It would not be the established, elegant Philadelphia she knew well but raw, new, unfinished Washington City on the Potomac River. The move propelled her into the national spotlight, which proved to be as harsh as it was warm. In Washington, she would develop new political skills, prove her mettle, and ultimately demonstrate the heroism that would spread her fame throughout the world.

Dolley Madison's first official call to national service came from the President's House just twenty-five days after her husband took office. Mr. Jefferson, it seemed, had a problem that neither he nor his secretary of state could solve. In his moment of need, the president turned to *Mrs.* Madison.

CHAPTER EIGHT

The Washington Quadrille

"Adieu, my beloved, our hearts understand each other."
—Dolley to James Madison, October 23, 1805

The President's House
Washington City
May 27, 1801

President Jefferson had a problem. A widower who rarely found it necessary to invite women to official functions, he had planned a dinner for twelve, including two spouses of his male guests. They were the wife of William Cranch, a Federalist who served as junior assistant judge of the Circuit Court of the District of Columbia, and Margaret Bayard Smith, wife of Jefferson's fellow intellectual and close friend, Samuel Harrison Smith, publisher of the *National Intelligencer*.

Protocol demanded that the president have an official hostess present when women were invited to formal gatherings at the President's House. Under normal circumstances, this would have been the president's wife, but Jefferson had none. His wife, Martha Wayles Skelton Jefferson, a tall, auburn-haired harpsichordist of queen-like carriage, might have been the perfect First Lady, but she had died in 1782, and he had not remarried. When Jefferson became president in 1801, he had been a widower for nineteen years. Within his own family, his feminine resources were slim. His daughter Martha (also known as Patsy) had married Congressman Thomas Mann Randolph, Jr. Daughter Mary (called Maria or Polly), who had married Congressman John Wayles Eppes, had young children and lived too far from the capital to carry out social duties in Washington, except on rare occasions.

With no wife or suitable female relative to fill the job, the president turned to the spouses of his cabinet officers. The next-ranking officer was his vice president, Aaron Burr, but his wife, Theodosia Bartow Prevost Burr, had died of stomach cancer in 1794, and Burr did not remarry until the last years of his life. Burr's daughter, Theodosia, would have been well suited for the job. Although only eighteen, she was a prodigy who had grown up in New York's high society, possessed a man's advanced education, spoke fluent French and Spanish, was well-acquainted with European nobility, and was highly skilled in the social arts. Unfortunately, she had just married southern planter Joseph Alston. Two weeks after her father took office, Theodosia moved to The Oaks, her husband's South Carolina rice plantation, and was unavailable to assist the president.

Next in line as candidate for official hostess was Dolley, the wife of Jefferson's long-time friend and now his secretary of state. On the forenoon of May 27, 1801, a warm, humid spring day in the grandly planned, sparsely inhabited new federal city, Dolley Madison received her first official summons to public duty. The brief note, written in the third person, stated "Thomas Jefferson begs that either Mrs. Madison or Miss Payne will be so good as to dine with him to-day, to take care of his female friends expected."[1] Whatever Dolley did at Jefferson's dinner on that evening, she impressed the president, who called on her to serve as his hostess for all eight years of his administration. The wife of the president had no title or formal duties. As the wife of the secretary of state, Dolley similarly had none, but as the president's official hostess, she assumed a unique position in Washington society.

It was quickly evident that Dolley had the perfect personality for the role. As one of her relatives wrote, "She was humble-minded, tolerant, and sincere, but with a desire to please, and a willingness to be pleased, which made her popular, and always a great friend and support to her husband. The power of adaptation was a life-giving principle in her nature, while an unusually attentive memory prevented her ever forgetting either names, faces, or the slightest incident connected with the personal history of any one."[2] In addition to receiving invitations to assist Jefferson in entertaining, Dolley and her husband were frequent guests at his afternoon dinners in their own right, sometimes as often as twice a week.[3]

Margaret Bayard Smith was one of the guests at the party where Dolley made her début as the president's hostess. Although she was the daughter of an active Federalist, she was impressed with Jefferson and became an ardent Republican. Jefferson reciprocated in his regard for the Smiths and introduced them to the Madisons. Margaret wrote to her younger sister, Maria Bayard. "I am highly pleased with her [Dolley]; she has good humour and sprightliness, united to the most affable and agreeable manners. I admire the simplicity and mildness of Mr. Madison's manners, and his smile has so much benevolence in it, that it cannot fail of inspiring good will and esteem."[4]

The day after the fateful party, Margaret gave a full report to her sister, Maria:

Since I last wrote I have formed quite a social acquaintance with Mrs. Madison and her sister; indeed it is impossible for an acquaintance with them to be different. Mr. Smith and I dined at the President's,—he has company every day, but his table is seldom laid for more than twelve. This prevents all form and makes the conversation general and unreserved. I happened to sit next to Mr. Jefferson and was confirmed in my prepossessions in his favour, by his easy, candid and gentle manners. Before and after dinner Mrs. Cranch and myself sat in the drawing-room with Mrs. Madison and her sister, whose social dispositions so made us well acquainted with each other. About six o'clock the gentlemen joined us, but Mr. Jefferson's and Madison's manners were so easy and familiar that they produced no restraint. Never were there a plainer set of men, and I think I may add a more virtuous and enlightened one, than at present forms our administration.[5]

In an age when women were chiefly viewed as social ornaments that stood behind the men they had married, Dolley created a new role for herself and the women who followed her in the President's House. As a farm girl in Virginia, she learned that hard work, diligence, and virtue were hallmarks of a respected person. From the Quakers, she learned the moral principles that governed the ethical choices she made in life. During her two years in Philadelphia as the wife of a congressman, she quickly adapted to the social demands of living among politicians and the sophisticated upper class. As mistress of Montpellier during her husband's four-year retirement, she mastered the art of entertaining often and on a large scale. When her husband was called to Washington, she brought all these traits and skills to bear on her new station in life: wife of the secretary of state and hostess for the president.

As the surrogate First Lady, she was thrust into the public eye and into the political world. Her greatest social skill was her ability to provide a warm and inviting space that enabled even the crustiest and sharpest-edged political adversaries to meet in peace. By the time her husband had served two terms as Jefferson's secretary of state, Dolley would accumulate a vast storehouse of social and political experiences, good and bad. These years, from 1801 to 1809, were the final training period for Dolley's ultimate personal challenge: her future role as the president's wife.

When the Madisons finally reached Washington on May 1, 1801, to begin James' service as secretary of state, Dolley was turning thirty-three, and her husband was fifty-one. Judge William Cranch administered the oath of office to Madison on May 2, and by May 14, all of Jefferson's key cabinet positions were filled.

Refreshed by his four-year immersion in the agricultural life, though suffering from the chronic rheumatic problems that would dog him for life, Madison was ready to reenter the world of Republican politics. Dolley's first cousin, Edward Coles, who met Madison about this time and who was to serve the Madisons in many responsible roles later in life, painted this portrait of his Virginia kinsman at the time Madison joined the Jefferson administration:

I never knew him to wear any other color than black; his coat being cut in what is termed dress-fashion; his breeches short, with buckles at the knees, black silk stockings, and shoes with strings or long fair boot tops when out in cold weather, or when he rode on horseback of which he was fond. His hat was of the shape and fashion usually worn by gentlemen of his age. He wore powder on his hair, which was dressed full over the ears, tied behind, and brought to a point above the forehead, to cover in some degree his baldness, as may be noticed in all the likenesses taken of him. . . . In height he was about five feet six inches, of small and delicate form, of rather a tawny complexion, bespeaking a sedentary and studious man; his hair was originally of a dark brown color; his eyes were bluish, but not of a bright blue; his form, features, and manner were not commanding, but his conversation exceedingly so and few men possessed so rich a flow of language, or so great a fund of amusing anecdotes, which were made the more interesting from their being well-timed and well-told. His ordinary manner was simple, modest, bland, and unostentatious, retiring from the throng and cautiously refraining from doing or saying anything to make himself conspicuous.[6]

The sight that greeted the Madisons upon their arrival in Washington was not impressive. Twenty years before becoming the nation's capital, the diamond-shaped, 6,000-acre piece of land that lay between the Potomac River and the Anacostia River (then known as the Eastern Branch of the Potomac)

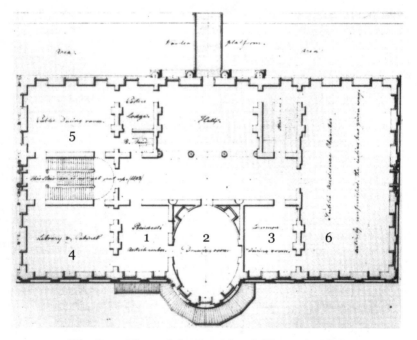

The State Floor of the President's House in 1803

During the Jefferson era, the rooms served the following purposes. **1** was the president's antechamber. **2** was the drawing room, where formal receptions were held. **3** was the dining room. **4** housed the library and cabinet officers. **5** was the public dining room. **6** was the East Room, labeled "Public audience chamber," was marked "entirely unfinished — the ceiling has given way."

had been a pleasant, wooded place. In 1790, when Major Pierre Charles L'Enfant, the man George Washington had chosen to lay out the city, visited the site, he fell in love with the landscape. Indeed, he became intoxicated with the possibilities, envisioning the federal city to be "the grand embodiment of a great nation yet to be," and imagined fountains, gardens, monumental architecture, and streets that, like his visions, reached "to far distant points of view."[7]

Two buildings would dominate the city: the hall of Congress and the president's official residence. The president's mansion that L'Enfant envisioned was to be five times the size of the current structure. President Washington approved the new residence in principle and authorized construction. The site was laid out and the cellars were dug, but the mansion was never completed as conceptualized. Nevertheless, it embodied the stately, high Federalist ideals that dominated the first years of the nation.

By the time Abigail and John Adams moved into the President's House, it was little more than an unfinished shell. Situated on its own hill, it commanded a beautiful view overlooking the Potomac. However, its first female occupant found it too large and too drafty and had to build thirteen fires to keep it warm. The largest public rooms were not plastered or painted and had no furniture. Abigail Adams strung a rope across the cavernous unfinished East Room to hang her clothes to dry, for that was the most practical use she could find for it.

Most of the people who worked in Washington lived in nearby Georgetown, which Abigail pronounced "the very dirtyest Hole I ever saw for a place of any trade....It is only one mile from me but a quagmire after every rain."[8] Virtually nothing had been constructed between the Capitol and the President's House, and the area was, for all practical purposes, a swamp.

By 1801, when Jefferson took office, the landscape had taken a decided turn for the worse. Although sections of many planned streets had not been opened, and some of the forest still remained, parts of the proto-city's land had been hacked clear. Nearly 3,000 people lived in 109 brick buildings and 263 poorly built, thrown-together wooden dwellings. For the city's first decades, the roads were rutted and littered with tree stumps. When the Madisons were preparing for their trip to Washington, the president cautioned them to come via Alexandria, lest their travel be frustrated by even worse routes to the city.

The President's House was still largely unfinished. Benjamin Latrobe wrote in 1803, "The surrounding Ground was chiefly used for Brick yards, it was enclosed in a rough post and rail fence.... During the short residence of President Adams at Washington, the wooden stairs & platform were the usual entrance to the house, and the present drawing room was a mere vestibule.... [The] Public Audience Chamber entirely unfinished, the ceiling has given way."[9]

Upon their arrival, the Madisons accepted Jefferson's hospitable offer and moved into the President's House until they could find suitable quarters of their own.[10] Though unfinished, the executive mansion offered ample space for Dolley; James; Dolley's son, Payne Todd; and her sister, Anna Payne. When the Madisons' carriage first pulled up in front of the building, the mansion was home to only two men: Jefferson and his private secretary, Charlottesville native Meriwether Lewis, and they were said to have rattled around the house "like two mice in a church."[11] Indeed, Jefferson described the place as "a great stone house, big enough for two emperors, one pope, and the grand lama in the bargain."[12]

Theodosia Burr Alston dined with Jefferson in October 1801, writing to her half-brother that she and her husband "had the felicity of dining with the president—it became lawful for me as my friend Mrs. Maddison was there—the house is really superb; it is built with a white stone which gives it an elegant appearance outside, inside it is well divided, but not as elegantly as it ought to be."[13]

Having no family in the immediate vicinity, Jefferson would have been delighted to have the Madisons remain in the presidential residence with him, but James and Dolley preferred to live in their own house. By May 26, they had rented and furnished a relatively small, new, three-story row house, one of a cluster known as "The Six Buildings" on M Street. It was located a short stroll down Pennsylvania Avenue, between Twenty-first and Twenty-second Streets, four blocks from the President's House in the direction of Georgetown.[14]

The house may have been small, but the neighbors were delightful. Albert Gallatin and his second wife, Hannah Nicholson Gallatin, lived next door. Ten years older than James Madison, Gallatin was a Swiss-born aristocrat and former Republican congressman from New York. Gallatin believed that people could run their own affairs without the governance of a hereditary elite, and he also championed the preservation of individual liberty within the context of a republic. He served as secretary of the treasury for most of the Jefferson and Madison administrations. Hannah Gallatin was the daughter of Commodore James Nicholson of New York, whose close ties with intellectual and political leaders, including Thomas Paine and Vice President Aaron Burr, provided her with a broad political education. In addition, she was described as the "most stylish woman in the drawing room" and dressed with "more splendour than any of the noblesse."[15] She and Dolley became close friends, and the Gallatins and the Madisons became mainstays of early Washington society.

*The Six Buildings
on Pennsylvania Avenue*

The relocation of the capital to Washington City was an enormous social boon for Dolley. Had either of the nation's first two capital cities, New York and Philadelphia, become the permanent seat of government, Dolley would have been at a serious disadvantage. Both of those places had long-established power structures and well-entrenched dynastic families who ruled the political and social life. As a former Virginia country girl who had recently married into the political and plantation aristocracy, Dolley would have been an outsider, excluded from the spheres of influence.

Washington City was perfect for her because it was virtually a blank slate. Not only were the city's physical, political, and social structures embryonic at best, the permanent population was so tiny that almost all social ties had to be created from scratch. Most of the congressmen were in the city for only four months each year, when Congress was in session, and they usually did not bring their wives or other family members with them. The core of Washington's high society consisted of the senior members of Jefferson's (and later Madison's) administrations; the financial elite, who could afford to live there permanently; and the foreign diplomatic corps. From 1801 to 1809, the entire group probably did not exceed one hundred and fifty people. It was also an intensely Southern city, not only because of its location but also because four out of the nation's first five presidents — and a large number of their cabinet members — were Virginians.

This atmosphere was ideal for someone like Dolley, who was part of the first two dozen government families wealthy enough to afford a permanent residence in the capital. She came to Washington in 1801 a perfect stranger. By the time her husband finished his service as president sixteen years later, Dolley had met an astonishing number of people and was arguably the best-known woman in America.

The Madisons spent May and June of 1801 in Washington. After Congress adjourned for the summer, they gave up their Six Buildings house and returned to Montpellier, where they stayed, enjoying the pleasures of country life and the companionship of their friends and relatives, until they returned to Washington in early October.

With the assistance of Dr. William Thornton and his wife, Anna, who became their neighbors and close friends, the

Madisons rented a three-story brick house now known as 1333 F Street. It stands between Thirteenth and Fourteenth Streets, just two blocks east of the President's House. The house had cellar rooms for both wine and coal, and, after the landlord agreed to build a stable and carriage house, it served the Madisons well for the remaining seven years of James' term as secretary of state.[16]

Dr. Thornton was a native of Tortola, a small island in the British West Indies. A Quaker, an architect, a physician, a painter, and an inventor, he had known the Todd and Payne families while living in Philadelphia. In Washington, he designed both the U.S. Capitol and The Octagon House (a later Madison residence), and was a consultant to Thomas Jefferson for the design of the University of Virginia. He and his wife, Anna Maria Brodeaux, a lifelong diarist, were both founders of Washington, which she referred to as this "dull tho' great City."[17]

Her culturally accomplished neighbors quickly became social assets for Dolley. Her friend Margaret Bayard Smith was a respected intellectual and soon-to-be-published author whose opinions were highly regarded by the growing flock of first-generation Washingtonians. In addition, Dolley's contact with Dr. Thornton broadened her knowledge of architecture and interior design, which she would put to good use when she later became the First Lady.

While Dolley was settling in, Thomas Jefferson set out to reform the formal models for social interaction, which were based on those of the European royal courts and had been established by the Washington and Adams administrations. As the first presidential couple, George and Martha Washington determined the structure of the social life at the President's House, then in New York. Martha was rightfully beloved by the veterans of the Revolution. During the war, she urged women to organize sick wards for wounded soldiers and roll handkerchiefs for use as bandages. In the field, she was conspicuously present at Washington's side at Valley Forge and at many of his other posts, where she was "saluted with the firing of cannon and small arms."[18] By the time her husband took office in 1789, she was known and respected throughout the new nation as "Lady Washington," a title that stuck with her for life.

The Washingtons moved to the new capital, Philadelphia, in 1790, where Martha soon settled into a daily schedule at her Federal-style house on High Street. She rose at dawn, had breakfast with the president, and returned to her chamber to have her hair set by her hairdresser while she read the daily newspapers. In her first years as the president's wife, she received callers on Tuesday and Friday afternoons, later restricting the callers to Tuesday. Supper, the main meal of the day, was held at three in the afternoon. When Congress was in session, evenings were filled with official dinners, except on Friday, Martha's reception night. In addition, the Washingtons went to the theatre, where their entry was "heralded by the playing of a grand air, 'The President's March,' at which the entire audience would rise."[19] They also attended assemblies, where the president danced minuets, although Martha never danced. Martha dressed tastefully, but simply, and supported a campaign to wear only American-made clothing.

At her extremely formal Friday night receptions, known as "levees" or "drawing rooms," Lady Washington ruled supreme and set a tone designed to establish respect for the new democracy's presidency. The formal Washington protocols mirrored those of the British and French royal courts and were specifically designed to impress the foreign diplomatic corps. *Rigid* is the only term accurate enough to describe the etiquette that Martha demanded at her Friday night levees.

Much as Martha is said to have protested some of the formality that characterized her husband's administrations, she savored her station in life and her privileges. Because George Washington was the wealthiest man ever to be elected president of the United States, there were *many* privileges. Martha relished the family's London-made cream-colored coach, whose four panels were lavishly illustrated with views of the four seasons created by famed Italian painter Cipriani. She never complained when Vice President Adams referred to her as "the presidentress" or when another gentleman addressed her as "Lady President." A wretchedly inaccurate portrait of her, engraved for public distribution with her blessing and titled "Lady Washington," firmly established her unofficial public title.[20]

The Federalists were highly pleased with the Washington administration's pomp and ceremony, but not the Republicans. Albert Gallatin mockingly referred to Martha as "our most gracious queen." Nevertheless, she was widely admired at home and respected abroad for her good deeds and high ideals, and the young nation easily survived its brief brush with the appearance of a nascent American royalty.

When Lady Washington was in a room, the chair to her right was reserved for Abigail Smith Adams alone, and anyone who unwittingly took that place was immediately instructed to move. Abigail found herself "much more deeply impressed [with Martha Washington] than I ever did before their Majesties of Britain."[21] Abigail wrote that the two women greatly enjoyed each other's company, although they rarely discussed politics. Born in Braintree, Massachusetts, in 1744, Abigail was the daughter of a well-to-do Boston merchant with close ties to England. By the time she married John Adams of neighboring Quincy, and later became his First Lady, she had become a staunch Federalist and was innately suspicious of the French. For that reason, she had no use for Francophile Republicans such as Jefferson, Madison, Burr, and Monroe. A rock-ribbed Federalist partisan, she was described by the ever-vigilant Albert Gallatin as "Mrs. President, not of the nation, but of a faction." Abigail was intensely interested in politics, and a senator noted of her, "the President would not dare to make a nomination without her approbation."

In letters, John and Abigail Adams addressed each other as "Dearest Friend," and John also referred to his wife with such terms as "my dearest partner," "my best, dearest, worthiest, wisest friend in this World," and wrote, "I think of thine as a Stateswoman." However, Abigail had a sharp tongue and showed little restraint in using it, other than that imposed by her husband.

When in Philadelphia, as First Lady, Abigail rose at 5:00 a.m. and concerned herself with household duties and correspondence during the morning. She received the public and returned social calls in the afternoons and dined with Adams every night except Tuesdays and Thursdays. On those nights, she held her drawing rooms. Lady Adams was a respected public figure. When she passed by in her carriage in Philadelphia, people bowed their heads and men doffed their hats.

To her credit, Abigail's advancing age did not harden her attitudes but rather opened her mind. During Jefferson's two terms, the Federalists watched in amazement as the nation failed to fall into anarchy, atheism, and ruin under the Republican government. To her great dismay, Abigail watched as her husband's party first turned against him and then their son, John Quincy. In 1809, displaying an amazing change of heart, the stalwart New England woman chose to support for president a man who was the political equivalent of the devil incarnate for the Federalists: James Madison, a Republican, a Virginian, and Thomas Jefferson's hand-picked successor.[22]

Thomas Jefferson spent little time in the company of women during his administration, which may have stemmed from the profound sense of loss he felt when his wife died. Whatever the reason, he certainly did not think that women should be involved in politics. He wrote in 1780, "The tender breasts of ladies were not formed for political convulsions and the French ladies miscalculate much their own happiness when they wander the true field of their influence into that of politicks."[23] He offered the hope that American women would not make the same mistake as their French contemporaries. "Our good ladies, I trust, have been too wise to wrinkle their foreheads with politics. They are contented to soothe and calm the minds of their husbands returning from political debate. They have the good sense to value domestic happiness above all other.... It is a comparison of Amazons to Angels," he wrote.[24]

Jefferson prized domestic felicity, believed that married bliss was grounded in women whose lives revolved around

Thomas Jefferson

their husbands, and vastly preferred women to be ornaments to their husbands' lives rather than intellectual partners. On the other hand, he bent his rules for Abigail Adams. With her, he corresponded about issues ranging from politics to the rearing of children.

Dolley seemed to be unaware of Jefferson's view that women should not be involved in politics because she demonstrated her eagerness to be informed and involved in the

political process. In 1805, while in Philadelphia recuperating from an ulcerated knee, she wrote to her husband, asking for political news, quickly assuring him that she would never be so bold as to express political views publicly. The last section of her deferential, self-effacing letter was an obvious attempt to mollify her husband so that that he would share the information she sought:

I wish you would indulge me with some information respecting the war with Spain and disagreement with England, as it is so generally expected here that I am at a loss what to surmise—You know I am not much of a politician but I am extremely anxious to hear (as far as you may think proper) what is going forward in the Cabinet—on this subject, I beleive you would not desire your wife the active partizan, such as her neighbor M^{rs}. L, nor will there be the slightest danger whilst she is conscious of her want of talents, and her diffidence in expressing her opinions always imperfectly understood by her sex.[25]

Jefferson might not have approved of Dolley's interest in politics, but he would have appreciated her understanding that women did not discuss such things in public. The role of women in politics was a minor matter for a man with a full national and international agenda demanding his attention. But his choice of Mrs. Madison as his on-call official hostess was both logical for him and a delight for Dolley. She was thirty-three, happily married, ebullient, cheerful, attractive, and well dressed. And although she had her own agendas, Dolley always loved a party.

As soon as he took office, Jefferson put a republican stamp on all things official. Pretentious ceremonies, elaborate formal protocols, and royal and aristocratic privileges would have no place in Jefferson's administration. In his first months in office, he rewrote the rules of protocol, which guided social conduct at all government functions. His key concept was the egalitarian idea that all official representatives of foreign governments were ambassadors of their countries and, therefore, should be treated as equals, regardless of their social status at home.

Until Jefferson's time, diplomats and titled aristocrats were treated as their official rank in society demanded. Thus, in diplomatic order of deference, a king would receive preference over a queen, a prince over a count or marquis, an ambassador over his chargé d' affaires. Jefferson ultimately codified his new rules of republican diplomatic protocol and published them as the *Cannons of Etiquette to be Observed by the Executive*. Jefferson initially misspelled the title as "Cannons of Etiquette," prompting social historian Catherine Allgor to write that the president's initial expression made for a "lovely martial image for the etiquette war."[26]

The canons demolished all customary differences in treatment based on rank, title, heredity, wealth, or other attribute of social status—and quickly brought on diplomatic chaos. The finished document was not published or distributed to the foreign diplomatic corps until the first weeks of 1804, after a series of dangerous diplomatic blunders. Although Dolley was primarily a spectator at the events to follow, she had a front-row seat for one of the most fiery and contentious diplomatic confrontations in the history of the new republic. It would forever be known as the "Merry Affair."

The world's diplomats did not flock to America's doorstep after the Revolution. Only about half of the major powers, notably England, France, Spain, and the colonies or vassal states they controlled, had any significant relationship with the new nation on the North American continent. The rest of the world, including most of Eastern Europe, Central and South America, Asia, and Oceania, was largely unaware of the United States of America. By 1802, nineteen years after the Revolutionary War had ended, only three nations—Britain, France, and Denmark—had diplomatic representatives in the new republic, and none of them held the rank of minister plenipotentiary, that is, an ambassador having the full authority to act as a representative of his government. Britain was represented by chargé d'affaires Edward Thornton, who still resided in Philadelphia; France by chargé d'affaires Louis-André Pichon, who lived in Georgetown; and Denmark by general consul Peder Blicher Olsen, who also resided in Philadelphia.

Olsen arrived in Philadelphia in the summer of 1801 and met President Jefferson in Washington on October 12, 1801. He took sick with yellow fever in 1803 and returned to Denmark that summer. Olsen was replaced by Peder Pedersen, who arrived in August and held the rank of consul general and chargé d'affaires.[27] Great Britain replaced its chargé d'affaires with a minister, Anthony Merry, late in 1803, and Merry moved the British delegation to Washington, an important sign of official recognition.

The European diplomatic corps operated by complicated rules of protocol based upon diplomatic rank and the current friend-or-foe status of each country. High-ranking ministers and their wives, for example, would be seated closest to the host, with deputies and aides at the far end of the table. Titled nobility would be seated by descending rank, with untitled guests at the end of the table or the back of the room. Ministers of nations at war with each other would not usually be invited to the same event, but if both countries were of equal importance to the host country, separate-but-equal events would be held for each.

These social protocols were followed at both private and state events. The rules of etiquette dictated who visited whom first, who was invited to what event, who was introduced first and by whom, who escorted whom where, and who was seated where. Violations of protocol could be, and often were, taken as national insults, and a failed introduction or improper invitation or seating arrangement could provoke an international incident.

Jefferson had been propelled into office by a republican tide that had no use for the trappings of monarchies. Accordingly, he went out of his way to let the world knew that under the new republican order, rank had no privileges. He banished the custom of formal drawing room evenings and substituted small dinners, usually all-male, held at round tables, with seating pêle mêle—first come, first seated —which ruled out any possibility of preference by rank, title, or social status. In his campaign to create a democratic, egalitarian atmosphere at every level of government, he neither sought nor took advice on how to go about it.

In matters of dress and personal deportment, the president exceeded the limits of good taste. He worked so hard to avoid ostentation that his mode of dress fell below plain to sloppy. Indeed, it sometimes seemed that in his rush to enforce republican virtues of equality and fraternity, he had completely forgotten that he was a Virginia gentleman of good parents, imbued with good taste, and trained from birth to provide polite, civilized hospitality for *all* his invited guests.

His first public display of poor taste came when the Danish chargé d'affairs, Peder Pedersen, replaced his predecessor and arranged via the secretary of state to present his credentials to the president. Madison briefed Pedersen that "the president keeps no etiquette and can be seen each morning from 9-12 by everyone." Thus warned, Pedersen appeared at the

President's House on October 1, 1803, and presented his credentials. Jefferson received him in house slippers.

Pedersen wrote to his superiors at the Royal Danish Foreign Office the next day, "The president received me in a simple, open and friendly manner that never fails to give one intimacy and confidence that seldom fails to win hearts." The meeting lasted about an hour, and Pedersen reported that "it gave me the most favorable idea about his excellent intellect and wide comprehensive knowledge."[28] The open-minded Dane may have thought the American president's dress a bit odd, but it is clear that he liked the chief executive. A short time later, however, Jefferson's casual treatment of the new British ambassador provoked quite a different reaction.

Anthony and Elizabeth Leathes Merry were not a couple to be trifled with. He was dignified, formal, rigid, plain, somewhat sullen, and passed "quite unnoticed" when in the company of his wife. She was intellectual, literate, tall, attractive, extremely fashionable, haughty, and had little use for the Americans or their Frenchified new government. Margaret Bayard Smith noted that Mrs. Merry was "entirely the talker and actor in all companies" and that "her good husband...is plain in his appearance and called rather inferior in understanding."[29]

Elizabeth Merry's tongue was as sharp as her quill, and she used both with great pleasure and frequency. Her comments, barbed though they were, reflected the viewpoint of the British aristocracy twenty years after the British lost their war with the American colonists and during a period when the United States was much warmer to France than to Great Britain.

The Merrys arrived in America late in 1803. In Alexandria, Virginia, they met Dr. William Thornton, the Madisons' next-door neighbor on F Street. Thornton invited the Merrys to ride with him to Washington in a coachee, a vehicle with which they were not acquainted. Thomas Moore, an Irish poet, had accompanied the Merrys on board ship. When the Merrys finally reached Georgetown, a few miles from the capital, Elizabeth wrote Moore a long letter, describing her distressed

first impressions of America. She began with a sour description of their arrival:

> Before this letter reaches you, you will have heard of
> our landing in Alexandria, after six days disputation
> with winds, tides, and ignorant navigators. The fol-
> lowing morning we set off for this place in a coachie.
> The cold was very severe, and the roads intolerable,
> nevertheless, I laughed every step of the way. Mr.
> Thornton met us at Alexandria, and advised this mode
> of conveyance as the best both for ease and quickness.
> Mr. Merry had never been in one of these vehicles,
> and his *quiet* astonishment and *inward groaning* gave
> rise to my mirth and risibility. On entertaining our
> apartments here, I asked the master of the house what
> he could give us for dinner. He immediately changed
> his position, walked to the fireplace, reclined his head
> on the chimney-piece, looked at me, or rather stared,
> and replied, 'Why, Mistress Merry, our custom is to
> give the best we have, but I keeps no schedule what-
> ever. My house is full; but you shall have yore dinner.'
> So we had, God knows! but neither his Britannic
> Majesty's Minister or Mistress Merry could eat a mor-
> sel that was served. A few days will, I hope, place us
> in a hovel of our own.[30]

She had only kind things to say of Dr. Thornton, whom
she described as "indefatigable in his endeavors to procure us
every comfort," but noted, "We have alarmed Congress itself
with the number of our servants and the immensity of our
baggage: the former they cannot account for; the latter, they
have ingeniously settled, is to be sold, and that their *home
markets* will be injured if foreign ministers are allowed to bring
over such profusion of luxuries for sale."[31]

Securing adequate housing in Washington—an endemic
problem for anyone moving into the city at that time—was
next on her list. "I should have told you the house you heard

talked of for us is not to be had for love or money. Mr. Merry
frets, and every moment exclaims, 'Why it [Washington] is a
thousand times worse than the worst parts of Spain!' I laugh,
and resolve to bear up *stoutly* against difficulties while Heaven
blesses me with health. I am now perfectly well, and to-mor-
row shall *exhibit* at the Capitol. The Capitol—good heavens,
what a profanation!! Here is a creek, too—a dirty arm of the
river—which they have dignified by calling it the Tiber. What
patience one need have with ignorance and self-conceit."[32]

On November 28, 1803, in the company of Secretary of
State James Madison, Ambassador Merry made the highly
important first official call to present his credentials. The ambassador was decked out in full diplomatic regalia, which
included a plumed hat and a large sword.[33] Like Peder
Pedersen before him, Merry was received by a casually dressed
president wearing slippers.

As if on cue, trouble erupted again three days later during a
dinner honoring the Merrys at the President's House. The
British and French were then at war, and the Merrys were
astonished to find that the French chargé d' affaires, Louis-
André Pichon, had been invited. Reeling from the insult, they
awaited the call to dine.

When the chief butler notified the president that dinner
was served, Jefferson turned to his hostess, Dolley Madison,
held out his arm, and escorted her to the table. Dolley whispered quickly, "Take Mrs. Merry," but Jefferson plunged
ahead. Since this was the Merrys' first official visit, both
European and American standards of normal protocol would
have demanded that the official host—the president—escort
Mrs. Merry to the table and that Ambassador Merry would,
in turn, escort the official hostess—in this case, Dolley. Except for Madison, the other cabinet officers were no help. Each
turned to the woman closest to him and escorted her to the
table. Madison ultimately escorted Mrs. Merry to the table,
leaving her husband to find a place for himself. Sally McKean
de Yrujo, Dolley's friend, now the wife of the Spanish ambassador, declared, "This will be the cause of war!"[34]

Shortly afterward, at the Madison residence on F Street, the diplomatic meltdown resumed. This time, the Merrys had accepted an invitation from the secretary of state and Mrs. Madison to dine at their home. Again, Jefferson's *Ninth Cannon of Etiquette*, the rule of pêle mêle and "gentlemen *en masse* giving place to the ladies *en masse*," was in play. That must have caused Dolley personal pain because she was always hospitable and sensitive to the needs of her guests. She and her husband had seen the bewilderment, chaos, and anger that Jefferson's rule of pêle mêle had brought about, and she had alerted the president to the potential damage. Yet she was bound by obligation to the president to enforce the new diplomatic etiquette.

When dinner was called at the Madison home, each man took the nearest woman to a chair. The result was entirely predictable. Mrs. Merry immediately reacted to the insult. She marched straight to her husband, took his arm, and he led her to the table. When the Merrys reached the table, they found Hannah Gallatin in the place of honor at the head, a clear violation of protocol. This time, Elizabeth Merry would not be humbled. She stood at the head of the table until Mrs. Gallatin offered her the chair and then "took it without prudency or apology."[35]

For the second time, Elizabeth Merry let it be known that she had been ill treated.[36] A woman of gourmet tastes, she commented negatively on Dolley's meal and how it had been served. Mrs. Madison set her table by Virginia standards, which emphasized an abundance of hearty food and drink, prepared from old plantation recipes, rather than a feast of rare European delicacies. The ambassador's wife implied that Americans were crude gourmands, and decried Dolley's table as being "more like a harvest-home supper, than the entertainment of a Secretary of State."[37]

Dolley promptly replied that "she thought abundance was preferable to elegance; that circumstances formed customs, and customs formed taste; and as the profusion, so repugnant to foreign customs, arose from the happy circumstance of the superabundance and prosperity of our country, she did not hesitate to sacrifice the delicacy of European taste, for the less elegant, but more liberal fashion of Virginia."[38]

For the wife of a cabinet member, the statement was more than a reply to a culinary observation. Returning the criticism of a foreign ambassador's wife to her face was a political act. In later days, the French military attaché, Colonel André de Bronne, recognized Dolley's supra-marital role when he stated that "Mrs. Madison has become one of America's most valuable assets. . . . The Secretary of State and his lady are so inseparable as his duty permits."[39]

Because of the vagaries of politics and human nature, and Dolley's hard work, Dolley and Elizabeth Merry later developed a personal relationship that bordered on friendship. In 1805, when Dolley was bedridden in Philadelphia with an ulcerated knee, she wrote to Anna Cutts, "the other Evening she [Mrs. Merry] came in high good humor to pass three hours with her patient, as she stile'd me."[40] In addition, despite her initial disgust with the primitive nature of the capital city, Elizabeth Merry's deep interest in botany led her to support Massachusetts Congressman Manasseh Cutler's efforts to establish a botanical garden in Washington.[41]

The Spanish ambassador, the Marquis de Yrujo, suffered from the same chaotic protocol as Anthony Merry, and the two ministers agreed that the treatment they had received was an insult to them personally and to their countries. Sally McKean de Yrujo saw Jefferson's new rules for what they were designed to be: an unmistakable demonstration of republican democracy in action. Her husband did not. A full-blown protocol war broke out in Washington when Merry and Yrujo retaliated. When the British and Spanish ambassadors entertained, none of the American cabinet officers' wives were escorted to the dinner table.

Madison ultimately viewed the Merry Affair as little more than a tempest in a teapot, but it was more than that. Jefferson's refusal to treat foreign emissaries with the respect they believed they deserved made both the Spanish and British ministers angry. This led directly to their forming bonds with Jefferson's opponents, namely the Federalists and his own scheming vice president, Aaron Burr. Burr, who had a keenly honed appreciation for women, may even have been doubly pleased with the rift, for he had taken an interest in the alluring, fashionable Mrs. Merry.[42]

Dolley Madison must have been saddened by the entire chain of events, for most of the Jeffersonian posturing was both unnecessary and uncivil. Yet, Dolley was always conciliatory and willing to waive her rights and give ground when a greater good could be achieved by doing so. In retelling her version of the Merry Affair, decades after the event during a dinner hosted by President James K. Polk, Dolley implied that what Merry believed was true: Jefferson's insults were deliberately planned to humiliate him and his country and put them in their place.

According to her niece, Mary Cutts, Dolley's recollection of the event went as follows. Mrs. Merry, feeling her own superiority, "publicly asserted that she intended to teach the Americans etiquette, and how to behave themselves. This was repeated to Mr. Jefferson, who instantly said, 'I will put her in Coventry' and secured Mrs. Madison's promise to dine with him the day after at a state dinner. She went. Jefferson advanced to hand her in. She stepped back and said, 'Take Mrs. Merry.' He answered, 'Not so,' and persevered handing in the lady of the secretary of state."[43] In telling Jefferson what to do, Dolley demonstrated the depth of her convictions because it was not any woman's place to tell the president of the United States how to act, especially in a politically sensitive situation.

We don't know exactly what Jefferson served his British guests at that infamous first dinner with the Merrys, but on January 10, 1802, Samuel L. Mitchill, a good-natured Republican politician, wrote to his wife, Catherine, about the conduct of Jefferson's normal daily dinners. "He has generally a company of eight or ten persons to dine with him every day. The dinners are neat and plentiful, and no healths are drunk at table, nor are any toasts or sentiments given after dinner. You drink as you please, and converse at your ease. In this way every guest feels inclined to drink to the digestive or the social point, and no further."[44]

While serving as the American minister to France between 1785 and 1789, Jefferson had acquired an amazing collection of recipes and the skills to prepare them. A month after the dinner described above, Congressman Manasseh Cutler, a Federalist who did not share Jefferson's tastes in politics but enjoyed his tastes in food, wrote the following review of the dinner he was served on February 6, 1802:

> Dined at the Presidents.... Rice soup, round of beef, turkey, mutton, ham, loin of veal, cutlets of mutton or veal, fried eggs, fried beef, a pie called macaroni which appeared to be a rich crust filled with strillions of on- ions or shallots, which I took it to be, tasted very strong, and not agreeable. Mr. [Meriwether] Lewis told me there were none in it; it was an Italian dish, and what appeared like onions was made of flour and butter, with a particularly strong liquor mixed with them. Ice cream very good, crust wholly dried, crumbled into thin flakes; a dish somewhat like a pudding—inside white as milk or curd, very porous and light, covered with cream sauce—very fine. Many other jim cracks, a great variety of fruit, plenty of wines and good.[45]

Dolley emulated Jefferson in being a lover of good food, and she has often been misidentified as the first woman to serve ice cream in the President's House. Although she en- joyed and helped to popularize the tasty treat, it was already well known to discriminating American palates by the time Dolley reached Washington. Sixty years before she became First Lady, ice cream recipes had been published in Europe.

The dessert was first described in America by Virginian Thomas Black, who enjoyed it at the Annapolis mansion of Governor Thomas Bladen in 1744, twenty-eight years before

Dolley was born. By 1777, it was being advertised in New York, and by 1786, a New York paper carried an advertisement from the City Tavern stating that they were serving it every day.[46] George Washington spent £51.6s.2d (about two hundred dollars) for ice cream in the summer of 1790 alone. He also owned his own ice-cream-making machine, as did fellow gastronome Thomas Jefferson, who had a sorbetière at Monticello and introduced vanilla-flavored French-style ice cream to his guests. On February 10, 1802, Samuel Mitchill again wrote to his wife, this time describing an amazing dessert Jefferson had served. "Among other things ice-creams were produced in the form of balls of the *frozen* material inclosed in covers of *warm pastry*, exhibiting a curious contrast, as if the *ice* had just been taken from the *oven*."[47] If Dolley had been unacquainted with ice cream before she came to Washington City, she quickly learned of it at Jefferson's table.

The eight years Dolley spent in Washington while Madison was secretary of state were filled with more than diplomatic tiffs and exotic food. An event that profoundly affected Dolley was the loss of her "sister-child," Anna Payne, to marriage. Anna, eleven years her junior, had shared Dolley's life and homes in Hanover County, Philadelphia, and Washington until she was twenty-five. Dolley had raised Anna as if she were her own daughter and deeply felt the pain of their separation, even though she and Anna were reunited whenever Congress was in session.

Anna was a belle of Washington society, and she so impressed Thomas Jefferson that he always chose her as his hostess for social events if Dolley was not available. On March 31, 1804, she married U.S. Representative Richard Cutts, thirty-three.[48] A very wealthy man, he was a solid Jeffersonian, born in Maine, which, until 1820, was a district of Massachusetts.

Three weeks after the wedding, Dolley responded to a letter from Anna, who was then on her bridal tour. Her reply speaks eloquently of the pain of Dolley's loss—and gratitude that Anna was constantly thinking of her. Only an hour after receiving the precious letter, Dolley wrote:

Tho few, are the Days, passed since you left me my dearest Anna they have been spent in anxious impatience to hear from you — your letter from Baltimore releaved my mind & the one from Philadelphia (this hour received) gives me the greatest pleasure — To trace you & your dear Husband in regretted City, where we have spent our early years to find that even there, you can recollect with affection the solitary being you left behind, reflects a ray of brightness on my somber prospect.[49]

Madison was initially close to Richard Cutts, whose membership in Congress gave the secretary of state valuable insights into the minds and inclinations of the legislators. Dissention over the War of 1812 created a schism between Cutts and the Madisons, which peaked around 1820. After Anna's death in 1832, Cutts resumed his ties with the Madisons and maintained contact with Dolley until his death in 1845.

Devoted as she was to Anna, Dolley had love to share with all of her friends and relatives. Martha, Thomas Jefferson's eldest child, had become Dolley's devoted friend during family visits. Martha accompanied her father in 1784, when he became the first U.S. minister to France, and she attended the convent school of the Abbé Royale de Panthemont, "one of the most fashionable schools in France."[50] With her knowledge of French and sophisticated upbringing, she would have been perfect to serve as the president's official hostess, had she not married her cousin, Thomas Mann Randolph, and immediately started raising a large family. Martha's sister, Mary Jefferson, had married Congressman John Wayles Eppes and had young children. She lived a considerable distance from the President's House and, following the tradition of congressmen's wives, did not come to live in Washington. Martha served as the president's hostess during the winter of 1802-1803, when she and Mary spent seven weeks with him. Mary died in 1804.

Dolley wrote that both of Jefferson's daughters were admirable women, but her friend, Margaret Bayard Smith, noted their different personalities. "Mrs. Eppes is beautiful, simplicity and timidity exemplified when in company, but when alone with you of communicative and winning manners," she wrote. "Martha is rather homely, a delicate likeness of her father, but still more interesting than Mrs. Eppes. She is really one of the most lovely women I have ever met with, her countenance beaming with intelligence, benevolence, and sensibility, and her conversation fulfils all her countenance promises."[51]

Martha "Patsy"
Jefferson Randolph

On January 17, 1806, on the second floor of the presidential mansion, Martha gave birth to a son, James Madison Randolph, her eighth child. Thus, Jefferson's grandson was the first child to be born in the President's House. The second child born there arrived in December 1806 and belonged to Fanny and Eddy, enslaved servants of the president.[52] That baby died two years later. Records kept by Jefferson's steward, Etienne Lemaire, noted on November 8, 1808, "Peter Lennox built the little coffin for Fanny's infant child."[53]

As both Jefferson daughters wished to maintain Washington's high fashion standards when they visited, Martha Jefferson Randolph wrote to her father, requesting him to ask Mrs. Madison for a favor. "Will you be so good as to send orders to the milliner—Madame Peck, I believe her name is,—through Mrs. Madison, who very obligingly offered to execute any little commission for us in Philadelphia, for two wigs of the color of the hair enclosed, and of the most fashionable shapes, that they may be in Washington when we arrive? They are universally worn, and will relieve us as to the necessity of dressing our own hair, a business in which neither of us are adepts."[54] This letter makes it clear that some of the most sophisticated women in Virginia plantation society trusted Dolley's knowledge of *haute couture* clothing and accessories to make sure that they dressed in the height of fashion.

Dolley played an even larger role in the life of Mary Jefferson Eppes' family in 1811. Congressman John Randolph—who caused considerable trouble for the Madisons—"so violently called the name of Eppes [that] the latter answered with a challenge to a duel," wrote Louis-Barbé-Charles Sérurier, the French minister to the United States. "These gentlemen will fight a duel at the end of the session next Monday and often what usually happens in these duels in America one can expect one of the two men will remain dead."[55] However, a few days later, Sérurier wrote to his superior in France, "The duel of the Messrs. Randolph and Eppes was converted into a compromise by Mrs. Madison. The Federalist [Randolph] apologized to the Republican [Eppes]. Everybody is astonished at a conclusion so contrary to custom. and all the credit of the affair remained Mrs. Madison's. Nobody knows what she said, but everybody can know what she accomplished."[56]

Although she loved them, Dolley did not confine her life and interests to children. A child of the Indian frontier, she became enraptured with the vision of Jefferson's aide, Meriwether Lewis, a former army officer, who yearned to explore the American West. On February 28, 1803, Thomas Jefferson convinced Congress to part with the pathetically small sum of $2,500 to explore the uncharted territory from St. Louis up the Missouri River to the Pacific Coast, in search of the existence of the much-longed-for 'Westward Passage." The trek was called the Corps of Discovery. When it was commissioned, two-thirds of all Americans lived within fifty miles of the Atlantic coast.

Dolley and the other wives of Jefferson's cabinet members were captivated by the grand, daring quest into the unexplored wilderness, but they were also concerned for the welfare of the expeditionary force and did everything possible to raise funds for their mission. Dolley focused her attention on equipping Meriwether Lewis, whom she knew well from their many meetings at the President's House, and his close friend, William Clark. She was present when the intrepid explorers were entertained prior to their departure and often worried about their safety. When the surviving members of the party returned four years later, Lewis and Clark bequeathed to Dolley some of the cooking utensils they had used during the journey.[57] In later years, she remembered them clearly and often spoke of them fondly.

Within months of Lewis and Clark's departure, the excitement generated by the expedition was almost totally eclipsed by an amazing offer from Napoléon that had a profound impact on the destiny of the United States. Jefferson wanted to buy the port of New Orleans to allow Americans to trade freely on the Mississippi River. Secretary of State Madison instructed Robert R. Livingston, the U.S. minister in Paris, to work out a satisfactory plan with France.

Emperor Napoléon Bonaparte, preparing for another war with the British, made a breathtaking offer. He would sell New Orleans—and all of the Louisiana territory that France claimed—for $15 million, about three cents per acre. Bonaparte was no fool. He knew that although France claimed the land, the Americans would surely overrun it in the near future, and France could not defend it. If he sold it to the Americans, they would look favorably at France—and less favorably at France's enemy, England. Jefferson pushed the treaty through Congress, in spite of doubts concerning its constitutionality. When the French Minister of Foreign Affairs; America's minister in Paris, Robert Livingston; and James Monroe signed the treaty on April 30, 1803, the size of the United States doubled—but the transaction was far from finished. It still needed to be ratified by Congress.

By the Fourth of July 1803, Jefferson made the public announcement of the great event, which was met with jubilation. Dolley, her husband, and the cabinet members all held their own celebrations. So did American residents in New Orleans, especially those looking for the new government jobs that would be available when New Orleans became part of the United States.

The perception that Dolley wielded political power is evident in a letter addressed to her by Thomas Randall, a New Orleans merchant who had met Dolley in Philadelphia years before. On August 23, 1803, before the Louisiana Purchase had even been ratified by Congress, he wrote, "It is many years since I had the pleasure of visiting you when in Philadelphia. Business has cast my Lot into this Place, & as it is likely to become annexed to the United States, & some officers necessary to be appointed for the Execution of its Laws; & having had a residence of Five Years, Knowing the customs & Habits of the People, I should hope through your Goodness & Influence to obtain some one of the offices that may be given Away."[58] He was probably not the first patronage seeker to write to Dolley, and she would deal with them by the hundreds during her years as Jefferson's hostess and as First Lady.

The combination of the Louisiana Purchase and the Lewis and Clark expedition led to greater diplomatic contact between the administration and the Native American nations. When Native American chiefs came to Washington, it was customary to entertain them in a manner similar to the way visiting foreign ministers were received. One evening, a group of Native Americans in full ceremonial dress attended a formal dinner at the Madisons' home. At the end of the evening, Dolley retired to her bedchamber. While standing at the mirror, removing her cap, she saw the reflected image of one of her guests, who had taken the wrong staircase when trying to depart. Always the thoughtful hostess, Dolley paused briefly so as not to alarm him. She walked calmly to the next room and pulled the rope that rang the servants' bell downstairs. Then she returned to her mirror until a servant arrived to show the guest the way to the exit.[59]

The complexity of the Louisiana Purchase treaty, the slowness of communication, and the ratification process itself, meant that Jefferson, Monroe, Madison, and Livingston were kept busy dealing with snags and unexpected problems. During the fall of 1803, with tension over the treaty running high, the Madisons and many of their friends found relief in one of Virginia's favorite forms of recreation: horse racing.

Jefferson, Madison, and many of the wealthy southern planters were avid horsemen. The Madisons' neighbor, Dr. William Thornton, owned his own racetrack, as did several of Madison's friends. Madison and Thornton jointly owned a racehorse named Wild Medley. The racing season attracted the cream of society, especially from the southern and middle states. Theodosia Burr Alston's father-in-law, Colonel William Alston, for example, came up from Charleston every year to attend the races and discuss politics, fine wines, and racehorses with his friend, Jefferson. Some of the racehorses were valued at more than $10,000 each.

The races were a grand opportunity to see and be seen, and Dolley and her friends looked forward to the season. In 1803, Congressman Manasseh Cutler described a day at the races:

> While the horses were running, the whole ground within the circus was spread over with people on horseback, stretching round, full speed, to different parts of the circus, to see the race. This was a striking part of the show, for it was supposed that there were about 800 on horseback, and many of them mounted on excellent horses. There were about 200 carriages and between 3,000 and 4,000 people—black, and white, and yellow; of all conditions, from the President of the United States to the beggar in his rags; of all ages and both sexes, for I should judge one-third were females.[60]

Dolley often attended the races, but her concern over social standing caused her to decline one opportunity because one of her finest horses had died, and she did not want to appear in a coach pulled by a horse that was "not an honor to the season."[61]

Attending the races was not Dolley's only diversion. She also enjoyed playing cards—for money. The secretary of state's wife enjoyed gambling. Her favorite card game was loo, which was favored by women and was played for a pool of money made up by bets and forfeits. Dolley also adopted a practice that had gained popularity among women after the French Revolution. In 1803, after dining with the Madisons, Theodosia Burr Alston, then twenty years old, wrote to her father, Aaron Burr, of thirty-five-year-old Dolley, "she is still pretty; but oh, that unfortunate propensity to snuff-taking."[62]

Dolley's snuff box.

A major event in Dolley's life came in the spring and summer of 1804, when she and her husband sat for the nation's most-acclaimed portraitist, Gilbert Stuart. Dolley found her husband's painting "admirable" and evidently also liked hers. For her sitting, she wore a high-waisted, white, Empire-style dress with a low-cut bodice. The dress featured short sleeves and was trimmed at the waist, bodice, and arms with gold braided cord and lace. A gold brocade shawl fell loosely around her back and over her right arm. She wore four dainty gold necklaces—two chokers and the other two, somewhat looser, a style that was one of her fashion signatures. She completed her toilette with red lipstick and heavily rouged cheeks, in the French style. On her left hand she wore a simple gold wedding band. Stuart posed her sitting in one of his favorite studio props: a Louis XVI gold armchair, with velvet back and armrests, which he painted in a color to compliment his sitter. Dolley was portrayed with a serene, small smile on her face, which expressed none of her effervescence and ebullience.

The portrait was adequate, but not one of Stuart's best. His choice of a dark, burnt umber background failed to separate Dolley's black hair from the drape behind it, leaving the dark hair to disappear into the dark drape. In addition, the artist painted a noticeable and distracting reflection near the bridge of her nose in her left eye socket. It gave the appearance of a skin abnormality, which, in turn, distracts the viewer's attention from her Irish blue eyes. For all his legendary artistic talent, Stuart sometimes produced attractive paintings that failed to capture the personality of the sitter. This rendering of Dolley was one of them, as was a lifeless portrait he produced in 1795 of the young Theodosia Burr, painted for her father.

In 1804, Aaron Burr himself provided the next round of controversy for the Jefferson administration, and Theodosia was at the heart of it. Burr was a Republican and Jefferson's vice president. Alexander Hamilton, who headed the Federalist opposition, detested Burr and attacked him in print on every possible occasion. Yet, no matter how often or how badly Burr was slurred by Hamilton, he chose not to respond—except once.

Everyone who knew Burr was aware that he and his daughter shared an intense emotional relationship. Theodosia's biographer referred to them as "emotional Siamese twins, joined at the heart."[63] After a dinner meeting with several of his fellow Burr-haters, one of Hamilton's friends wrote to another Hamilton disciple describing the discussion. The writer recited the usual allegations of Burr's character flaws and faults, but added the statement, "I could detail to you a still more despicable opinion which General Hamilton has expressed of Mr. Burr."[64]

The letter was published in the _Albany Register_ on April 24, 1804.[65] The four words, "still more despicable opinion," published for the world to see, were the flashpoint for Burr. In another letter, Hamilton had expressed the belief that Burr had an improper, perhaps even incestuous, relationship with his teenaged daughter. Burr demanded that Hamilton disavow the remarks attributed to him in the newspaper. Hamilton declined.

Unable to gain a retraction, Burr challenged Hamilton to a duel for having defamed him in public. Hamilton accepted the challenge, thereby acknowledging that Burr had a legitimate complaint against him that could be settled no other way. The duel was held on the morning of July 11, 1804, at Weehawken, New Jersey, a short rowboat ride from Manhattan. After careful preparations, the word was given, and each man stepped off ten paces, turned, and, at the command, "Present!" fired. Hamilton shot first, and missed; Burr fired second, and did not. Hamilton fell, mortally wounded, and died the next day.

Although it had been a completely fair fight, the world never forgave Burr for killing Hamilton. After slipping away for several weeks to Georgia while the public's fever cooled—and to temporarily distance himself from warrants for murder that had been sworn out against him in New Jersey and New York—he calmly returned to Washington and resumed his role as vice president of the United States and president of the Senate.

The Burr-Hamilton duel was a great political embarrassment to Jefferson and Madison, but Dolley had conflicting emotions. Burr had, after all, lived with her mother, helped Dolley with her legal problems after John Todd died, served as her orphaned son's designated guardian, introduced Dolley to Madison, and been a close friend ever since the dreadful yellow fever days in Philadelphia.

Five days after the fatal duel, Dolley briefly touched on the tragic subject, stating, "You have herd no doubt of the terrible duel & end of poor Hamilton."[66] Her letter masks the deep personal pain she must have felt over the crisis her friend and protector now faced, but as bad as Burr's plight was, this would not be the last time that Dolley, Theodosia, and Aaron Burr would have serious issues to deal with.

Burr had developed a contentious relationship with Jefferson during their first administration and was discarded for his fellow New Yorker, George Clinton, when Jefferson chose his running mate for his second term. His reputation sullied by the duel, Burr could not return to his law career on the East coast. In the spring of 1805, he set out on the first of two year-long scouting trips throughout the West and Southeast. The purpose: to make contacts, acquire land, build alliances, and investigate the possibility of creating his own country to rule by liberating Spanish Mexico—and perhaps adding to it a large part of the Louisiana Purchase.

Although the exact extent and goals of his ambitious plans remain unclear even today, the date of his intent to strike out on his own is well known. One of Burr's friends and confederates, Englishman Charles Williamson, a secret agent in the British government, reported Burr's plans for conquest to Anthony Merry. On August 6, 1804, Merry dutifully passed along the information to London. The letter was a bombshell, for it declared that Aaron Burr, who was still at that time the sitting vice president of the United States, wished to make a treasonous alliance with the British government. Merry wrote:

> I have just received an offer from Mr. Burr, the actual Vice President of the United States (which situation he is about to resign), to lend his assistance to his Majesty's Government in any Manner in which they may see fit to employ him, particularly in an endeavoring to effect a separation of the Western part of the United States from that which lies between the Atlantick and the Mountains, in its whole Extent.[67]

Subsequent events showed how serious Burr's plans were. In August 1804, Burr, carrying a travel permit bearing the name of the Marquis de Yrujo, headed south to visit (and survey, for the benefit of his planned invasion) "West Florida," then claimed by Spain. Upon his return to Washington, he carried out his official duties as vice president until his term ended in March 1805. Burr's self-serving actions set the stage for painful choices that his friends the Madisons would have to make in the very near future.

In just four years, Dolley Madison had become the most important woman in Washington society. With everything that had happened during her husband's first term as secretary of state, Dolley must have thought she was prepared for whatever Washington could throw her way. But as her husband's political star rose in the heavens, she quickly learned how vicious the capital could be to a man in high position—and to the woman closest to him.

Drawn by J.Herring after J.Wood.   Engraved by J.F.E.Prudhomme

D. P. Madison

CHAPTER NINE

Our Hearts Understand Each Other

Washington City
March 4, 1805

By the time James Madison was sworn in for his second term as Thomas Jefferson's secretary of state, Dolley's life had become less complicated — or so it seemed. There was no house hunting to do or furniture to buy. Dolley and James were settled into their well-established home on F Street and had formed a large, active network of friends and professional acquaintances. The diplomatic protocol crises of the Merry-Yrujo era were past. Save for the formality of the swearing-in itself, and the rounds of congratulations and parties that followed, the Madisons' lives the day after his second inauguration were much the same as the day before. Yet the next four years were to be a coming-of-age period in Dolley's life, as challenging on the personal level as the first four had been in the political arena.

One of Dolley's first orders of business was to find a proper school for her son. Payne was her only surviving child, and the only living link to her much-loved first husband, John Todd.

This made him very precious to her, and Dolley was obsessed with his health. She also indulged most of his wishes and overlooked his shortcomings, practices that would fuel severe problems in the future.

As was his mother's, Payne's early life is thinly documented and described chiefly in anecdotes. Nevertheless, Payne's formative years seem to be consistent with those of a boy of his times and circumstances. On Walnut Street in Philadelphia, where he was born and lived as a toddler, and later at Montpellier and Washington, where he grew into his teens, he always had the warm companionship—and watchful eye—of his young aunt, Anna Payne, thirteen years his senior. His stepfather, James Madison, always treated Payne as if he were his own natural son, and one of those close to him saw that he learned to play the piano.[1]

Montpellier was a child's paradise that featured acres of land to roam, trees to climb, and a massive portico on which children could play hopscotch, marbles, and other games, even when it rained. Given the enormous extent of Madison's connections, Payne's playmates included the children of the Chews, the Jeffersons, and many other neighbors and relatives. Payne and Anna were always welcome at the slave village, Walnut Grove, adjacent to the big house, where they often played with the enslaved children. The Madison fruit gardens, tended by Monsieur Bizet and the slaves he had trained, offered a riot of colors and smells in the fall, when the grapes were bursting with juice and the peach and fig trees were heavily laden with sweet fruit, there for the picking.

Payne also enjoyed the stories his grandmother told about Madison's youth, particularly one where "the Princeton boys went out one night, young Mr. Madison among them, and built a bonfire to burn 'in effigy' the letter of the New York merchants who loved money better than they did their country, and broke their word after the colonies had solemnly promised one another not to buy anything from Great Britain, and wrote the Boston merchants that _they_ should buy from England all they pleased."[2] Payne was impressed with the good fun it must have been to build bonfires and burn letters, but, as with most young boys, he had little interest in the causes of the Revolution or the concepts that drove it. His later life would confirm that he was an adventurer, not an intellectual.

Payne's education started at his mother's knee, aided, no doubt, by his young aunt, Anna. James Madison, with his keen mind, undoubtedly formulated the plan for his stepson's schooling. Dolley did not possess the sophisticated literary tastes of her college-educated husband, but she did read frequently, chiefly novels. Although her formal education did not extend past grade school, her grammar, spelling, and handwriting improved after her marriage to Madison. By the time the Madisons entered the President's House as its chief residents, Dolley's letters were a credit to any educated woman of her time. During the summer of 1804, when her son was twelve, Dolley wrote to Anna that "Payne continues weak & sick—my prospects rise & fall to sadness as this precious Child recovers or declines!"[3] Payne recovered, and the Madisons turned their attention to his schooling.

Washington did not yet have any private schools of high academic standing, and Payne needed formal schooling. After consulting Dolley's friend, Betsy Patterson Bonaparte, a native of Baltimore, Dolley and James sent Payne to be educated there. After initial difficulties making contact with Bishop John Carroll, Payne was successfully enrolled in St. Mary's College in early December 1805.[4] It was a preparatory seminary that accepted both Protestant and Catholic boys, was operated by Carroll's diocese, and was headed by the Reverend William Louis Du Borg.[5] Shortly after Payne was enrolled, Madison wrote to Dolley that he was trying to keep her son "in some sort of attention to his books."[6] Payne seems to have applied himself to his schooling because headmaster Du Borg reported to Dolley in June 1807 that "Payne does us honor." She noted that she had "never had courage to leave M[ontpellier?] to visit but expect him to pass 5 weeks with us in Augus & September," which he did.[7]

At the time he moved to school in Baltimore, Payne was thirteen and impressionable. The Madisons' choice put Payne's teenage development under the direct supervision of one of high society's most flamboyant, provocative, sensual, and controversial women. In 1803, Betsy Patterson had married Jérôme Bonaparte, Napoléon's younger brother, when both were in their late teens. Napoléon opposed the marriage, which ended in a divorce that he demanded in 1813. Payne probably first met the "little Duchess of Baltimore," known far and wide for her scant and revealing clothing, when she and Jérôme dined at the President's House during the early years of the Jefferson administration. The lovely Mrs. Bonaparte, then in her early twenties and described as a "goddess of wit and beauty," taught Payne everything she knew best: the charm, polish, and enjoyment of high society.[8] From Betsy, the handsome young man learned French, dancing, etiquette, and self-indulgences. Soon it was Betsy and women like her, rather than his hard-working, disciplined mother and aunt, who dominated and defined his fancy. Until her final days, Dolley remained oblivious to his quickly developing flaws of character, and never ceased to expect great things from the unworthy son she adored.

Anna Payne's life at this point was quite different from that of her young nephew. As he entered school, she entered the social world, where she shined as brightly as her older sister, Dolley. When she and the Madisons were living in Philadelphia, Anna was in her teens, with hopeful beaus already vying for her attention. By the time they moved to Washington City in 1801, she was a sought-after young society woman of twenty-one. Always popular, she was described as "gay and fond of dancing, and a smiling and sympathetic talker."[9]

Dolley was now in her mid-thirties and generally enjoyed good health, although her husband constantly battled recurrences of chronic bouts of weakness, which she called his "old complaint." With the exception of her eyesight, which proved to be a continuing problem, and a sprained ankle, Dolley had relatively few serious medical complaints until 1805. The eye problem resembled recurring conjunctivitis, which produces various combinations of burning, itchy eyes; redness; copious tears; and a light discharge of sticky mucus, depending upon the source of the condition, which can be a bacterial infection or an allergic reaction. This eye ailment afflicted Dolley all her life. She had many days when she could not open her eyes without excruciating pain and was forced to spend long periods of time in a darkened room. Like her husband, she had several attacks of liver complaints, or "bilious fever," and was once struck with a sudden attack of deafness. This deafness distressed her more than anything else that ever ailed her because Dolley was an inveterate talker and a listener. Often when she was sick she imagined that she would never be well again, but Dolley was nothing if not resilient.[10]

In 1805, Dolley's life was threatened by an ulcerated knee, which caused her serious pain and nearly led to a leg amputation. The problem arose in late May and became so painful that she asked her husband to take her back to Philadelphia, where Dr. Philip Syng Physick treated her for months. During her treatment and recovery, she resided at Gray's Ferry, just across the Schuylkill River. The resort, where she had picnicked with other Quaker children in her teens, was now her hospital ward — and a grim reminder of the time she spent there twelve years before, during the yellow fever epidemic that had claimed the lives of many of her loved ones in 1793.

On June 4, 1805, Dolley wrote to her sister, Anna, "I now write you from my bed to which I have been confined for Ten days with a sad knee — it became a painful Tumour, & 2 Doctors were call'd in, & their applications of caustick [caustic soda][11] & so forth gives me hopes of getting well but heaven knows when as it promises to be Tedious." [12] A month later, she was still confined to bed. Although she thought the tumor was better, it had in fact become worse. "I am reduced & weak & think a little more confinement & calomil would throw me into a decline," she wrote.[13]

President Jefferson was evidently unaware of the seriousness of Dolley's condition, for he wrote two letters in quick succession, asking her to obtain things in Philadelphia for his son-in-law's younger sister, Virginia Randolph, who was soon to marry Wilson Jefferson Cary at Monticello. On July 8, Dolley wrote to Anna, "I had a friendly note from the President yesterday beging me to get Virgineas wedding garments with trinkets & dresses for all the family—I shall ride to the stores, but cannot get out to shop for them."[14] Even in severe pain, Dolley was ready to help a friend—or president—in need.

During virtually all of her recuperation, her husband was faithfully at her side. "Mr. Madison does a profusion of business here—he writes Volumes," Dolley noted.[15] He spent his time with her talking, writing, and sometimes reading, but always ready to attend to her needs and comfort her, despite problems with his own fragile constitution.

Dolley's knee worsened. At the end of July, her physician immobilized her leg with a yard-long, wooden splint wrapped tightly with cloth.[16] Dolley wrote to Anna:

> Doctor Physick has seen it, & says he will cure me in a month—this aught to comfort me—but Anna, if I was not afraid of death I could give way to most immoderate greaf—but fool that I am—here is my beloved Husband siting anxiously by me & who is my unremiting Nurse—but you know how delicate he is I tremble for him—on our way one night he [was] taken very ill with his old bilious complaint I thought all was over with me, I could not fly to him & aid him as I used to do—but Heaven in its mercy restored him next Morning & he would not pause until he heared my fate from Doctor Physick.[17]

According to a Quaker visitor, throngs of Philadelphians dropped by to see Dolley, but the crowd of well-wishers was wearying to the ailing patient. With the events of 1793 clearly in mind, Dolley was constantly worried about her husband. Of the yellow fever threat, she wrote: "I enquire every day & they tell me there is not a single case. Mr. Madison goes out a

great deal, & does not tell me he hears of it—he is very subject
to bilious attack's & I am often miserable with fears for his
health, as I have been the cause of bringing him here at this
dangerious season, he laugh's at my anxieties & our acquaintances aid him in persuading me that we are both in safety."[18]

Dolley's crisis bound the Madisons together until late
October, when James had to return to his official duties in
Washington. The separation, although only a few weeks long,
was the longest time the couple had ever been apart and would
be the longest time they would ever be separated. Condemned
to bed, unable to move her infected leg, Dolley dearly missed
her husband. Their letters tell the story of their mutual devotion. "A few hours only have passed since you left me my
beloved, and I find nothing can relieve the oppression of my
mind but speaking to you in this manner," she wrote on October 23, finishing the letter the next day. She noted that her
knee was finally healing and closed her letter, "Adieu, my
beloved, our hearts understand each other."[19]

Her natural interest in politics surfaced again during this
period of recuperation. On November 1, from Philadelphia,
she made a deferential but specific inquiry about diplomatic and
military events that were preoccupying her husband.[20] Reflect-
ing his appreciation of her carefully understated interest,
Madison provided Dolley with a detailed, thoughtful analysis of the political climate in his return letter the next week.[21]

Her recovery was sufficiently complete that she was able
to return to Washington in late November, and the knee did
not bother her again. Reunited with her husband at their home
on F Street, Dolley gratefully resumed her place in Washington society. As soon as she returned, Dolley had to face a new
problem: her profligate younger brother, John Coles Payne,
then twenty-three, who liked gambling as much as strong
drink. Both Madisons were concerned about his addictions and
the company he kept. They hoped that a change of residence
and the influence of sober, responsible people would aid in his
reform. In 1806, Madison arranged for John to serve as the
secretary to George Davis, the American consul in Tripoli,

D. P. Madison

then one of the Barbary pirate states on the Mediterranean coast. The assignment, which put him out of reach of the watchful eyes of the family, only exacerbated his problems.

After John's departure, Dolley wrote to him regularly but received few replies. An 1809 letter to him expressed the longing of a loving sister that her wayward brother would return to the fold, healed of his demons. "You promised to return to us long before this," Dolley wrote, "& I hope & trust that if you are disappointed in your prospects where you are, that you will not suffer those weak refections, on yourself, which affect me, in your letter, to stay you one moment from my arms & heart, that are open to receive you. You would return to sisters & Brothers that love you & whose happiness it would be to do every thing for you."[22]

Dolley went on to say that she had paid off some of his debts "& will take every care of your interest as much as if it was my own son's, who is by the bye, a fine fellow, & who remembers & talks of you with the tenderest affection—& indeed so do all your old acquaintances, many of them have written to you, & I truly believe that you left no enemy behind you."[23] Sadly, both Dolley's profligate brother and son accepted her help, support, and money, but neither returned her affections or generosity in any proportion to what they had been given.

Dolley's relatives were not the only source of potential problems. Her friendship with Aaron Burr also came back to haunt her. As Madison was preparing to be sworn in for his second term as secretary of state in the spring of 1805, Burr was packing his bags. Although the vice president had won the respect of the Senate as its presiding officer, his relationship with the president had been stormy. Jefferson ignored Burr's friends and colleagues when patronage jobs were handed out. Burr was charged with having Federalist sympathies. When the Republicans caucused in Washington in February 1804 and re-nominated Jefferson for president, Burr was passed over in favor of New York's aging George Clinton. Disgusted but undaunted, Burr ran for governor of New York, but lost. He had survived the duel with Hamilton with his body intact, but his reputation was in tatters. His time on the national political stage had come to an end. Or so everyone thought.

By 1806, Aaron Burr had resurfaced in the national limelight, and again, the news was bad: his conspiracy to conquer Spanish Mexico had become the nation's worst-kept secret. In the early spring of 1807, Burr, who had dipped deeply into the pockets of his wealthy South Carolina son-in-law, Joseph Alston, to finance the operation, set off from Philadelphia on flatboats with the first contingent of a rag-tag private army and navy to invade Mexico. Along the Ohio River, he picked up other settler-soldiers and then dropped off his daughter, Theodosia; his grandchild, Aaron Burr Alston; and his son-in-law, Joseph Alston, at Blennerhassett Island in the Ohio River opposite Parkersburg, West Virginia. There the Alstons were entertained by Harman Blennerhassett, Jr., one of Burr's chief co-conspirators, and his alluring wife, Margaret.

Burr had enlisted many shady co-conspirators, including Brigadier General James Wilkinson, then commander of all U.S. military forces in the West. Burr was unaware that Wilkinson was also a well-paid spy, known to the Spanish minister, the Marquis de Yrujo, as "Agent Number 13." Burr and his flotilla continued downstream to the Mississippi and were on their way to New Orleans when Jefferson had Burr arrested for treason. Wilkinson had informed on Burr to save his own neck.

Under a heavily armed military guard, Burr was transported on horseback across half the country to the federal penitentiary at Richmond. Dolley related the news to Anna Cutts in March 1807.[24] At Burr's trial, Chief Justice John Marshall threw out the charge of treason based on lack of evidence. Acquitted but not exonerated, Burr fled to Europe in the summer of 1808, leaving his forlorn daughter, Theodosia, behind. The entire spectacle was a great embarrassment to Dolley, who had not forgotten the kindness Burr had shown her in the past and the pleasant, if brief, social relationship she had shared with his daughter, Theodosia. When the news arrived that Burr had slipped out of the country, Dolley must have been relieved, but within a short time, he would again be an issue she would have to deal with.

Burr's disgrace, though personally painful to her, was hardly the saddest event in Dolley's life during this period. She lost two Jackson nieces (both her namesake, Dolley Payne Jackson, and her sister, Lucy Jackson) in 1806. Worst of all in 1807, her mother died after a two-year struggle with tuber-culosis. Dolley's uncle, Isaac Winston, wrote eloquently about his sister's lifelong devotion to Dolley:

> To you, she was a tender, affectionate, and most ex-cellent Parent—through the whole course of your life, with impassioned fondness, she pressed you to her tender Bosom & never for a Moment lost sight of your best and dearest Interests—from your earliest Infancy, with ineffible goodness, she impressed on your tender mind, the sublime principles of Piety & virtue—with unabated Ardor she pursued with unerring prudence, the means best calculated to induce to the Prosperity & Happiness of yourself and the rest of the children; and in the attainment of these important objects she was deeply rewarded in you, by your Gratitude [and] your assiduous and affectionate attention.[25]

In the depths of her grief, Dolley opened her heart to her old friend, Eliza Collins Lee. "When I trace the sad events that have occured to me, I feel as if I should die two [too]. My Husband is nearly well & I have exerted all my fortitude, all my religion, in order to live for him & my son. Alass! my friend, I used to think that I could not survive the loss of my Mother . . . yet am I still here; & in all the bitterness of mourn-ing striveing to reconcile my heart to the greatest misfortune!"[26]

The next year she lost her sister, Mary Payne Jackson, to tuberculosis. From her correspondence, it is clear that the loss of each relative, no matter how distant the relation-ship, was experienced as a personal blow by Dolley, who never let any passing of any friend or relative go unnoticed. Each was treated as if the deceased had genuinely been the most important person in her life.

By the spring of 1808, when she was forty, Dolley's once-large family had been reduced to her husband, James; her sisters, Anna Payne Cutts and Lucy Payne Washington; her problematic absent brother, John Coles Payne; and her son, Payne, at school in Baltimore. She had also recently lost one of her old friends to the necessities of being married to a diplomat. Her fun-loving friend, Marchioness Sally McKean Yrujo, was embarking with her husband for Spain, "greaved beyond measure at leaving her country and friends."[27]

With this new loss, and having recently survived her own brush with death during the knee infection, Dolley would have had every right to feel fearful and vulnerable. A flare-up of inflammatory rheumatism in the summer of 1808 produced extreme pain, which was not lessened when her doctor bled her. It did not help that the attack, which caused her to faint and also rendered it impossible for her to move her right arm for some time, happened at Montpellier when she was in the midst of entertaining fifteen or twenty members of the Madison family and their connections.[28] Nevertheless, James' career was on the rise, and the bustle of politics, and her resultant social responsibilities, left Dolley little time to grieve her losses. Her workhorse attitude enabled her to rise above her emotional and physical ailments and do what needed to be done.

As 1808 progressed, it was clear that Thomas Jefferson was preparing for his retirement and that Madison was the logical Republican candidate to take his place in the President's House. The fact that Dolley was a major asset to Madison's candidacy is apparent in a letter written on Monday, November 23, 1807, by Dr. Samuel Mitchill, U.S. Senator from New York, to his wife, Catherine. Mitchill described his encounter with Dolley after church on the previous day:

> [I] had the honor of escorting Mrs. Madison through
> the crowd to her carriage. She inquired kindly after

you and so did Mrs. Cutts. The former of these ladies has the prospect of being *Lady President*. Mr. Jefferson is moving away his things gradually to Virginia, with intent of retiring at the expiration of his term. Mr. Madison and Mr. Clinton are the two prominent characters talked of to succeed him. The former gives dinners and makes generous displays to the members. The latter lives snug at his lodgings, and keeps aloof from such captivating exhibition. The Secretary of State has a wife to aid his pretensions. The Vice-President has nothing of female succor on his side. And in these two respects Mr. Madison is going greatly ahead of him.[29]

It is clear that a candidate's wife could be a major political asset, and Dolley had already become a political force to be reckoned with. First and foremost, she was friends with everyone and everyone was on friendly terms with her. She maintained, with varying degrees of success, close relationships with all the wives of the European diplomats: the haughty Elizabeth Merry, wife of the British minister; the elegant Emilie Pichon, wife of Louis-André Pichon, the French minister; Dolley's audacious friend, Sally McKean de Yrujo, wife of the Spanish minister; and the sad, tormented Louise Henriette, the physically abused spouse of Louis-Marie Turreau de Garambouville, successor to Pichon. Madame Turreau's extensive and ongoing abuse, which included being whipped in front of their servants, was well-known to the women of Washington. The situation presented Dolley with a special dilemma, one common to those in diplomatic circles. If she was to openly side with the poor woman, whom she adored, pitied, and visited with almost every day, would the act be viewed as one of compassion for a victim of domestic violence, or as a condemnation of the French minister and his government?[30]

Dolley had far fewer problems with the diplomats themselves, half of whom were married. The others, notably the Danish bachelor, Peder Pedersen, and Augustus John Foster, an unmarried Englishman who served under the British minister, Anthony Merry, also admired her. Foster later wrote a book about his experiences in America, which included visiting Montpellier while Madison was secretary of state. There he experienced both the Madisons' legendary hospitality and, the previous day, the virtues of a Virginia mint julep, which a kindly neighbor had served him before breakfast.[31] Indeed, the bachelors in Dolley's orbit were especially fortunate, for she had already developed a solid reputation as Cupid's helper and was always happy to introduce a young man of good character to suitable female companions. Throughout Washington, and for hundreds of miles in all directions, it was well known that the home of the secretary of state was a happy place where everyone, regardless of rank, would find a warm and genuine welcome.

When it came to her own domestic partnership, Dolley and her husband were an inseparable team. He considered her "a thing of beauty and a joy forever." When she was present, gaiety and good will abounded, and Dolley was always willing to offer advice on any problem that concerned James. She was his hostess and political informant. She dressed his long hair, read to him, wrote letters for him when he was ill, and was ever-watchful for ways to assist the man she so dearly loved.

From every quarter came assurances that Dolley made a warm impression on the hearts of her friends. Emilie Pichon and her husband had been recalled to Paris by the spring of 1807 but wrote to Dolley about the loss of her companionship. "It is very happy for foreigners [from France], that while they are deprived of Mr. Jefferson's society they are to enjoy yours. It surely is great comfort for them when they leave their country & relatives to have such happy prospects abroad."[32]

When the Republicans caucused at the Capitol at the end of January 1808 to nominate candidates to lead the nation, James Madison was to be president and George Clinton was to be vice president. Clinton, who was serving as Jefferson's vice president, felt that he deserved the nation's top leadership post by right of succession and bristled at the thought of remaining in second position as someone else was installed over him. In July 1807, a surprise loomed up when James Monroe let his name be circulated for nomination.

At Dolley's request, James Monroe had often sent her elegant French gowns while the Monroes were in Paris. Thinking that James' wife, Elizabeth Kortright Monroe (who considered Dolley "too countrified"), had instigated Monroe's candidacy, Dolley confided to her sister Anna that she had never really trusted "la belle Américaine," the name Napoléon had given Elizabeth. According to John Quincy Adams' diary, Dolley had "no hesitation in speaking upon the electioneering now so warmly carried on, in which she spoke very slightingly of Mr. Monroe."[33]

The venerable Senator Mitchill was convinced of Madison's imminent success, however, and wrote to his wife in January 1808, "As I foretold you in my former letters, Mrs. Madison has a bright prospect of becoming Lady Presidentress and of being mistress of the sumptuous mansion on Palatine Hill for four years."[34] Indeed, she did, but not before surviving serious attempts to assassinate her character.

Madison's Federalist opponents circulated "lewd rumors of a graphically scandalous nature," suggesting a litany of sexual compromises by the gregarious, buxom secretary of state's wife. They included allegations that Dolley had been Jefferson's lover when the Madisons moved into the President's House before finding their own house. Rumors also alleged that the Madisons were childless because Jemmy was impotent, that Dolley was oversexed, and that Madison had both Dolley and Anna dispense sexual favors to Jefferson, fellow Republicans, and foreign diplomats in return for votes and support.

The attack was furthered by Virginia's own John Randolph, who spread the rumors in Congress and wrote of Madison's "unfortunate matrimonial connection."[35] In 1805, when the gossip began, Dolley quickly reacted to put herself out of reach of any further allegations. She wrote to her husband that the French minister, General Louis-Marie Turreau, and several Frenchmen had arrived at their house and that they wished to see her, but "I declined seeing them as you were absent and I upstairs, the General sent word up that he was anxious to see and speak to me, but I resolved not to admit a gentleman, into my room, unless entitled by age and long acquaintance."[36]

Dolley was deeply hurt by the allegations. Her sister Anna was also shocked, as it had been said that she, with Dolley's approval, had been intimate with Madison and that Richard Cutts, her husband, had married her only with the entice-ment of a cabinet position. When the editor of *The Boston Globe* reprinted the claims, Cutts challenged him to a duel.[37]

In the spring of 1809, James Madison ran against his Federalist opponent, South Carolina Governor Charles Cotesworth Pinckney, who lost. Pinckney clearly acknowl-edged Dolley's strong influence on the election. "I was beaten by Mr. and Mrs. Madison," he lamented. "I might have had a better chance had I faced Mr. Madison alone."[38] Dolley was jubilant. This time when they moved back into the President's House, she knew they had at least a four-year lease. And there was even a chance that the lease might be renewable.

The room was so terribly crowded that we had to stand on the benches; from this situation we had a view of the moving mass; it was nothing else. It was scarcely possible to elbow your way from one side to another, and poor Mrs. Madison was almost pressed to death, for every one crowded round her, those behind pressing on those before, and peeping over their shoulders to have a peep of her, and those who were so fortunate as to get near enough to speak to her were happy indeed. As the upper sashes of the windows could not let down, the glass was broken, to ventilate the room, the air of which had become oppressive.[4]

Madison was escorted to the front of the chamber by a committee of congressmen, who showed him to the central chair. Jefferson sat to his right; Supreme Court members sat in front; and Representatives sat in their places on the floor of the House. Jefferson nodded toward Madison and remarked that "he was much happier at this moment than my friend."[5]

Madison was dressed in his usual dark clothing, but he relaxed his severe style a notch by wearing a handsome ivory-colored six-button vest, embel-

Dolley Madison

lished by an elegantly embroidered vine-and-flower garland, which ran down the lapels and across the waist.

After a ten-minute speech, which paid tribute to his predecessor, declared basic republican principles, but offered no insight into any future policies, Madison was sworn in by Chief Justice John Marshall, an ardent Federalist, who took no pleasure in installing his political foe as chief executive.

The new president left the hall to the sound of booming cannon salutes, and the militia lined his route back to his residence on F Street, where the Madisons held open house.[6]

After the inauguration, Margaret Smith and her husband
followed the throng to the Madison's house. "The street was
full of carriages and people," she wrote. "We had to wait near
half an hour, before we could get in, — the house was completely filled, parlours, entry, drawing room and bed room."
Not everyone was comfortable with the revealing French
dresses Dolley now wore at almost all formal occasions. Just
prior to the inauguration in 1809, Ruth Hooper Dalton Deblois,
the daughter of a Washington merchant and a friend of
Dolley's, sent her a package and a note. "Accept and wear
for the sake of the donor the enclosed Handkerchief it claims
no other Merit then being thought worthy of my Valuable
friend Mrs Madison, of shading her lovely bosom from the
admiration and gaze of the Vulgar."[7]

Dolley, who by now had a clear vision of her tastes, made
her own fashion choices. After the inauguration ceremony,
Margaret Smith recalled, "Near the door of the drawing room
Mr. and Mrs. Madison stood to receive their company. She
looked extremely beautiful, was drest in a plain cambric dress
with a very long train, plain round the neck without any handkerchief, and beautiful bonnet of purple velvet, and white
satin with white plumes."

Elaborate turbans soon became Dolley's fashion signature.
At the president's New Year's Eve reception in 1812, she wore a
pink, satin, ermine-trimmed robe with gold chains, and a turban "topped by nodding ostrich plumes."[8] Turbans had become
stylish in the first years of the nineteenth century, and Dolley
commented on them as early as 1804. In 1813, she asked Betsy
Bonaparte to be alert for fine accessories for her. "I will avail
myself of your taste, in case you meet with any thing eligant, in
the form of a Turban, or even any thing <u>briliant</u> to make me —
such as gause or lace flower'd with Gold or silver."[9] In virtually
every image created of her after she became First Lady, Dolley
is wearing one of her elaborate, brightly colored turbans.

She considered herself to be "an economist" in all financial matters, but her clothing bills spoke otherwise. In 1811, she had the U.S. consul at Bordeaux scurry around Paris for two months, collecting clothing catalogues and illustrations from which two of Dolley's French friends selected the fashions to fill her extensive shopping list. The import duties on this one shipment of clothes alone cost $2,000, and although Madison fumed, he paid. By 1813, new shipments were already on their way to the well-dressed First Lady.[10]

On the evening of the inauguration, Dolley Madison initiated her golden reign over Washington. It commenced at an inaugural ball for four hundred invited guests, held at Long's Hotel on Capitol Hill, and was the first ever held in this country. Each of the previous three presidents had closed his inauguration day by going to bed early. Presidents Washington and Adams had been inaugurated at temporary capitals, and Jefferson would have been aghast at any pageantry that was so plainly modeled along royal patterns. Madison's inauguration was quite different. The capital was now nine years old, and its residents were starting to claim the right to do whatever they wished. In addition, every American in Washington over the age of thirty-two had been born a royal subject, and dancing was a time-honored tradition in royal courts. All of this led to the Madisons' inaugural ball. Since that night in the spring of 1809, every president of the United States has finished his inauguration day at a ball like the Madisons'.

The guests came from far and wide, but most were from Washington City, Virginia, and Maryland. Baltimore was at least a full day's trip away, and it took more than a week to come from New York. Unless the visitors had friends to stay with, they fared badly at the crowded boardinghouses and hotels of the still-primitive capital.

The ball started precisely at seven o'clock, and the band struck up "Jefferson's March." The man who had been president only hours before entered the room with his private secretary, Dolley's cousin, Isaac A. Coles. "Am I too early?" Jefferson asked. "You must tell me how to behave, for it is more than forty years since I have been to a ball."[11]

Next the band played "Madison's March," and the new president entered the hall, along with Dolley and Anna Cutts, escorted by the ball managers. Dolley's costume that night reflected what the country would come to expect of the "Presidentress," as one commentator had dubbed her. It caused a sensation. She wore a pale buff-colored velvet dress with a very long train; a Parisian turban of the same buff-colored velvet and white satin, with two Bird of Paradise plumes; and a pearl necklace, earrings, and bracelets as accents. Margaret Smith wrote that "she looked and moved like a queen."[12] On that momentous day in her life, Dolley was two months shy of her forty-first birthday. However, the transition from Dolley Payne, the Quaker farm girl, to Dolley Payne Todd Madison, First Lady of the United States, was now complete.

A problem quickly arose. Quaker farm girls were not taught how to dance. At the inauguration ball, when the managers presented Dolley with the first dance, she whispered to them, "I do not dance."

One of the managers, British-born Captain Thomas Tingey, commandant of the Washington Navy Yard, said, "Give it to your neighbor."

"Oh, no," said Dolley. "That would look like partiality."

"Then I will," said Tingey, and he presented the honor of the first dance to Anna Payne Cutts."[13]

At the dinner that followed, Dolley demonstrated how quickly she and her husband had discarded Jefferson's confrontational *Canons.* Jefferson had taken office as president when the nation was young and unestablished on the international stage, and when implementing republican concepts was a new responsibility. When the Madisons took over in 1809, the country was a full member of the international community. It no longer needed to impress the world with its republican principles, which were now well known, and its capital was starting to acquire a semblance of polish. Washington's residents, as well as the foreign diplomatic corps, now expected a higher level of sophistication. Dolley Madison, a peerless hostess and a woman of exquisite common sense, was the perfect person to lead Washington society.

At the inauguration ball that evening, she was led to dinner by the French minister, General Louis-Marie Turreau de Garambouville, who was decked out in full diplomatic splendor, his costume replete with gold and diamonds. Turreau had a fiery temper and was widely known as a wife-beater. Although Dolley personally disliked him, his presence was essential. She mustered her poise and charm and glided to the table. Her sister, Anna Payne Cutts, was escorted to the table by the English minister, David Montagu Erskine, Anthony Merry's successor. Madison escorted Margaret Bayard Smith. Dolley sat at the center of the crescent-shaped table, with the French and English ministers at each hand. Anna Cutts was next on her right; Margaret Smith was next on her left; and her husband was next to Mrs. Smith on the other side of the table, opposite Dolley. Jefferson was also at the table. Margaret Smith said of him, "I do believe that father never loved son more than he loves Mr. Madison, and I believe too that every demonstration of respect to Mr. Madison gave Mr. Jefferson more pleasure than if paid to himself."[14]

Everyone in Washington was fascinated with the new couple. Although Dolley, with her colorful clothing, effusive warmth, and great energy, attracted far more attention than her quiet, black-clad husband, Mrs. Frances Few, the sister-in-law of Albert Gallatin, took care to describe them both:

> Mr. Madison the President-elect is a small man quite devoid of dignity in his appearance—he bows very low and never looks at the person to whom he is bowing but keeps his eyes on the ground. His skin looks like parchment—at first I thought this appearance was occasioned by the small-pox but upon nearer approach, I found this was not the case—a few moments in his company and you lose sight of these defects and will see nothing but what pleases you—his eyes are

penetrating and expressive—his smile charming—his manners affable—his conversation lively and interesting. Mrs. Madison is a handsome woman—looks much younger than her husband—she is tall and majestic—her manners affable, but a little affected. She has been very much admired and is still fond of admiration—loads herself with finery and dresses without any taste—and amidst all her finery you may discover that in neatness she is very deficient. Her complexion is brilliant—her neck and bosom the most beautiful I ever saw—her face expresses nothing but good nature. It is impossible however to be with her and not be pleased. There is something very fascinating about her—yet I do not think it possible to know what her real opinions are. She is all things to all men—not the least of a prude as she one day told an old bachelor and held up her mouth for him to kiss.[15]

At the ball, Madison seemed "spiritless and exhausted" and wanted to retire immediately after dinner, which he did. The guests danced until the musicians stopped playing at midnight, but without the president or his presidentress, who were already in bed, sound asleep.[16]

One week after the inauguration, Mrs. William Thornton noted in her diary, "Mr. and Mrs. Madison went to the Great House."[17] As queenly as Dolley appeared on inauguration day, the "President's Palace," as some called the executive mansion, bore little resemblance to a royal residence at the time the Madisons moved in. It was still a shabby, unfinished building, surrounded by lumber piles and heaps of stone. Congress had not appropriated enough money to even finish, not to mention furnish, the President's House, so its first occupants had to provide most of their own furniture. Since Jefferson had taken all his furniture back to Monticello, the few rooms that were furnished greatly needed more furniture.

When the Madisons moved into the house in 1809, Washington City was still a "series of disjointed villages separated by great distances."[18] The executive mansion was by far the finest and most natural meeting place for what became known as the "Republican Court." The building was informally being referred to as the "White House" as early as May 19, 1809.[19] The popular title was "fully entrenched," by 1820, though only in unofficial use. The executive mansion was not officially designated The White House until 1901.[20]

The term "First Lady" had a similar evolution, partly because the president's spouse is not a government officer, and the role is neither named nor defined in the Constitution. "The Presidentress" or the "Lady Presidentress" were both terms of address and reference used during the Madison era. "First Lady" did not become a common title until after the Madisons left the White House, but both "Presidentress" and "First Lady" will be used here for convenience.

During her husband's first presidential administration, Dolley's greatest joy was the opportunity to make a permanent mark on history by decorating the President's House. She crafted the interior of the national symbol to reflect both traditional elegance and American simplicity. Working with master architect Benjamin Henry Latrobe, with input from his wife, Mary Elizabeth Hazlehurst Latrobe, a childhood friend of hers from Philadelphia, Dolley carefully cultivated an image for the new nation. She chose each of the tables, chairs, sofas, mirrors, carpets, tables, table linens, plates, glasses, knives, forks, spoons, and saltcellars to reflect the values of the new republic.

To the extent possible, Dolley and Latrobe chose American-made goods for the White House. The state dining service was English Staffordshire, although the Madisons had other china of French origin. Although some French-made furniture had come with the house, the Madisons bought little more from France, even though they were decidedly Francophiles. Virtually all of the standing furniture came from American craftspeople and merchants. This was as much an attempt to deny the Federalists an excuse to criticize the Madison administration for pro-French bias as it was to demonstrate national pride. On the other hand, Dolley employed a French *major domo*, John Sioussat, to run the White House domestic staff; dressed in the latest Parisian fashions to receive her guests at her weekly drawing rooms; and served French meals prepared by her French chef, Pierre Roux, with the finest French wines.

Latrobe, who was born and trained in England, came to the United States in 1796. His first impression of the city that he would later help to build was anything but positive. He took one look and dismissed it as a "wretched and desolate place," containing half-finished houses "tumbling to ruins, which the madness of speculation has erected."[21]

The next year, he undertook his first major architectural work in this country, the Virginia State Penitentiary, where Aaron Burr was imprisoned in 1807 while awaiting his trial for treason. In 1803, President Jefferson—himself an extraordinary architect—named Latrobe Surveyor of the Public Buildings, with the responsibility for finishing work on both the President's House and the Capitol. A month before his inauguration as president, Madison asked his friend to become the agent of the President's Furniture Fund, which Congress provided for each president. John Adams had received $14,000 for his single term. Jefferson was given $29,000 for his two terms, and the Madisons received $20,000 for their two terms.

In furnishing the White House, Latrobe would report directly to Madison, but all of the actual arrangements would be handled by Dolley. "Assigning the entire regulation of the household to the First Lady was a clear indication of Madison's abiding confidence in his wife's capabilities," wrote Conover Hunt-Jones, a scholar who researched the history of the Madison White House. "Few American men of that era would have entrusted the task to a woman."[22]

An inventory of the furnishings showed that twenty-three of the rooms were adequately furnished and that only the oval drawing room was not. Latrobe and the First Lady jumped into the decorating design work with enthusiasm. Latrobe brought his formal training and classical ideals to the task, and Dolley added her enthusiasm and delight in pairing intense colors. They had $20,000 to work with prior to the burning of the White House, and they spent a bit more than $12,000 of that. All of the funds expended went to decorating two major rooms: the ladies' drawing room, also known as "Mrs. Madison's parlour," now known as the Red Room, and the large oval drawing room, now known as the Blue Room.

Latrobe had begun preparing for the work before the inauguration, and he had the ladies' drawing room ready for Dolley's first gala drawing room on May 31, 1809. When the guests walked in, they were greeted by furniture in the "very latest Sheraton style" and window treatments that reflected Dolley's unique preferences:

> The curtains in the room were made of sunflower yellow damask with a valence of swags and draperies topping each window. This valance continued all around the top of the room, the stiff festoons looping up to a pole placed near the ceiling line. The fringe with which all the draperies and valances were trimmed caused a mild furor; it was made of long and short drops, silk over bits of wood, and must have enhanced the elegance of the room. In front of the fireplace, "on a fireboard' beneath the mantle the same yellow damask was arranged in a fluted pattern known as a 'rising sun.' The furniture of the room was upholstered in bright yellow satin; the high-backed sofas and stiff chairs were elegant with no pretense of comfort. The room's furnishings were completed with a new carpet, a few pier tables and card tables, and a fine guitar ordered expressly by Mrs. Madison.[23]

In this setting, the First Lady received her guests, often dressed in buff or yellow satin, or in a contrasting crimson. Indeed, Dolley accessorized the ladies' drawing room with herself.

The large oval drawing room required considerably more work, but it was ready for a formal reception just seven months later, on New Year's Day, 1810. Madison quickly learned that his architectural genius would have to be kept on a short financial leash. Only a week after the inauguration, Latrobe casually informed the president that he was making haste to acquire the basic necessities for the house, which would include spending $3,150 for four pairs of looking glasses (mirrors). Latrobe and Dolley had no shortage of good taste, but the initial $5,000 authorized for the decorating was gone in less than two months, and they needed nearly $4,000 more. Latrobe scoured Philadelphia, New York, and Baltimore for the furniture they needed. Dolley decided that an elegant pianoforte was necessary so that the young women of Washington could properly entertain guests at her drawing rooms. They initially selected one for $650, but they settled for another for $450. Mary Latrobe was delegated the responsibility for choosing the guitar, as she was skilled in playing that instrument.[24]

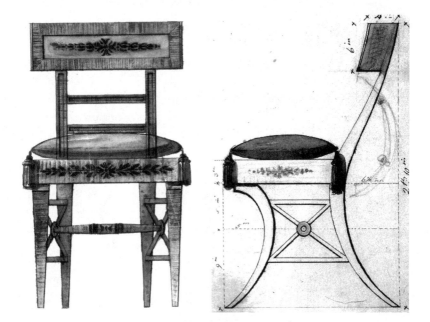

Chair designed by Benjamin Latrobe
for the Oval Drawing Room of the White House

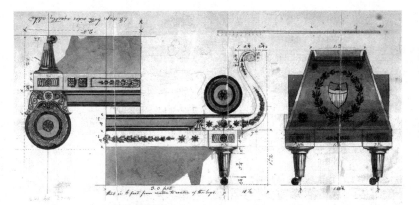

*Sofa designed by Benjamin Latrobe
for the Oval Drawing Room of the White House*

Latrobe designed the chairs and sofas in the Greek style he so much respected, and his designs closely followed those that appeared in an 1807 cabinetmaker's guide published in London. His plans were executed by the shop of John and Hugh Finlay of Baltimore, which was renowned for handsome painted furniture. Latrobe chose paint in preference to heavy gilt, as the latter, then popular in Europe, was considered too courtly for the residence of the president of the American republic. In September 1809, the Finlays billed Latrobe $1,111 for thirty-six cane-seat chairs "made to a Grecian model, painted, gilded and varnished, with the United States arms painted on each," two matching sofas, and four matching settees.[25]

Latrobe's correspondence with Dolley in the spring and summer of 1809 demonstrates what a well-matched and hard-working team they were. Dolley wanted silk damask curtains for the three windows and two alcoves in the oval drawing room, but Latrobe could not find enough fabric. "There is no Silk Damask to be had either in New York or Philadelphia, & I am therefore forced to give you crimson Velvet curtains of which I can get plenty," Latrobe wrote to her."[26] This posed no real problem for Dolley, who adored crimson and had used it as the primary color throughout her bedchamber at Montpellier.

Nine days later, when Latrobe saw the cloth, he wrote in despair, "The curtains! Oh the terrible velvet curtains! Their effect will ruin me entirely, so brilliant will they be." He was half right. They were brilliant indeed—and the effect of their bright, bold simplicity complimented the exquisitely detailed painted furniture he had designed. The floor of the room was covered with "169 yards of Brussels carpet," hand-woven on a draw loom, and thirty yards of matching border. The room was a triumphant masterpiece for both its designers.

The impressive, life-size, full-length portrait of George Washington painted by Gilbert Stuart, which was the first to show him as president of the nation rather than general of the army, was hung in the dining room. The majority of Latrobe's work was finished by the end of 1809, after he had designed a carriage and a chariot for the Madisons, along with the livery costumes to be worn by their coachmen and drivers.[27]

Dolley held her first levee, which she called her "weekly drawing room," on Friday, March 31, 1809, three-and-a-half weeks after her husband's inauguration. These events were

The Reign of Dolley Madison

later held on Wednesdays. The name was derived from the French *levé* ("to rise"), the morning reception received by a sovereign or person of high rank from his courtiers when rising from bed in the morning. The European practice evolved into a reception or assembly held by the president, his wife, or other high official. The stunning success of the first one, and that of the dozens that followed during the next eight years, permanently established Dolley as the queen of Washington society, a title she would enjoy for the rest of her life.

An illustration (shown at left) published by *Puck* magazine captured the essence of Dolley's popular levees. The poem that accompanies the cartoon reads: "They say when Dolly Madison / Wore, quite by right, the social bays, / That laughter bubbled, overrun, / The Washington of other day; / That mirth prevailed where now you'll find / Sedate and staid sobriety; / They did not then so strictly mind / The cannons of Society. / Less heed they paid to rank and station / In Madison's administration. / They say that Dolly Madison / Was wont on country legislators / To lavish smiles, and plain homespun / Was not tabooed by style's dictators, / That brains instead of clothes were prized— / A things that's very hard to credit! / That with applause they recognized / The apt remark—not he who said it! / Ah! Sad's the change throughout the nation / Since Madison's Administration!"[28]

George and Martha Washington—a very wealthy family— introduced the levee to the national government, much to the chagrin of Washington's successor, John Adams. It was impossible to cover the costs of lavish dinners from the president's salary, and Martha's levees were paid for out of Washington's own wallet. In Washington's wake, Abigail Adams, whose husband's pockets were not nearly as deep as those of the gentleman planter from Mount Vernon, complained to her sister about the Fourth of July celebration they were to host in 1797. "As we are here we cannot avoid the trouble nor the expense. I have been informd the day used to cost the late President 500 dollars. More than 200 wt. [pounds] of cake to be expended, and 2 quarter casks of wine besides spirit. You will not wonder that I dread it, or think President Washington to blame for introducing the custom, if he could have avoided it."[29]

Dolley's drawing rooms were markedly different from those of the Washington, Adams, and Jefferson administrations. She had a specific goal in mind: to create a climate that reflected the Republican simplicity of American social values yet projected a sense of refined elegance and high fashion. In the Madisons' time, the United States was still a great experiment, where men like Jefferson and Madison were seeking to create an efficient national government and implement the egalitarian principles they both held so dear.

No written invitations were issued and none were needed. Dolley banished the formal receiving lines, personally greeted and spoke to everyone, and freely made introductions all around. No one was a stranger at one of her drawing rooms for more than five minutes. Every guest was treated as if he or she were a long-lost friend or close member of the family. Dolley's extraordinary memory enabled her to make virtually anyone feel welcome, and she empathized with every problem of the human condition as if it were her own. Her tact directed her to pursue or deflect any given subject of conversation, thus defusing potential confrontations before they occurred. She was, indeed, the perfect hostess for her understated husband.

Benjamin Latrobe wrote to a friend, "Mrs. Madison gives drawing rooms every Wednesday. The first one was very numerously attended by none but respectable people. The Second, La La," in other words, not nearly as exclusive a clientele. He described the third as being attended by "a perfect rabble in beards and boots."[30]

Washington Irving was one of many to describe the splendors of Mrs. Madison's drawing room hospitality.

Washington Irving

He wrote to a friend, "Here I was most graciously received, found a crowded collection of great and little men, of ugly old women and beautiful new ones, and in ten minutes was hand and glove with half the people in the assemblage." He described Dolley, then forty-one, as "a fine, portly, buxom dame who has a smile and a pleasant word for everybody. Her sisters, Mrs. Cutts and Mrs. Washington, are like the two merry wives of Windsor; but as to Jemmy Madison—ah! poor Jemmy!—he is but a little withered apple-John." Irving was aware of Dolley's influence with her husband, and a month later, when he was hoping to receive a diplomatic appointment, he wrote, "The President, on its being informed to him, said some very handsome things of me, and I make no doubt will express a wish in my favor on the subject, more especially as Mrs. Madison is a sworn friend of mine, and indeed all the ladies of the household and myself are great cronies."[31]

William C. Preston, a proud, feisty, college-age man who was a distant relative of Dolley's through his great-uncle, Patrick Henry, left his own description of the grand affairs. "The drawing room when I entered was ablaze with brilliant uniforms and gorgeous toilets [costumes, hairstylings, and makeup], made doubly dazzling by the reflection of many mirrors. In the center I saw Mrs. Madison, a tall, portly, elegant lady, with a turban on her head and a snuffbox in her hand. She advanced straight toward me and extending her left hand said 'Are you William Campbell Preston, the son of my old friend and most beloved kinswoman, Sally Campbell? Sit down, my son, for you are my son, and I am the first person who ever saw you in this world.'" Dolley then turned with a graciousness that charmed the young man, and introduced him to the young women around him.[32] Her pervasive and genuine warmth to everyone, offered as it was during a period when vitriolic public attacks and rabid party politics reigned unchecked, firmly established Dolley's reputation and set the standard against which first ladies of the future would long be measured.

Her warmth was not limited to politicians and her extended family. Indeed, Dolley was as kind to total strangers as she was to her closest friends. One day, two old ladies stopped in unannounced at the President's House while the family was still having breakfast. Dolley, wearing a simple gray dress, a large apron, and a linen kerchief pinned around her neck, greeted them warmly, spoke to them at length, and then bade them good-bye. The teller of this story noted that "her simplicity of manner and attire completely swept away their awe, and before departing one of them found courage to exclaim, 'Perhaps you wouldn't mind if I kissed you, just to tell the folks about it.'"[33]

During both presidential administrations, the Madisons spent their summers at Montpellier, and no sooner did they arrive than flocks of their friends and connections descended on the plantation. In August 1809, Margaret Bayard Smith and her husband were among them. After a three-day visit with Jefferson at Monticello, from which she departed only with the regret that it could not have lasted longer, Margaret recorded in her notebook a detailed description of the warm reception they received at Montpellier:

> The sadness which all day hung on my spirits was instantly dispelled by the cheering smile of Mrs. Madison and the friendly greeting of our good President. It was near five oclock when we arrived, we were met at the door by Mr. Madison who led us in to the dining room where some gentlemen were still smoking segars and drinking wine. Mrs. Madison entered the moment afterwards, and after embracing me, took my hand, saying with a smile, 'I will take you out of this smoke to a pleasanter room.' She took me through the tea room to her chamber which opens from it. Everything bespoke comfort. I was going to take my seat on the sopha, but she said I must lay down by her on her bed, and rest myself, she loosened my riding habit, took off my bonnet, and we threw ourselves on her bed.
>
> Wine, ice, punch and delightful pine-apples were immediately brought. No restraint, no ceremony.

Hospitality is the presiding genius of this house, and Mrs. Madison is kindness personified. She enquired why I had not brought the little girls; I told her the fear of incomoding my friends.

'Oh,' said she laughing, 'I should not have known they were here, among all the rest, for at this moment we have only three and twenty in the house.'

'Three and twenty,' exclaimed I! 'Why where do you store them?'

'Oh we have house room in plenty.' This I could easily believe, for the house seemed immense.... Mrs. Cutts soon came in with her sweet children, and afterwards Mr. Madison, Cutts, and Mr. Smith. The door opening into the tea room being open, they without ceremony joined their wives. They only peeked in on us; we then shut the door and after adjusting our dress, went out on the Piazza — (it is 60 feet long). Here we walked and talked until called to tea, or rather supper, for though tea hour, it was supper fare. The long dining table was spread, and besides tea and coffee, we had a variety of warm cakes, bread, cold meats and pastry. At table I was introduced to Mr. William Madison, brother to the President, and his wife, and three or four other ladies and gentlemen all near relatives, all plain country people, but frank, kind, warm-hearted Virginians. At this house I realized being in Virginia, Mr. Madison, plain, friendly, communicative, and unceremonious as any Virginia planter could be — Mrs. Madison, uniting to all the elegance and polish of fashion, the unadulterated simplicity, frankness, warmth, and friendliness of her native character and native state. Their mode of living, too, if it had more elegance than is found among the planters, was characterized by that abundance, that hospitality, and that freedom, we are taught to look for on a Virginian plantation.

We did not sit long at this meal — the evening was warm and we were glad to leave the table. The gentlemen went to the piazza, the ladies, who all had children, to their chambers, and I sat with Mrs. Madison till bed time talking of Washington. When the servant appeared with candles to show me my room, she insisted on going up stairs with me, assisted me to undress and chatted till I got into bed. How unassuming, how kind is this woman. How can any human being be her enemy. Truly, in her there is to be found no gall, but the pure milk of human kindness....

The next morning Nany called me to a late breakfast, brought me ice and water, (this is universal here, even in taverns) and assisted me to dress. We sat down between 15 and 20 persons to breakfast — and to a most excellent Virginian breakfast — tea, coffee, hot wheat bread, light cakes, a pone, or corn loaf — cold ham, nice hashes, chickens, etc.[34]

In the spring of 1811, an off-again, on-again wedding spiced up life at the White House. Supreme Court Associate Justice Thomas Todd of Kentucky had been courting Lucy Payne Washington, who had been a widow since the death of her first husband, George Steptoe Washington, in 1809. George's passing left Lucy a wealthy widow with three sons, and she spent much of her widowhood living in the White House, enjoying the love and warm surroundings of her sister and brother-in-law.

Under the impression that Lucy Washington had rejected his affections, the disconsolate justice headed back to his home in Lexington, but he was soon intercepted by a fast rider, who caught up with him at Lancaster, Pennsylvania. Lucy had changed her mind. The wedding was on again! The decision had been difficult for Lucy, who was of two minds about the chance to remarry, which meant leaving her home at Harewood and her family.[35] Dolley had her own mixed feelings because the marriage would mean that her beloved sister would leave to live at the far western edge of the United States. She wrote to her sister, Anna, "the Brother we shall acquire as a Supreme Judge he is oblidged, to come here for 2 months every winter & he binds himself to bring her to her friends when she pleases to come.... Lucy is in deep distress & you may suppose that my greaf is not slight—My nights are miserable & so are my days."[36] At a quiet family ceremony, the president gave the bride away on March 29, 1812. It was the first wedding to be held in the White House. The next day, the bridal couple headed for Harewood, where they picked up Lucy's sons for the trip to Pittsburgh, and the great adventure of floating down the Ohio River to their new Kentucky home.[37]

There were other, more constant, tugs on Dolley's heartstrings. One of the most vexing problems the new First Lady had to deal with was the unending stream of patronage-seekers and others who attempted to exploit their connections—if any— with her. Friends, relatives, acquaintances, and complete strangers all had a common goal: to obtain Dolley's assistance. Many people were simple and straightforward, asking only that Dolley put in a good word for a relative seeking a federal job. Others sought to gain commercial advantage through her endorsement. The most desperate were people who had encountered tragedy in their lives, had forsaken all hope, and now turned to the First Lady because they had nowhere else to go for aid.

A typical petition for help came from Samuel Todd, a nephew from her first marriage. Samuel, the son of James Todd, Dolley's former brother-in-law, lived under the dark cloud of his father, who embezzled more than $3,000 from the Philadelphia Bank and fled to Georgia, never to reappear, leaving his family in humiliation. Dolley wrote to him, "Nothing would gratify me more than to be of use in promoteing your wishes & your good. Independent of my love for you and your Mother & every individuel of your family I feel truly anxious for the welfare of you all." Samuel had good luck. Dolley was able to help him find a job as a clerk in the Navy Department.[38] However, she was not always successful. She sought to obtain posts for her cousin, Isaac Coles, and her brother, John Coles Payne, with the U.S. legation in Paris, but failed.[39]

In desperation, Patsy Jefferson Randolph pleaded with Dolley to help her nephew, Beverley, obtain a clerkship so that he could help support the family. Patsy wrote, "you have no doubt heard of the total ruin of David M. Randolph. he is himself gone to England upon a scheme so little likely to succeed, that nothing but dispair could have suggested it. his family in the mean time entirely destitute."[40] Patsy went on to say that her sister, Mary (Molly) Randolph, who had married her cousin, David Mead Randolph, U.S. Marshal of Virginia, was destitute after her husband's bankruptcy. Molly was forced to open a boardinghouse to make ends meet, a fate Dolley knew all too well from her own mother's experience. Whether Dolley was able to secure a clerkship for Beverley Randolph is not known.

What must have been similarly distressing to Dolley was a June 24, 1809, letter from Theodosia Burr Alston, the beloved daughter of former vice president Aaron Burr. "You may, perhaps, be surprised at receiving a letter from one with whom you have had so little intercourse for the last few years," she wrote. "But your surprise will cease when you recollect that my Father, once your Friend, is now in exile; and that the President only can restore him to me & to his country."[41] Using an assumed name, Burr had fled to Europe in the summer of 1806 to escape his creditors and, he hoped, to find support abroad for his schemes to conquer Mexico. By 1809, he was destitute and *persona non grata* in most of Europe. In the United States, he was technically a fugitive from justice, as he had jumped bail and left the country, failing to appear for trial in an Ohio federal court on local charges relating to his western conspiracy.

Theodosia dearly hoped that her father's friend, Dolley, could persuade Madison to pave the way for Burr's return. She received the bad news three months after her request; her plea had been tactfully declined. She wrote to her half-brother, Frederick Prevost, "The long expected answer from Mrs. Madison was such as reason & experience unmixed with hope might have led us to suppose it. She expresses great affection for me, calling me her 'precious friend,' pays me some compliments badly teared; & regrets that Mr. Madison finds it impossible to gratify my wishes &c."[42]

Some of the requests that Dolley received were much less grave than those of Patsy Randolph or Theodosia Alston. Her status as a national tastemaker led a steady stream of people to her door, all looking for an endorsement for their products. One was Joseph Milligan, a publisher, renowned bookbinder, and owner of a circulating library in Georgetown. He wrote to Dolley in 1809, enclosing a novel for her to read. Then he made his pitch. "J. Milligan has now in the press Tales of Fashionable Life by Miss [Maria] Edgworth which he intends to offer amongst his friends for subscription [price to Subscribers ... 2 Dollars] if Mrs. Madison should think fit to begin the list he has no doubt [that] most of the Ladies would follow her Example."[43] Dolley's response has not survived.

John Jacob Astor, a man who would play a large part in Dolley's future, also regarded her as a trendsetter. Astor, who had cultivated strong political connections with the Madison administration, was a millionaire by 1807, thanks to his success in the international fur trade. To promote his products, the clever businessman enlisted Dolley as a fashion model.

"I have taken the liberty of sending a Box to the care of M[r]. Henry Payson of Baltimore, addressed to you, containing a Muff & Tippet made of Silver Fox Skins, the produce & Manufacture of our own Country," he wrote. "The American Fur Company, an infant Establisment in this City, request, that you will be so obliging as to wear it from Motives of Patriotism, and to give encouragement to the Manufactures of our Country, by introducing and giving example, which I know your goodness will incline you to do."[44]

Dolley was happy to oblige and responded three weeks later, "Mrs. Madison presents her best respects and thanks to her friend Mr. Astor, & begs the favor of him, to assure the American Fur company, of her grateful acceptance of the beautiful Muff & Tippet, she has lately received from them."[45]

The red velvet and gold brocade tunic from the Bey of Tunis, c. 1805

Even before Madison became president, Dolley received some astonishingly beautiful and highly exotic fashion gifts. In 1805, while Madison was secretary of state, Tobias Lear, U.S. consul general to Algiers, sent her a burnoose—a long cloak with a hood, worn by Arabs and Moors—and a pair of Turkish slippers.[46] At the turn of the nineteenth century, when Jefferson took office as president, the Bey of Tunis, the Dey of Algiers, and other rulers of the Barbary States on the north coast of Africa extorted a hefty fee from any nation that wanted to conduct business in the Mediterranean. If a country did not pay this annual tribute, its vessels were subject to being attacked by Barbary pirates, who would seize the ships, imprison the crews, and hold them for ransom or sell them into slavery. The United States, along with most European nations, found it cheaper to pay the money rather than lose the right to trade in the Mediterranean or provoke the Barbary States into a costly war.

In November 1805, the Bey of Tunis sent his ambassador, Sali Sulliman Melli Melli, to the United States aboard a returning American warship, the frigate *Congress*, "to ascertain what sort of country America was, and if really such a nation as the United States existed."[47] He arrived wearing a vest embroidered with gold and a red skullcap. As a gesture of goodwill, he brought two Arabian horses for President Jefferson—one black, the other a bay mare—along with other presents.

Madison immediately directed that those gifts given to him should be sold and the proceeds deposited in the federal treasury, as the Constitution forbids government officials from accepting presents.[48] One of the presents was evidently a stunning red velvet tunic embroidered with nearly a pound of gold thread. Dolley was thoroughly unhappy when her husband instructed her to return the foreign gifts. Dejected but defiant, she wrote to her sister, Anna, "Mr. Madison has made me send in to the office my Bournouse which I cabbaged [concealed or appropriated] so snug. he was plaguy inquisitive about two other things, & I expect yet to be oblidged to refund."[49] The stunning red-and-gold tunic was one of the items she successfully cabbaged.[50]

Unfortunately, there were far graver concerns than successful levees or unwanted foreign tribute to bedevil President Madison. Two years after his inauguration, he had a residence decorated as splendidly as many in Europe, a wife enraptured with her roles as interior designer and hostess, a cabinet in total disarray, and two plates full of international crises. Unlike his predecessor, Jefferson, Madison had not chosen wise men of sound judgment and firm commitment to help run his government. As one commentator noted, "his cabinet was stocked with some bumbling incompetents and at least one avowed opponent."[51]

Madison's own party soon split over issues of trade and possible war with England, and, while trying to find a cabinet he could work with, he went through two secretaries of state, three attorneys general, and four secretaries each of the departments of the treasury, war, and navy in rapid succession. Intellectual genius though he was, Madison was not a strong political leader. Instead of consulting with Congress, he remained aloof and wrote pamphlets on issues and had them published in Samuel Harrison Smith's *National Intelligencer*. The president became so disliked that his personal secretary would not dare make the journey to Capitol Hill for fear of the epithets that would be directed at him.

During this period, a primary American dilemma was how to retain neutral status during the Napoleonic Wars. The nation was caught between superpowers Britain and France, each of which demanded that America cease all trade with the other. If America did not defend its rights, its very existence as a sovereign nation would come into question. If it asserted its rights too vigorously, war with either nation—or both—might be the result.

Since the end of the American Revolution, the British had been a thorn in the nation's side. The Jay Treaty had accomplished virtually nothing. In 1806, Napoléon banned British goods from being landed in Europe, and American ships were caught in the middle when the British responded with a blockade of France. Both Britain and France confiscated American vessels found to be dealing with the opposing country. Between 1803 and 1812, British captains impressed thousands of captured American seamen, forcing them to serve on British warships. In 1807, after the American ship refused to be boarded, the British warship *Leopard* fired on the U.S. ship *Chesapeake* only three miles off the Virginia coast, killing three Americans and wounding eighteen more.

Thomas Jefferson's Embargo Act of December 1807, designed to use "peaceful coercion" to force the British to cease impressing seamen and confiscating ships and cargo, backfired when it resulted in economic disaster for American merchants trading with England. Inside the United States, "war hawk" legislators, including Henry Clay and John C. Calhoun, fed up with the British insults and fearing that the British would incite Indian attacks in the upper Midwest, pressed for a declaration of war against England. Madison asked for the declaration on June 1, 1812, even though all of the Federalists opposed it. It quickly passed Congress and Madison, who "viewed the declaration with sadness and regret," signed it and formally declared war on England on June 18, 1812.[52]

The British were involved in a full-scale war with France and did not immediately send ships or troops across the Atlantic to fight. Nevertheless, British troops from Canada invaded U.S. territory in August 1812 and captured Ft. Mackinac in Michigan. There, U.S. attempts to invade Canada all failed in 1812, leaving the country distraught over what was now being called "Mr. Madison's War."

Dolley was worried not only about her husband, whose health was never vigorous, but also about her son Payne. He had finished his schooling in Baltimore, and Betsy Bonaparte and the Pattersons had turned him into a full-blown socialite, with polished manners in the ballroom and drawing room. He had, however, little ambition to become the junior James Madison. His academic performance at his preparatory school had been sub-par, and plans to send him to his stepfather's *alma mater*, Princeton, had to be scrapped. Payne was spending his time enjoying all the privileges of the White House, with no corresponding responsibilities. Madison's personal secretary, Edward Coles, fell ill in 1813, and Payne temporarily took his place. But Payne was much fonder of Washington's dinners and balls than of work, and he seemed headed down his uncle John C. Payne's self-destructive path.

The temptations of being the handsome, charming, socially polished son of the president were many and obvious. Dolley adored Payne, and both she and James sought ways to give him a sense of purpose. A window of opportunity opened — or so it seemed — in the spring of 1813. Czar Alexander I of Russia had offered to broker a peace treaty between the Americans and the British. Madison, realizing that the recent defeat of Napoléon by the British at Waterloo would soon free thousands of British troops for the war with America, appointed Secretary of the Treasury Albert Gallatin to head a peace commission and join John Quincy Adams, the U.S. minister in St. Petersburg. In order to have a bipartisan commission, Madison chose Federalist Senator James A. Bayard as a second commissioner. Bayard took along two aides, and Gallatin took his son. Payne spoke French, the language of the Czar's court, and although he did not want to leave the comforts of home and accompany the peace commission, his parents made the choice for him.

The handsome, six-foot-tall attaché, wearing the splendid, custom-made uniform of a third lieutenant of cavalry, took ship with the rest of the peace commission at New Castle on the Delaware River. In his pocket, Gallatin had his orders from Madison—and a bank draft for $800 to use on Payne's behalf. Amazingly, Gallatin also had *carte blanche* to draw on Madison's personal bank account if further funds were needed.[53] Why James Madison, a prudent man with full knowledge that he had an under-motivated, under-achieving, dissipated stepson on his hands, turned him loose on foreign soil with access to that much money may never be known.

As Payne's departure neared, Dolley must have cringed to think that he might suffer the same fate as her brother, John Coles Payne. While serving in Tripoli, John had run up great debts through his gambling and drinking. When his appointment in Tripoli ended in 1811, he fled back to the United States, where he was forced to sell everything he owned and move in with the Madisons. Dolley wrote to Anna Cutts, "I have paid 100$ for him since he got home & advanced 50$ for his current expences alass! I wish, often that he had been never in Triploa with [George] Davis—I know not what to wish—for the past, more than that he had allways been prudent & wise. he is now entirely dependent even if he sells his lands to advantage—but let me stop—you are at a distance & so is Lucy."[54] Dolley thought of the trip to Russia as a marvelous cultural enrichment for Payne, and beseeched him to write frequently. It was all that she could do.

Madison closed out his first term a troubled man with a worried wife. His apprehensions revolved around his concern for the pathetic state of American defenses, his belief that a British fleet would soon land soldiers on American soil, and his fear that his stepson would succumb to temptation while away from his parents' watchful eyes for six months to a year. In addition, Madison's party was fractious and the opposition, contentious. The Federalists did not put up a man to run against him; rather, they backed DeWitt Clinton, a New York Democratic-Republican—a man of Madison's own party—to run. Nevertheless, Madison prevailed, and after a low-key inauguration, he returned home to the White House.

On May 9, 1813, John Payne Todd, age twenty-one, sailed with Commissioners Gallatin and Bayard aboard the *Neptune,* bound for Russia. The parting must have been intensely painful for Dolley, who was now losing sight of her only remaining child, off on a long, dangerous sea voyage. A month later, her husband was severely afflicted with malaria, and she nursed him around the clock as he hovered between life and death. On July 29, an exhausted Dolley wrote to Hannah Gallatin, "You have heared no doubt, of the illness of my Husband but can have no idea of its extent, and the dispair, in which I attended his bed for nearly five weeks! even now, I watch over him, as I would an infant, so precarious is his convalessence— added to this, the disappointments & vexations, heaped upon him by party spirit."[55]

Buffeted as she was by personal tempests from all points of the compass, Dolley may well have invoked the ancient mariner's prayer, "God leash all storms!"

Painted by Stuart.   Eng.d by J.B. Longacre.

CHAPTER ELEVEN

From Hostess to Heroine

Chesapeake Bay, Maryland
Aboard the H.M.S. *Albion*
Tuesday, August 16, 1814

John S. Skinner was the first man to hear directly from the mouth of the enemy the dreaded words no one in Washington wanted to hear. And when he reported the chilling news to his superiors, few of them were convinced that what he had been told was true. Skinner's job was to negotiate the return of impressed American seamen. For more than a year, a British blockading squadron had been patrolling the North American coast between Charleston and Boston, sending landing parties ashore at will to loot villages and plantations and to intercept every ship it saw and force it to heave to for inspection. If the ship had legitimate business in America, and was not carrying contraband, that is, goods coming from or destined for France or French-controlled ports, it was allowed to pass. If it was carrying contraband, it was seized and escorted to Bermuda as a prize of war, where the ship and its cargo would be sold, or it was scuttled and sunk on the spot.

Vice Admiral Sir George Cockburn, the man who burned Washington

Either way, the crew would be impressed into the service of the Royal Navy.

By 1810, more than 5,000 men had been taken from American ships. The British eventually released 1,361 of these men after admitting that the seamen were Americans.[1] Skinner was negotiating with Rear Admiral Sir George Cockburn, a tall, lean, professional soldier with no use whatsoever for Americans. His powerful flagship, the seventy-four-gun *Albion*, was just one of the great, dark, menacing weapons of doom that lay waiting at anchor in Chesapeake Bay and at the mouths of the Patuxent and Potomac Rivers. The forty-two-year-old Cockburn, with his sunburned face and gold-trimmed hat, was the pride of the British navy. A veteran of many months at the North American station, Cockburn delighted in the raids, skirmishes, and battles he led. One historian succinctly described Cockburn's style of combat: "He fought war with gusto, and he played very, very rough."[2] He was also so despised for burning and looting settlements along the banks of the Chesapeake that an American had offered a reward of "$1,000 for the admiral's head and $500 for each of his ears."[3]

When Skinner concluded his negotiations and left the admiral's flagship that day, he asked casually what might lie in the future. Cockburn's reply sent a chill down his spine. The man in the imposing, black, dress uniform looked him in the eye and said, "I believe, Mr. Skinner, that Mr. Madison will have to put on his armour and fight it out."[4]

A well-chosen legion of British spies, aided by captured American sailors and local Americans who opposed the war, had provided Cockburn and his superior, Admiral Sir Alexander Cochrane, commander of all forces in North America, with excellent intelligence about the region. The British had a good idea of the navigability of the Chesapeake Bay. They had soundings of its depth and accurate maps. However, instead of the immediate armed opposition the British expected, they experienced … nothing. Renegade guides had been easy to hire.[5] As soon as the fleet dropped anchor, small boats flying white flags came out from shore, filled with people offering to sell food, water, and beer to the invaders.

The naval officers were quickly able to verify that Washington was half empty and that it was poorly defended by a loose coalition of marginally trained, under-supplied, under-equipped militia units with no central command. Furthermore, the landscape was not intimidating, and the numerous farms and plantations between their anchorage and Washington offered ample sources of food and water. In short, Washington was a soft target: easily attacked, largely undefended. As the nation's capital, it offered enormous propaganda value. It was also the home port of the American navy, which could easily be bottled up in the shallow, narrow Patuxent River, where most of the ships lay at anchor at Pig Point.

The plan to occupy the Chesapeake Bay had been chosen by Admiral Cochrane before the fleet left England and was based on Admiral Cockburn's first-hand knowledge. Cochrane's orders from the Crown were explicit: destroy settlements along the coast, burn public buildings, humiliate the American government, and secure the subjugation of the United States. Admiral Cockburn had informed his commander, "I feel no hesitation in stating to you that I consider the town of Benedict in the Patuxent, to offer us the advantages for this purpose beyond any other spot within the United States.... Within forty-eight hours after the arrival in the Patuxent of such a force as you expect, the City of Washington might be possessed without difficulty or opposition of any kind."[6]

On August 1, 1814, Major General Robert Ross, commander of the British army units that would lead the fighting, finished loading his soldiers aboard transport ships and was piped aboard Admiral Cochrane's flagship, the *Tonnant*. With Cochrane's red flag flying from the foremast, the eighty-gun warship weighed anchor and sailed into the Atlantic, leading the convoy west. The invasion of America was on, and British warships filled the Chesapeake Bay less than three weeks later.

Immediately upon his return to Washington, John Skinner reported Admiral Cockburn's alarming statement to his superiors. President Madison took it seriously, but few others took it at face value. Cockburn was well known for his arrogance and disdain. No one thought that the huge fleet, which now numbered over fifty warships, would attack Washington City. As was the custom, a large part of the population had already left the city to escape the summer heat. Congress was adjourned, and the wealthy local planters were already away in the mountains or the spas of Virginia and New England or were making summer tours of Europe. Those who were left behind carried out their lives in the stifling, dusty heat, believing that the attack, if any, would certainly be launched on Baltimore, as the secretary of war, General Armstrong, firmly insisted. Others thought the target would be Annapolis.

At 9:00 a.m. on Friday, August 19, only three days after Skinner's conversation with Cockburn, the British fleet sailed up the Patuxent River. One of U.S. Commodore Joshua Barney's lookouts picked up a shocking piece of intelligence, which evidently had come from a nearby planter who was on good terms with Cockburn. The haughty admiral, it was said, planned to destroy Commodore Barney's flotilla in the Patuxent and "dine in Washington on Sunday."[7] Cockburn only missed his scheduled dinner engagement by four days.

By 2:00 that afternoon, a rider brought news of the invasion to the capital. Secretary of the Navy William Jones ordered the American fleet to move as far as possible upriver. If the worst came to pass, his orders to Commodore Barney were to burn the ships and pull their crews back into Washington City to fight at the U.S. Navy Yard. Given the size of the British fleet, and its total blockade of the river, the American navy was doomed.

Jones next put out calls to the militia units in the region, just as the city was learning that the main force of British troops had landed at Benedict, Maryland, on the west bank of the Patuxent, forty-five miles from Washington. Good news of a great victory arrived from Canada hours later: the British had

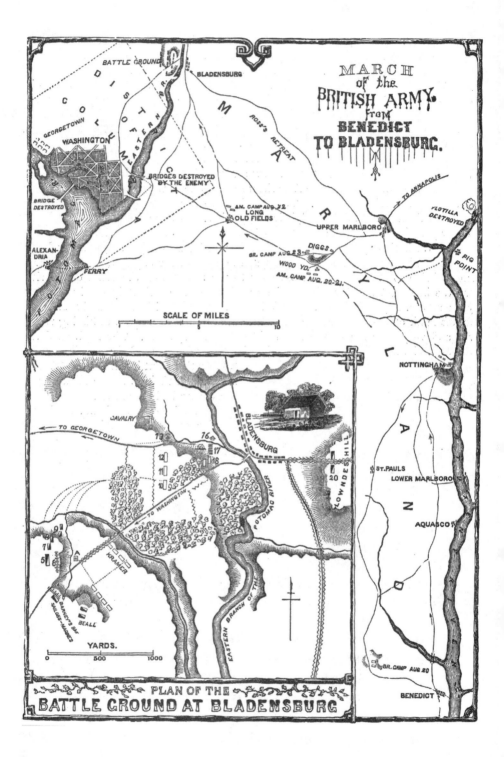

MARCH of the BRITISH ARMY from BENEDICT TO BLADENSBURG.

BATTLE GROUND

BLADENSBURG

DIST

COLUMBIA

GEORGETOWN

WASHINGTON

EASTERN BR.

ROSS'S RETREAT

BRIDGES DESTROYED BY THE ENEMY

BRIDGE DESTROYED

AM. CAMP AUG 22
LONG
OLD FIELDS

MARYLAND

TO ANNAPOLIS

FLOTILLA
DESTROYED

ALEXANDRIA

FERRY

BR. CAMP AUG 23

UPPER MARLBORO

DIGGS

WOOD YD.

AM. CAMP AUG. 20-21.

PIG
POINT

SCALE OF MILES

5   10

NOTTINGHAM

TO GEORGETOWN

CAVALRY

13

16

17

12

18

11

10

TO WASHINGTON

BLADENSBURG

POTOMAC RIVER

LOWNDES HILL

20

ST. PAULS

LOWER MARLBORO

9

7

5

KRAMER

BARNEY'S BAT

SAILORS MARINES

BEALL

EASTERN BRANCH OF THE

AQUASCO

YARDS.

0   500   1000

BR. CAMP AUG 20

PLAN OF THE
BATTLE GROUND AT BLADENSBURG

BENEDICT

been beaten back at Fort Erie. The militiamen were ecstatic, and vowed to do the same if the British attacked Washington. However, they had only to look around at the defenders of Washington to achieve a more realistic viewpoint.

The District's militia had immediately heeded Jones' call and assembled for duty at the foot of Capitol Hill on the night of August 19. "Perhaps it was in haste," wrote military historian Joseph Lord, "but they were never in worse shape. Some had no shoes, others lacked weapons. Captain John J. Stull's company of riflemen had not a rifle among them."[8] They were about to fight 4,500 of the best-equipped, best-trained, best-commanded soldiers in the Western world. The fight would pit raw militiamen against battle-hardened professional soldiers. Given the complete futility of the fight, it was perhaps just as well that the Americans had no idea what they were up against.

On August 20, Ross' and Cockburn's troops marched north, paralleling the Patuxent River. By the night of August 21, they had marched sixteen miles and camped at Nottingham. The next day it was six more miles north-northwest to Upper Marlboro, Maryland, where they received food and drink from Dr. William Beanes, a Scotsman, a Federalist, and a foe of the war. The invasion of the capital seemed imminent to both sides. And it was almost called off at the last moment.

As the sky lightened on Monday morning, August 22, Admiral Cockburn led a flotilla of fourteen large rowboats, each capable of holding forty to sixty men, up the shallow waters of the Patuxent. His objective was Pig Point, where he sought to corner Commodore Barney and destroy his anchored ships. He could see the commodore's flag flying from his topsail sloop, the *Scorpion*. Before Cockburn could land troops on the shore or fire a shot, smoke rose from Barney's ship, and there was a massive explosion. One by one, powder charges planted by the Americans on their ships were ignited, and within minutes, the disappointed invaders saw that there would be no U.S. Navy to fight, capture, or destroy. All but one warship was blown up, but the British captured thirteen merchant schooners, which lay upstream. The best of these ships were loaded with tobacco for shipping home as war prizes; unseaworthy schooners were torched. The British achieved the total destruction of the U. S. Navy at Pig's Point without a single shot being fired.

On the ground, the invaders had their work cut out for them. On Tuesday, August 23, they marched west past Long Old Fields, just six miles due east of Washington, where they met determined—but futile—resistance. All of the American troops had been massed at Bladensburg, Maryland, the site of the northernmost two bridges on the Eastern Branch of the Potomac River. President Madison and his advisors observed the situation and offered comments to the American commanders from a position scarcely a mile behind the likely line of battle. Because they were only a few miles from Washington, the American defenders knew that if they could not hold the bridges, the capital city was doomed. Madison conferred with Secretary of War John Armstrong and asked if he had any advice to give or plan to offer. Armstrong had none.

The night of August 23 was quiet. The only man with a mission that evening seemed to be Admiral Cockburn's aide, Lieutenant Scott. The young officer had been sent to advise Admiral Cochrane, at anchor off Benedict, that the U.S. Navy's ships at Pig's Point had been destroyed. He brought back to Cockburn the most astonishing orders: call off the invasion of Washington and return to the fleet. The point had been made. The greatest part of the American fleet had been destroyed, a greater goal than had been anticipated. Cockburn was on no account to proceed any further. Instead, he should turn his troops and head back to re-embark at Benedict. Cockburn was incensed. He wanted to smell the total humiliation of the Americans in the smoke from its capital.

That same evening, Madison was back in the White House, having dinner after a long day in the field. Colonel George Minor of the Tenth Virginia militia appeared at the door to plead with the president for arms but was told by Madison that munitions were the responsibility of the secretary of war. Undaunted, Minor tracked down Secretary Armstrong at his boardinghouse up Pennsylvania Avenue, and he asked again. Armstrong agreed, but said that he would not take action that night. There would be adequate time to get Minor's troops armed the next day. Minor grumbled that this indifference "could only lead to losing the city."[9]

Dolley Madison was more well liked by the troops than was her husband. Madison's servant, Paul Jennings, who showed unbounded admiration for her, said, "She was beloved by every body in Washington, white and colored. Whenever soldiers marched by, during the war, she always went out and invited them to take wine and refreshments, giving them liberally of the best in the house."[10]

෧෨ஃ෪

Wednesday morning, August 24, 1814
Bladensburg village, five miles from the White House

At first light, drums rolled in the British camp. The troops fell in, and excitement rippled through the ranks. They were professional soldiers, trained to fight. The scorching heat had taken its toll, but the line had been drawn at Bladensburg, and it was time for a battle. In the early dawn, fire from the burning of the upper river crossing, known as Stoddert's Bridge, lit up the sky. The fire had been ordered by U. S. General William Henry Winder, who torched the bridge to deny the British easy access to Washington. Because the water was deeper at the remaining southern bridge at Bladensburg, it would be nearly impossible for the British troops to ford the river at that point. The invaders would be forced to cross the bridge, thereby funneling them into a narrower field of fire and making them more vulnerable to American artillery.

Winder then decided to plant explosives under the southern bridge, with orders to destroy the structure if the British advanced that far. He quickly made his way to the Navy Yard, where he woke up Captain Thomas Tingey, commander of the yard, and Commodore Barney. Winder did not leave until Tingey promised to send several kegs of gunpowder to the bridge immediately. He then rode back to bridge, reaching it, totally exhausted, about 3:00 a.m. A few hours later, after only an hour's sleep, Winder gave the order: the American forces would make a stand at the Bladensburg Bridge. The various units pulled back to the west (Washington) side of the river and dug in. Winder caught a few more hours of sleep.

Early that morning, Admiral Cockburn received the letter from his commander that made his blood boil. Cockburn and Ross were to pull back their troops immediately and head for the fleet at Benedict. There was to be no attack on Washington City. Cockburn was stunned, and he handed the note to General Ross. To Ross, an order was an order, and there was nothing to debate. Cockburn fumed. "No," he said. "We can't do that. We are too far advanced to talk retreat."[11]

The two veteran officers left their tent and conversed intently. If they disobeyed orders and lost the battle, they would both return to England in leg irons. If they disobeyed orders and were successful, the disobedience would probably be far outweighed by the magnitude of their accomplishments. These two sober, professional, military men considered their orders, their mission, and their training. They decided to attack.

On August 24 at daybreak, Madison embraced his fearful wife, kissed her, and told her that he and his officers would be back for a late dinner, probably about four o'clock instead of the usual time, three. Then he walked out of the White House, took the reigns of his horse from Paul Jennings, and headed off to the anticipated battlefield at the Bladensburg Bridge. He was accompanied by General Armstrong, General Winder, Colonel Monroe, other cabinet members, and several friends.[12]

At about the same time, the British broke camp and headed off on a fifteen-mile march to Bladensburg. The morning was cool, but after five hours, the sun was cooking the soldiers inside their wool uniforms, and many dropped from heat prostration. The battle broke out between noon and one o'clock, when a disciplined column of British regulars marched over the crest of Lowndes Hill. In plain sight of the American defenders, they headed directly for the bridge. Through a telescope from the American side, Madison's cabinet officers could see British soldiers falling from the effects of the patriots' cannon fire, but then, the infernal howling of explosive Congreve rockets roared over the heads of the Americans and into the soldiers' ranks.

Madison, watching from a position about a mile behind the bridge, wisely decided that experienced military commanders should direct the fighting, and he motioned to General Armstrong and Colonel James Monroe to ride back with him. Just then, the British troops stormed the bridge, and soon a flood of red-and-blue uniforms streamed across it. One witness wrote that the British "moved as steadily and undismayed as though there were no opposition."[13]

At the river, the American defenders fell back. Several times they tried to muster their troops and cannon fire, but it was soon hopeless. They turned and started to flee, disappearing into the trees and running across the fields. Their heels and the hooves of their horses kicked up such a mighty cloud of dust that it could be seen from any high point in the capital. Washington's last hope had just dissolved in a panicked mob of fleeing soldiers.

When the American lines broke, and the militiamen started their hasty retreat, Madison, Monroe, and the rest of the president's party retreated to Washington to regroup and make new plans. Henry Adams, a Madison biographer, described the scene:

> The President left Bladensburg battlefield toward two o'clock. He had already ridden in the early morning from the White House to the navy-yard, and thence to Bladensburg, — a distance of eight miles at the least. He had six miles to ride, on a very hot August day, over a road encumbered by fugitives. He was sixty-three years

D. P. Madison

old, and had that day already been in the saddle since eight o'clock in the morning, probably without food. Soon after three o'clock he reached the White House, where all was confusion and flight.[14]

For Madison, it was a complete disaster. For Cockburn and Ross, it was a triumph. Their soldiers and sailors had defeated an American force twice their size.[15] The admiral and the general would go home in glory, not in irons.

⤳⤺

Wednesday afternoon, August 24, 1814
Inside the White House

About three o'clock that afternoon,[16] a frenzied James Smith, the president's messenger, galloped up to the White House, his horse frothing at the mouth, panting from the heat and exhaustion. Smith ran inside without bothering to knock and thrust a paper into Dolley's hand. The message was simple: "Run for your life or be taken prisoner by the British." She knew the directive was final. The remaining citizens and defenders of Washington were evacuating in frenzied droves. Even the one hundred soldiers who were supposed to defend the White House with their lives had evaporated into the dust, along with their commander, Colonel Carberry, who had not bothered to say good-bye to the First Lady or ask if he could assist with her departure.

She was overwhelmed with the choices that faced her. What to take? What to leave behind? Where to go? How to get there? The decisions she made would forever define Dolley Madison as a woman of strength and honor. On that searing-hot, dust-saturated day, she proved herself to be so totally devoted to her country that she was willing to sacrifice every-thing precious to her in order to save as many of the nation's treasures as possible.

The time was critically short, help was scarce, and the means of transportation was even scarcer. The only other people left in the building that afternoon included the White House *major domo*, "French John" Sioussat; Madison's fifteen-year-old mulatto body servant, Paul Jennings; a maid, Sukey; a cook; Thomas McGraw, the Irish gardener; John Freeman (an enslaved butler), his wife, and his child; and Joe Bolin, a coachman. The treasures of the nation, housed in a building that the British troops—now only minutes away—had sworn to burn to the ground, were entrusted to Dolley. She was the only person empowered to choose what would be preserved and what would be defaced, stolen, or destroyed by the enemy.

The first bewildering choice was what to take and what to leave behind. Dolley was the sole guardian of the public trust. She wrote to her sister: "I am accordingly ready; I have pressed as many cabinet papers into trunks as to fill one carriage; our private property must be sacrificed, as it is impossible to procure wagons for its transportation. I am determined not to go myself until I see M^r. Madison safe, and he can accompany me, as I hear of much hostility towards him. Disaffection stalks around us."[17] In other words, the citizens were already blaming Madison for the defeat.

Dolley immediately decided that the single most important item in the White House was Gilbert Stuart's magnificent portrait of President George Washington. It was one of four full-length "Lansdowne portraits," so named because the first had been commissioned in 1796 for Lord Shelburne, first Marquis of Lansdowne, a British admirer of Washington. The portrait had been purchased by the government in 1800 and hung in the state dining room. Preparing it for safe transport proved to be a nearly impossible challenge. It was enormous: 106 inches high by 61 inches wide. Its canvas was stretched across a wooden stretcher frame, wrapped around the stretcher, and secured with hundreds of furniture tacks. The stretcher was, in turn, placed inside a large, heavy, wooden gilt frame, which, because of its size and weight, was bolted to the wall instead of being hung from wires.

D. P. Madison

By now, the smell of gunpowder saturated the White House. In her letter to Anna Cutts, Dolley described the frantic scene:

> Our kind friend, Mr. [Charles] Carroll, has come to hasten my departure, and is in a very bad humor with me because I insist on waiting until the large picture of Gen. Washington is secured, and it requires to be unscrewed from the wall. This process was found too tedious for these perilous moments; I have ordered the frame to be broken, and the canvass taken out it is done, and the precious portrait placed in the hands of two gentlemen of New York, for safe keeping. And now, dear sister, I must leave this house, or the retreating army will make me a prisoner in it, by filling up the road I am directed to take. When I shall again write you, or where I shall be tomorrow, I cannot tell!![18]

George Washington,
by Gilbert Stuart, 1797

As she mentioned in her letter, when unscrewing the huge frame from the wall proved to be too time-consuming, Dolley had French John and Thomas McGraw break the frame apart with an axe and free the canvas on its stretcher frame.[19] One story tells that Dolley stood by with a carving knife, ready to cut the picture out of its stretcher frame if the portrait could not otherwise be saved.[20] A tale later surfaced that French John had cut the canvas loose and rolled it up, but that never happened.[21]

By good fortune, two New Yorkers, Jacob Barker, a financier, and Robert G. L. DePeyster, a merchant and friend of James Monroe, arrived at the White House with a cart, just in time to help French John remove the portrait from the wall. "Save that picture," Dolley said to them. "Save that picture, if possible; if not possible, destroy it."[22] She knew that the portrait would be a choice morsel for the British troops, and wanted to make certain that they could not hold it up as an object of ridicule.

The only portrait that the British were able to steal was a miniature of Dolley, which was returned to the White House in 1827.[23] The miniature had been acquired "as a prize of war," under circumstances "the citizens of the U.S. will ever regret," wrote Christopher Hughes, a friend of Payne Todd (with whom he was then in Brussels), to S. Gardiner, a British soldier who was evidently in contact with Todd. Hughes wished to have the miniature returned to the Madisons. He wrote Gardiner, "Intrinsically, the portrait, as an object of art had little value; and therefore you *lose* nothing; only *do not lose* an opportunity of doing a chivalrous thing in a gallant and chivalrous manner." On November 17, 1827, Gardiner assured Hughes that the portrait would be returned. The preservation of this correspondence suggests that the miniature was repatriated to Todd, but no one knows how Gardiner originally acquired it; whether or not Payne received it, and, if so, what he did with it.[24]

As Ann Marie Thornton, the Madisons' former neighbor from F Street, later wrote, she was "*escorted* out of town by our defeated troops." Along the way, she saw "General Washington's picture, & a cart load of goods from the president's House in Company." This would have been the cart provided and accompanied by Robert DePeyster and Jacob Barker. If the portrait had been cut from its stretcher frame and rolled up, Mrs. Thornton could not have identified it. Its two guardians took the portrait to a private house in nearby Maryland, where it remained for a few weeks until the danger had passed.

D. P. Madison

Then it was returned to government custody. It was reinstalled in the White House in 1817, after the executive mansion was rebuilt.[25]

In 1848, the Madisons' friend, Charles Carroll, claimed that he had saved the portrait, and someone else accused Dolley of trying to steal credit for the patriotic act. Dolley wrote DePeyster, "I acted thus because of my respect for General Washington—not that I felt a desire to gain laurels; but should there be a merit in remaining an hour in danger of life and liberty to save the likeness of anything, the merit in this case belongs to me."[26] An enslaved White House servant, Nace or Nance Rhodes, had the same selfless motives as Dolley. In 1815, he was paid $5.00 for returning "urns, branch candlesticks, waiters, etc." that he had removed for safekeeping on the day of the invasion.[27] Had he acted for personal gain, he could have sold the fine silver for much more than the insignificant $5.00 reward.

Stuart's portrait of Dolley was never in danger, as it was hanging at Montpellier at the time of the burning. Some have credited Dolley with being the savior of the Declaration of Independence, but that honor goes to Stephen Pleasanton, a brave clerk in the secretary of state's office. Despite the scorn of Secretary of War Armstrong, who scoffed at any danger of invasion, Pleasanton and other clerks "stuffed bags with the Declaration of Independence, the Constitution, international treaties, and the correspondence of George Washington."[28] These documents were hidden in Leesburg, Virginia, until the British departed and were then, as was the Washington portrait, returned to federal custody.[29]

The history of the frantic afternoon of August 24 survives in scattered accounts by a number of witnesses, some of which conflict on minor points. However, all of these stories taken together paint a picture of imminent danger, absolute terror, and immense pressure to do the right thing and place the public good above personal needs. Later that afternoon, Dolley again wrote to Anna Cutts, stating that she had "pressed as many cabinet papers into trunks as would fill one carriage," adding that "our private property must be sacrificed, as it is impossible to procure wagons for its transportation."[30]

The evidence of danger increased by the minute. The next state treasure to be saved—an incomprehensible choice by some standards and perfectly logical by others—was the magnificent set of red velvet drapes from the oval drawing room, which Dolley had personally chosen. French John fetched a ladder, took down the drapes, and he and Dolley hurriedly stuffed them into trunks and loaded them aboard Dolley's carriage. The curtains were later stored at the Madisons' temporary residence after the war, but their history after that point has been lost.[31]

Next, wrote Paul Jennings, "Mrs. Madison ordered her carriage, and passing through the dining-room, caught up what silver she could crowd into her old-fashioned reticule [a netted handbag], and then jumped into the chariot with her servant girl Sukey, and Daniel (probably Charles) Carroll, who took charge of them."[32] Dolley's most complete inventory of what she saved was recorded in a letter she wrote on December 13, 1814, to her friend, Mary Elizabeth Latrobe:

> Two hours before the enemy entered the city, I left the house where Mr. Latrobe's elegant taste had been so justly admired, and where you and I had so often wandered together, and on that *very day* I sent out the silver (nearly all)—the velvet curtains and Gen. Washington's picture, the cabinet papers, a few books, and the small clock—left everything else belonging to the publick, our own valuable stores of every description, a part of my clothes, and all my servants' clothes, &c, &c., in short, it would fatigue you to read the list of *my* losses, or an account of the general dismay, or particular distresses of your acquaintance.[33]

A small piece of good luck came Dolley's way, and about three o'clock that afternoon, she wrote to her sister, "At this late hour a wagon has been procured, I have had it filled with the [silver] plate and most valuable portable articles be-longing to the house; whether it will reach its destination; the Bank of Maryland, or fall into the hands of British soldiery, events must determine."[34] This must have been the wagon used by DePeyster and Barker.

Then the few people remaining in the White House began to leave. The next person to depart was John Freeman, who tied a feather bed to a coachee and departed, with his wife, child, and a servant in tow.[35] The last person to evacuate the president's mansion was French John. Before doing so, he carefully hid some gold and silver and then put buckets of water and wine outside for the thirsty American soldiers who might stop by. When he left the building, he was carry-ing an odd piece of cargo to safety. Knowing how dearly Dolley valued it, he did for Mrs. Madison what she in good con-science could not do for herself. He took Dolley's pet macaw, Polly, to John Tayloe's Octagon House, which had been taken over as the temporary official residence of the French minis-ter, Louis-Barbé-Charles Séurier. There, French John entrusted the bird to the minister's cook.[36] This act made Polly a posses-sion of the French minister, and thereby afforded the animal diplomatic immunity from harm by the British. Dolley had shown her devotion to the nation by risking her life to save the nation's treasures instead of her own. Now French John, also in the midst of imminent danger, showed his devotion to the Madisons by risking his own life to save Dolley's beloved pet.

One more item made the list of surviving White House treasures, but Dolley was probably not even aware that it had been taken to safety. In fact, the squirreling-away was prob-ably also the work of French John. We only know of it from a brief note that Dolley wrote in the fall of 1814 to Minerva Denison Rogers, wife of Commodore John Rogers. It was sent in thanks for a courtesy paid to Dolley just after the burning. It read, "I beg you and my estimable friend, your husband, to accept a demijohn [large bottle] of pure wine saved from the President's House the morning of its destruction."[37]

Having saved the First Lady's macaw, French John had returned to the White House for a final inspection. There, the dedicated and sophisticated Frenchman might well have chosen a fine bottle from the White House wine cellar so that his president and the First Lady would have something to celebrate with in the better times that he hoped lay ahead. In any case, he carefully closed all the windows, locked the front door, and left the key to the empty White House with a servant at the nearby residence of Andrei Dashkov, the Russian minister, who, wisely, had already fled to Philadelphia with his wife, Eugenia.

As soon as Dolley and the other White House staff departed, Paul Jennings noted that "although the British were expected every minute, they did not arrive for some hours; in the mean time, a rabble, taking advantage of the confusion, ran all over the White House, and stole lots of silver and whatever they could lay their hands on."[38]

About 4:30 in the afternoon, about half an hour after Dolley raced off to Georgetown, Madison and his counselors reached the White House. Having escaped the British onslaught on horseback, Madison had transferred to a carriage and was now rolling along Pennsylvania Avenue, accompanied by Richard Rush, General John Mason, Charles Carroll, and several other aides. The fleeing crowd murmured, "There goes the President."[39]

When Madison and his party walked into the White House, a bizarre sense of suspended animation pervaded the building. Although the British were expected to literally burst through the door at any time, Madison and his party paused to rest. Jacob Barker and Robert DePeyster were still collecting a few valuables. "For more than an hour," a historian wrote, "the group sat around exchanging experiences. It was an odd interlude, with the British just over the horizon and the city clearly doomed, and can best be explained by the sixty-three-year-old president's desperate need for rest after his full day in the saddle, hounded by disaster."[40]

Madison's illusions about yeomen volunteers, fighting for their homeland, besting trained, professional soldiers had been dashed. The father of the Constitution told Barker, "I could never have believed that so great a difference existed between regular troops and a militia force, if I had not witnessed the scenes of this day."[41] Looking back on the day's events some time later, Barker was more impressed with the heroism of the president's wife than with the president's troops. He later named one of his merchant ships the *Lady Madison*.[42]

Then it was time to go. A half hour after the men departed, Mordecai Booth, chief clerk at Captain Tingey's Navy Yard—and one of the last committed defenders of the city— knocked on the door of the White House. He yelled for French John, hoping the president was inside, able to tell them what to do. The door was locked; the house was dark; and there was no reply. The silence and the darkness made Booth's blood run cold. He realized that the capital of his country had been completely abandoned by its government.[43]

The British marched into the nearly deserted city at dusk, led by General Ross himself. To a military man, Washington City was a bizarre scene. The streets and houses were deserted, save for roaming cows and pigs. The advance unit

The Capture and Burning of Washington

consisted of Ross, Cockburn, and a small portion of the fresh, rested, 1,460-man Third Brigade. The troops headed down Maryland Avenue, directly toward the Capitol, seeing little but nevertheless wary. When they were 200 yards short of the Capitol, a volley of shots rang out from a darkened private home. Ross' horse was shot out from under him. The British immediately retaliated, but by the time they entered the residence, it was empty. Cockburn ordered his men to fire Congreve rockets into the house, and it was soon in flames. The troops had firm orders: destroy public buildings and protect all private property — unless it held arms or was being used by the enemy to attack His Majesty's forces. The greatest flames and explosions, however, came from Captain Tingey's Navy Yard, which Tingey himself had ordered destroyed. It was 8:20 p.m.[44]

At the Capitol, the Third Brigade formed a line and, on command, fired a volley into the windows of the building. After they battered down the doors, the wondering soldiers explored the great halls. Then they went to work. In the House and Senate chambers, they stacked desks, chairs, and bookcases into a tall pile and added large quantities of gunpowder from their rockets. Then they fired more rockets into the pile, and the flames did their job. The clock above the Speaker's chair read 10:00 as it started to melt.[45] The next stop was the White House.

&&&

Wednesday evening, August 24, 1814
Inside the White House

Admiral Cockburn personally led a detachment of 150 men up Pennsylvania Avenue at 10:30 p.m. They stopped at the boardinghouse of Mrs. Barbara Suter, where they ordered a meal to be served to Cockburn's staff when they returned, and they moved on. Because Cockburn was uncertain whether

Dolley Madison was in the White House or not, a messenger was sent to offer her safe passage to the place of her choice.

Many years later, according to Pennsylvania Congressman Charles J. Ingersoll, a friend of the Madisons, Dolley confirmed to him that British troops had indeed offered to escort her to a place of safety. They allegedly also offered the president the option of saving the public buildings by paying a ransom. Ingersoll stated that Dolley rejected both offers "with contempt."[46] It was likely that she was speaking solely for herself, for the president was not with her to speak on the subject of a ransom. There is no known evidence that Dolley ever spoke with British troops before or during her flight from the White House, so we can only speculate on the events that she described.

With the White House empty, there was no further need for social amenities. Cockburn's troops entered the president's mansion and were amazed at the dinner waiting for them. Captain Harry Smith thought the cold cuts excellent and the Madeira, "super-excellent."[47] The troops hoisted their crystal goblets and raised a toast to "the health of the Prince Regent and success to His Majesty's arms by sea and land."

Roger Chew Weightman, a Washington bookseller that the British had pressed into service as a guide, was forced to sit in a chair in the White House and drink a toast "to Jemmy," as Cockburn liked to refer to the president. Then the admiral invited Weightman to choose a souvenir of the night. Weightman asked for something expensive. Cockburn said that only trinkets could be liberated. Valuables were to be consigned to the White House funeral pyre. The admiral chose one of Madison's tri-cornered hats and a cushion from Dolley's chair. One British soldier chose a small medicine chest belonging to the president; another, Madison's sword.

One man who was in a good position to observe the burning was Captain Harry Smith, junior adjutant to General Ross. He was one of many fortunate soldiers to dine at the White House that night. He wrote, "We found supper all ready, which was sufficiently cooked without more fire, and which many of us speedily consumed, unaided by fiery elements and drank some very good wine also. I shall never forget the destructive majesty of the flames as the torches were applied to the beds, curtains, etc. Our sailors were artists at the work."[48]

Another diner described the meal in much the same manner:

> You will readily imagine, that these preparations were beheld, by a party of hungry soldiers, with no indifferent eye. An elegant dinner, even though considerably over-dressed, was a luxury to which few of them, at least for some time back, had been accustomed; and which, after the dangers and fatigues of the day, appeared particularly inviting. They sat down to it, therefore, not indeed in the most orderly manner, but with countenances which would not have disgraced a party of aldermen at a civic feast; and having satisfied their appetites with fewer complaints than would have probably escaped their rival *gourmands*, and partaken pretty freely of the wines, they finished by setting fire to the house that had so liberally entertained them.[49]

After sitting at the president's table, eating his food, and drinking his wine, a soldier collected all the plates and silver into the tablecloth and hauled everything off. The next step was to pile everything combustible into the oval drawing room. Nothing was held back. Into the pile went all of Latrobe's Greek-influenced furniture, the red velvet cushions, the pianoforte, and even the guitar. Then the invaders added a large dose of gunpowder, fired a Congreve rocket into the huge pile, and voila! A royal bonfire. The White House was consumed by flames in less than an hour. Every scrap of wood was burnt; the roof disintegrated onto the top floor; the top floor collapsed onto the bottom. Miraculously, the exterior stone walls and some of the vertical partitions survived.

Madison was almost taken prisoner by the British during the invasion. Lieutenant Beauchamp Colclough Urquhart wrote of that evening, "Before [in front of] the door there was a coach, into which some of the movables had been placed by the servants, but which they had abandoned. The soldiers amused themselves, by knocking the coach to pieces with the but-ends of their muskets. If there had been any cavalry on the spot, Madison might have been taken a prisoner, for the officers of the 85th [Regiment, King's Light Infantry] distinctly saw him mount his horse when the militia took to their heels. He was accompanied by two others. Mr. Urquhart has got Madison's fine dress sword, which he took out of his house."[50]

Cockburn's men then went on to the long, brick Treasury Building. The troops were disgusted when they found no money, only books and ledgers, which burned brightly, as did the rest of the building. By midnight, the fires in Washington were burning so fiercely that they could easily be seen in Baltimore, forty miles away.[51] Then the heavens opened up in an enormous thunderstorm, and rain dampened the fires, preventing them from spreading to the city at large.

The next morning, August 25, Cockburn's troops finished destroying what had been spared the previous night. What the Americans had not blown up, the British put to the torch. On Pennsylvania Avenue, they set fire to the brick building that housed the departments of state, war, and the navy. Through the ingenious arguments of Dr. William Thornton, the Office of Patents was saved. Not so the office of the *National Intelligencer*. Because of pleas from neighbors, who feared that a fire would spread to their houses, Cockburn agreed to destroy the newspaper office through other means. The presses were demolished and the type thrown out the window. Cockburn specifically instructed the troops to destroy all the *c*'s so that his name could not be maligned.

In the midst of this British wave of destruction, things turned ominous. Thunder sounded, lightning flashed, and the sky became the color of India ink. The storm of all storms hit Washington like an omen. In addition, a huge explosion, resulting from the improper detonation of American powder stores, killed dozens of men.

Cockburn realized that his job was done. He sent officers to spread rumors that he was about to lead his troops in a dozen different directions. Then he set an 8:00 p.m. curfew for all Americans. Secrecy was of overriding importance. No one must know of the impending British retreat. By midnight, the invaders were back at Bladensburg, and they quickly made their march all the way back to Benedict. By August 30, the British troops were sleeping on clean sheets in their ships. The battle for Washington was complete.

❧

About sundown on August 24, approximately six hours after the battle of Bladensburg ended, Paul Jennings walked to the Georgetown ferry, where he found the president surrounded by the men he had left with earlier that morning. These men now served as Madison's personal bodyguards. Such was the state of the national defenses that there was no military guard of any kind for the president of the United States, in his own capital city, while under direct attack by a foreign army. The ferry soon arrived, and the president and his escorts were rowed across the Potomac. Leaving the servants to fend for themselves, the president's party went elsewhere to confer and returned a short time later.

❧

The first person to see Dolley in flight was a Miss Brown, who wrote that she, her mother, and her sister saw "Mrs. Madison in her carriage flying full speed through Georgetown, accompanied by an officer carrying a drawn sword." Dolley headed first for the Georgetown home of Secretary of the Navy William Jones. She found him there, having completed the destruction of the U.S. Navy Yard to prevent its capture by the British. Jones and Navy Department clerk Edward Duvall

D. P. Madison

Belle Vue, Charles Carroll's House, now the Dumbarton House, Washington

joined Mrs. Madison and proceeded to Belle Vue, the Georgetown home of Charles Carroll, where other Jones and Carroll family members had rendezvoused.[52] There, Jones received a message that he could meet Madison in Georgetown at the Foxall's Foundry, the largest manufacturer of munitions in the country. At about five o'clock, Jones set off with Dolley, her entourage, Carroll, and Duvall in search of the president, somewhere in Georgetown or on the road that paralleled the Potomac.

In a memoir describing the chaos of August 23-24, a Mr. Williams recorded the following after seeing the cloud of dust from the fleeing American troops. "About three o'clock the white flag was floating from the tops of windows of several private dwellings in the city, and a few minutes after our troops entered Georgetown in full flight, while women and children were everywhere running through the streets almost frantic, and crying and screaming." Williams had the foresight to place a small boat on the Potomac, ready to take him and his family four miles upriver, where a cart was waiting to take them to Loudoun County, Virginia. Williams continued:

> Proceeding up the river half a mile, to the narrows, where the road lay along the bank, I perceived the President's carriage opposite to us, with Mrs. Madison in it, accompanied by Mr. [John] Graham — chief clerk of the State Department — and one or two other

gentlemen, on horseback. The carriage stopped occasionally while Mrs. Madison looked out toward the city. Presently a military officer, of the District militia, rode up at great speed, proclaiming to the fleeing inhabitants hastening them along the road, that 'General Winder was defeated, routed, and in full retreat through Georgetown, closely pursued by the enemy.'

Dolley was already fully alarmed, for she had not heard from her husband in person since breakfast that morning, before the battle. After hearing the news from the militia officer, she was extremely concerned for Madison's safety. Fearing that his delay in meeting her meant that he had been captured by the enemy, "she sprang out of the carriage into the road, screaming and wringing her hands. Mr. Graham, dismounting, endeavored to pacify her and quiet her fears, and succeeded so far as to persuade her to get into the carriage again and proceed up the river."[53]

Dolley and James had their joyous reunion on the bank of the Potomac River south of Washington later that night, but it was necessarily brief. Madison needed to regain control of his troops and his government, both of which were in total disarray. The situation was devastating for both of them. As historian Conover Hunt-Jones wrote, "The British invasion of Washington was a humiliating insult to the citizens of Washington, and to the American public at large, but it was particularly devastating for the Madisons. They were burned out of their home and suffered severe losses of valuable personal property. Still they were expected to act as courageous models for an outraged public."[54]

They had to part quickly, agreeing to meet at Salona, an estate in McLean, Virginia, belonging to the Reverend Mr. John Maffit. From there they would travel to a tavern at Great Falls. Instead, for reasons unknown, Dolley chose to spend the night with her friend, Matilda Lee Love, in nearby Rockeby, a mile from Salona. From the open window, she could see the great fires burning her house, the Capitol, and the Navy Yard. When

Madison arrived at Salona, the designated meeting place, Dolley was not there, but Madison spent the night anyway.

The next day, August 25, Madison retraced his route, trying to find Dolley. When he again reached Salona, he found that she was headed to the tavern in Great Falls, the place they were next supposed to meet. Up arriving at the tavern, Dolley went upstairs to wait for Madison. She was quickly confronted by the indignant owner, who screamed, "Miss Madison! if that's you, come down and go out! Your husband has got mine out fighting, and damn you, you shan't stay in my house; so get out!"[55]

The ranting litany was taken up by other female refugees, who believed that Madison had brought about the war that now left them homeless. Charles Ingersoll noted, "Ladies who had partaken at Mrs. Madison's drawing-room, the welcome of the President's mansion, and who lived to become sensible of their error, prejudiced by party, embittered by hostilities, and maddened by expulsion from their homes combined to refuse her admission here." Dolley had come face to face with the enmity that resulted from the burning of Washington during "Mr. Madison's War."

The next few days were confusing, exhausting, and demoralizing. Chaos reigned. No one had any idea where the British would strike next. The American army—if it could be called an army at all—had completely dissolved. Its commanders, when they could be found, could scarcely muster ten percent of their troops, and even then, they had no food, few weapons or supplies, and no orders to proceed anywhere or do anything.

James and Dolley traversed the landscape around Washington in search of each other, the one always arriving someplace an hour after the other had left. Madison had equal bad luck in finding General Winder, the commander of his troops. On August 27, after learning that the British were on their ships, Madison sent letters to his scattered cabinet officers, asking them to return to Washington. The same day, he sent a note to Dolley, asking her to do the same. The main topic

D. P. Madison

*The President's House after the Conflagration
of the 24th of August, 1814*

was where to sleep, for the President of the United States and his First Lady were now homeless. "I know not where we are in the first instance to hide our heads; but shall look for a place on my arrival," Madison wrote. "Mr. Rush offers his house in the six buildings and the offer claims attention. Perhaps I may fall in with Mr. Cutts, and have the aid of his advice. I saw Mr. [Abraham] Bradley at Montgomery Court House who told me that Mrs. Cutts was well. James [probably a Madison slave] will give you some particulars which I have not time to write."[56]

Madison was able to return to the smoldering ruins of Washington that night. Wholesale plundering was going on. No public building, store, or sleeping room was safe from looters. Initially, Dr. William Thornton, the superintendent of patents, took charge of the city, posted guards, and tried to impose order. The next day, Mayor James Blake returned and took over. By 5:00 p.m. on August 27, when the president returned to his capital, the city was quiet.

The next days brought further disappointments. Alexandria, Virginia, surrendered without a shot being fired, and the enemy troops spent three hurried days totally restocking their supply of food and water. Instead of worrying about a reappearance of the British in the city, many Washingtonians simply wanted to surrender. Anne Marie Thornton noted in her diary on August 28, "The people are violently irritated at the thought of our attempting to make any more futile resistance."[57]

That same day, Madison got the best possible news of all: his "dearest wife" was back. The reunion was emotional and gave them both hope, but the grueling events of the previous week had left them emotionally exhausted. Dolley's characteristic grace was now lost in depression and anger against the British. As she saw a group of American soldiers walk by, she cried that she wished she had 10,000 such men "to sink our enemy to the bottomless pit."[58]

The Madisons took solace with Anna and Richard Cutts for several weeks. On August 30, Margaret Smith visited Mrs. Madison and wrote to Mrs. Kirkpatrick, "Mrs. Madison seem'd much depress'd, she could hardly speak without tears. She told me she had remained in the city till a few hours before the English enter'd. She was so confident of Victory that she was calmly listening to the roar of cannon and watching the rockets in the air, when she perceived our troops rushing into the city with the haste and dismay of a routed force."[59]

Accompanied by Navy Department clerk Edward Duvall, Dolley had her carriage drive past the smoldering ruins of the White House. She must have been reduced to tears at the sight of her former home. Attorney William Wirt, who had helped to try the government's unsuccessful treason case against Aaron Burr, surveyed the destruction and wrote to his wife, "I went to look at the ruins of the President's house. The rooms which you saw so richly furnished, exhibited nothing but unroofed naked walls, cracked, defaced, and blackened with fire."[60] Two months later, Madison was told that rebuilding the White House would cost an estimated $292,000.

Overwhelmed by the public cries for his skin and the efforts to restore effective government and reorganize the nation's defenses, Madison appointed a committee to oversee

rebuilding the capital. There was even strong talk—predictably, along regional lines—about moving it altogether. The
third and final vote to do so failed by a narrow margin. In the
interim, the patent office was hastily refitted so that Congress
could squeeze in. The Madisons moved in with Richard and
Anna Cutts, and everyone in the city learned to make do despite the temporary chaos. Inconvenient though it was for
all, the most important matter had been settled: Washington
would be rebuilt.

Immediately after the news of the burning spread, James
Madison and his administration were hated men. Newspapers everywhere decried the incompetence of the government
and its military leaders. On August 27, The *Richmond Enquirer*
mourned, "The blush of shame, and of rage, tinges the cheek
while we say that Washington has been in the hands of the
enemy." The editor of the *Winchester* (Virginia) *Gazette* minced
no words. "Poor, contemptible, pitiful, dastardly, wretches!
Their heads would be but a poor price for the degradation
into which they have plunged our bleeding country!" The
United States Gazette in Philadelphia wanted vengeance. It

The Fall of Washington, or Maddy in Full Flight

demanded that the nation's leaders resign, and if they did not, "they must be constitutionally impeached and driven with scorn and execration from the seats which they have dishonored and polluted." [61]

The publishers did not stop at words. Madison was personally ridiculed for leaving Washington in the midst of his fleeing troops. In a widely distributed British cartoon titled "The Fall of Washington, or, Maddy Takes Flight," Madison, with British ships bobbing behind him and Washington in flames, is shown rushing off, trailing state papers in his wake. One character asks another, "Where thinkest thou our President will run to now!" His neighbor replies, "Why verrily to Elba, to join his bosom friend," referring to Napoléon Bonaparte, who had been exiled by the British to the Isle of Elba.

After the forced resignation of Secretary of War Armstrong, under whom few officers wanted to fight again, Madison appointed James Monroe to the post. Monroe rallied the troops, pulled together the artillery, placed it at strategic points on the Potomac River, and pounded the departing warships, though with little effect. Nevertheless, this demonstrated that the Americans, though down, were not out.

The British next tried to take Fort McHenry at Baltimore, but failed. During their attempt, on September 13-14, Francis Scott Key, a Georgetown lawyer watched the start of the battle from his flag-of-truce boat. He was so inspired by the American defense that he composed a poem immortalizing the words "and the rockets' red glare / the bombs bursting in air / gave proof through the night / that our flag was still there." The poem was set to match the melody of the English drinking song, "To Anacreon in Heaven," and it became our national anthem.

The stubborn resistance of the defenders ultimately led Admiral Cockburn to declare a cease-fire, withdraw his ships, and return with them to the main fleet. The British sailed away and continued their coastal harassment, but they did not make any major strikes until one fateful day in December 1814. It would be their last blow.

D. P. Madison

Dolley Madison, age 48, in 1816

Gradually, the outrage over the American humiliation was replaced by resolve. Men with cooler heads spoke out in the newspapers about coming together, raising a proper army, learning the ways of war, and preparing the nation—one nation, indivisible—to thwart any further British predations. The vitriolic anti-Madison rhetoric was calmed by stories of the First Lady's strength and honor under fire, and soon she was being recognized as a national heroine.

The Madisons were never to live in the White House again, and it was not fit for habitation until Madison's successor and friend, James Monroe, was sworn in. On September 18, 1814, three weeks after the burning, the Madisons moved from the Cutts' residence into Colonel John Tayloe's splendid mansion, the Octagon House. Located on the corner of New York Avenue and Eighteenth Street, it had been designed by Dr. William Thornton and was completed in 1800. After the White House, the Octagon House was the finest residence in the city.

The Octagon House

It was designed for entertaining on a large scale, was fully furnished, "and boasted a series of well-appointed interior rooms that were quite suitable to the needs of the chief executive and his family."[62] This was due in no small part to the fact that Tayloe was one of the wealthiest men in America, with an income easily triple that of the president. At the outbreak of hostilities, the Tayloes had moved to Mt. Airy, their expansive country estate in Virginia, where the colonel bred internationally renowned racehorses.

Because the ceilings of the Octagon House were lower than those in the White House, Dolley was unable to hang the precious red velvet drapes she had saved from the inferno. Nevertheless, knowing that the eyes of Washington were on them, and realizing the importance of putting on a good face, Dolley opened the Octagon House for her first weekly drawing room on November 2, 1814.[63]

It was an enormous success, with record attendance. However, the publishers of the Washington *City Gazette*, competitors of the *National Intelligencer* (published by the Madisons' friend, Samuel Harrison Smith) were not thrilled with the reappearance of Dolley's levees. On September 19, 1814, the *Gazette* stated, "The destruction of the President's House cannot be said to be a great loss in one point of view, as we hope it will put an end to drawing-rooms and levees; the resort of the idle, and the encouragers of spies and traitors."[64] Most of the city, however, shrugged off the *Gazette*'s opinion as the complaints of old curmudgeons and flocked to Dolley's door.

Before, during, and after the British invasion, Dolley had kept a level head and faced the disaster with bravery and dignity. Most of her contemporaries would have agreed with the comment made by Charles Hurd, a chronicler of Washington history, who wrote, "Next to Joshua Barney she was the bravest American soldier,"[65] Others went further and declared her *the* heroine of the War of 1812, and so she is often remembered today.

Dolley, forty-seven-years old and decked out again in her stylish dresses, turbans, drapes, ribbons, and even black pearl necklaces, now returned to her favorite roles: hostess and peacemaker. With her smile and a good word for all, friend or foe, the people of Washington were grateful to have her back. Through her obvious personal compassion for those who had lost so much in the brief attack, Dolley overcame much of the hostility that many held for her aloof husband. She was so highly regarded by the end of her husband's second term that she might have been elected president herself if her female contemporaries had been able to vote and hold office.

Across the Atlantic, another kind of peace was being made. On December 24, 1814, the second American Peace Commission, this one meeting with its British counterparts at Ghent, Belgium, signed the Treaty of Ghent, which ended the costly, deadly hostilities between the United States and Great Britain. Because ship-borne mail was the only means of communication, the treaty did not arrive in New York until February 10, 1815, and the news did not reach the Octagon House until February 15. After a careful review, Madison signed the treaty, and Dolley "threw open the mansion's handsome door to welcome adherents of all political persuasions."[66]

Paul Jennings left a more specific account of the day the treaty was received. He recalled, "When the news of peace arrived, we were crazy with joy. Miss Sally Coles, a cousin of Mrs. Madison, and afterwards wife of Andrew Stevenson, since minister to England, came to the head of the stairs, crying out, 'Peace! peace!' and told John Freeman (the butler) to serve out wine liberally to the servants and others. I played the President's March on the violin, John Susé [Sioussat] and some others were drunk for two days, and such another joyful time was never seen in Washington." Then the Madisons' faithful servant carefully noted, "Mr. Madison and all his Cabinet were as pleased as any, but did not show their joy in this manner."[67]

Although the British had sailed out of Chesapeake Bay and no longer directly menaced Washington and Baltimore, the war was still underway. British frigates raided coastal villages in Maine and elsewhere along the Atlantic coast. In Jamaica, where the British fleet was supposed to rendezvous in November 1814, Admiral Cochrane was planning an invasion to capture the richest prize on the North American continent: New Orleans, the gateway to the central and western two-thirds of the continent. The amphibious attack was launched in December and was finally repulsed by General Andrew Jackson's troops on January 8, 1815. The news of the American victory reached Washington a month later, on February 4. But the war had officially ended on December 24. All the men killed on both sides of the heated battle of New Orleans had died in vain. Because of the lack of information, both sides had needlessly spilled each other's blood.

The Madisons left for Montpellier in March 1815, while their new residence was being prepared. The block on the corner of Nineteenth Street and Pennsylvania Avenue, which

The Seven Buildings

came to be known as "The Seven Buildings," had been built in the mid-1790s as part of the initial construction boom in the embryonic capital city. The three-and-a-half-story corner house, Number 1901, was the most elegant and boasted five bays instead of three. After the Madisons returned from Montpellier, where they had spent the summer of 1815, Number 1901 became their home, and they lived there until Madison left office in March 1817.

The treasury department issued warrants for a total of $7,577 to refurbish the new executive mansion. For reasons unknown, the money for rent and repairs came from another fund, administered by none other than Dolley's fiscally irresponsible son, Payne Todd, now back from Europe and his stint as attaché to the first peace commission. While overseas, he had lived like a prince and ran up debts of $6,500, which Madison had to cover.

The funds appropriated by Congress for furnishing the new dwelling were wholly inadequate, and the Madisons had to settle for inferior carpeting and second-hand furniture purchased at auction They made up the deficit in furnishings by drawing on their private stock of furniture at Montpellier. Dolley also was creatively frugal. One historian wrote, "The First Lady's practical approach to creating a place out of ashes and thin air is a notable testament to her talents as an ingenious shopper. In the front door painted imitation mahogany and the simulated damask curtains in the drawing room, visitors to the President's House found evidence of Dolley's valiant attempts to stretch the buying power of the dollar."[68]

In the late fall of 1816, James Monroe was elected president, much to Madison's delight. John Adams wrote to Thomas Jefferson, analyzing Madison's eight-year record. "Not withstanding a thousand faults and blunders, his administration has acquired more glory, and established more Union, than all his three Predecessors., Washington, Adams, and Jefferson, put together."[69]

In March 1817, the Madisons watched with pride as Monroe, their colleague, friend, and neighbor, was inaugurated as the fifth president of the United States. At a post-inauguration reception, Harrison Gray Otis, a hard-shell Federalist was moved to note, "Mrs. Madison behaved with her usual civility, she always finds time & occasion to speak to everybody, & what is a little remarkable never forgets the name of any one to who she has been introduced — she as well dressed rather more pensive than common, but more interesting we all thought than ever. Mr. Madison was quite cheerful and conversible even complimentary — apparently glad to be rid of his Laborious State."[70]

The Madisons had vacated the Seven Buildings and moved in with the Cuttses so that Monroe could hold a reception there. They briefly attended Monroe's inauguration ball and then retired for the evening. Her heart filled with pride, Eliza Collins Lee wrote to Dolley on March 4, 1817 to congratulate her.

On this day eight years ago I wrote...to congratulate you on the joyful event that placed you in the highest station your country can bestow. I then enjoyed the proudest feelings—that my friend—the friend of my youth, who had never forsaken me, should be thus distinguished and so peculiarly fitted to fill it. How much greater cause have I to congratulate you, at this period for having so filled it as to render yourself more enviable this day, than your successor, as it is more difficult to deserve the gratitude and thanks of the community than their congratulations—You have deservedly received of all.[71]

Washington society did not let the Madisons slip off the stage unnoticed. Dolley was deluged with heartfelt letters of thanks, goodwill, and congratulations. On March 13, the citizens of Georgetown held an elaborate farewell ball for them, at which they presented Mrs. Madison with of a portrait of herself. Beneath the painting were inscribed the following lines:

The Power divine when Time begun,
Bade charming WOMAN and the SUN
Illumine the Terrestial Ball:-
A charming WOMAN still we find,
Like the bright SUN, cheers all Mankind,
And, like IT, is admired by all![72]

The Madisons had spent sixteen years in Washington. During that time, they experienced every high and low, exhilaration and depression that the human spirit can embrace. With strength and honor, they faithfully discharged their duties to the high offices they held. Now it was time for them to slip quietly out of the limelight to retire in privacy to their paradise in the Blue Ridge Mountains. They had every right to believe that they would spend the rest of their days in peace and comfort. There, within a squirrel's jump of heaven, the ex-president could find the peace he dreamed of, harness undisturbed his extraordinary mind, and prepare his professional papers for publication and preservation for generations to come. Surrounded by extended family and the Madison connections, Dolley must have looked forward to renewing old ties, enjoying her gardening, entertaining her guests, and savoring the matchless presence of her "great little Madison." Unfortunately, fate had other plans.

CHAPTER TWELVE

Adam and Eve in Paradise

Montpellier Plantation
April 1817

T he sweet perfume of honeysuckle was luxuriant at Montpellier in March 1817, when James Madison passed the republican torch to his friend, James Monroe, but the Madisons would not be able to enjoy it until a full month later. The month after Monroe's inauguration was filled with farewell parties, balls, and dinners for the Madisons. When all was done, the former president and presidentress boarded a Potomac River steamboat for their voyage to Aquia Creek, where a carriage would take them back to their country home.[1] James K. Paulding, a naval officer and Madison appointee to the Board of Naval Commissioners, accompanied them as they headed down the Potomac for home. This time it would not be just a summer vacation but a one-way trip. Madison was clearly elated. Paulding wrote, "if ever a man rejoiced sincerely at being freed from the cares of public life it was he. During the voyage he was as playful as a child; talked and joked with everybody on board, and reminded me of a schoolboy on a long vacation."[2]

After eight years in Washington, the work of moving was immense. Furniture had to be packed or sold. Hundreds of well-wishers wrote to Dolley and James, and Dolley sought to answer each of them. From the great George Towne ball, they brought back numerous messages of love, "spelled out in transparencies, paintings, and verses executed on white velvet and most richly framed."[3] Little of Dolley's correspondence from this period survives to describe the ordeal of relocating and the relief that certainly followed as they finally settled into a permanent home.

The arrival at Montpellier had a different effect on each of the Madisons. James had grown up on the plantation before Montpellier, which he expanded twice, was even built, and like an arrow shot from a bow, he sped there at every opportunity. He reveled in the life of a Jeffersonian intellectual country gentleman. While Madison was enjoying his customary summer vacation, six months before he left office, Attorney General Richard Rush stopped in Orange County to pay him a visit and wrote that he had never "seen Mr. Madison so well fixed anywhere."[4] Even Dolley's colorful macaw, Polly, repatriated from the French minister's cook after the British invasion, also seemed to enjoy his new home with its view of the Blue Ridge Mountains.

Aside from summer visits, Dolley, on the other hand, had lived at Montpellier for only four years, from the time her husband finished his term as a congressman in 1797 until he went back to Washington as Jefferson's secretary of state in 1801. Although she had spent most of her life living in the country, by the time her husband finally retired, she was more an urban society woman than a rural planter's wife. And she was certainly not the mistress of Montpellier. That role belonged exclusively to her mother-in-law, Nelly.

Upon leaving Washington, the Madisons had regretfully dismissed their extraordinary French chef, Pierre Roux, whom Madison had loaned $150 to start a restaurant, and French John, the man who *really* ran the White House.[5] Dolley's maid, Sukey, and Madison's butler, Paul Jennings, returned with them to Montpellier, where they later married. Of Madison's closest two intellectual soulmates, he had lost Monroe to the White House, but he and Jefferson, who was only thirty miles away, were both free from the turmoil of politics.

For Madison, Montpellier signified everything that was good, substantial, natural, and satisfying. For Dolley, now forty-nine-years old and an intensely social creature at heart, it represented peace, but also isolation; a simpler, less-demanding life, but one that lacked the international sophistication to which she had become accustomed. She often wrote to her nieces in Washington requesting news—any news— that would help alleviate her sense of isolation. In all, the transition from Washington to Montpellier was easier for James than for Dolley.

Then there was Payne. When his stepfather answered Jefferson's call and moved to Washington, Payne was nine years old. He quickly came to like being pampered by the people, especially the women, who filled his parents' social circle in the capital city. When his father became president, he was seventeen. His life as the privileged son of one of Washington's most-respected families had opened many doors that might better have been left shut, especially the portals of the taverns

John Payne Todd

of Pennsylvania Avenue, where Payne became well known. During his two years of service as an attaché with the peace commission, he showed little interest in the proceedings of the commission but great interest in the ballrooms of St. Petersburg. There, he distinguished himself in the drawing room and ballroom for the "perfection of his manners before royalty, acquiring among his new acquaintances the title of 'The American Prince.'"[6] Payne left St. Petersburg for Paris before the rest of the commission members, without telling his parents, with whom he seldom bothered to correspond. Undaunted, Dolley wrote to him constantly, with rarely a reply. What little she did learn came through one of the commissioners, Albert Gallatin, usually relayed through his wife, Hannah, with whom she was in close contact.

A year after Payne left for Russia, Dolley wrote to him, "Early in July I wrote to you my dearest Payne by Mr. Carraman—I hope you have the letter by this day—I wrote also by Mr. Hughes & Mr. Carrol. Not a line from you has reached us since you left St. Petersburg. How impatient I am, you aught to immagin—I am consoled for your absence & your silence by the impression that you are engrossed by the variety of objects in Europe which are to enlighten & benefit you the rest of your life."[7]

Instead of educating his mind while in Paris, Payne sought to duplicate his social successes in Russia. In this regard, he was successful. In France, he kept company with royals and courtiers and flirted, danced, drank, and gambled himself into heavy debts, which Madison discreetly paid.

When he returned to Washington, Payne's parents hoped that he would find a good wife, settle down, cut back on his drinking, raise tobacco, and rear a proper family. Their prayers were not answered. In 1816, Dolley's cousin, Edward Coles, then traveling through the South, explained that he, too, rarely heard from Payne, even though Coles had frequently written to him. Noting that he had, regretfully, ceased trying to maintain a correspondence with Payne, Coles wrote, "I beg you to inform him of this, and to say to him that I have not been less mortified than disappointed by his conduct."[8] Coles noted that he had heard Payne was courting a young woman who lived on F Street in Washington, but he put little stock in the story.

Five years later, in 1821, Dolley pleaded for Payne's help, but heard nothing. "I write you at W[ashington?] at Philadelphia & at Baltimore.... It was short, & in my great alarm, it contain a request that you would come to me, as I had a wish to travel a distance from home on account of the

Typhus fever—but that fear, has been dissipated for the present, by the children in the house getting well, & the negros also."[9] His reply the next week was a request for money.[10]

Wherever he went, Payne left a trail of drinking, gambling, and debt in his wake. In 1825, Madison paid out $500 for his debts at a Washington lottery house; in 1827 another $1,000; then $600 to John Jacob Astor, who loaned Payne money, which he also lost in gambling. As bad as Payne's behavior was, Dolley never knew even the half of it. Madison shielded her from the mortification of knowing the extent of her son's wasted life by paying out more than $20,000 to cover Payne's debts without ever telling her. In all, Madison shouldered the burden of about $40,000 between 1813 and 1836, a huge sum in good times, and nearly a catastrophe in his retirement years.[11] Sometimes, the truth was unavoidable. In 1829, and again in 1830, Payne was thrown into debtor's prison in Philadelphia, which was a "crushing blow" to Dolley. In complete mortification, she wrote to Anna Cutts:

> I enquired of you if you had heard from or of my dear Child—you say nothing—& since that letter, I received one from him, in which he tells me that he was boarding within Prison bounds! for a debt of 2—or 300$ he has submitted to this horrid—horrid situation—It allmost breaks my heart to think of it Mr Cutts owed him more than this, of the money P[ayne] entrusted to him, to place in the Bank—but <u>he</u> owes you even more I know, still <u>that</u> is not the purpose— I don't know that I shall send you this letter— in truth I feel as if I could not write a letter— My pride— my sensibility, & every feeling of my Soul is wounded. Yet we shall do something—what or when depends on Mr. Madison's health, & strength, to do business— his anxiety, & wish to aid, & benefit Payne is as great as a Fathers— but his ability to command mony in this country, is not greater than that of others.[12]

Her son's imprisonment for debt totally demoralized Dolley. For a time, she lost all interest in speaking to anyone or going anywhere. She doubted her faith "in everything and everybody"[13] Edward Coles likened Payne's visits to Montpellier to those of "a veritable serpent in the Garden of Eden.'"[14] Nevertheless, Payne's long-suffering mother kept up a brave front, always opening her heart to him, reaching out, hoping for the best, despite the many whispered reports of him and his personal demons. When the distresses that Payne brought to her and her husband came up in discussion among her intimates, she would invariably say of him, "Forgive his eccentricities, for his heart is al right," and would repeat one of Madison's favorite quotations, which he himself had used to console Dolley: "Errors like straws upon the surface flow / Those who would seek for pearls must dive below."[15]

When the Madisons arrived at Montpellier in the spring of 1817, James' mother Nelly was eighty-six-years old, still animated, and definitely the mistress of Montpellier. James Sr. had died in 1801, just before his son became secretary of state. When James K. Paulding visited in 1817, he wrote that Nelly was "thin and spry as a bird, and, reading without glasses, she kept abreast of the times."[16] The elder Mrs. Madison inhabited the south wing of the mansion and maintained her own lifestyle, garden, and slaves. At two o'clock, she welcomed her daily guests, who always included Dolley, James, and whomever was visiting that day. Her ancient _major domo_, Old Sawney, lived solely to pass her a glass of water when needed. At three, her dinner was brought up from her private kitchen in the basement below. She always doted on Payne.[17] But she adored and appreciated Dolley even more and was delighted to have such a warm and attentive daughter-in-law in the household. With great affection, she looked at Dolley one day and said, "You are _my_ Mother now, and take care of me in my old age."[18]

As Dolley adjusted to a comfortable retirement at Montpellier, her chatty, charming sister, Lucy Payne Washington Todd, was in despair. No law required a justice of the U. S. Supreme Court to live in Washington, and Lucy's husband

Montpellier in 1836

preferred his home in Kentucky. But she longed for the comforts of her sister and family in Virginia. Dolley's other sister,
Anna Cutts, however, was able to maintain a close relationship
with her famous sibling.

When Anna and Richard Cutts came to visit, the plantation glowed with energy. Anna now had a brood of children
ranging from three to twelve years old, and Dolley treated
them as if they were her own. In turn, the rambunctious lot
of them loved listening to the stories that Aunt Dolley and
Uncle Jemmy told, and there was universal sadness each time
the Cutts family left Montpellier. Cutts, who held a government staff position, was building a large two-story brick house
on the northeast corner of the President's Square, with a
double parlor and a large garden with fruit trees and berry
bushes. The Cutts family clearly wanted a home where they
could welcome Dolley and her husband when they visited
the capital. The house would play a major role in Dolley's
later life, but not in the way that either family expected.

Whenever the Madisons were home in Montpellier, a constant flow of guests — one, two, or two dozen at a time, many of whom stayed for a week or three — made the pilgrimage to see them. Groups of well-wishers flowed in and ebbed out like the tide — except for those who did not seem to know when it was time to leave. Barbecues for multiple dozens of guests took place. Formal dinners with two dozen guests at the table were not uncommon, and there was no lack of either quantity or quality in the meals. In 1825, Congressman George Ticknor wrote that the food at Montpellier was "not only abundantly, but handsomely provided; good soups, flesh, fish and vegetables, well cooled — desert and excellent wines of various kinds."[19] Sometimes, James and Dolley worried that they literally would be eaten out of house and home.[20]

Madison generally let his guests roam free and amuse themselves during the day, while he was seeing to his crops and editing his professional papers, but at dinner time, which was four o'clock in the afternoon, everyone assembled to enjoy

The Montpellier dining room as it may have looked in the 1820s

the lavish hospitality for which the Madisons were always known. During and after dinner, the conversation flowed as liberally as the fine wines. Here the visitors found Dolley and Madison at their respective bests: Dolley as the turbaned, fashionable, gracious hostess; Madison as the wry raconteur and purveyor of philosophy, wit, and droll humor that larger groups seldom saw. His favorite subject was, of course, constitutional history, and to discuss this topic, he was frequently willing to stay up and converse until the wee hours of the morning. Count Carlo Vidua, who visited Montpellier in 1825, described Madison as possessed with "an indescribable gentleness and charm," which the count "thought impossible to find in an American."[21] When the Marquis de Lafayette enjoyed the hospitality of Montpellier during his 1824 national tour, he rested, and shared a private dinner with Dolley and James, Anna and Richard Cutts, and Lucy Payne Todd on November 17.

As ingrained as this lavish style of entertaining was, it was also costly. While in office, Madison had not been able to put aside any of his $25,000 presidential salary, for, as he quickly discovered when he entered the White House, the presidency was a charity job: it cost more than it paid. Superb as he was as a hands-on plantation manager, he had been away in Washington for sixteen years. After his brother, Ambrose, died in 1793, Madison stepped in as on-site manager from 1797 to 1801. But when he was called to Washington as secretary of state, and then was promoted by the public to president, he had to rely on overseers to handle most of the management duties, and Montpellier's production suffered considerably. In addition, the European trade wars, which had blocked exports, combined with the burden of Payne's debts, reduced crop prices, the maintenance of an enslaved labor force of more than 100 men and women, the extensive entertaining, and his considerable expenditures for books and wine severely taxed Madison's ability to keep up with the demands on his finances. By the 1830s, visitors were commenting that the mansion was still handsome but was in need of maintenance and no longer in its prime.

A female visitor to Montpellier in 1819 wrote to Dolley's friend, Eliza Collins Lee, that "I spent 2 days with Mr. & Mrs. Madison — they enquir'd kindly after you. Her soul is as big as ever and her boddy has not decreased. Mr. Madison is the picture of happiness and they look like Adam and eve in Paradise."[22] Indeed, Dolley no longer sported the twenty-three-inch waist of her second wedding dress — but not many fifty-one-year-old women maintained the waistlines they had at twenty-six. However, the financial realities of their retirement years had sunk in. Dolley was acutely aware that the days of $2,000-a-year clothes-shopping sprees were over. Buying new Parisian dresses was financially out of the question. Consequently, fabric panels known as gores were added to one of her favorite gowns, a red velvet Empire dress, to make it fit better.

Her brother-in-law, Richard Cutts, had his own financial problems. After losing a great deal of money during the War of 1812, and making some bad investment decisions, not even his government job was enough to keep him financially afloat. In 1819, his creditors forced him into bankruptcy, which, in turn forced him to sell his home, for which Madison had loaned him money. Dolley convinced her husband to buy the house on Lafayette Square, which kept the Cutts family from losing their home.

She also had to deal with her brother, John C. Payne, whose alcoholism continued after his return from Tripoli in 1806. He ultimately married and moved to a plantation close to Montpellier, but Dolley was never able to rely on his help when she needed it. He did, however, prove to be a valuable assistant to Madison and helped to edit the notes James had kept during the constitutional convention in 1787.

Editing and publishing his private journals of the debates during the framing of the Constitution were James Madison's main goals during retirement. He knew that if the papers were properly prepared and preserved in print, his final gift to the nation would be complete. Madison came from healthy stock. In an age when men died of old age at sixty, his father lived until his seventy-seventh year, and Nelly had celebrated her ninety-seventh birthday before she died in 1829. Despite his relatively good health in the 1820s, when Madison was in his early seventies, he felt the press of time. All of his long-term, recurring debilities continued to haunt him, and even with the constant, doting attention of Dolley, his "affectionate nurse," Madison was starting to feel his age.

He dug into the main part of his work in 1823. To aid him in the enormous task of dictating, writing, arranging, and editing his papers, he had several able assistants. First and foremost was Dolley, who typically worked as his amanuensis—his scribe and personal secretary—from ten in the morning until three o'clock in the afternoon, right before dinner was served. He was always a gracious host, but the constant interruptions necessitated by social intercourse kept him away from his work, and he once remarked that "some visits were taxes and others bounties."[23] He relished the winters, when the roads were bad, which slowed the flow of visitors down to a trickle, enabling him to spend long periods of uninterrupted time at his writing and editing. Three years into the work, Dolley wrote of the magnitude of the project, and her sense of being trapped by it, to Sally Coles Stevenson:

> I have just now reccd. by post your welcome letter my ever dear cousin, and cannot express my anxiety to embrace you once more! But a spell rests upon me from those I love best in this world—not a mile can I go from home—and in no way can I account for it, but that my Husband is also, fixed there. This is the third winter in which he has been engaged in the arrangement of papers, and the [work?] appears to accumalate as he proceeds—so that I calculate its out-lasting my patience and yet I cannot press him to forsake a duty so important, or find it in my heart to leave him during its fulfillment.[24]

D. P. Madison

James Madison in 1833

In the early 1830s, as Madison turned eighty, his health began to decline. He had just bailed Payne out of debtor's prison for the second time and was forced to sell off land in Kentucky and mortgage half of Montpellier just to keep his head above water. In 1834, he was forced to do something even more painful: sell off a parcel of slaves. Madison counted on selling his papers to the government and selling the rights to publish the papers to a commercial publisher. This would provide a financial cushion and trust fund for his wife, but the going was difficult. His health declined precipitously in the mid-1830s, by which time he had edited his papers through 1787.

What to do with his slaves upon his death presented both a moral and practical dilemma for Madison. He viewed the system of slaveholding to be a "dreadful evil," but his father and grandfathers had been slaveowning Virginia planters. Madison issued orders to his overseers to "treat the Negroes with all the humanity and kindness consistent with their necessary subordination and work."[25] Even visitors who abhorred slavery were forced to admit that the master of Montpellier "treated his slaves with a consideration bordering on indulgence."[26] Paul Jennings left this assessment of his former owner:

> Mr. Madison, I think, was one of the best men that ever lived. I never saw him in a passion, and never knew him to strike a slave, although he had over one hundred; neither would he allow an overseer to do it. Whenever any slaves were reported to him as stealing or 'cutting

up' badly, he would send for them and admonish them privately, and never mortify them by doing it before others. They generally served him very faithfully.[27]

Madison saw the obvious incongruity between slavery and the professed ideals of the Revolution when he opposed a plan to give slaves as a bounty to army recruits.[28] He was a leader in the American Colonization Society, which sought to buy the freedom of slaves and repatriate them to Africa — an idea from which his own slaves recoiled. Yet he owned slaves.

Ultimately, he held an amalgamation of different viewpoints on the peculiar institution. Yet in the end, Madison did not know how to get rid of slavery, and never freed his slaves. Instead, he passed the dilemma on to his wife, to whom he willed his plantation, his Washington house on Lafayette Square, and his slaves. As he stated in his will, "I give and bequeath my ownership in the negroes and people of coulor held by me to my dear wife," adding "but it is my desire that none of them should be sold without his or her consent, or in case of their misbehaviour; except that infant children may be sold with their parent who consents for them to be sold to him or her, and who consents to be sold."[29]

By 1834, Madison could no longer leave his bed, and in 1835, Dolley wrote to her niece, Dolley Cutts, "*My* days are devoted to nursing and comforting my *patient*, who walks only from the bed in which he breakfasts, to one in the little chamber."[30] Save for a bout of influenza and her recurring eye problems, Dolley remained in good health. The pains she felt most were the losses of loved ones close to her.

Despite his weakened condition, Madison was too polite to turn away most requests. In 1835, crippled with rheumatism and unable to do his own writing, he nevertheless made a generous reply to a letter directed to him:

Dear Sir, I have received your letter of April 29th. In my present condition crippled as it is by a chronic complaint with the addition of a new inroad on my health, and the addition of both to the enfeebling effects of my very advanced age, I cannot undertake a compliance with your request on the important and controverted subjects to which it relates. I can only therefore with this apology tender my acknowledgements for the kind sentiments you have impressed and a sincere return of my best wishes for your welfare.[31]

Even at the age of eighty-four, crippled with rheumatism, Madison managed a clear signature in dark ink. Dolley hovered over her husband in his last years, caring for his every need. Paul Jennings and his wife, Sukey, also cared for him throughout the last decades of his life. Jennings wrote:

I was always with Mr. Madison till he died, and shaved him every other day for sixteen years. For six months before his death, he was unable to walk, and spent most of his time reclined on a couch; but his mind was bright, and with his numerous visitors he talked with as much animation and strength of voice as I ever heard him in his best days. I was present when he died. That morning Sukey brought him his breakfast, as usual. He could not swallow. His niece, Mrs. Willis, said, 'What is the matter, Uncle Jeames?' 'Nothing more than a change of *mind,* my dear.' His head instantly dropped, and he ceased breathing as quietly as the snuff of a candle goes out.[32]

On June 28, 1836, the day James Madison slipped away from earthly life at his beloved Montpellier, Dolley Madison, the daughter of a man who had sacrificed the prosperity of his family to perform the noble deed of emancipation, became the legal owner of more than one hundred enslaved human beings. The nation deeply mourned the Father of the Constitution, as he was then being called. He was eulogized not only for his brilliant mind but also for his devoted service as rector of the University of Virginia, Virginia legislator, U.S. congressman, secretary of state, and president. In the wake of Madison's death, letters of condolence flocked in from around the world. Predictably, Dolley replied to every one of them.

A month after the funeral, James Laurie, president of the board of managers of the American Colonization Society, wrote to console Dolley for her loss. In the process, he recognized her immense importance to her late husband. "The loss we deeply deplore. And what Citizen of this great Republic, which he did so much to form and to elevate deplores it not? But what loss, Madam, which we so greatly feel, must be felt with an intensity of which we can form no adequate conception, by you; you who were his companion in the journey of life, you who shared so richly in the exercise of his social and domestic virtues—his Partner in sorrow and joy."[33]

The marriage had been strong and loving for forty-two years, during which time James and Dolley had rarely been separated. Her union with the "great little Madison" had provided a fertile field in which she grew and blossomed. As she developed new skills and abilities—qualities quite unknown, and many unsought, in the quiet world of the Quakers from whence she had come—she put them into use not for herself, but for the benefit of her family, her husband, her connections, and for the nation. Now she was again widowed, but remarriage was not a serious option. She would have to face the rest of her life on her own.

She had lost her life's partner. In 1832, she had lost her beloved sister, Anna Payne Cutts, who died three years after Dolley's adored mother-in-law, Nelly. Her home, Montpellier, was partially mortgaged, as was the Cutts house in Washington. Her son, Payne, was completely incompetent as a farmer and seemed hell-bent on destroying his life one drink and one wager at a time. Dolley would find the ebb tide of her life more grueling than any period she had ever experienced.

CHAPTER THIRTEEN

Days of Grace and Honor

D olley smiled as the conductor of the Marine Band raised his baton and struck up the music as President James K. Polk entered the outer hall of the president's mansion on Wednesday, February 7, 1849. The venerable lady, now well into her eightieth year, was a guest of honor at this fashionable levee, attended by a large assembly of foreign ministers, judges, members of both houses of Congress, and ordinary citizens. In a description of that night, Polk wrote in his private journal, "Towards the close of the evening I passed through the crowded rooms with the venerable Mrs. Madison on my arm. It was near twelve o'clock when the company retired."[1] Thirty-two years after her husband left office, Dolley was still lively and an important leader in the capital's social circles. Whenever anyone important visited Washington to see the president, his or her second stop was invariably at Lafayette Square to visit Mrs. Madison. She was the oldest living widow of a Founding Father, the oldest surviving First Lady, a *grande dame* of Washington high society—and a woman with a mission: to finish her husband's work and keep his memory and ideals alive.

About a year before Polk's party, the famous daguerreo-typist, Matthew Brady, had asked Mrs. Madison to sit for him. The tediously long exposure time necessary made it impossible for him to capture more than a suggestion of her usual jolly smile, and she seemed tired. Indeed, she was. She was nearing the end of her long life. She wore one of her signature turbans, a simple white one with silk tulle netting. In earlier days, her turbans were solely ornamental. Now they concealed her white hair with cleverly designed false black curls, which peeked out from under them. Gone were the Empire dresses, which emphasized cleavage. Now she wore high-necked scarves to cover the wrinkles of her neck. For the picture, Dolley had chosen a brocade Jacquard shawl to wear over the shoulders of her black dress, and white gloves to cover her arthritic hands. But white hair and wrinkles were superficial physical characteristics common to women of her years. Dolley's unique dynamic personality was still intact, if a bit muted by age.

After her husband's death, Dolley became a guest of honor at the majority of the special events that took place in Washing-ton. The social invitations and high-level attention she received notwith-standing, Dolley knew that her most important mission for the rest of her life was to preserve Mad-ison's works. She became the torchbearer of his dream. Her reverence for Madison shines forth in a letter she wrote in 1838 to Charles Ingersoll, a close friend of her husband's, who was evidently pre-paring something for print and had inquired about Madison's religious beliefs.

Dolley Madison's white turban, with tulle netting

Dolley replied, "To your further enquiry into the religion, domestic life, and acquirements of my dear husband, I lament that I have not the power—the capacity to do him justice—I can only feel that he was good and perfect in all these, and that nothing short of true religion can make man perfect. He was accomplished in literature and sciences as his writings manifest and as you sir, so eloquently proved in your beautiful sketch of his life in 1836 for the Portrait Gallery."[2]

Maintaining her legendary vivacity and enthusiasm for life, and continuing to provide the hospitality for which she was famous, was arduous in the wake of James' death. Her advancing age, failing income, and mounting debts, and the incessant demands and numerous problems caused by her dissolute son, were challenges that she spent her last thirteen years trying to survive. Her helper at Montpellier, and later in Washington, was her niece, Anna Coles Payne, whom Dolley had virtually adopted, knowing that her own son would be of little

Anna Coles Payne

help. Anna, who became her aunt's closest companion, was born in 1810 and was twenty-six when James Madison died in 1836. Dolley was sixty-eight.

Anna was the daughter of Dolley's troubled brother, John Coles Payne, who had unsuccessfully farmed near Montpellier, later helped Madison edit his papers, and stayed on for a time after Madison's death to help ensure that the papers were copied for publication. John then moved to Kentucky, and eventually, he and his family ended up in Illinois, where he died about 1841. Anna Payne, whom Dolley called "a sterling girl," remained with Dolley and was always at her aunt's side until Dolley died in 1849.[3] Without Anna as a compassionate and loving companion, Dolley would certainly have succumbed to depression. A year after Dolley died, Anna married Dr. Thomas H. Causten, but she lived only two more years after her wedding.

After laying her husband to rest in the Madison family cemetery at Montpellier, little more than a hundred yards from Ambrose Madison's first house on the property, Dolley's first priority was money. For all practical purposes, she had none. Madison had left bequests totaling almost $15,000 to the American Colonization Society, the University of Virginia, and his *alma mater*, the College of New Jersey at Princeton, but there was little cash to pay the everyday expenses of life, never mind the noble bequests.

Dolley was so totally blinded by her love for her son—and so deeply in need of help—that she installed Payne as the manager of Montpellier so that she could concentrate on selling the publication rights to Madison's papers to a New York or Philadelphia publisher. As with everything else entrusted to Payne, this was a tragic mistake.

John Payne Todd had already failed to make a success of the farm his stepfather had given him, but his mother's love could not be diminished by reality. After years in public life, concealing her private thoughts from others, she was probably unaware that she was also concealing them from herself. The enormity of Payne's selfishness and insensitivity to the needs of others, as well as his own self-destructive traits, were hard to overestimate by anyone who knew him—except his mother.

Payne was truly a tortured man. At Montpellier, after his stepfather retired, he deteriorated rapidly. He could not forget the high life in Europe, where he had been fêted, flattered, and received in the royal families; where he had danced with the czar's daughter in St. Petersburg; and where he had been entertained by the Count and Countess D'Orsay in Paris.[4] The isolated life that kept him out of the taverns of Washington and Baltimore forced him into tortured introspection. By now, he was a full-blown alcoholic, but because alcoholism was considered to be a moral disease, there were no treatment programs.

At Montpellier, Payne chronicled his obsessions, his self-loathing, and his battles with his personal demons in a journal describing his tortured life.[5] Katharine Anthony wrote:

> With his diary for his only companion, he struggled against temptation, but always unsuccessfully. In his scrawling hand, now large, now extremely small, he set down his successive falls from grace. He fought as confusedly and as desperately against tobacco as against drink. His untidy notes reveal a state of depression rarely so mercilessly exposed to the light. Whether he was a genuine invalid or hypochondriac does not make much difference. Engaged constantly with his symptoms, he complained in turn of pains in his teeth, pains in his back, rheumatic pains in his legs, of heartburn, nausea, mysterious inflammations — many of which were no doubt very real. There was no regularity in his habits. He slept and rose at all hours, sometimes rolling himself in a blanket in front of the fire and staying there indefinitely. His meals were erratic, and what he ate seemed to him to be of great importance. His primary concern was how he felt after drinking, or, on rare occasions, after refraining from drink.... His feelings of inferiority could not be borne without compensations. An illusion of self-importance helped to bolster him up. Todd invented a cipher [code] for his diary which, applied to the most trivial matters, gave them the mock importance of Madison's official documents.... His letters and diary of the Montpellier period are those of a shipwrecked and floundering soul.[6]

The sale of the publication rights for Madison's papers was to have provided the funds to pay Madison's bequests

and debts and to provide his widow with a comfortable retirement. He had expected that the sale would net $100,000,
which would have been more than enough to accomplish all
of these goals.

Although Dolley had no experience in publishing, she had
many friends who did, and she sent out inquiries to them
about how to contact and negotiate with the nation's major
publishers. Her contacts included wise and knowledgeable
businessmen such as James K. Paulding, who got in touch
with Jared Sparks, former editor of the *North American Review*. Sparks, who had visited Montpellier, became one of the
leading literary figures in Boston. In 1837, he published a
twelve-volume edition of the papers of George Washington,
making him the perfect person to contact. Dolley's brother,
John Coles Payne, undertook the huge task of supervising the
transcriptionists, who were making accurate copies of all
the papers for publication, as the originals were to be sold to
the government.

Then Dolley made a grave mistake. Instead of entrusting
the negotiations with the publishers to an experienced literary hand, she gave the responsibility to her son. The result,
predictably, was a disaster. Paulding, a prominent writer and
literary figure, wrote to Sparks, asking him for the "particulars
of your agreement with the Publishers of the Washington
papers" so that he could give Payne advice on how to negotiate
the contract on behalf of his mother. Paulding knew Payne
well, and had little confidence in him. Paulding confided to
Sparks, "if you are acquainted with him, you need not be told
that he is the last man in the world to compass [direct] such a
business."[7] He was correct in his assessment.

By the end of 1836, Payne had alienated every one of the
large publishers, and thereby lost any hope of seeing the
$100,000 his mother counted on. Some smaller literary houses
nibbled, but the Madison papers would never be published
within Dolley's lifetime. This caused Dolley added stress and
anxiety because her friends, and the nation, expected the
publication to take place. After James' death, she had assumed

the mantle of protector of the family, and the public had high expectations of her. Now she had no resources left, financially or emotionally.

Finally, she had a stroke of good luck. In 1837, Congress accepted the proposal to publish the first three volumes of Madison's papers in return for a payment of $30,000 to Dolley. These volumes appeared in 1840. A woman of honor, Dolley used the money to pay off her debts and to pay the bequests specified in her husband's will. In the fall of 1837, she chose to move to the Cutts' house in Washington to resume her previous lifestyle: fall and winter in the capital; late spring and summer at Montpellier. She left her son in charge of the plantation.

The Richard Cutts House was free of debt when Dolley and Anna Payne moved in. An early pencil-and-watercolor sketch of the house, painted by the Baroness Hyde de Neuville, showed it as a relatively narrow, two-story building with an attic, a gable roof, dormer windows, and chimneys at both ends. It sat on a large, open lot and was accessible by dirt roads running past the front and to the left side.

The house, which Richard Cutts built for his bride, Anna Payne, was one of the most pretentious in the city when Cutts built it. It overlooked Lafayette Square, and its beautiful garden, full of flowers and fruit trees, attracted swarms of butterflies, which Dolley so adored that she had them embroidered on many of her fanciest dresses and turbans. Anna Payne Cutts died in 1832, and Richard Cutts was a widower when his son, James Madison Cutts, married Ellen O'Neale and took her to Montpellier to spend

The Richard Cutts House, Washington

their honeymoon days with Aunt and Uncle Madison. Ellen became mistress of the Cutts mansion when they returned from Montpellier, and in 1835, Adèle Cutts was born. Richard Cutts had mortgaged the house to James Madison before Madison died and was not able to pay off the mortgage before his own death in 1845.[8]

Dolley Madison and Anna Payne, about 1848

When Dolley took up residence in the house in 1837, at the age of sixty-nine, Adèle was only two years old, but Dolley, always a friend of children, was delighted with her great-niece, as was Anna Payne, then twenty-seven. With the exception of two years and several visits spent at Montpellier, Dolley lived at the Cutts' house for the rest of her life. In Washington, she was welcomed back like a long-lost friend and instantly was deluged with invitations to dinners, parties, and balls. Within a year, she had more social engagements than she could possibly handle. Most were from old friends and acquaintances, but many were from people who had heard the legends about her and simply wanted to meet her. Dolley, now turning seventy years old, was a full-blown Washington celebrity again.

An intensely gregarious person since birth, Dolley did not let her financial difficulties dampen her enthusiasm for social events, even though now she could not return them in kind. As Ethel Arnett noted, "She was invited to practically all affairs, public and private, and her natural enthusiasm for gatherings of all kinds prompted her to attend almost any event to which she was invited."[9]

Businessman William Kemble, forty-four, the New York agent for the DuPont de Nemours chemical company, met Dolley at a party hosted by his relative, James K. Paulding, then secretary of the navy. He was seated next to her, and he left the following description of the meeting: "The old lady is a very hearty, good looking woman of about 75. — Soon after we were seated, we became on the most friendly terms & I paid her the same attentions I would have done a girl of 15 — which seemed to suit her fancy very well and after eating about 20 plates — each with the smallest slice of something on it & drinking as many glasses of wine, the company rose & we adjourned to the drawing room for Coffee."[10] The only part of his recollection that would have displeased Dolley was the statement about her age. She was only seventy-one at the time.

Within a few years, a general economic downturn forced her to rent out the Cutts' house in 1840 and 1841 and live at

Montpellier. She could not collect funds owed to her, and the lack of income caused by Payne's mismanagement of the plantation precluded her from paying her own debts. Her downward economic spiral had begun, but she bore it with her usual fortitude. Often entertained but rarely cared for, yet always the caregiver herself, Dolley took in her aging sister, Lucy in the summer of 1840. Lucy had lost her husband, Judge Thomas Todd, in 1826 and now suffered from what appeared to have been a heart attack.

Payne continued his dissipated life, always with a hand out to his mother, and never a hand offered to help her. Dolley often named Payne as her business agent. As a result, many transactions were either botched or rigged in his financial favor. Dolley continued to turn a blind eye to his character defects, even though they were well known to all of her friends. Indeed, when Congress bought the first portion of Madison's papers in 1837, one of Dolley's friends wrote, "this money will in all likelihood be lost to Mrs. Madison if he [Payne] has any power over it."[11] By 1841, the reality of Payne's corrosive effect on her finances set in, and Dolley rewrote her will, placing her assets in a trust. In a rare trip outside her home area, she paid a visit to New York, where she reunited with friends. She also accepted a $3,000 loan in return for a mortgage on the Cutts' house from John Jacob Astor, who was acutely aware of her need for cash.[12]

Although her real need was for money to pay her debts, she was, instead, flooded with presents of good will and tokens of respect. During the War of 1812, a controversy had arisen between Commodore Oliver Hazard Perry and Commodore Jesse D. Elliott concerning Elliott's conduct during the Battle of Lake Erie. Some officers believed that Elliott had intentionally kept his

Jesse D. Elliott
commemorative medal

vessel, the *Niagara*, out of the fight, leaving Perry to take the full force of the British fire. They charged that Elliott only engaged the enemy when he believed that Perry was dead so that Elliott could take all the credit for winning the battle. The argument raged, in varying degrees of intensity, for several years. James Fenimore Cooper defended Elliott, and a commemorative medal was struck to honor Elliott's bravery. Elliott sent a copy of the medal to Cooper for his "disinterested vindication of his brother sailor, Jesse D. Elliott."[13] Other copies were distributed to historical societies and foreign ministers, and one was given to Dolley Madison. As a heroine of the War of 1812, only Mrs. Madison received a medal struck in silver, confirming once again her popularity and place in Washington's political society.

If there was any doubt about Dolley's official recognition for her life's work, it was dispelled in January 1844, when a message reached Dolley from the House of Representatives. She had visited the gallery of the House on several occasions, and an honor of unprecedented significance was bestowed upon her—the highest political compliment ever paid to any other woman until that time. The impressive document, delivered personally by Dolley's friend, former congressman Charles J. Ingersoll, read, "Resolved, unanimously, that a committee be appointed on the part of the House to wait upon Mrs. Madison, and to assure her that, whenever it shall be her pleasure to visit the House, she be requested to take a seat within the Hall."[14]

On May 24, 1844, another recognition of Dolley's high standing came in the Supreme Court room of the Capitol. There, Samuel F.B. Morse, a nationally renowned portrait painter turned inventor, was prepared to make the first public demonstration of his electric recording telegraph. Wires had been strung between Washington and an office in Baltimore. In Washington, Morse had assembled sixteen people to witness the historic event, including Henry L. Ellsworth, the commissioner of patents; his daughter, Annie; and Dolley Madison. The first words to be sent to Baltimore, and then sent back to confirm the transmission, were dictated by Annie Ellsworth and came from the biblical book of Numbers, 23:23: "What hath God wrought?" The communication was successful. The test had worked! Then Morse turned to Dolley and asked if she wished to send a message. Knowing that a Baltimore cousin of hers, the wife of U.S. Representative John Wethered, was present at the other end, she asked Morse to send the following: "Message from Mrs. Madison. She sends her love to Mrs. Wethered." With this transmission, Dolley became the first person to send a personal message by telegraph.[15] The next day, the *Baltimore Patriot* exclaimed, "This is indeed the annihilation of space."[16]

Dolley got another lift in spirits from American soldiers and sailors in 1846. That year, the United States declared war on Mexico. Unlike 1814, when American troops abandoned the battlefield and deserted their posts at the White House, the soldiers setting off for war against Mexico marched past Dolley's home on Lafayette Square, cheering and saluting their heroine. Elizabeth Dean wrote, "They showed their admiration and respect to one who, more than thirty years before, had shown no lack of courage when a foreign enemy not only entered Washington, but also marched upon her very home."[17]

While these honors were pouring in, money was not. After Congress had purchased the first installment of Madison's papers, Dolley had negotiated an agreement to publish the second lot, amounting to four volumes, with Harper and Brothers, one of the largest publishers in the country. By 1840, the first of these volumes had not yet appeared, and Dolley grew fearful over the delays. She was seventy-two, and her mission remained as clear as ever. By 1844, the first volume lacked only two pages to be complete, but the books were never published.

Determined to see Madison's work preserved, she returned to Virginia in 1842. She rented out the Cutts' house again and lived at Montpellier. Then she made an excruciatingly difficult decision to sell half of Madison's beloved plantation to Richmond merchant Henry W. Moncure. The money from the sale proved insufficient for her needs, but she held onto the rest of the property — or tried to. She moved back to Washington in December 1843, her debts somewhat lessened, but still substantial, and all of her property was subject to the demands of her many creditors.

By this point, Dolley, a cosmopolitan woman at heart, had little but sentimental value for Montpellier, having lived there in the last few years chiefly because it was less expensive than Washington and was a place where the slaves willed to her by Madison could remain together. Then, in the summer of 1844, alarming news arrived. On July 5, Sarah, an educated Madison slave, wrote an urgent and profoundly distressing letter to Dolley, begging her to stop the sale of the slaves at Montpellier:

> My Mistress: I dont like to send you bad news but the condition of all of us your servants is very bad, and we do not know whether you are acquainted with it. The sheriff has taken all of us and says he will sell us at next court unless something is done before to prevent it — We are afraid we shall be bought by what are called negro buyers and sent away from our husbands and wives. If we are obliged to be sold perhaps you could get neighbors to buy us that have husbands and wives, so as to save us some misery which will in a greater or less degree be sure to fall upon us at being separated from you as well as from one another. We are very sure you are sorry for this state of things and we do not like to trouble you with it but think my dear mistress what our sorrow will be. The sale is only a fortnight from next monday but perhaps you could make some bargain with somebody by which we could be kept together.[18]

That summer, Dolley was forced to sell the rest of the plantation, its slaves, and other personal property to Moncure, with the stipulation that she held the right to buy it all back within five years. Her financial circumstances rendered that impossible. She lived out the last years of her life trying bravely to stay calm and positive in the face of overwhelming money problems.

A favorite nephew, James Madison Cutts, son of Anna and Richard, was born at the Cutts' house and was a frequent visitor to Montpellier. He recalled with sadness Dolley's last years:

> I remember her best in the last years of her life, when I often looked into her face and with a child's instinct knew she was in distress, and my father told me she was poor, and often being the bearer from him of small sums of money, I knew that she was in need and want, and well do I remember running from the Senate chamber as an avant-courier of my father the moment the Senate by its vote passed the appropriation of $20,000 to purchase the remaining letters and papers of Mr. Madison. Thus did Congress and a grateful country relieve her last distresses, and I arrived out of breath, the first to bring her the glad tidings which made us all happy for her dear sake.[19]

The sale of Madison's remaining papers came about in May 1848, just as Dolley was turning eighty. It provided $5,000 immediately and the interest income from a $20,000 trust fund set up in her name so that Payne could not get his hands on it. Her debts still greatly outdistanced the new funds, and she began selling off personal items, such as paintings and other furnishings, to pay the clamoring crowd of debtors.

In her last years, few of those who had the money or positions that provided them with the greatest ability to ease her life did anything to help her. These were the people who had flocked to her drawing rooms and partaken of her hospitality and generosity. Now they turned their backs. Much simpler folk, including Madison's enslaved valet, Paul Jennings, whom Dolley had inherited, and French John, were kinder and more helpful.

About 1840, Dolley had sold Jennings to Senator (later Secretary of State) Daniel Webster for $120 to enable Jennings to work himself out of slavery. In 1856, Webster wrote, "I have paid $120 for the freedom of Paul Jennings; he agrees to work out the same at $8 per month, to be furnished with board, clothes, washing, &c."[20] Jennings wrote the first memoir about life inside the White House, which was published in New York in 1865. From his unique vantage point as a former Madison slave, a former White House servant, and a freedman, he speaks eloquently of his love for the Madisons:

> In the last days of her life, before Congress purchased her husband's papers, she was in a state of absolute poverty, and I think sometimes suffered for the necessities of life. When I was a servant to Mr. Webster, he often sent me to her with a market-basket full of provisions,

President James K. Polk (center), Dolley Madison (second from right), Anna Payne (second from left), and others in 1846 or 1847

and told me whenever I saw anything in the house that I thought she was in need of, to take it to her. I often did this, and occasionally gave her small sums from my own pocket, though I had years before bought my freedom of her.[21]

Even in the last few years of her life, Dolley was vigorous, active, and mobile. She was an honored guest at the 1845 inauguration of President James K. Polk, the last president she would meet. In all, she lived through the terms of eleven of them: George Washington, John Adams, Thomas Jefferson, James Madison, James Monroe, John Quincy Adams, Andrew Jackson, Martin Van Buren, William Henry Harrison, John Tyler, and James K. Polk. In addition, she outlived all but the last three. In 1848, she served as honorary chair of a womens' group to raise funds for the Washington Monument and was a special guest at the ceremony when the cornerstone was laid on the Fourth of July.

One of her last major private acts was to join the Protestant Episcopal Church. Dolley had been unchurched since being ejected by the Quakers for marrying Madison in 1794. She had attended Episcopal church services in Washington numerous times with her husband. On July 15, 1845, both Dolley and Anna Payne were confirmed and formally welcomed into the membership of St. John's Episcopal Church in Washington. On the twenty-seventh, she complied with a request from the rector, the Reverend Mr. John Pyne, to state her full name to be entered into the church's confirmation

St. John's Episcopal Church, Washington

register. She wrote it out in a clear, even hand, "Dolley Payne Madison."

In 1849, Anna Payne and those close to Dolley noticed that she was losing strength, although her mind remained clear. Her niece, Mary E.E. Cutts, saw her often in the last years of her life and recorded many of the stories Dolley told her. One day, while a loved one was reading the Bible to her, Dolley fell asleep. She slept for eighteen hours, and her alarmed family called for a doctor. He called in specialists, and they concluded that Dolley was suffering from apoplexy — paralysis or unconsciousness from a stroke.

Relatives and old friends soon gathered at her side. Her son, Payne, happened to be there, and when she heard his voice, said Mary Cutts, "she gave utterance to these words, 'My poor boy.'"[22] Eliza Collins Lee was with her in the last hours, and occasionally Dolley would awaken for a short time, "smile her long smile, put out her arms to embrace those whom she loved and were near her, then gently relapse into that rest which was peace."[23] Eliza had the reassurance that Dolley was conscious and not in pain during her last hours. She later wrote to her son, Zaccheus Collins Lee, "When frequently requested to open her eyes by her Niece Annie Payne — she at length did so — and looking round on the Ladies around her Bed — *she* caught *my eye* — when I said to her do you know me. She said with a distink'd voice and sweet smile — 'Do I *know* you, my dear Betsey — Yes, and I love you.'"[24]

Dolley Payne Todd Madison died between ten and eleven p.m. on Thursday, July 12, 1849. Her remains were prepared and placed in a coffin at her home. Friends and family paid their last respects at the Cutts' house for several days. The coffin was moved to St. John's church on the morning of Monday, July 16, where Dolley lay in state until four o'clock that afternoon. During the day, hundreds of people paid their respects to their former friend and the nation's former presidentress. The last rites of the church were performed at four o'clock. In the large, solemn gathering, two elderly people sat together in the pew immediately behind the one reserved for family and relatives. In the days to come, there would be a national outpouring of grief for the woman who had inspired and touched the hearts of so many thousands of people, but no one would miss them more than the frail old man who held the hand of the fragile old woman in the second pew.

When the ceremony was over, the funeral procession, which was said to have been larger than any ever seen in the city, accompanied the casket to a vault in the Congressional Cemetery. The procession included the clergy, ten pallbearers, the family, the president and his cabinet, the diplomatic corps, the members of the Senate and the House of Representatives, the justices of the Supreme Court, officers of the army and navy, the mayor of Washington, thousands of strangers, and Dolley's two dear, elderly friends from the second pew at St. John's Church.

Save for James Madison himself, there were no other people who could possibly have better appreciated the life and value of Dolley Payne Todd Madison than those two: Eliza Collins Lee, seventy-nine, and Anthony Morris, eighty-three, who had been maid of honor and best man at Dolley's first wedding, fifty-nine years before.

Epilogue

J ust before Dolley died, she signed a will that replaced one that Payne Todd had written for her and persuaded her to sign on June 11, 1849. His version, to no one's surprise, left all of Dolley's estate to him. Dolley signed the final will, drawn up during her death vigil by her closest friends, on July 9, three days before her death. The final will directed that Payne receive all her belongings except the $20,000 placed in trust for Dolley by Congress, which was to be equally divided between Payne and Dolley's niece-companion, Anna Payne. Payne contested the will, claiming Anna Payne's share as his own. In 1851, the courts decided that the last will, favoring Anna Payne, was valid.

Always ambivalent about owning slaves, Madison did not emancipate his slaves in his will, as George Washington had, but passed them on to Dolley. In order to keep them together, she sold them along with the plantation in 1844, but retained some slaves in Washington. An inventory of her personal property taken after her death shows that her Washington slaves (probably three to five) were valued at $2,000.[1]

Anna Payne moved out of the Cutts' house after Dolley died and, a year later, married Dr. James H. Causten, Jr. As

359

the administrator of the estate niggled with Anna Payne Causten over the ownership of several small items Dolley had given her during their time together, Payne was injured in a fall and sought treatment in Boston. There he contracted typhoid fever and, in weakened condition, returned to Washington. He died on January 16, 1852. His funeral was to be attended by Clara Wilcox Payne, widow of John C. Payne, and Anna Payne Causten and her husband. But the weather was bad, and the only people who attended were Dr. Causten, two of Payne's other male relatives, his administrators, some of his past companions, and a few gentlemen, who out of respect for his mother, paid the last duty to his remains.[2] He was interred in the Congressional Cemetery.

Because Payne had substantial debts, his few personal assets — including family paintings and Dolley's dresses — were sold at public auction. Dr. Causten arranged for these items to be purchased at the auction to keep them in the family.

The monuments to Dolley (left) and James Madison at Montpelier

He also arranged to have Dolley's remains moved from the Congressional Cemetery — Payne's choice — to a private vault, awaiting negotiations to inter her at the cemetery at Montpellier, which was no longer in family hands. The negotiations were successful, and Dolley's casket was removed from the Causten family vault on January 12, 1858, and interred adjacent to the remains of her beloved husband.

The rest of Payne's estate, which included furniture and personal effects from Montpellier, had been taken to Toddsberthe, Payne's nearby plantation house, in 1844.

Anna Causten arranged for her husband to buy as much of the estate as possible, including the Gilbert Stuart portraits of James and Dolley.

Anna and James Causten had a daughter, Mary, who was born in 1851, shortly before her mother's death. Anna died in 1852 and was interred in the Causten family vault next to her famous aunt, until Dolley was reinterred at Montpellier. Mary Causten inherited Dolley's treasures, and she married John Kunkel in 1873. In 1899, Mary Kunkel decided to sell many of the Dolley Madison heirlooms and had a catalog printed. The remaining portion of Dolley's things passed to Mary's son, John Baker Kunkel III, who married Neva Ryder. Hard times during the Depression caused the Kunkels to sell a portion of Dolley's possessions. The remainder was stored in the couple's home. John died in 1944 and was survived by his wife. In 1956, she and her dog and cat were all found in her house, dead of malnutrition.

A workman hired to clean out the house had been alerted by the estate attorneys that the contents might include historical items related to Dolley Madison. He found family portraits and an old trunk containing the remainder of Dolley's possessions, including Matthew Brady daguerreotypes (reproduced in this book), letters, records, and clothing. In 1958, the entire collection was sold to a newly formed nonprofit corporation, The Dolley Madison Memorial Association, Inc., for $10,000. After detailed consultations with the Greensboro Historical Museum, the collection was transferred there in 1963. Following a meticulous inventory by Caroline Bivens, the museum opened a permanent display of Dolley's portraits, dresses, and personal memorabilia as a memorial to her.

After 1844, Montpellier went through six owners in the next fifty-seven years. In 1901, the property, by then known as "Montpelier," with a single "l," was purchased by William duPont, Sr., and the duPonts nearly doubled its size and substantially altered the interior. William's daughter, Marion, inherited the estate in 1928 and added two horse-racing tracks to the property, along with numerous working buildings. Marion duPont Scott died in 1983, deeding Montpelier to the National Trust for Historic Preservation. It was opened to the public in 1987, and in 2000 The Montpelier Foundation became steward of the property.

Marion duPont Scott directed that Montpelier be restored "in such a manner as to conform as nearly as possible with the architectural pattern which existed when said property was owned and occupied by President Madison." The restoration will reduce the house from the duPont-era's fifty-five rooms to the twenty-two-room configuration that the Madisons knew in the 1820s. The deconstruction and restoration of the house started in 2004.[3]

The intellectual preservation of Dolley's legacy began in earnest in 1956, when the Papers of James Madison project decided to give Dolley's papers the same care and attention as those of her husband. The primary objective—to publish scholarly editions of all Madison's papers—has already resulted in twenty-three volumes. The project also nourished two other notable Madison books: Ralph Ketcham's *James Madison: A Biography* (1971) and David B. Mattern and Holly C. Shulman's *The Selected Letters of Dolley Payne Madison*, both published by the University of Virginia Press.

The availability of the James and Dolley Madison papers, from which this book draws deeply, will continue to encourage potential authors of new books on the Madisons. Dolley's memory and legacy will flourish and grow, given this rich new source of the details of her life.

One delightful piece of Dolleyania has defied accurate documentation to this day: the belief that it was Dolley who inaugurated the tradition of the annual White House Easter egg roll on Easter Monday. Neither Dolley nor any of her contemporaries mentions this event in any document located to date, but true or not, the tradition is now firmly attached to Dolley's White House years.

Ethel Stephens Arnett, one of Dolley's more recent biographers, wrote that young John Payne Todd had heard that an egg hunt or roll had been practiced by the Egyptians and suggested that his mother adopt the game for him and his friends. "Dolley liked the idea," Arnett wrote, "and with her own hands tinted hundreds of hard-boiled eggs in bright colors, invited the children of the area to come and play with them, and thus started the Easter Egg Hunt on the White House Lawn." [4] She is said by some to have started the tradition on the grounds of the Capitol.

In the original version of the egg roll, children brought baskets of colored hard-boiled eggs and sat in long rows, one line at the upper terrace of the slope; another at the bottom. Those at the top sent the eggs rolling to the bottom, where the recipients scrambled for the hopping eggs and ran them back to the top, shrieking with laughter. As the merriment progressed, the children started rolling along with the eggs, and great fun was had by all. White House historian, William Seale, researched the tradition and wrote that President Rutherford B. Hayes "had begun the tradition of rolling Easter eggs on the White House lawn. This Easter Monday custom had originated at the Capitol many years before; no one remembering exactly when." [5] The popular children's event has continued, despite wartime interruptions, to this day.

Hundreds of newspaper and magazine articles and books have been written about Dolley in the more than 150 years since she died, but nowhere is Dolley more popular than in the realm of children's literature. Dolley, who had always wanted to have more children, surrounded herself with young people as much as she could, and children were drawn to her. Many fine women have served as "presidentress" since Martha Washington, but more children's books have been published about Dolley Madison than about any other First Lady. The former Quaker farm girl from North Carolina would have liked that.

Acknowledgements

B ooks such as this one come to life only with the help of an army of generous, selfless scholars, librarians, archivists, curators, archaeologists, photographers, and digital media specialists who collect, preserve, and willingly share their knowledge. I am deeply indebted to the following people and institutions for helping me understand Dolley Madison's world. But in the end, everything written here is the product of the author, who is solely responsible for any errors of omission or commission.

From abroad, Diane Claeys, of Claeys Antiques, Brugge, Belgium, provided me with information on Madison's Mechlin lace, and Henrik Stissing Jensen, Assistant Archivist of the Royal Danish National Archives, Copenhagen, furnished information about Danish diplomatic representatives in the United States during the Madison period.

In South Carolina, the staff of Corinthian Books worked with unexcelled efficiency to produce this book. They included my veteran "dream team" publishing colleagues: Diane Anderson, senior editor; Betty Burnett, Ph.D., associate editor; Rob Johnson, graphic designer; and Steve McCardell, typesetter;

along with researchers Nadia Shamsedin, Susann D. Gilbert, and Jennifer L. North. In addition, I had the usual heroic help from the Charleston County Library system, from Valerie Perry of The Historic Charleston Foundation, and from Marge McNeill, Registrar of the Theodosia Burr Chapter of the National Society of the Daughters of the American Revolution.

In Kentucky, Manuscript Librarian Claire McCann of the Special Collections and Archives Department, Margaret I. King Library, University of Kentucky, Lexington, helped me locate a rare letter. At the Maryland Historical Society, Elizabeth Proffen and Ruth Mitchell helped me locate letters and images. In New Jersey, William Mason, Site Administrator, and Beverly Weaver, Director of the Office of Historic Sites, furnished information and images of The Indian King Tavern Museum.

In North Carolina, at The Greensboro Historical Museum, Susan Webster, Registrar; Stephen Catlett, Archivist; and Jon Zachman, Curator of Collections, helped me understand Dolley's physical legacies, while Brooke Martin assisted with my photography. At Guilford College, Gwen Gosney Erickson, Librarian of The Friends Historical Collection, Hege Library, and her veteran predecessor, Carol Treadway, guided me through the manuscript records and the intricacies of life of the early North Carolina Quakers of the New Garden Monthly Meeting. And in Philadelphia, Andrea Ashby of the Independence National Historical Park rushed me photographs and documents from their collections.

Nowhere did I receive more help or a warmer welcome than in Virginia, where Dolley spent most of her life. In Richmond, Catherine E. Dean, Curator of Collections, and Chandler Battaile, Director of Development of the Association for the Preservation of Virginia Antiquities (A.P.V.A./Preservation Virginia), reviewed my data and furnished theirs on Scotchtown plantation's chain of title. At The Valentine Richmond History Center, Richmond, Teresa Roane, Director of Archives and Photographic Services, located more valuable Dolley letters, as did the reference staff of The Library of Virginia.

At Scotchown, in Hanover County, Site Administrator Susan V. Nepomuceno explained the intricacies of daily life at Patrick Henry's home, which was acquired, restored, and is operated as a museum by A.P.V.A./Preservation Virginia. By far the most fruitful and interesting part of my research was the weeks spent at that mother lode of all things Madisonian: the Alderman Library of the University of Virginia in Charlottesville. To work in a single building that housed four massive scholarly projects, namely the Papers of James Madison, the Papers of Dolley Madison, the Papers of George Washington, and the Papers of Thomas Jefferson, and to have access to the staffs of all four, was a once-in-a-lifetime research experience.

At the Alderman Library, I met Dr. Holly Cowan Shulman, Research Associate Professor in the Studies in Women and Gender program, as well as the director of The Dolley Madison Project. I owe particular thanks to Dr. David B. Mattern, Associate Editor of the Papers of James Madison, and to Mary A. Hackett, Assistant Editor, for sharing their comprehensive knowledge and insights, and also to Dr. Angela Kreider, Assistant Editor, and research assistant, Wendy Ellen Perry. Down the hall, Dr. Frank E. Grizzard, Jr., Senior Associate Editor of the Papers of George Washington, and his colleagues, Beverly H. Runge, Associate Editor, and Dr. John C. Pinheiro, Assistant Editor, fielded my questions about contacts between the Madisons and the Washingtons. Michael Plunkett, Director of the Albert and Shirley Small Special Collections Library, explained the intricacies of their Dolley and James Madison holdings.

In Orange County, at James Madison's Montpelier, Lee Langston-Harrison, Curator; Allison Enos, Associate Registrar; Beth Taylor, Director of Education; Dr. Matthew D. Reeves, Archaeologist; and Ann L.B. Miller, Research Scientist, shared their extensive data and expanded my understanding of Dolley and James Madison's relationship with Montpelier and the senior Madisons. At George Washington's Mount Vernon, Mary V. Thompson, Research Specialist with the Mount

Vernon Ladies' Association, helped me understand the Washingtons' relationship with Dolley, and at Belle Grove Plantation, Ed Presley furnished me with portraits of James Sr. and Nelly Madison. Diane P. Elliott, Photography Manager at James Madison University Photographic Services, provided Madison wine bottle images, and Kenneth M. Clark, Historian, The James Madison Museum, in Orange, was very helpful. In West Virginia, my good friend, Dr. Ray Swick, located two marvelous nuggets of Madisonia for me at his *alma mater*, Miami University, Oxford, Ohio. At Harewood House, where Dolley and James were married, Mr. Walter Washington, a descendant of President George Washington, led me to a fine photograph of the room where the wedding took place.

In the nation's capital, the Photoduplication Service of the Library of Congress fielded numerous image inquiries in record time. In the Manuscripts Division, Fred Bauman took special care in copying for me the August 23-24 letter from Dolley to her sister, which immortalizes the peak of her heroism in the war of 1812. At The Octagon House, the museum of the American Architectural Foundation, Mari Nakahara, Assistant Collections Manager, quickly provided the images I needed. At the Smithsonian's National Museum of American History, Lisa Cathleen Grady furnished valuable information about Dolley's dresses. Jennifer Robertson, Rights and Reproductions Coordinator, National Portrait Gallery, helped me locate yet another portrait of Dolley. Harmony Haskins, Photo Archivist at the White House Historical Association, helped me obtain the stunning image of Dolley by Gilbert Stuart.

Mary-Beth Kavanaugh and Jill Reichenbach of the New-York Historical Society gave me rapid access to three other Madison portraits, as did Ryan Hyman, F.M. Kirby Curator of Collections, and Janice Ranger, Visitor Services & Public Programs Coordinator of the Macculloch Hall Historical Museum in Morristown, New Jersey. At The Schlesinger Library, Radcliffe Institute for Advanced Study, Harvard University, I cannot fail to thank Kathryn Allamong Jacob, Johanna-Maria Fraenkel Curator of Manuscripts, for explaining the myster-

D. P. Madison

ies of the Mary Estelle Elizabeth Cutts Papers. Many other archives, libraries, and institutions also furnished invaluable assistance, but the names of the staff members who helped so much were not provided.

Numerous other people, including book and manuscript dealers, auctioneers, collectors, genealogists, and practitioners of a dozen arcane specialties, each contributed to the information in this book. They included Tim Berschauer, Richard W. Spellman, Jane M. Roberts, Diane Payne, Leslie Bailey, Gary Savoy, Peterson Clarence, Al Miedma, Darren Kister, Chandler A. Peterson, Amy Orr, Jos Vanderhoydonk, Richard R. Rogers, Diane Moore Woodruff, Lawrance Bernabo, and the inimitable Peter Tavino. I thank them one and all.

Illustration Credits

When the image is a photograph taken by the author or made from an original print or engraving in the author's collection, it is identified as (RNC). Images from the Prints and Photographs Division of the Library of Congress are identified as PPD (DLC), and images from the Greensboro Historical Museum are identified as (GHM). The sources of all other images are specified in full. Dolley, regardless of her marital status at the time, is noted as DM; her husband, James, is noted as JM. Each image was researched to determine the copyright holder. Please notify the author concerning any omissions or inaccuracies, which will be corrected in the next edition.

Dust jacket. Front cover and spine: DM by Gilbert Stuart, courtesy of the White House Historical Association (White House Collection); background: The Burning of Washington, as depicted in *The Stationer's Almanack,* London, 1815 (DLC). Back cover: DM by George Catlin, courtesy of the Macculloch Hall Historical Museum. Front flap: DM by Bass Otis, collection of the New-York Historical Society.

Front matter. Page ix, DM, engraver unknown, after an 1812 portrait by William Chappell (RNC); xii: JM, engraving by Sealy (RNC).

Chapter 1: In Harm's Way. Page xx: DM, engraver unknown, after a painting by Alonzo Chappel, published by Johnson, Wilson & Co., New York (RNC); 2: telescope photograph by RNC, courtesy of Blennerhassett Island Historical State Park; 3: JM, engraved by H. B. Hall after an unknown artist (DLC); 6: The President's House in 1807, from Charles William Janson, *The Stranger in America*, 1807.

Chapter 2: A Child Among Friends. Page 14: George III, engraved by C. Warren after a portrait by R. Corbould; published by J. Stratford Holburn Hill, London; 25: maps from Stephen B. Weeks, *Southern Quakers and Slavery*, 1896; 34: An artist's conception of the Paynes' house, drawing by Anna Belle Bonds, from Ethel Stephens Arnett, *Mrs. James Madison: The Incomparable Dolley*, 1972.

Chapter 3: The Flower of Youth. Page 42: Dolley Madison's needlework, photograph by Margaret Boylan Smoot (GHM); 44: Scotchtown Plantation, and 45: The ladies' parlor, photographs by RNC, courtesy of Scotchtown Plantation / APVA Preservation Virginia; 51: A child ought to have pretty trinkets to wear, drawing by Sandra James in *Dolley Madison, Quaker Girl*, 1944; 52: The Cedar Creek Meeting House, from Bell, *Our Quaker Friends*, 1905; 57: The Indian King Tavern Museum, courtesy of the New Jersey Division of Parks and Forestry; 68: Quaker silhouette from Robert Wilson, *Philadelphia Quakers, 1681-1981*.

Chapter 4: Love, Marriage, and Yellow Fever. Page 72: Second Street North from Market St. with Christ Church. Philadelphia, drawn and engraved by W. Birch & Son, published by R. Campbell & Co., Philadelphia (DLC); 74: The City of Philadelphia, base map: Map of Philadelphia in 1776, drawn by P.C. Varte, engraved by Scott (DLC); 76: Independence Hall, Philadelphia, engraved by J. Rogers (RNC); 86: Mary Payne's boarding house, from Allen C. Clark, *The Life and Letters of Dolly Madison*, 1914; 88: The Pine Street Meeting House, drawing by an unknown artist, from Ella Kent Barnard, *Dorothy Payne, Quakeress*, 1909; 89: Elizabeth ("Eliza") Collins Lee, from Clark, *Life and Letters*; 91: John Todd, Jr., by Charles Willson Peale, courtesy of Macculloch Hall Historical Museum; 91 & 92: John and Dolley Todd's house, also The Todd family's kitchen, Philadelphia, courtesy of Independence National Historical Park, Philadelphia; 106: Aaron Burr, mezzotint engraving by E. Gridley (RNC).

Chapter 5: In Second Blush. Page 110: Dolley's wedding dress for her marriage to James Madison, photograph by Margaret Boylan Smoot (GHM); 113: JM, engraved by Johnson, Fry & Co., New York, after a painting by Alonzo Chappel (RNC); 115: Martha Washington, engraved by Johnson, Wilson & Co., Publishers, New York; published by Johnson, Fry & Co. (RNC); 120: Dolley's engagement ring, photograph by RNC, courtesy of the National Trust for Historic Preservation; 122: The drawing room of Harewood House, photograph by Van Jones Martin, courtesy of Walter Washington; 124: signatures of DM (GHM); 125: James Madison's vest, photograph by Margaret Boylan Smoot (GHM); 126: A fluting iron, photograph by RNC, courtesy of Scotchtown Plantation / APVA Preservation Virginia; 127: DM by James Peale (DLC).

Chapter 6: Mrs. Madison's Debut. Page 130: DM by Gilbert Stuart, courtesy the White House Historical Association (White House Collection); 138: James Madison, Sr., also 139: Nelly Conway Madison, both by Charles Peale Polk, courtesy Belle Grove Plantation, a National Trust Historic Site; 142: James Madison, Sr's, wine bottle, photograph by Diane P. Elliott, courtesy of James Madison University Photographic Services, Harrisonburg, Virginia; 146: James Monroe, engraved by Johnson, Fry, & Co., New York, after a painting by Alonzo

Chappell (RNC); 151: Mary Wollstonecraft by John Opie, courtesy of The Tate Gallery, London; 155: Dolley's calling card case, photograph by RNC (GHM); 160: Sarah (Sally) McKean Martínez, Marchioness de Casa Yrujo, engraved by D. Appleton & Co., New York, for Griswold's *The Republican Court*, 1861; 161: Carlos Fernando Martínez, Marquis de Casa Yrujo, from Clark, *Life and Letters*; 162: Abigail Adams, engraved by G.F. Storm after a painting by Gilbert Stuart (RNC).

Chapter 7: Within a Squirrel's Jump of Heaven. Page 172: Montpelier—The Home of President Madison, woodcut by Pierson Eng. New York, (RNC); 175: base map: school textbook, c. 1870 (RNC); 178: JM and 179: DM, both by James Sharpeles, Sr., courtesy of Independence National Historical Park; 182: Montpellier floorplan, courtesy of The Montpelier Foundation; 184: The Temple, photograph by RNC courtesy of The Montpelier Foundation.

Chapter 8: The Washington Quadrille. Page 198: Thomas Jefferson, after an engraving made by Charles B. J. F. de Saint-Mémin (RNC); 204: The State Floor of the President's House, 1803, by Benjamin Latrobe (DLC); 207: The Six Buildings on Pennsylvania Avenue, from Clark, *Life and Letters*; 213: Thomas Jefferson, engraved by Sealy (RNC); 226: Martha "Patsy" Jefferson Randolph, 1861 engraved by J. Rogers after a painting by Thomas Sully for Griswold's *The Republican Court*, 1861; 231: Dolley's snuff box, photograph by RNC (GHM).

Chapter 9: Our Hearts Understand Each Other. Page 236: DM, engraved by J.F.E. Prud'homme after a drawing by James Herring after a portrait by Joseph Wood (RNC).

Chapter 10: The Presidentress. Page 252: tunic from the Bey of Tunis, photograph by RNC (GHM); 254: JM, and 255: DM, both by Thomas Christian Lübbers, accession numbers 1939.243 and 1939.244, collections of The New-York Historical Society; 264: chair designed by Benjamin Latrobe and 265:

sofa designed by Benjamin Latrobe, both courtesy of the Maryland Historical Society, Baltimore, Maryland; 266: The Reign of Dolly Madison, engraved by L. M. Glacksing, poem by Roy Farrell Greene, in *Puck*, April 24, 1901; 268: Washington Irving, engraved by Moseley Isaac Danforth after a painting by Charles Robert Leslie, published by James Herring, New York (RNC); 276: tunic from the Bey of Tunis, photograph by RNC (GHM).

Chapter 11: From Hostess to Heroine. Page 282: JM and the Burning of Washington, engraved by R.E. Babson after a painting by Gilbert Stuart, published by Walker & White, Boston, New York, Phil. & Baltimore (RNC); 284: Vice Admiral Sir George Cockburn, mezzotint by C. Turner from a portrait by J. J. Halls in The National Maritime Museum, London (DLC); 288: March of the British Army from Benedict to Bladensburg, from Benson J. Lossing, *The Pictorial Field-Book of the War of 1812*; 296: George Washington, by Gilbert Stuart, PPD (DLC); 302: The Capture and Burning of Washington, woodcut, 1876, from Richard Miller Devins, *Our First Century*, 1876, PPD (DLC); 308: Belle Vue, from Clark, *Life and Letters*; 310: The Taking of the City of Washington in America, London: published by G. Thompson; 312: The President's House after the Conflagration, engraved by William Strickland after a drawing by George Munger, PPD (DLC); 314: The Fall of Washington, or Maddy in Full Flight, cartoon published in London by S.W. Fores, PPD (DLC); 316: DM by Bass Otis, collection of the New-York Historical Society; 317: The Octagon House, photographed by Robert C. Lautman, courtesy of the Prints and Drawings Collection, The Octagon, The Museum of the American Architectural Foundation, Washington, D.C.; 320: The Seven Buildings, from Clark, *Life and Letters*.

Chapter 12: Adam and Eve in Paradise. Page 324: DM by George Catlin, courtesy of the Macculloch Hall Historical Museum; 327: John Payne Todd, by William Kurtz, in Clark, *Life and Letters*; Montpellier in 1836, engraved by J.F.E.

Prud'homme, after a drawing by John G. Chapman (RNC); 332: The Montpellier dining room, photograph by Michael Remorenko, courtesy The Montpelier Foundation and the National Trust for Historic Preservation; 336: JM, engraved by Thomas B. Welch after a drawing by James B. Longacre (RNC).

Chapter 13: Days of Grace and Honor. Page 340: daguerreotype of DM by Matthew Brady (GHM); 342: Dolley Madison's white turban, photograph by RNC (GHM); 343: Anna Coles Payne, by Charles Bird King, photograph by RNC (GHM); 347: The Richard Cutts House, PPD (DLC); 348: DM and Anna Payne, by Matthew Brady (GHM); 350: Jesse D. Elliott medal, photograph by RNC (GHM); 355: DM and President James K. Polk group photo, daguerreotype by G.P.A. Healy(?), courtesy of the George Eastman House; 356: St. John's Episcopal Church, from Clark, *Life and Letters*.

Epilogue: Page 360: The monuments to Dolley and James Madison, photograph by RNC, courtesy The Montpelier Foundation.

$\mathscr{Source}\ \mathscr{Notes}$

CHAPTER 1: In Harm's Way

1 Benson J. Lossing, author of *The Pictorial Field-Book of the War of 1812* (New York: Harper & Brothers, 1868), 922, put the American force at about 7,000 men, of whom 900 were trained enlisted men and 400 were cavalry. Their artillery firepower consisted only of twenty-six cannons, twenty of which were only small six-pounders.

2 James Pack, *The Man Who Burned the White House: Admiral Sir George Cockburn, 1772-1853* (Annapolis: Naval Institute Press, 1987), 14.

3 It was the first and last time that a sitting American president ever took the field of battle in command of his troops. Population ratios: Anthony S. Pitch, "The Burning of Washington," in *Journal of the White House Historical Association*, Fall 1998, 9.

4 JM, at Mr. William's about 6 or 7 miles from Washington, to DPM, August 23, 1814, noted as item 91 in Frederick B. McGuire-Madison catalog dated February 26, 1917.

5 DPM to Lucy Payne Washington Todd, August 23, 1814. DMP (DLC).

6 John Van Ness statement, November 23, 1814, *American State Papers*, Mil. 16, 1:581, in Pitch, "The Burning of Washington," 9.

7 Eleanor Young Jones, Washington, to DPM, August 23, 1814, transcribed by Mary Estelle Elizabeth Cutts, in Mary E. E. Cutts Memoir I (MCR-S). Mary Cutts (1814-1856), Dolley's favored niece, was the daughter of Anna Payne and Richard Cutts. Mary saved and transcribed many of her letters, and wrote two very respectful versions of the life and times of her beloved aunt. The first, a thirty-two page manuscript, was written in the early 1850s and includes intimate details of Dolley's life that only she could have told her niece. Because the manuscript was not sequentially paginated, no page numbers are being cited here. This collection is known as Mary Estelle Elizabeth Cutts Papers (A/C 991), Schlesinger Library, Radcliffe Institute, Harvard University, and will be cited as Cutts Memoir I (MCR-S). Mary Cutts later produced an edited version, which added historical background but cut out many of the personal details. This second version consists of sixty-one pages and was microfilmed by the Library of Congress as Cutts Memoir microfilm, part II (M-96) from originals owned by the George B. Cutts family. It will be cited as Cutts Memoir II (DLC). The first published work to embody information from Mary Cutts' two manuscripts was Lucia B. Cutts, *Memoirs and Letters of Dolly Madison* (Boston: Houghton Mifflin and Company, 1888). Lucia Cutts, Dolley's grandniece, heavily edited, rewrote, and Bowdlerized many of the letters Mary Cutts had transcribed. In this book, I have quoted from the best available manuscript version (original, photocopy, or scholarly transcription) of all letters, except as noted.

8 Ralph Ketcham, *James Madison: A Biography* (Charlottesville: University of Virginia Press, 1990), 577.

9 Walter Lord, *The Dawn's Early Light* (New York: W. W. Norton Co., 1972), 101.

10 Lord, 101.

11 Paul Jennings, *A Colored Man's Reminiscences of James Madison* (Brooklyn: George C. Beadle, 1865), 8.

12 *National Intelligencer*, Washington, August 24, 1814.

13 DPM to Edward Coles, May 13, 1813 (NjMoMHH).

14 DPM to Hannah Nicholson Gallatin, July 28, 1814, Albert Gallatin Papers, no. 113 (NHi).

15 DPM to John Payne Todd, August 6, 1814, Albert Gallatin Papers (NHi).

16 Alexander Cochrane to the Earl of Bathurst, July 14, 1814, War Office 1: Secretary of War (DLC), Library of Congress, in Pitch, "The Burning of Washington," 9; also Lord, illustration opp. p. 192.

17 Lord, 15.

18 Garry Willis, *James Madison* (New York: Times Books / Henry Holt & Co., 2002), 137.

19 Anthony S. Pitch, *The Burning of Washington: The British Invasion of 1814* (Annapolis: Bluejacket Books / Naval Institute Press, 1998), 88-89.

20 Lord, 145.

21 Jennings, 8-9.

22 Lord, 146.

23 Jennings, 9.

24 DPM to Mary Elizabeth Hazlehurst Latrobe, December 3, 1814, in Allen C. Clark, *Life and Letters of Dolly Madison* (Washington: Press of W. F. Roberts Company, 1914), 166. Hereafter cited as Clark. Anthony S. Pitch stated that he was "unable to locate the original or a handwritten copy of this much-quoted letter." As of June 2004 the author could not locate the original or any copy in any library or archive.

25 Spiking is the process of disabling a cannon by driving an iron spike into a cannon's touch-hole and then breaking off the remainder, thereby making it impossible to ignite the powder charge and fire the weapon.

26 DPM to Lucy Payne Washington Todd, August 23, 1814, DMP (DLC). Transcript made by Dolley Madison for Margaret Bayard Smith in 1836. For an analysis of this letter, see David B. Mattern, "Dolley Madison Has The Last Word: The Famous Letter," in *Journal of the White House Historical Association*, Fall 1998, 38-41.

27 DPM to Lucy Payne Washington Todd, August 23, 1814, DMP (DLC).

CHAPTER 2: A Child Among Friends

1 Claude G. Bowers, editor, *The Diary of Elbridge Gerry, Jr.* (New York: Brentano's, 1927), 178-179.

2 The term "vast cousinage," which so aptly characterizes the complex relationships resulting from the extensive intermarriage of families during the colonial period, was coined in the 1970s by Dr. Walter Edgar, head of the Institute for Southern Studies of the University of South Carolina.

3 Elizabeth Lummis Ellet, *The Queens Of American Society* (New York, Charles Scribner and Co., 1867), 239.

4 Maud Wilder Goodwin, *Dolly Madison* (New York: Charles Scribner's Sons, 1896), 4.

5 Cutts Memoir I (MCR-S).

6 The penciled notes of Dolley's grandniece, Mary Causten (Mrs. John) Kunkel, d. 1919, are the stated (and undocumented) source of the Pocahontas connection to Anna Fleming Payne. Kunkel Collection (NcGHM).

7 Ella Kent Barnard, *Dorothy Payne, Quakeress. A Side-Light Upon the Career of "Dolly" Madison* (Philadelphia: Ferris & Leach, 1909), 21.

8 Will of Josias Payne, *The Virginia Magazine of History and Biography*, VII: 80-81.

9 The will of Josias Payne, of Pittsylvania County, Virginia, was dated January 12, 1785, and proved December 19, 1785. *VMHB*, VII: 80-81. The children listed as heirs were George, Josias, John (who married Mary Coles), Susannah (who married William Heale), Anna (who married William Harrison), William, and Robert.

10 Barnard, 21-22.

11 Barnard, 22. The lieutenant governor, Spotswood, was the highest-ranking officer residing in Virginia during that part of the Proprietary period because the governor, the Earl of Orkney, remained in Britain and never visited the colony.

12 Lucia Beverly Cutts, ed., *Memoirs and Letters of Dolley Madison, Wife of James Madison, President of the United States.* (Boston: Houghton Mifflin Company, 1886), 4, states that William Coles' first wife bore the maiden name of Philpot and was an aunt of Patrick Henry, but provides no source.

13 Barnard, 33.

14 Barnard, 29.

15 Barnard, 29-30.

16 Barnard, 28-29.

17 Ethel Stephens Arnett, *Mrs. James Madison: The Incomparable Dolley* (Greensboro, North Carolina: Piedmont Press, 1972), 22.

18 Arnett, 22.

19 John Payne's birth date: New Garden Monthly Meeting records, vol. 1 (1743-1783), 29, FHC (NcGG). Great Britain ceased using the Julian, or "old style," calendar in 1752, as it had over the centuries accumulated an eleven-day lag. The adoption of the Gregorian calendar added eleven days to the old style date and changed the first day of the new year from March 25 to January 1. For some time after the official conversion, dates continued to be stated in the old style and were often annotated (o.s.).

20 Arnett, 20-21.

21 Barnard, 21.

22 Various sources (including Barnard, 26, and Arnett, 22) state that Coles Hill plantation was located in Hanover County, but *Old Homes of Hanover County, Virginia* (Hanover County, Virginia: The Hanover County Historical Society, 1983), makes no mention of it, perhaps because no dwelling house has survived. No history of Coles Hill plantation is known to exist.

D. P. Madison

23 "The Payne Family of Goochland," *VMHB* VI: 315.

24 "The Payne Family of Goochland," *VMHB* VII: 80-81.

25 Arnett, 2.

26 Seth B. Hinshaw, *The Carolina Quaker Experience, 1665-1985. An Interpretation* (North Carolina Yearly Meeting: North Carolina Friends Historical Society, 1984), 9.

27 Katharine Anthony, *Dolly Madison, Her Life and Times* (Garden City, New York: Doubleday & Co., 1949), 23.

28 Stephen B. Weeks, *Southern Quakers and Slavery: A Study in Institutional History* (Baltimore: The Johns Hopkins Press, 1896), 127-128.

29 Hinshaw, 30.

30 William M. Hale, ed., *The Colonial Records of North Carolina* (Raleigh, North Carolina: P.M. Hale, 1886) 1: (1662-1712), 45.

31 Hinshaw, 8, 12.

32 Hinshaw, 14-15.

33 James Pinckney Pleasant Bell, *Our Quaker Friends of Ye Olden Times. Being in Part a Transcript of the Minute Books of Cedar Creek meeting, Hanover County, and the South River meeting, Campbell County, Va.* (Lynchburg, Virginia.: J.P. Bell Co., Publishers, 1905), 145-157, *passim*.

34 Bell, 161-166, *passim*.

35 Weeks, 126.

36 Arnett, 16, citing Cedar Creek Monthly Meeting Minutes.

37 Arnett, 17.

38 Goodwin, 14.

39 Arnett, 3; Hiram H. Hilty, *New Garden Friends Meeting. The Christian People Called Quakers* (Greensboro, North Carolina: North Carolina Friends Historical Society, 1983), 68.

40 J. Hector St. John deCrèvecoeur, *Letters from an American Farmer; And, Sketches of Eighteenth-Century America* (London, 1782); reprinted (London: J.M. Dent & Sons), 1912, 133.

41 New Garden Monthly Meeting, Minutes, vol. 1 (November 1765–September 1775), FHC (NcGG).

42 Arnett, 3-4.

43 Arnett, 3-4, citing Register of Deeds, Rowan County, Salisbury, North Carolina, Deed Book VI: 250, 252, and 402.

44 Arnett, 6.

45 The tribe, whose name has been variously recorded as Keyawee, Kewawee, Keiauwee, and Kiawah, lived in the central portion of North and South Carolina between 1700 and 1750.

46 Arnett, 6, citing John Lawson, *A History of North Carolina* (1709, reprinted Richmond, Virginia: Garrett & Massie, 1951), 48-52.

47 Arnett, 5, citing Rowan County Deeds Book VI:402-403 and 575.

48 Arnett, 455n2.

49 Arnett, 6-7.

50 Arnett, 7.

51 Arnett, 8.

52 New Garden Monthly Meeting Records vol. 1 (1743-1783), FHC (NcGG).

53 Walter Payne's namesake: Arnett, 9.

54 New Garden Monthly Meeting Records vol. 1 (1743-1783), FHC (NcGG).

55 Goodwin, 2.

56 Archibald Henderson, "Dolly Madison Gave Her Age Wrong; Cut Off Four Years for Vanity's Sake," *Greensboro* (North Carolina) *Daily News*, June 3, 1928.

57 DPM, July 27, 1845, to The Rev. Smith Pyne, St. John's Church, Washington. In 1958, Margaret Brown Klapthor, The Smithsonian Institution's associate curator of history, contacted the newly established the Papers of James Madison project about her name. The staff of the Madison Papers confirmed her research: Dolley was indeed Dolley. The news made the front page of the June 13, 1958, issue of the *New York Times*, as well as the April 21 issue of *Time* magazine.

58 Arnett, 14-15, citing New Garden Monthly Meeting Records, FHC (NcGG).

59 Arnett, 456n14, citing Rowan County, N.C., Register of Deeds, Book VI, 575. The final transfer of the land did not take place until July 7, 1770, when a second deed was issued. By that time, John and Mary Payne had already returned to Virginia.

60 New Garden Monthly Meeting Records, vol. 1 (1743-1783), FHC (NcGG).

61 David B. Mattern and Holly C. Shulman, eds., *The Selected Letters of Dolley Payne Madison* (Charlottesville: University of Virginia Press, 2003), 10-11.

62 North Carolina. Historic Sites Section. *Alamance Battleground: Where the Regulators and Militia Met to End the War of the Regulation* (Raleigh, North Carolina: North Carolina Historic Sites, 1980).

63 Hilty, 18.

64 New Garden Monthly Meeting Minutes, vol. 1 (1743-1783), FHC (NcGG).

65 Margaret Bayard Smith, *The First Forty Years of Washington Society* (New York, Charles Scribner's Sons, 1906), 351.

66 Archibald Henderson wrote, "Dolly Madison was a wonderful, gracious, large-minded, and generous woman. But she had her little vanities — as we all have. And one of these was in regard to her age. She always said she was born in 1772, thus cutting off at a stroke four years from her age. Pardonable fib!"

67 Margaret Bayard Smith, "Mrs. Madison," *The National Portrait Gallery of Distinguished Americans* (New York: Herman Bancroft, 1836), III: 1-10.

68 Arnett, 17; also Barnard, 33, citing Cedar Creek Monthly Meeting Records, April 28, 1769.

CHAPTER 3: The Flower of Youth

1 The first record in which Dolley is quoted as having lived at Scotchtown is vague, and the details stated are inaccurate, save one. It appears in Cutts

𝒟. 𝒯. Madison

Memoir I (MCR-S) as follows: "[John Payne was a] resident of North Carolina, where his father had given him a plantation, but soon after his [1761] marriage he purchased an estate in Hanover County, Virginia, twenty miles from Coles Hill, the residence of William Coles. Later in life [when] Mrs. Madison was asked to describe this homestead, she said, 'I can just remember the mantel pieces, they were of black marble supported by white figures, there were twenty rooms on a floor, every one had marble hearths and mantels—it was built by an English nobleman and was called Scotch town because of the emigrants, and was surrounded with small brick houses attached to the main building.' It was purchased by her father from Peter Randal—or Randolph as he afterwards spelt his name." Because of the recollection of the black mantels, many hearths, and the sense that the house was very large (as most children think their houses are!), Dolley's description bears some similarity to Scotchtown. Its original mantels were indeed black marble, and all the living rooms did have hearths, but the house had eight rooms per floor, not twenty, and the outbuildings were not attached to the main house. No Randolphs appear in the documented chain of title, and the entire Payne connection to Scotchtown is ephemeral. Nevertheless, in Dolley's defense, it must be noted that she was but a toddler when she is believed to have briefly lived there, and there is no evidence that she returned to visit in later life to update her early childhood memories of the place.

2 *Virginia: A Guide to the Old Dominion* (Washington: Federal Writer's Project, 1941), 353-354.

3 Norine Dickson Campbell, *Patrick Henry: Patriot and Statesman* (Old Greenwich, Connecticut: Devin-Adair Co., 1969), 93, citing *Journal of the House of Burgesses*, 1766-1769, 281.

4 Scotchtown, in Beaverdam, Hanover County, Virginia, was deeded to APVA Preservation Virginia, Richmond, in 1958. They restored the house to its Patrick-Henry-era appearance, and it is now open as a public museum.

5 Barnard, 34. These fireplaces, altered during the Victorian period, have been reconstructed to their Henry-era configuration.

6 Robert D. Meade, *Patrick Henry, Patriot in the Making* (Philadelphia: J. B. Lippincott, 1969), 279.

7 Madeira was the favored wine of the southern colonies because of its unique quality: unlike most wines, it aged best when stored hot. For the unique place of Madeira wine and wine garrets in Southern history, see Richard N. Côté, "Fine Wines and Thoroughbreds: The Correspondence Between Thomas Jefferson and Col. William Alston," American Wine Society *Journal*, vol. 28, no. 4 (Winter 1996), 112.

8 Campbell, 17.

9 Interview by the author with Susan V. Nepomuceno, Site Administrator, Scotchtown Plantation, April 24, 2004.

10 Sarah's death date: Campbell, 122n8.

11 Campbell, 94; also interview with Susan V. Nepomuceno.

12 Campbell, 94n30, citing William Coles of St. Martin's Parish to his daughter, Mary Payne, 176 acres, purchased from William Winston, Jr.,

deceased. Hanover County Court Records, 1783-1792, 110, dated September 5, 1771.

13 Arnett, 18.

14 Barnard, 37.

15 DPM to Anna Payne Cutts, August 19, 1805. DMC (#1661), Tracy W. McGregor Library (ViU).

16 J. William Frost, *The Quaker Family in Colonial America* (New York: St. Martins Press, 1973), 70-80.

17 Jessamyn West, *The Quaker Reader* (New York: Viking, 1962), 222.

18 Goodwin, 5.

19 Cutts Memoir I (MCR-S).

20 Bell, 104, 132-135.

21 Barnard, 33, citing Cedar Creek Monthly Meeting Records.

22 Anthony, 3.

23 Goodwin, 10.

24 Goodwin, 10.

25 Jay Worrall, Jr., *The Friendly Virginians: America's First Quakers* (Athens, Georgia: Iberia Publishing Co., 1994), 250.

26 Accessions NT1987.13.a-b in the collection of James Madison's Montpelier (ViMpMPL). Both Hannah and Rachel were friends from Burlington, New Jersey.

27 Arnett, 29.

28 DPT, Hair-wood, September 16, 1794, to Eliza Collins Lee, Loudoun County, DMP (DLC).

29 Arnett, 29.

30 Barnard, 54.

31 Arnett, 28.

32 Barnard, 54-56; Arnett, 26-27.

33 Conover Hunt-Jones, *Dolley and the "Great Little Madison"* (Washington: American Institute of Architects Foundation, 1977), 7-8.

34 Judith Richardson (1763-1852) married Judge Charles Smith of New Kent and lived at Wakefield plantation, Hanover County, Virginia. She died without issue. Annotation by Valentine Museum, Richmond, of transcript of a letter from DPM, to Judith Richardson, June 1783 (ViRVal).

35 Dolley Payne to Judith Richardson [Smith], Rocky Hills, Virginia, March 1, 1800 (ViRVal).

36 Robert Douglas Roller, *Richardson-DePriest Family* (Charleston, West Virginia: privately published, 1905), 10. A photostatic copy of the entire letter is on file at the Valentine Richmond History Center, Richmond, Virginia (ViRVal).

37 Harriet Tayloe Upton, "The Family of James Madison," in *Wide Awake* (Boston, May 1888), 382.

38 See for example DPM to John Payne Todd, Mechanic Hall Place, New York, April 9, 1823 (ViU).

39 W. Jay Mills, *Historic Houses of New Jersey* (Philadelphia: J. B. Lippincott, 1902), 328. Like so many other details about Dolley's early life, these traditional stories recorded by W. Jay Mills about her relationship

with the Creightons and their tavern are undocumented. Since 1903, the tavern has been owned and operated as a New Jersey state historical site and is open to visitors.

40 Hoag Levins, "Indian King Tavern Museum," n.d.

41 Levins.

42 George R. Prowell, *The History of Camden County, New Jersey* (Philadelphia: L. J. Richards & Co., 1886), 113.

43 Mills, 329.

44 Anthony, 11.

45 Bell, 104.

46 Worrall, 196.

47 Worrall, 197.

48 Worrall, 207.

49 Bell, iii.

50 Anthony, 16-17.

51 Cutts Memoir I (MCR-S). Dolley's grandniece, Lucia B. Cutts, did not perpetuate this myth in her 1888 biography.

52 DPM to Elizabeth Lummis Ellet, cited in Anthony, 17.

53 Anthony, 17.

54 Ellet, 238-257.

55 Allegations that John Payne served as a Revolutionary War soldier had ceased by 1886. In her *Memoirs and Letters of Dolly Madison*, Dolley's grandniece, Lucia Beverley Cutts, made no mention of John Payne's life during the Revolution. Ella Kent Barnard (1909) a well-informed local historian, and Allen C. Clark (1914), a compiler of Dolleyania, similarly made no service claims. Elizabeth Lippincott Dean (1928) said nothing. Katharine Anthony (1949) thought through the subject carefully and concluded that he did not serve. Ethel Stephens Arnett (1972) said nothing, and James Madison's biographer, Ralph Ketcham (1975), stated that "like most of his Quaker brethren, he refused to serve in the revolutionary army." The author commissioned searches of the Daughters of the American Revolution lineage records and a National Archives search of Revolutionary War military service records. Neither produced any evidence that Dolley's father ever bore arms in the conflict.

56 Hiram S, Hilty, *By Land and by Sea: Quakers Confront Slavery and its Aftermath in North Carolina* (Greensboro, North Carolina: North Carolina Friends Historical Society, 1993), 19.

57 Arnett, 458n42.

58 Arnett, 458n42. The first U.S. census, taken in 1790, came seven years after John Payne manumitted his slaves and, therefore, did not enumerate his slaves. Since he freed them before his death, they likewise were not listed in the personal property inventory made when his will was probated.

59 Mattern and Shulman, 12.

60 John H. Russell, *The Free Negro in Virginia*, 1619-1865 (Baltimore: The Johns Hopkins Press, 1913), 43.

61 Worrall, 250.

62 Arnett, 24.

63 R. A. Brock, "Prefatory Note to The Fourth Charter of the Royal African Company of England," *Collections of the Virginia Historical Society,* VI:18-19.

64 Ellet, 240. Five hundred dollars would have been an incredibly large amount of money for a freed slave to have accumulated, whatever the circumstances. Ellet offers no documentation for the amount, and her claim must be considered in that light.

65 Arnett, 30, citing Cedar Creek Meeting Records.

66 Anthony, 18, citing Cedar Creek Meeting Records. Quaker diarist Elizabeth Drinker does not note his presence until March 5, 1781. Elizabeth Forman Crane, editor, *The Diary of Elizabeth Drinker* (Boston: Northeastern University Press, 1991, 3 vols.), I:384. Elizabeth Drinker lived from 1735 to 1807. Her first dated journal entry was made October 8, 1758, when she was a few weeks shy of turning twenty-three. She spent the last half of her life "an invalid, confined pretty closely to her chamber."

67 Arnett, 30.

68 Drinker, 1:ix-xxxiv.

69 Goodwin, 23.

70 Drinker, I:343.

71 Drinker, I:384. Elizabeth Drinker recorded the name of Mary Payne, as "Molley," but there were several common nicknames for Mary (including Molly, Molley, Polly, Polley, and Maimie). Mary may have been introduced to Mrs. Drinker as any one of them.

72 Drinker, I:410, 411.

73 Weeks, 212.

74 This sum is conjectural, based on the assumptions that an average enslaved worker was valued at $500 and that John Payne owned 50 slaves.

75 Arnett, 31, citing Cedar Creek Monthly Meeting Records.

76 Arnett, 31.

77 Ketcham, 377.

78 Goodwin, 16-17.

79 Clark, 13.

CHAPTER 4: Love, Marriage, and Yellow Fever

1 John Harvey Powell, *Bring Out Your Dead. The Great Plague of Yellow Fever in Philadelphia in 1793* (New York: Time-Life Books, 1965), xviii.

2 Goodwin, 19.

3 Mattern and Shulman, 13.

4 Philadelphia Payne evidently died in early childhood. She is noted only in the certificate of transfer granted to John and Mary Payne's family by the Northern District Monthly Meeting to the Pine Street Monthly Meeting in 1786. Barnard, 59.

5 Drinker, I:431.

6 Arnett, 33.

7 Arnett, 33.

8 Katharine Anthony, in *Dolly Madison, Her Life and Times*, 11, stated that Mary Payne "was the mother of nine children, besides three who had died," but the author did not name them or provide a reference. As they were all buried in Virginia, they would have not have been noted as part of the Philadelphia family.

9 Anthony Morris erred by a year. Dolley was fifteen when she arrived in Philadelphia. Anthony Morris, Highland, Georgetown, D.C., to Anna Payne, June 26, 1837, in Grace Dunlop Peter, "Unpublished Letters of Dolly Madison to Anthony Morris Relating to the Nourse Family of the Highlands," in *Records of the Columbia Historical Society of Washington, D.C.*, 44-45 (1944): 219.

10 "The Tavern's Legendary Visitor," Haddonfield, New Jersey: Indian King Tavern Museum, n.d.

11 Goodwin, 20.

12 Goodwin, 19-20.

13 Cutts Memoir I (MCR-S).

14 Drinker, 424.

15 Drinker, 155, 166.

16 Mills, 329.

17 Mills, 328.

18 Arnett, 35.

19 David McCullough, *John Adams* (New York: Simon & Schuster, 2001), 424.

20 McCullough, 426.

21 DP, Philadelphia, to Eliza Brooks, Junr. [Elizabeth Brooks Ellicott], c. December 1788. Formerly on deposit at the University of Kentucky Presidential Memorabilia Collection, Special Collections (KyU); present owner unknown.

22 *ibid.*

23 John Todd's birth date: Clark, 15.

24 Barnard, 73n1.

25 Clark, 14.

26 The 1899 auction catalog detailing the possessions of Mrs. Mary C. Kunkel, daughter of Anna Payne, lists as item #5 a "Beautiful Ivory Miniature of John Todd, First Husband of Dolley P. Madison. Painted by Charles Willson Peale. Gold Mounted." *Estate of Mrs. Dolley P. Madison, wife of President James Madison.* DMC (GHM). It is now owned by the Macculloch Hall Historical Museum.

27 Cutts, *Memoirs and Letters*, 10.

28 Arnett, 39.

29 Arnett, 39.

30 Robert H. Wilson, *Philadelphia Quakers, 1681-1981* (Philadelphia: Philadelphia Yearly Meeting of the Religious Society of Friends, 1981), 66-67.

31 Barnard, 61, 65-66.

32 Arnett, 40.

33 Goodwin, 32.

34 Weeks, 126.

35 Weeks, 127.

36 Barnard, 68.

37 The names of the attendants, Elizabeth Collins and Anthony Morris, were "stated by descendants." Clark, 14.

38 Sarah Parker to Elizabeth Brooke, December 7, 1789, in Barnard, 66.

39 Barnard, 66.

40 This is an excerpt from Bayard Taylor's poem, "The Quaker Widow," in Edmund Clarence Stedman, ed., *An American Anthology*, 1787-1900 (Boston: Houghton-Mifflin Co., 1900), #456.

41 Barnard, 63-64n.

42 Accession records of the Macculloch Hall Historical Museum, Morristown, New Jersey.

43 The Dilworth-Todd-Moylan House, Philadelphia, is a public museum owned and administered by the Independence National Historical Park.

44 Isaac Heston: Arnett, 48-49.

45 Arnett, 45.

46 Inventory of estate of John Todd., Jr., December 7, 1793, W. Parsons Todd Collection (PPIn).

47 Barnard, 72n1.

48 John Todd, Jr., Chester, to DPT, July 30, 1793 (NjMoMHH).

49 Cutts, *Memoirs and Letters*, 11.

50 Minutes of the Philadelphia Monthly Meeting. Adjourned meeting, 13th of 8 mo. 1793, transcribed in Anthony, 44-45.

51 Arnett, 47.

52 Goodwin, 35-36.

53 Clark, 16.

54 Will of John Payne, September 2, 1792, DMC (NcGHM).

55 Bob Arnebeck, "Destroying Angel: Benjamin Rush, Yellow Fever, and the Birth of Modern Medicine," 1999, and online October 10, 2003 at http://www.geocities.com/bobarnebeck/fever1793.html.

56 Drinker, I:494.

57 Drinker, I:495.

58 Thomas Jefferson to James Madison, September 8, 1793, in Anthony, 47.

59 Anthony, 48.

60 Arnebeck, Chapter 1, p. 7.

61 Arnebeck, Chapter 1, p. 8.

62 Drinker, I:497.

63 Wormwood and absinthe are often inaccurately described in modern writings, which frequently perpetuate erroneous myths about both. According to Mordantia Bat, author of "Wormwood Articles," in Absinthe Reference at Le Fee Verte (online at http://www.feeverte.net/worm-idx.html on October 8, 2003), "The toxicity of wormwood is attributed to a compound it contains called Thujone. Thujone can be toxic to the brain and liver. The leaves of the wormwood plant also contain a substance called santonin, which is said to cause vertigo and delusion in overdoses. Thus,

this is possibly why the excessive and chronic use of absinthe was sometimes reported to cause a wide variety of symptoms and maladies, including convulsions, hallucinations, tremors, and sometimes paralysis."

64 Drinker, I:497.

65 Jim Murphy, *An American Plague: The True and Terrifying Story of the Yellow Fever Epidemic of 1793* (New York: Clarion Books, 2003), 40.

66 Arnett, 50; 460n21.

67 In a copy of the letter written by John Todd to his first cousin, William Linn, the clerk's name is listed as "Isaac Hastings." W. Parsons Todd Collection, catalog #633 (PPIn).

68 Isaac Heston to his brother, September 19, 1793. W. Parsons Todd Collection, catalog # 2203 (PPIn).

69 DPT to James Todd, Darby, 4th day Evening 9 oclock [October 1793] (NjMoMHH).

70 The illness, treatment, and death of young Edward Frost occurred on October 19, 1871, in Charleston, S.C., which demonstrates how little medical knowledge had advanced since the Philadelphia yellow fever epidemic seventy-eight years earlier. Richard N. Côté, *Mary's World: Love, War, and Family Ties in Nineteenth-Century Charleston* (Mt. Pleasant, S.C.: Corinthian Books, 2000), 320-321.

71 James Todd, Philadelphia, to William Linn, December 9, 1793. W. Parsons Todd Collection, catalog #633 (PPIn). James Todd was Dolley's brother-in-law; William Linn was James' first cousin.

72 *Yellow Fever*, Virginia Department of Health, June 1998.

73 Mary Coles Payne, n.p., to her nurse in Philadelphia, c. October 25, 1793, W. Parsons Todd Collection, catalog # 629 (PPIn).

74 The 1793 Philadelphia city directory lists "Mary Payne, widow, boarding house, 96 N. Third St." That address had been renumbered 150 North Third St. by 1912.

75 Ray Swick, *An Island Called Eden: The Story of Harman and Margaret Blennerhassett* (Parkersburg, West Virginia: Blennerhassett Island Historical State Park, 2000), 37.

76 Gamaliel Bradford, *Wives* (New York: Harper & Brothers, 1925), 133.

77 Goodwin, 46.

78 DPT, October 28, 1793, to James Todd, W. Parsons Todd Collection (NjMoMHH).

79 DPT to James Todd, Darby, October 31, 1793, W. Parsons Todd Collection (NjMoMHH).

80 The inventory of John Todd's estate was dated November 21, 1793. Photocopy of typescript copy, DMC (GHM).

81 W. Parsons Todd Collection, catalog # 638 (PPIn).

82 DPT to James Todd, March 18, 1794 (NjMoMHH).

83 Goodwin, 43.

84 Milton Lomask, *Aaron Burr* (New York: Farrar, Strauss, Giroux, 1979) I:161-162.

85 Will of Dolley Payne Todd, Philadelphia, May 13, 1794 (NjMoHP).

86 "preserved a gentlemanly silence": Lomask, I:162.

87 Cutts, *Memoirs and Letters*, 14.

88 Ketcham, 110.

89 Ketcham, 110.

90 Ketcham, 110, citing Thomas Jefferson to JM, August 31, 1783.

91 The earliest source located for this excited plea, which would inaugurate forty-two years of devoted marriage, is Cutts, *Memoirs and Letters*, 15.

CHAPTER 5: In Second Blush

1 Ketcham, 379.

2 Goodwin, 55.

3 All the traditional accounts of this romantic introduction place it at Dolley's house on Fourth and Walnut in the spring of 1794. The earliest is in Cutts Memoir I (early 1850s), which stated "In this first interview, at her own house, she conquered the recluse bookworm, Madison." Financial records state that on March 10, 1794, Dolley received three months' rent from Richard Elliott and on April 25, agreed to lease the house to Margaret Grant. This suggests that the meeting took place in late February or early March, just before Dolley rented out her house. If spring 1794 is the correct time for the meeting, it could not have taken place at her mother's boardinghouse (as has sometimes been stated), for Mary Payne had sold it and moved in with Lucy and George Steptoe Washington at Harewood plantation in December 1793.

4 Cutts, *Memoirs and Letters*, 15.

5 Ketcham, 379.

6 Goodwin, 50-51.

7 Harrison Gray Otis to his wife, February 23, 1815, in Samuel Eliot Morison, ed., *The Life and Letters of Harrison Gray Otis, 1765-1848* (Boston and New York: Houghton Mifflin Co., 1913), II:168.

8 Conover Hunt-Jones, 11, citing the "Diary of Lord Francis Jeffrey" (typewritten excerpt), The White House, Washington.

9 Arnett, 58, references a June 1828 letter in the Edward Coles Papers, Princeton, for Madison's 5'6" to 5'6-1/2" height. Ketcham, 89, states that he was "five feet six inches tall and slightly built," but most of his contemporaries do not credit him with that much height. Clark, 495, states Dolley's height at 5'6". Based on her dresses, that figure seems about right.

10 Cutts Memoir I (MCR-S). In fact, he was seventeen years, two months her senior.

11 Samuel L. Mitchill, "Dr. Mitchill's Letters from Washington,1801-1813, *Harper's New Monthly Magazine* (April, 1879), 742.

12 Cutts Memoir I (MCR-S). An embellished version of the conversation was published in Cutts, *Memoirs and Letters*.

13 Goodwin, 57.

14 Mary Payne to John Parrish, August 19, 1794, Cox-Parrish-Wharton Papers, microfilm reel #8 (PHi).

15 Catharine Coles, Philadelphia, to DPT, June 1, 1794, DMP (ViU).

16 Catharine Coles, Philadelphia, to DPT, June 1, 1794, DMC (#1664), Special Collections, Tracy W. McGregor Library (ViU).

17 JM, Orange, to DPT, August 18, 1794, JMP (DLC).

18 Ketcham, 381.

19 William W. Wilkins to DPT, Philadelphia [probably before August 1794] (ViU).

20 William W. Wilkins, Philadelphia, to DPT, Martinsburg, Virginia, August 22, 1794, DMP (DLC).

21 William W. Wilkins, Philadelphia, to DPT, Martinsburg, Virginia, August 22, 1794, DMP (DLC).

22 The eight irregular, unmatched, mill-cut diamonds are embedded directly into the surface of a black substance, which was bonded to a simple, rose-gold finger ring. At some later date, the ring's original band was replaced with one of yellower gold. National Trust / Montpelier accession record #NT1985.15. Photographed at Montpelier by Richard N. Côté.

23 Meade, 22.

24 The Virginia Annual Meeting set the minimum mourning period prior to remarriage at twelve months. Weeks, 127.

25 Arnett, 61. This letter has not survived, but one can deduce that it was delivered from surviving letters and Dolley's subsequent actions.

26 Ketcham, 381.

27 Madison spelled it Harriott. JM, Harewood, to James Madison, Sr., October 5, 1794, *PJM* 15:361.

28 The marriage date of James Madison, Sr., and Nelly Conway is from a manuscript copy of the Madison family Bible records written in the hand of James Madison, Sr., DMC (NcGHM).

29 Ludwell Lee (1760-1836), son of Richard Henry Lee, was a Virginia planter, congressman, and senator. He married his first cousin, Flora Lee Lee, and lived at Belmont Plantation, near Ashland, which she had inherited.

30 DPM, Hair-Wood, to Eliza Collins Lee, Loudoun County, Virginia, September 15/16, 1794, DMP (DLC). Dolley first dated the letter "15th," then changed it to read "16th." She most likely wrote the body of the letter before the ceremony, when she was still Dolley Todd, and finished that evening, when she was Dolley Madison. The meaning of "Alass!" remains an intriguing mystery, as the last page of the letter was damaged, probably removing part of the postscript.

31 Ketcham, 382, citing photostat of the Balmain Account Book (DLC).

32 Cutts Memoir I (MCR-S). The light and elegant laces from Mechlin, Belgium, were hugely fashionable in the 18th century, and were favored by the royal courts of Europe as a decoration for their clothes. Courtesy Diane Claeys, lace historian, Claeys Antiques, Katelijnestraat 54, 8000 Brugge, Belgium.

33 Arnett, 63. The 1794 wedding dress and wreath are in the Dolley Madison Collection at the Greensboro Historical Museum. The white satin shoes are also part of the collection but have not been positively identified as those she wore at her wedding to Madison.

34 Barnard, 82 and 82n1. Barnard states that "the mosaics of the necklace represent the Temple of Minerva, Tomb of Cæcelia Nutallis, Bridge of Colla, Pontius Luganus, Colosseum of Flavius Vespanius, Pontius Salasius, Temple of Vesta, Temple of Venus, Tomb of Caius Cœustus, Temple of Jupiter Tonans, and the Temple of Jupiter Stattor."

35 James Peale, the youngest brother of the famous portraitist, Charles Willson Peale, lived most of his life in Philadelphia. Peale's elder brother had painted the miniature of Dolley's first husband, John Todd., Jr.

36 JM, Harewood, to James Madison, Sr., October 5, 1794, in Ketcham, 383.

37 This James Madison will be identified as the Reverend or Bishop Madison in this volume.

38 The Reverend James Madison, Williamsburg, Virginia, to JM, November 12, 1794, Hubbard Taylor Papers (KyU).

39 Mitchill, 743.

CHAPTER 6: Mrs. Madison's Debut

1 Ellet, 242.

2 Anthony, 92. Saint-Méry lived in Philadelphia from October 1794 to August 1798.

3 Philadelphia Monthly Meeting, Southern District. Men's Minutes, 1781-1793.

4 Drinker, I:638.

5 *PJM*, 1:3.

6 For a more detailed exploration of James Madison's "connections," see Ralph Ketcham's *James Madison: A Biography.*

7 Ketcham, 3.

8 Ketcham, 2-3.

9 James and Dolley Madison invariably spelled the name of their plantation Montpellier, the same as the well-known French town, noted as a health resort and seat of learning. Its name is associated with clean, invigorating air, as noted on July 6, 1781, by Madison's cousin, Edmund Pendleton. He wrote Madison about the "Salubrious Air of this fine Seat, not to be exceeded by any Montpelier in the Universe" (*PJM* 3:172-173). In 1836, Margaret Bayard Smith wrote, "The extreme salubrity of the situation induced the proprietor to call it Montpellier." The present "one-l" spelling of the property's name came into use after Dolley sold the plantation in 1844. See Montpelier Fact Sheet #5: Origin of the Montpelier Name (Montpelier Foundation, November 1994). The "two-l" spelling will be used when referring to the plantation during the lifetime of Ambrose, James Sr., James Jr., and Dolley Madison. The "one-l" spelling will be used when referring to the present-day historical complex, known as "James Madison's Montpelier."

10 Ann L. Miller, *The Short Life and Strange Death of Ambrose Madison* (Orange, Virginia: Orange County Historical Society, 2001), 26-27.

11 James Madison, Sr., (1723-1801) will be referred to as James Sr., in this book; his son, James Jr., (1751-1836), the future president, will be referred to as "James Madison," "James Jr.," or "Madison."

12 Matthew Reeves, "Examining a Pre-Georgian Plantation Landscape in Piedmont Virginia: The Original Madison Family Plantation, 1726-1770. Delivered at the 2003 Society for Historical Archaeology Conference, Providence, Rhode Island (Orange County, Virginia: The Montpelier Foundation, 2003), 3.

13 Reeves, 2-3.

14 Misattribution of names seems to be a curse of the Madison family. Nelly's name was never "Eleanor Rose." Her name is recorded as Nelly Conway in the James Madison, Sr., family Bible, and as Nelly Madison in her will, November 28, 1807, and September 16, 1808, at the Orange County Court House, Orange, Virginia.

15 *Women Through Fredericksburg's History* (Fredericksburg, Virginia: Historic Fredericksburg Foundation, Inc., 2004).

16 Interview by the author with Matthew Reeves, Ph.D., Director of Archaeology at James Madison's Montpelier, April 23, 2004.

17 James Madison, Sr.'s, original account books, 1755-1765, 1769-1770, 1799, and 1801: Shane Collection, reel 17, m-265 (PPPrHi).

18 Ketcham, 11.

19 Ketcham, 12.

20 John Finch, *Travels in the United States and Canada.* (London: Longman, Rees, Orme, Brown, Green, and Longman, 1833), 244.

21 Cutts Memoir II (DLC).

22 W. E. Kennaugh, Washington, to Payne Todd, March 16, 1850, DMP (DLC).

23 Meade, 294, cites Goochland County records of 1733. He states that "Two Negroes found guilty of felonious murder were ordered to be hanged and their 'heads and quarters' set up in several parts of the county, in accordance with a gentle practice inherited from England." For the practice Meade cites the *Virginia Gazette*, July 27, 1769.

24 Ketcham, 12; Barnard, 36.

25 Ketcham, 6.

26 *PJM* 15:139, 152.

27 *PJM* 15:152.

28 An ell was a unit of measure of cloth, roughly an arm's length. James Monroe, Paris, to JM, October 23, 1795, Rives Collection, JMP (DLC).

29 JM to James Monroe, Philadelphia, March 16, 1795, JMP (DLC) and James Monroe to JM, Paris, October 23, 1795, and November 18, 1795, JMP (DLC).

30 James Madison to James Monroe, Paris, January 20, 1796, JMP (DLC).

31 Hunt-Jones, 19.

32 DPM to unknown recipient, Washington, May 15, 1839 (NNPM).

33 J.L. Cathcart, shipment of six pipes of Madeira wine for James Madison and Lucy Cathcart, September 18, 1811, JMP (DLC), illustrated in Hunt-Jones, 20.

34 Hunt-Jones, 26.

35 Hunt-Jones, 20.

36 John Swanwick, Philadelphia, to JM, June 14, 1795, JMP (DLC).

37 Martin J. I. Griffin, "Stephen Moylan," in *The American Catholic Historical Researches*, Vol. 5, No. 2 (April 1909), 231-235.

38 Stephen Moylan, Philadelphia, to JM, February 2, 1797 (OclWhi).

39 PJM 16:452n, citing James and Dolley P. Madison *v.* Edward Heston, January 10, 1797, Philadelphia Court of Common Pleas.

40 Thomas Jefferson, Monticello, to JM, December 28, 1794, *PJM* 15:234.

41 Susan Branson, *These Fiery Frenchified Dames: Women and Political Culture in Early National Philadelphia* (Philadelphia: University of Pennsylvania Press, 2001), 12.

42 Branson, 32-33.

43 Drinker, II:795.

44 Robert Honyman to DPM, July 19, 1799, DMC (#1664), Special Collections, Tracy W. McGregor Library (ViU).

45 Robert Honyman to DPM, January 25, 1795, DMC (#1664), Special Collections, Tracy W. McGregor Library (ViU).

46 Dance information courtesy The English Quadrille, Wellington Museum, Apsley House, London, and the StreetSwing.com Dance History Archives.

47 For most of his life, Virginia planter George Washington used enslaved blacks as his coachmen. The primary exception to that rule was during his presidency, when he had hired four white coachmen in succession. He may have used these four in Philadelphia to get around the laws there regarding the freeing of slaves. Mary V. Thompson, Research Specialist, Mount Vernon Ladies' Association, to the author, May 10, 2004; also Beverly H. Runge, Ph.D., Associate Editor, and John Pinheiro, Ph.D., Assistant Editor, Papers of George Washington, University of Virginia, to the author, May 10, 2004.

48 *PJM* 15:505.

49 Susan Gray Detweiler, *George Washington's Chinaware* (New York: Harry N. Abrams, Inc., 1982), 73 & 76.

50 DPM to Mrs. R.B. Lee, DMP (DLC). Elizabeth "Eliza" Collins (1769-1858) married Richard Bland Lee in 1794 and was also read out of meeting.

51 Rufus Wilmot Griswold, *The Republican Court, or, American Society in the Days of Washington* (New York: D. Appleton and Company, 1861), 330.

52 Goodwin, 70.

53 Probably Anne, the wife of merchant William Bingham, *saloniére femme extraordinaire* of Philadelphia.

54 Sally McKean, Philadelphia, to Anna Payne, June 10, 1796, in Cutts, *Memoirs and Letters*, 18-19.

55 *PJM* 15:374n9.

56 Sally McKean to DPM, September 3, 1796. This extract was part of the printed description of a letter offered for sale in the Frederick B. McGuire-Madison catalogue, February 26, 1917. Sally covers many of the same topics in her letter to Anna Payne, in Cutts Memoir I, noting that she had written three letters already that day, including one to Dolley.

57 Anthony, 96.

58 Sally McKean, Philadelphia, to Anna Payne, September 3, 1796, Cutts, *Memoirs and Letters*, 21.

59 Goodwin, 68.

60 Thomas J. Fleming, *The Duel: Alexander Hamilton, Aaron Burr, and the Future of America* (New York: Perseus Publishing, 1999), 129-130.

61 Abigail Adams, Philadelphia, to Mary Cranch, March 18, 1800, in Stewart Mitchell, ed., *New Letters of Abigail Adams, 1788-1801* (Boston: Houghton Mifflin Co., 1947), 241-242.

62 John Adams, Philadelphia, to Abigail Adams, 27 February 1796 (online digital edition). *Adams Family Papers: An Electronic Archive.* Massachusetts Historical Society. http://www.masshist.org/digitaladams/

63 Worrall, 280.

64 JM, Philadelphia, January 18, 1797, to James Maury, Liverpool, *PJM* 16:462-463.

65 Cincinata: the Society of the Cincinnati, a private, hereditary, patriotic society made up of former officers who served in the American Revolution and their male descendants.

66 Mrs. Friere was the wife of Cypriano Riberio Freire, Portuguese minister to the United States.

67 Edmond Charles Genet, Jean Antoine Joseph Fauchet, and Pierre Auguste Adet were successively French ministers to the United States.

68 Possibly Martha Wharton, daughter of Samuel and Sarah Lewis Wharton, who married Samuel B. Shaw in 1801.

69 lives at service: is employed as a servant.

70 "Signora Catoni" (Sally McKean), Philadelphia, August 3, 1797, to DPM, near Orange Court House, via Fredericksburg, Virginia (MdHi).

71 Cutts Memoir I (MCR-S).

72 José Ignacio de Viar to DPM, February 16, 1796 (NN).

73 JM, Philadelphia, to James Monroe, Paris, April 7, 1796, JMP (DLC).

74 JM, Philadelphia, January 18, 1797, to James Maury, Liverpool, *PJM* 16:462-463.

75 *PJM*, 17:36n1.

76 Volney, Costantin Francois Chassebœuf, comte de, *The Ruins, or, Meditation on the Revolutions of Empires: And the Law of Nature* (London, J. Johnson, 1792), xvii.

77 *PJM* 17:xix.

CHAPTER 7: Within a Squirrel's Jump of Heaven

1 DPM to Anna Payne Cutts, July 5, 1820. The earliest version of this letter, quoted here, is in Cutts Memoir II (DLC). It also appears, in modified form, in Cutts, *Memoirs and Letters*, 174, and in Clark, 212.

2 Ketcham, 389.

3 Ketcham, 67.

4 Manuscript journal of John Hough James, volume 7 (December 17, 1831–April 27, 1833), The Walter Havighurst Special Collections, Miami University Libraries, King Library, Oxford, Ohio, courtesy of Ray Swick, Ph.D., Blennerhassett Island Historical State Park, Parkersburg, West Virginia.

5 Ketcham, 45.

6 Goodwin, 76

7 Clark, 32.

8 Ann L. Miller, *Historic Structure Report: Montpelier, Orange County, Virginia. Phase II: Documentary Evidence Regarding the Montpelier House, 1723-1983* (Orange County, Virginia: James Madison's Montpelier, July 1990), 2. Hereafter cited as Miller, *Historic Structure Report, Phase II.*

9 *PJM* 17:141n1.

10 The valuation is from fire insurance policies issued to Madison in the stated years.

11 Monroe acquired his plantation, "Highland," in 1793 for £1,000. Its northern neighbor was Jefferson's Monticello. The Monroe family moved there in 1799, and it remained their home until 1823. It was sold to pay off debts in 1826. By that time, Monroe was living at his Loudoun County plantation, Oak Hill, which he acquired in 1794. Monroe built a new brick house there in 1822. It served as his primary residence from 1823 until his death in 1831. Courtesy James Monroe's Ash Lawn-Highland and the College of William and Mary.

12 James Monroe, Albermarle County, to JM, February 6, 1798. Owned by the Reverend David H. Coblentz, Williamsburg, Virginia in 1966.

13 Courtesy of The Montpelier Foundation.

14 Cutts Memoir II (DLC).

15 Smith, *First Forty Years,* 234.

16 Cutts Memoir II (DLC).

17 Cutts Memoir II (DLC).

18 Cutts Memoir II (DLC).

19 Cutts Memoir II (DLC).

20 Cutts Memoir II (DLC).

21 Cutts Memoir II (DLC).

22 "last of the Romans": last of the Founding Fathers.

23 "Visit to Mr. Madison. From the correspondent of the Portland Avertiser [sic]. Orange Court House, Va. May 23, 1833," in *Niles [Weekly] Register,* August 17, 1833, 409-411.

24 Cutts Memoir II (DLC).

25 The aphorism, "within a squirrel's jump of heaven," attributed to Madison, is from Goodwin, 61, with no source cited. Although the source may be apocryphal, the description is exquisitely descriptive of Montpellier and the Madisons' opinion of it.

26 Edmund Pendleton to JM, July 6, 1781. Montpelier fact sheet #5: The Origin of the Montpelier Name. Montpelier Foundation, November 1994.

27 *PJM* 17:36n1.

28 Cutts, *Memoirs and Letters,* 25.

29 *PJM* 17:378-379; also Edmund Berkeley, Jr., "Prophet without Honor: Christopher McPherson, Free Person of Color," *VMHB,* 77 (1969): 180-190.

30 The long-standing Jackson family tradition that Mary Payne's wedding to Jackson was the first to be performed in the President's House (the White House) is incorrect. James Madison did give the bride away, but he

was not yet living with Jefferson at the President's House at the time of the ceremony, which took place shortly after September 25, 1800. Mary was "fast recovering" from the birth of her first child as of August 3, 1801. The wedding was most likely held at Montpellier or at Harewood, where Mary resided. Stephen W. Brown, *Voice of the New West: John G. Jackson, His Life and Times* (Macon, Georgia: Mercer University Press, 1985), 10; John George Jackson to DPM, September 25, 1800, Thomas J. Jackson Papers (DLC).

31 Ketcham, 387.

32 Joseph Dougherty to Thomas Jefferson, May 15, 1809, Thomas Jefferson Papers (DLC).

33 Arnett, 72-73.

34 His salary: Dean, 194; the bonnet: Cutts Memoir II (DLC).

35 Cutts Memoir II (DLC).

36 JM, Richmond, to DPM, December 2, 1799, M.E.E. Cutts Papers (MCR-S).

37 DPM, n.p., to Eliza Collins Lee, January 12, 1800, DMP (DLC).

38 Aaron Burr, New-York, to Joseph Alston, January 15, 1801, Matthew L. Davis, *Memoirs of Aaron Burr, With Selections From His Correspondence* (New York: Harper & Brothers, 1837 & 1838), II:144.

39 José Ignacio de Viar, Philadelphia, to DPM, May 20, 1801, DMC (#1664), Special Collections, Tracy W. McGregor Library (ViU).

CHAPTER 8: The Washington Quadrille

1 Thomas Jefferson to DPM, May 27, 1801, in Cutts, *Memoirs and Letters*, 28.

2 Cutts, *Memoirs and Letters*, 26.

3 Thomas Jefferson to DPM, June 4, 1801, in Cutts, *Memoirs and Letters*, 28.

4 Margaret Bayard Smith, Washington, to Maria Bayard, Smith, *The First Forty Years*, 27-28.

5 Margaret Bayard Smith to Maria Bayard, May 28, 1801, Smith, *First Forty Years*, 29.

6 Edward Coles to Hugh Blair Grigsby, December 23, 1854 (VHi).

7 William Seale, *The President's House. A History* (Washington: The White House Historical Association, 1986) I:3-4.

8 Lynne Withey, *Dearest Friend. A Life of Abigail Adams* (New York: Simon & Schuster, 1981), 275.

9 Caption from drawing, "The White House ('President's House') Washington, D.C. Principal story, measured floor plan. Plan of the Principal Story in 1803" (DLC).

10 *PJM-SS*, 1:112-113.

11 Dumas Malone, *Jefferson and His Time* (Boston: Little, Brown & Co., 6 vols., 1948-81), IV:40.

12 That Jefferson would be familiar with the leader of the Buddhist faith in 1801, when that religion was practiced almost exclusively in East Asia, demonstrates the incredible breadth of his knowledge.

13 Theodosia Burr Alston, Dumfries, Virginia, to A.J.F. Prevost, New Rochelle, New York, October 1, 1801 (MoSW).

14 *PJM-SS*, 1:113n1.

15 Raymond Walters, Jr., *Albert Gallatin: Jeffersonian Financier and Diplomat* (New York: Macmillan Company, 1967), 53-54, 214.

16 *PJM-SS* I:113n1 and 3:341.

17 Anna Maria Brodeaux Thornton to DPM, August 24, 1802, DMC (#1664), Special Collections, Tracy W. McGregor Library (ViU).

18 Carl S. Anthony, 42.

19 Carl S. Anthony, 43-44.

20 Carl S. Anthony, 46.

21 Carl S. Anthony, 49.

22 Withey, 297.

23 John Chester Miller, *The Wolf by the Ears: Thomas Jefferson and Slavery* (Charlottesville: University Press of Virginia, 1995), 180.

24 Joseph J. Ellis, *American Sphinx: The Character of Thomas Jefferson* (New York: Alfred A. Knopf, 1997), 91.

25 DPM, Philadelphia, to JM, November 1, 1805, Cutts Memoir II (DLC).

26 Catherine Allgor, *Parlor Politics: In Which the Ladies of Washington Help Build a City and a Government* (Charlottesville: University Press of Virginia, 2000), 39.

27 Henrik Stissing Jensen, Assistant Archivist, National Danish Archives, Copenhagen, to the author, June 23, 2004.

28 Peder Pedersen, Washington, to the Royal Danish Foreign Office, October 2, 1803 (in French). Copy and translation for the author courtesy of Henrik Stissing Jensen, Assistant Archivist, National Danish Archives, Copenhagen, June 23, 2004.

29 Clark, 60-61.

30 Elizabeth Leathes Merry, George Town, near Washington, to Thomas Moore, "Sunday, 1804," in Clark, 57-59.

31 Clark, 57-59.

32 Clark, 57-59.

33 Allgor, 36.

34 Allgor, 37.

35 Ketcham, 432.

36 DPM to Anna Payne Cutts, June 4, 1805, Cutts Memoir II (DLC).

37 Arnett, 32.

38 Margaret Bayard Smith, "Mrs. Madison," in *The National Portrait Gallery of Distinguished Americans* (New York: Herman Bancroft, 1836), III:4.

39 Carl S. Anthony, 77.

40 DPM to Anna Payne Cutts, June 4, 1805, Cutts Memoir II (DLC).

41 Arnett, 468n27.

42 *PJM-SS*, 6:xxvii.

43 Cutts Memoir II (DLC).

44 Mitchill, 744.

45 Arnett, 140.

46 John F. Mariani, *The Dictionary of American Food and Drink* (New York: Hearst Books, 1994), 159.

47 Samuel Latham Mitchill, Washington, to Catherine Akerly Cook Mitchill, Mitchill, 744.

48 The *National Intelligencer,* published on Wednesday, April 4, 1804, stated "Married, on Saturday last...," which would have been Saturday, March 31.

49 DPM to Anna Payne Cutts, April 26, 1804, DMC (#1661), Tracy W. McGregor Library (ViU).

50 Margaret W. Brown, *The Dresses of the First Ladies of the White House* (Washington: Smithsonian Institution, 1952), 11.

51 Smith, *The First Forty Years,* 34.

52 Seale, 101.

53 Seale, 101.

54 Goodwin, 96.

55 Arnett, 102.

56 Arnett, 102-103.

57 Cutts Memoir II (DLC).

58 Thomas Randall, New Orleans, to DPM, August 25, 1803, collection of Charles M. Storey, Boston, Massachusetts.

59 Cutts Memoir II (DLC).

60 Arnett, 147.

61 Arnett, 149.

62 Theodosia Burr Alston, Washington, to Aaron Burr, October 16, 1803, in Matthew L. Davis, ed., *Memoirs of Aaron Burr, With Selections from his Correspondence* (New York: Harper & Brothers, 1838), II:241-242.

63 Richard N. Côté, *Theodosia Burr Alston: Portrait of a Prodigy* (Mt. Pleasant, South Carolina: Corinthian Books, 2002), ix.

64 Harold C. Syrett and Jean G. Cooke, eds., *Interview in Weehawken: The Burr-Hamilton Duel* (Middletown, Connecticut: Middletown University Press, 1960), 45.

65 Herbert S. Parmet and Marie Hecht, *Aaron Burr: Portrait of an Ambitious Man* (New York: Macmillan Press, 1967), 202.

66 DPM to Anna Payne Cutts, July 16, 1804, Cutts Memoir II (DLC).

67 Anthony Merry, Washington, to Lord Harrowby, London, August 6, 1804, in Milton Lomask, *Aaron Burr: The Conspiracy and Years of Exile, 1805-1836* (New York: Farrar, Straus, Giroux, 1982), 34.

CHAPTER 9: Our Hearts Understand Each Other

1 DPM to Anna Payne Cutts, May-June, 1806, Cutts Memoir II (DLC).

2 Harriet Tayloe Upton, "The Family of James Madison. The Children of the White House," in the Boston *Wide Awake,* 380.

3 DPM to Anna Payne Cutts, July 16, 1804, Cutts Memoir II (DLC).

4 DPM to JM, October 26, 1805, Cutts Memoir II (DLC); JM, Washington, to DPM, October 31, 1805 (NjP); JM to DPM, November 1805 (MHi).

5 JM, Washington, to DPM, October 28, 1805, Cutts Memoir I (MCR-S).

6 JM to DPM, c. November 2, 1805, DMC (#1661), Special Collections, Tracy W. McGregor Library (ViU).

7 DPM to Anna Payne Cutts, June 18, 1807, Cutts Memoir II (DLC); Richard Forrest to DPM, September 21, 1807, Madison Miscellany (DLC).

8 Mary Phelps, "The Spoiled Son of Dolly Madison," in *The Mentor*, July 1929, 15-16.

9 Upton, 380.

10 Arnett, 80.

11 Caustic soda, or lye (sodium hydroxide, NaOH), burns away living tissue by chemical action and is extremely dangerous and painful. In the nineteenth century, it was used to clean wounds. In the present day, it is banned for medical use but is used to clean clogged pipes, ovens, and as an industrial solvent to strip floors and clean brick.

12 DPM to Anna Payne Cutts, June 4, 1805, Cutts Memoir II (DLC).

13 Calomel, a powerful purgative and laxative, was a commonly used, multi-purpose remedy found in most American homes until the late nineteenth century. Calomel pills contained mercuric oxide, a poisonous white powder that can cause decreased urine output, salivation, mouth sores, difficulty breathing, swelling of the throat, abdominal pain, and vomiting. DPM to Anna Payne Cutts, July 8, 1805, DMC (#1661), Special Collections, Tracy W. McGregor Library (ViU).

14 DPM to Anna Payne Cutts, July 8, 1805, DMC (#1661), Special Collections, Tracy W. McGregor Library (ViU).

15 DPM to Anna Payne Cutts, September 23, 1805, Cutts Memoir II (DLC).

16 DPM to Anna Payne Cutts, July 31, 1805, Cutts Memoir II (DLC).

17 DPM to Anna Payne Cutts, July 29, 1805, DMC (#1661), Special Collections, Tracy W. McGregor Library (ViU).

18 DPM to Mary Smith Pemberton Morris, August 20, 1805 (DNCD).

19 DPM, Philadelphia, to JM, October 23, 1805, Cutts Memoir II (DLC).

20 DPM to JM, November 1, 1805, Cutts Memoir II (DLC).

21 JM to DPM, November 6, 1805, Dolley Madison Memorial Association (NcGG).

22 DPM to John Coles Payne, with the American Consul at Tripoli, September 21, 1809. Letter owned by Nathaniel E. Stein, New York, N.Y., in 1961.

23 DPM to John Coles Payne, Tripoli, September 21, 1809, letter owned by Nathaniel E. Stein, New York, N.Y., in 1961.

24 DPM to Anna Payne Cutts, March 27, 1807, DMC (#1661), Special Collections, Tracy W. McGregor Library (ViU).

25 Isaac Winston, Auburn, to DPM, January 30, 1808, Cutts Memoir II (DLC).

26 DPM to Elizabeth Collins Lee, February 26, 1808, DMP (DLC).

27 DPM to Anna Maria Brodeaux Thornton, May 18, 1808, DMC (#1664), Special Collections, Tracy W. McGregor Library (ViU).

28 DPM to Anna Payne Cutts, Saco, Maine, June 3, 1808, DMC (#1661), Special Collections, Tracy W. McGregor Library (ViU).

29 Mitchill, 752.

30 DPM to Anna Payne Cutts, May 22, 1805, Cutts Memoir II (DLC); DPM to Anna Payne Cutts, June 4, 1805, Cutts Memoir II (DLC).

31 Augustus John Foster, *Jeffersonian America. Notes on the United States of America, Collected in the Years 1805-06-07 and 11-12* (San Marino, California:

The Huntington Library, 1954). Edited by Richard Beale Davis. Madison's Scottish neighbor, a Mr. Downie, offered Foster the "mint julap" which, Downie told him, "the Virginians were in the habit of taking before breakfast." Then, as now, it consisted of brandy, sugar, mint leaves, and water. Foster, 138. This visit by Foster—there may have been several—may have taken place over a six-day period in late August 1807. DPM to Anna Maria Brodeaux Thornton, August 26, 1807 (NcGHM).

32 Alexandrine-Emilie Pichon, Paris, to DPM, April 18, 1807, DMC (DLC).

33 Carl S. Anthony, 80.

34 Mitchill, 752.

35 Carl S. Anthony, 80.

36 DPM to JM, October 30, 1805, Cutts Memoir II (DLC).

37 Carl S. Anthony, 80.

38 Allgor, 77.

CHAPTER 10: The Presidentress

1 Margaret Bayard Smith to Susan B. Smith, March 4, 1809, Smith, *First Forty Years*, 58.

2 Elizabeth Collins Lee to DPM, March 2, 1809, Cutts Memoir II (DLC).

3 Margaret Bayard Smith to Susan B. Smith, March 4, 1809, Smith, *First Forty Years*, 59.

4 Margaret Bayard Smith to Susan B. Smith, March 4, 1809, Smith, *First Forty Years,* 60-61.

5 Ketcham, 475.

6 Ketcham, 474-475.

7 Ruth Hooper Dalton Deblois to DPM, February 18, 1809 (PPPrHi).

8 Virginia Moore, *The Madisons: A Biography.* (New York: McGraw-Hill Book Company, 1979), 284.

9 DPM to Elizabeth Patterson Bonaparte, November 24, 1813 (MdHi).

10 Much of the information about furnishing the White House before and after the burning comes from the extensive study of the subject by Conover Hunt-Jones, *Dolley and the "great little Madison,"* (Washington: American Institute of Architects Foundation, 1977). Hunt-Jones, 34.

11 Gaillard Hunt, "The First Inauguration Ball," in *The Century Magazine*, March 1905, 755.

12 J. Madison Cutts, Jr., "Dolly Madison," *Records of the Columbia Historical Society*, III: 53. Hereafter cited as J. Madison Cutts; also Margaret Bayard Smith to Susan B. Smith, March 4, 1809, Smith, *First Forty Years*, 62.

13 Margaret Bayard Smith to Susan B. Smith, March 4, 1809, Smith, *The First Forty Years*, 62.

14 Margaret Bayard Smith to Susan B. Smith, March 4, 1809, Smith, *The First Forty Years*, 62-63.

15 Ketcham, 476, citing Diary of Frances Few, March 3, 1809, Georgia Department of Archives and History.

16 Margaret Bayard Smith to Susan B. Smith, March 4, 1809, Smith, *The First Forty Years*, 63.

17 Hunt-Jones, 29, citing the diary of Mrs. William Thornton, March 11, 1809 (DLC).

18 Hunt-Jones, 29.

19 Hunt-Jones, 126, Chapter IIIn1.

20 Seale, 163, 654.

21 Hunt-Jones, 21.

22 Hunt-Jones, 35-36.

23 Margaret Brown Klapthor, *Benjamin Latrobe and Dolley Madison Decorate the White House, 1809-1811* (Washington: The Smithsonian Institution, 1965), 157.

24 Hunt-Jones, 36.

25 Klapthor, 160.

26 Benjamin Henry Latrobe, Philadelphia, to DPM, March 22, 1809 (NHi).

27 Benjamin Henry Latrobe, Philadelphia, to DPM, April 21, 1809 (NN).

28 "The Reign of Dolly Madison," poem by Roy Farrell Greene, in *Puck*, April 24, 1901.

29 Stewart Mitchill, ed., *New Letters of Abigail Adams, 1781-1801* (Boston: Houghton Mifflin Co., 1947), 98-99.

30 Benjamin Latrobe to George Harrison, June 30, 1809, in Talbot Hamlin, *Benjamin Henry Latrobe* (New York: Oxford University Press, 1955), 311.

31 J. Madison Cutts, 54.

32 J. Madison Cutts, 55.

33 J. Madison Cutts, 54-55.

34 Margaret Bayard Smith's notebook entry, August 4, 1809, in Smith, *The First Forty Years*, 81-83.

35 Moore, 260.

36 DPM to Anna Cutts, March 20, 1812, DMC (#1661), Special Collections, Tracy W. McGregor Library (ViU).

37 Moore, 261-262.

38 Mattern and Shulman, 98; DPM to Samuel Poultney Todd, March 16, 1809, DMP (DLC); DPM to Samuel Poultney Todd, March 31, 1809, DMP (DLC); DPM to Samuel Poultney Todd, May 5, 1809, DMP (DLC).

39 Mattern and Shulman, 98.

40 Martha (Patsy) Jefferson Randolph to DPM, Cutts Memoir II (DLC).

41 Theodosia Burr Alston, Rocky River Springs, North Carolina, to DPM, June 24, 1809, in Charles Burr Todd, *The True Aaron Burr. A Biographical Sketch* (New York: A.S. Barnes & Co., 1902), 68-70.

42 Theodosia Burr Alston to Frederick Prevost, September 12, 1809, Burr-Purkitt Family Papers (MoSW).

43 Joseph Milligan to DPM, December 13, 1809, Cutts Memoir II (DLC). Maria Edgeworth, a popular Irish novelist, wrote *Tales of Fashionable Life: Moral Tales for Young People*, a three-volume set, for juvenile readers.

44 John Jacob Astor, New York, to DPM, February 20, 1811, Cutts Memoir II (DLC). A muff is a cylindrical hand-warmer; a tippet is a long scarf-like garment, made of animal skins sewn together head-to-tail, which is worn around the neck and hangs down in front.

45 DPM, Washington, to John Jacob Astor, March 13, 1811, Lee Kohns Memorial Collection (NN).

46 Tobias Lear to DPM, September 2, 1805 (CSmH).

47 Foster, 47; also Janson, *The Stranger in America*, 225-230.

48 Foster, 47.

49 DPM to Anna Payne Cutts, May 3, 1806, Cutts Memoir II (DLC).

50 The red tunic with the gold embroidery is preserved at the Greensboro Historical Museum.

51 Hunt-Jones, 34.

52 Ketcham, 529.

53 Moore, 287-288.

54 DPM to Anna Payne Cutts, July 15, 1811, Cutts Memoir II (DLC).

55 DPM to Hannah Nicholson Gallatin, July 29, 1813, Albert Gallatin Papers (NHi).

CHAPTER 11: From Hostess to Heroine

1 Pitch, *The Burning of Washington*, 12.

2 Lord, 51.

3 Pitch, *The Burning of Washington*, 19.

4 Lord, 27.

5 Pitch, *The Burning of Washington*, 20.

6 Lord, 48.

7 Lord, 59.

8 Lord, 61.

9 Lord, 92.

10 Jennings, 14.

11 Lord, 97-98.

12 Jennings, 8.

13 Lord, 140.

14 Henry Adams, *History of the United States of America During the Administrations of James Madison* (1889-1891, 4 vols; republished by Literary Classics of the United States, 1986), 1016.

15 Lord, 139.

16 The exact times of the start and end of battles, the movements of officials and troops, and the comings and goings of Dolley and the president sometimes appear to overlap and some statements contradict each other. Such conflicts are sometimes unavoidable in the writing of stories based on multiple sources and conflicting accounts, some of which were not recorded until many months—or even many decades—after the event took place.

17 DPM to Dear Sister, August 23 and 24, 1814, DMP (DLC). How Dolley found the time to write this detailed letter in the midst of an attack and evacuation remains a mystery.

18 The only surviving copy of this letter, which may have been written to either Anna Payne Cutts or Lucy Payne Todd, is a copy in Dolley's hand of the original. The original has not survived. Whether it was, in fact, written on the date of the catastrophe or at some later date is discussed in David

B. Mattern, "Dolley Madison Has The Last Word. The Famous Letter," in *White House History*, Fall 1998, 38-43. A facsimile of part of this letter Dolley copied in her own hand, now in the Dolley Madison Papers (DLC), was used as the endpapers for this volume.

19 McGraw's role comes from Jennings, 13.

20 Arnett, 241.

21 In 1978, and also 108 years before, art conservators examined the painting and found no evidence that the canvas had ever been cut or otherwise removed from its original stretcher frame. Marion Mecklenburg and Justine S. Wimsatt, "The White House Full Length Portrait of George Washington by Gilbert Stuart: Conservation Treatment Report and Commentary, " 1978. Unpublished. Office of the Curator, the White House. Cited in *White House History*, Fall 1998, 35. Also Clark, 184n-185n, Citing Laura Carter Holloway, *Ladies of the White House* (San Francisco: H. H. Bancroft, 1870).

22 Arnett, 242.

23 Hunt-Jones, 47.

24 Hunt-Jones, 47, citing PJM (DLC).

25 Betty C. Monkman, "Reminders of 1814,"*White House History*, Fall 1998, 35.

26 DPM to Robert DePeyster (DLC), cited in Arnett, 242.

27 Hunt-Jones, 47.

28 Pitch, "The Burning of Washington," 12.

29 Pitch, "The Burning of Washington," 12.

30 DPM, August 23-24, 1814, to Lucy Payne Washington Todd, DMP (DLC).

31 Hunt-Jones, 48. A red velvet Empire period (1800-1820) dress belonging to Dolley is preserved at the Greensboro Historical Museum. A scarlet velvet dress is mentioned in an inventory of Mrs. Madison's furniture in her Washington house. The dress also appears in the Kunkel Sale Catalog of 1899. Some have said that this dress was made from the red velvet curtains which hung in the oval drawing room of the White House before the fire. Dolley evacuated those curtains on August 24, 1814, but their later fate remains a mystery. Research conducted by Susan Joyce Webster, Curator of the Greensboro Historical Museum, established that the red dress at the museum was made from silk velvet fabric, which would be appropriate for clothing. This does not, however, rule out the possibility that the dress was made from the oval drawing room curtain material. Susan Joyce Webster to the author, August 2, 2004.

32 Jennings, 9. Jennings' account was published in 1865, fifty-one years after the event. He is probably referring to Charles Carroll, whom Dolley reported as being there when the portrait was taken down.

33 DPM to Mary Elizabeth Hazlehurst Latrobe, December 3, 1814, in Clark, 166.

34 DPM to Anna Payne Cutts, August 23-24, 1814, DMP (DLC).

35 Jennings, 9.

36 Hunt-Jones, 45-46.

37 DPM to Minerva Denison Rogers, Monday [September-December 1814], transcript in the John Rogers papers, 1st series, vol. 2 (DLC).

38 Jennings, 9-10.

39 Lord, 150.

40 Lord, 151.

41 Lord, 151.

42 Carl S. Anthony, 84.

43 Lord, 158.

44 Lord, 161.

45 Lord, 164.

46 Arnett, 244.

47 Lord, 167.

48 Captain Harry Smith, Junior Adjutant to Major General Robert Ross, "Eyewitness Accounts of the Burning of the White House. They Were There," *White House History*, Fall, 1998, 56.

49 Lieutenant James Scott, Adjutant to Admiral Sir George Cockburn, "Eyewitness Accounts of the Burning of the White House. They Were There," *White House History*, Fall, 1998, 56.

50 *Courier* (London), October 3, 1814, British Museum. Cited in Lieutenant G. R. Glieg, with the British Forces at the Battle of Bladensburg, "Eyewitness Accounts of the Burning of the White House. They Were There," *White House History*, Fall, 1998, 59.

51 Lord, 168-171, *passim*.

52 Belle Vue, now known as Dumbarton House, has been restored and is now the national headquarters for The National Society of The Colonial Dames of America. Located at 2715 Q Street N.W., Washington, the society's museum house is open to the public.

53 S. Williams, "Leaves from an Autobiography," in *The Ladies' Repository* (Cincinnati, Ohio), XIV (1854), 159, courtesy of Dr. Ray Swick, State Historian, Blennerhassett Island Historical State Park, Parkersburg, West Virginia.

54 Hunt-Jones, 48.

55 Arnett, 246.

56 JM, Brookville, Maryland, to DPM, August 27, 1814, JMP (DLC).

57 Lord, 202.

58 Lord, 204.

59 Margaret Bayard Smith to Mrs. Kirkpatrick, August 30, 1814, in Smith, *The First Forty Years*, 110.

60 William Wirt to Elizabeth Washington Gamble Wirt, October 14, 1814, in Clark, 186.

61 Lord, 215.

62 Hunt-Jones, 51.

63 Hunt-Jones, citing Edward Coles to John Coles, November 2, 1814, Edward Coles Collection (PHi).

64 Arnett, 249-250.

65 Arnett, 250.

66 Hunt-Jones, 51.

67 Jennings, 13-14.

68 Hunt-Jones, 57.

69 John Adams to Thomas Jefferson, February 2, 1817, *Adams-Jefferson Letters*, II:507-508.

70 Mrs. Harrison Gray Otis, Lancaster, Pennsylvania, to her father, Otis, II:206.

71 Elizabeth Collins Lee to DPM, March 4, 1817, Cutts Memoir II (DLC).

72 DMC (NcGHM).

CHAPTER 12: Adam and Eve in Paradise

1 Mattern and Shulman, 216.

2 Ralph L. Ketcham, ed., "An Unpublished Sketch of James Madison by James K. Paulding," *VMHB* 67:432-437.

3 Moore, 371.

4 Hunt-Jones, 74.

5 Moore, 371.

6 Mary Phelps, "The Spoiled Son of Dolly Madison," *The Mentor*, July 1929, 16.

7 DPM to John Payne Todd, August 6, 1814 (NjMoMHH).

8 Edward Coles, near Statesburg, South Carolina, to DPM, February 22, 1816 (NN).

9 DPM to John Payne Todd, in care of Anna Payne Cutts, Washington, May 24, 1821, DMP (DLC).

10 DPM to John Payne Todd, May 28, 1821. Present owner unknown.

11 Ketcham, 615-616.

12 DPM to Anna Payne Cutts, June 6, 1829, Cutts Memoir II (DLC).

13 Arnett, 285.

14 Ketcham, 616.

15 J. Madison Cutts, 49.

16 Ketcham, "An Unpublished Sketch of James Madison," 434.

17 Moore, 373.

18 Ketcham, 620.

19 George Ticknor, *Life, Letters, and Journals of George Ticknor* (Boston: James R. Osgood, 1876), I:347.

20 Arnett, 311.

21 Ketcham, 620-621.

22 Elizabeth Collins Lee to DPM, March 30, 1819 (DLC).

23 Arnett, 311.

24 DPM to Sarah (Sally) Coles Stevenson, c. February 1820, last owned by Richard J. Hooker, Chicago, Illinois.

25 Ketcham, 374.

26 Moore, 381.

27 Jennings, 15.

28 Ketcham, 148.

29 Extract from the will of James Madison, in Drew R. McCoy, *The Last of James Madison and the Republican Legacy* (New York: Cambridge University Press, 1989), 256.

30 DPM to Dolley Cutts, May 11, 1835, Cutts Memoir I.

31 JM, Montpellier, to an unknown recipient, possibly Thomas G. Addison, May 11, 1835. Present owner unknown.

32 Jennings, 81.

33 James Laurie, Washington, to DPM, July 24, 1836, DMC (#1664), Special Collections, Tracy W. McGregor Library (ViU).

CHAPTER 13: Days of Grace and Honor

1 Goodwin, 266.

2 Ingersoll wrote the biographical sketch of Madison for the *National Portrait Gallery of Distinguished Americans*, which also contained a sketch of Dolley by Margaret Bayard Smith. DPM, Washington, to Charles J. Ingersoll, Philadelphia, June 15, 1838, C. J. Ingersoll Collection (PHi).

3 Arnett, 329.

4 Barnard, 114.

5 Brief excerpts from John Payne Todd's personal journal(s) appear in Katharine Anthony's 1949 biography, *Dolly Madison: Her Life and Times*, chiefly on pp. 361-364. To the best of the author's knowledge, they are not cited in any later works. Anthony did not use footnotes or endnotes, but under the heading, "Documents" in her bibliography, she cites "Library of Congress: Manuscript Division. Letters and Memoranda of John P. Todd." The author found Anthony's citation only days before this book went to press and did not have the opportunity to read these Todd manuscripts.

6 Anthony, 361-363.

7 James Kirke Paulding to Jared Sparks, September 11, 1836, in Ralph M. Alderman, ed., *The Letters of James Kirke Paulding* (Madison: University of Wisconsin Press, 1962), 182-183.

8 Virginia Tatnall Peacock, *Famous American Belles of the Nineteenth Century* (Philadelphia: J.B. Lippincott, 1901), 177-179.

9 Arnett, 352.

10 William Kemble to William Kemble, Jr., January 26, 1839, Alderman, 243.

11 George W. Featherstonehaugh to William Cabell Rives, April 6, 1837, Rives Papers (DLC).

12 Arnett, 345.

13 James Franklin Beard, *The Letters and Journals of James Fenimore Cooper* (Cambridge: Harvard University Press, 1960), 5:ix.

14 Arnett, 347, citing the *Washington Globe*, January 8, 1844.

15 Bayard, 122-123.

16 Arnett, 352-353.

17 Dean, 225.

18 Sarah, a slave of Dolley Madison at Montpellier, to DPM, July 5, 1844, in Clark, 341-342.

19 J. Madison Cutts, "Dolly Madison," 50-51.

20 Jennings, iv.

21 Jennings, 14-15.

22 Arnett, 391.

23 Arnett, 391-392.

24 Elizabeth Collins Lee to Zaccheus Collins Lee, 1849 (ViU).

EPILOGUE

1 Barnard, 112.

2 Arnett, 396-400, *passim.*

3 Courtesy of The Montpelier Foundation.

4 Arnett, 281.

5 William Seale, *The President's House: A History* (Washington: The White House Historical Association, 1986) I:504. There are many variations of the Easter Egg Roll story, most of which are not supported by documentary evidence. In 2000, a White House web page stated, "The first egg rolls, largely family affairs, seem to have been held during the administration of President Andrew Johnson. Youngsters of the President's family dyed eggs on Sunday for the Monday rolling, which the First Lady would watch from the South Portico. A family member has attested to hearing the stories of such activity from Andrew Johnson Patterson, the President's grandson, who lived at the White House while his mother served as White House hostess on behalf of her invalid mother, First Lady Eliza Johnson. Although small groups of egg rollers were reported on the White House grounds under the presidency of General Ulysses S. Grant, the majority of egg rolling activity and all day picnics took place at the Capitol." http://clinton3.nara.gov/WH/glimpse/Easter/.

Bibliography

PRIMARY SOURCES

In the manuscript source citations, standard MARC repository codes have been used when available. When MARC codes were not available, the full name of the holding institution or last known owner has been provided. The author thanks the following organizations for permission to publish from their collections.

MiDbEI   Edison Institute, Henry Ford Museum and Greenfield Village Library, Dearborn, Michigan.

NcGG   Friends Historical Collection, Guilford College, Greensboro, North Carolina. New Garden, North Carolina Monthly Meeting records, vol. 1 (1743-1783) and minutes (November 1765– September 1775).

NcGHM   Greensboro Historical Museum, Greensboro, North Carolina. The Dolley Madison Collection and the Kunkel Collection.

MCR-S   Harvard University. Schlesinger Library, Radcliffe Institute. The Mary Estelle Elizabeth Cutts Papers (A/C 991). Cited as Cutts Memoir I.

CSmH   Henry E. Huntington Library, San Marino, California.

PHi   Historical Society of Pennsylvania, Philadelphia. The Cox-Parrish-Wharton Papers, microfilm reel #8; C. J. Ingersoll Collection.

PPIn   Independence National Historical Park, Philadelphia. The W. Parsons Todd Collection.

ViMpMPL	James Madison's Montpelier, Montpelier Station, Virginia. Matthew B. Reeves, "Examining a Pre-Georgian Plantation Landscape in Piedmont, Virginia: The Original Madison Family Plantation," presented at the 2003 Society for Historical Archaeology Conference, Providence, Rhode Island. Ann L. Miller, "Historic Structure Report: Montpelier, Orange County, Virginia. Phase II: Documentary Evidence Regarding the Montpelier House, 1723-1983. Also curatorial files, architectural renderings, and accession records.
DLC	Library of Congress. The James Madison Papers, the Dolley Madison Papers, the Mary E. E. Cutts memoir and letters (microfilm roll M-96), The Thomas J. Jackson Papers, and the Rives Papers.
Vi	The Library of Virginia, Richmond, Virginia.
NjMoMHH	Macculloch Hall Historical Museum, Morristown, New Jersey.
MdHi	The Maryland Historical Society.
OoxM	Miami University, Oxford, Ohio. Journals of John Hough James.
NjMoHP	Morristown National Historical Park, Morristown, New Jersey.
NjHi	New Jersey Historical Society, Newark, New Jersey.
NHi	New-York Historical Society, New York City. The Albert Gallatin Papers.
NN	New York Public Library, New York City.
PPPrHi	Presbyterian Historical Society, Philadelphia. James Madison, Sr.'s, account books, 1755-1765, 1769-1770, 1799, and 1801: Shane Collection, reel 17, m-265.
NjP	Princeton University, Princeton, New Jersey.
KyU	University of Kentucky, Lexington, Kentucky.
ViU	University of Virginia, Charlottesville, Virginia. The Papers of James Madison and The Papers of Dolley Madison.
ViRVal	Valentine Richmond History Center, Richmond, Virginia.
ViHi	Virginia Historical Society, Richmond, Virginia.
MoSW	Washington University Libraries, St. Louis, Missouri.
CtY	Sterling Library, Yale University, New Haven, Connecticut.

SECONDARY SOURCES

Adams, Henry. *History of the United States of America During the Administrations of James Madison.* 4 vols., 1889-1891; republished in one volume by Literary Classics of the United States, 1986.

Alderman, Ralph M., ed. *The Letters of James Kirke Paulding*. Madison: University of Wisconsin Press, 1962.

D. P. Madison

Allgor, Catherine. *Parlor Politics: In Which the Ladies of Washington Help Build a City and a Government.* Charlottesville: University of Virginia Press, 2000.

Anthony, Carl Sferrazza. *First Ladies: The Saga of the Presidents' Wives and Their Power, 1789-1961.* New York: William Morrow and Company, 1990.

Anthony, Katharine. *Dolly Madison: Her Life and Times.* New York: Doubleday and Company, 1949.

Arnebeck, Bob. "Destroying Angel: Benjamin Rush, Yellow Fever and the Birth of Modern Medicine." Unpublished manuscript, online July 4, 2003, at http://www.geocities.com/bobarnebeck/table.htm.

Arnett, Ethel Stephens. *Mrs. James Madison: The Incomparable Dolley.* Greensboro, North Carolina: Piedmont Press, 1972.

Bagby, George William (attributed to). "The Home of Madison in 1871." *Lippincott's Magazine*, vol. 9 (April 1872), 473-477.

Barnard, Ella Kent. *Dorothy Payne, Quakeress. A Side-Light upon the Career of "Dolly" Madison.* Philadelphia: Ferris & Leach, 1909.

Bell, James Pinckney Pleasant. *Our Quaker Friends of Ye Olden Times. Being in Part a Transcript of the Minute Books of Cedar Creek meeting, Hanover County, and the South River Meeting, Campbell County, Va.* Lynchburg, Virginia: J. P. Bell Co., Publishers, 1905.

Berkeley, Edmund Jr. "Prophet without Honor: Christopher McPherson, Free Person of Color." *Virginia Magazine of History and Biography* 77 (1969): 180-190.

Bowen, Catherine Drinker. *Yankees From Olympus, Justice Holmes and His Family.* Boston: Little, Brown & Co., 1944.

Bowers, Claude G., editor, *The Diary of Elbridge Gerry, Jr.* New York: Brentano's, 1927.

Bradford, Gamaliel. *Wives.* New York: Harper Brothers, 1925.

Branson, Susan. *These Fiery Frenchified Dames: Women and Political Culture in Early National Philadelphia.* Philadelphia: University of Pennsylvania Press, 2001.

Brock, R.A. "The Fourth Charter of the Royal African Company of England, September 27, 1762, with Prefatory Note, Exhibiting the Past Relation of Virginia to African Slavery." *Virginia Historical Collections*, VI:18-19.

Brooks, Geraldine. *Dames and Daughters of the Young Republic.* New York: Thomas Y. Crowell, 1901.

Brown, Margaret W. The *Dresses of the First Ladies of the White House.* Washington: Smithsonian Institution, 1952.

Brown, Stephen W. *Voice of the New West: John G. Jackson, His Life and Times.* Macon, Georgia: Mercer University Press, 1985.

Butterfield, Lyman H., et al., eds. *Adams Family Correspondence.* Cambridge: Harvard University Press, 1963. 2 vols.

Campbell, Norine Dickson. *Patrick Henry: Patriot and Statesman.* Old Greenwich, Connecticut: Devin-Adair Co., 1969.

Clark, Allen C. *Life and Letters of Dolly Madison.* Washington: Press of W. F. Roberts Co., 1914.

Côté, Richard N. *Mary's World: Love, War, and Family Ties in Nineteenth-century Charleston.* Mt. Pleasant, South Carolina: Corinthian Books, 1999.

Côté, Richard N. *Theodosia Burr Alston: Portrait of a Prodigy.* Mt. Pleasant, South Carolina: Corinthian Books, 2001.

Crane, Elaine Forman, ed. *The Diary of Elizabeth Drinker.* Boston: Northeastern University Press, 1991. 3 vols.

Cutler, Manasseh. *Life, Journals and Correspondence of Rev. Manasseh Cutler.* William P. and Julia P. Cutler, eds. Cincinnati: Robert Clarke and Co., 1888. 2 vols.

Cutts, J. Madison. "Dolly Madison," *Records of the Columbia Historical Society,* III:28-72.

Cutts, Lucia Beverley, ed. *Memoirs and Letters of Dolley Madison, Wife of James Madison, President of the United States. Edited by her grandniece.* Boston: Houghton Mifflin Company, 1886.

Daniels, Jonathan. *The Washington Quadrille: The Dance Beside the Documents.* Garden City, New Jersey: Doubleday, 1968.

Davis, Matthew L., ed. *Memoirs of Aaron Burr, With Selections from his Correspondence.* New York: Harper & Brothers, 1837 & 1838. 2 vols.

Dean, Elizabeth Lippincott. *Dolly Madison, The Nation's Hostess.* Boston: Lothrope, Lee, and Shepard Co., 1928.

deCrèvecoeur, J. Hector St. John. *Letters from an American Farmer; And, Sketches of Eighteenth-Century America.* London, 1782; reprinted London: J.M. Dent & Sons, 1912.

Detweiler, Susan Gray. *George Washington's Chinaware.* New York: Harry N. Abrams, Inc., 1982.

Ellet, Elizabeth Lummis. *The Queens Of American Society.* New York: Charles Scribner and Co., 1867.

Ellis, Joseph J. *American Sphinx: The Character of Thomas Jefferson.* New York: Alfred A. Knopf, 1997.

Finch, John. *Travels in the United States of America and Canada.* London: Longman, Rees, Orme, Brown, Green, and Longman, 1833.

Fleming, Alexander H. *Duel: Alexander Hamilton, Aaron Burr, and the Future of America.* New York: Perseus Publishing, 1999.

Foster, Augustus John. *Jeffersonian America. Notes on the United States of America Collected in the years 1805-6-7 and 11-12 by Sir Augustus John Foster, Bart.* Richard Beale Davis, ed. San Marino, California: The Huntington Library, 1954.

Frost, J. William. *The Quaker Family in Colonial America.* New York: St. Martin's Press, 1973.

Goodwin, Maude Wilder. *Dolly Madison.* New York: Charles Scribner's Sons, 1896.

Griffin, Martin I.J. "Stephen Moylan," in *The American Catholic Historical Researches,* vol. 5, No. 2 (April 1909), 231-235.

Griswold, Rufus Wilmot. *The Republican Court, or, American Society in the Days of Washington.* New York: D. Appleton and Co., 1861.

Hale, William M., ed. *The Colonial Records of North Carolina.* Raleigh, North Carolina: P. M. Hale, 1886.

D. P. Madison

Hamlin, Talbot. _Benjamin Henry Latrobe._ New York: Oxford University Press, 1955.

Hanover County Historical Society. _Old Homes of Hanover County, Virginia._ Hanover, Virginia: Hanover County Historical Society, 1983.

Henderson, Archibald. "Dolly Madison Gave Her Age Wrong; Cut Off Four Years For Vanity's Sake." _Greensboro Daily News,_ June 3, 1928.

Hilty, Hiram H. _By Land and By Sea. Quakers Confront Slavery and its Aftermath in North Carolina._ Greensboro, North Carolina: North Carolina Friends Historical Society, 1993.

Hilty, Hiram H. _New Garden Friends Meeting: The Christian People Called Quakers._ Greensboro, North Carolina: North Carolina Friends Historical Society, 1983.

Hinshaw, Seth B. _The Carolina Quaker Experience, 1665-1985._ Greensboro, North Carolina: North Carolina Friends Historical Society, 1984.

Hinshaw, Seth B., and Mary Edith Hinshaw. _Carolina Quakers: Our Heritage of Hope._ Greensboro, North Carolina: North Carolina Yearly Meeting, 1972.

Hinshaw, William W. _Encyclopedia of American Quaker Genealogy._ Ann Arbor, Michigan: Edward Brothers, 1936.

Hunt, Gaillard. "The First Inauguration Ball." _The Century Magazine,_ March 1905, 754-760.

Hunt-Jones, Conover. _Dolley and the "Great Little Madison."_ Washington, D.C.: American Institute of Architects Foundation, 1977.

Jennings, Paul. _A Colored Man's Reminiscences of James Madison._ Brooklyn, New York: George C. Beadle, 1865.

Ketcham, Ralph. _James Madison. A Biography._ Charlottesville: University Press of Virginia, 1990.

Ketcham, Ralph L., ed. "An Unpublished Sketch of James Madison by James K. Paulding." _Virginia Magazine of History and Biography,_ 67:432-437.

Klapthor, Margaret Brown. _Benjamin Latrobe and Dolley Madison Decorate the White House, 1809-1811._ Washington: The Smithsonian Institution, 1965.

Kolatch, Alfred J. _The Jonathan David Dictionary of First Names._ Middle Village Way, New York: Jonathan David Publishing Co., 1980.

Lancaster, Robert Bolling. _Old Homes of Hanover County, Virginia._ Hanover, Virginia: Hanover County Historical Society, 1983.

Lindsay, Kenneth C. _The Works of John Vanderlyn: From Tammany to the Capitol._ Binghamton, New York: University Art Gallery, State University of New York at Binghamton, 1970.

Lomask, Milton. _Aaron Burr: The Conspiracy and Years of Exile, 1805-1836._ New York: Farrar, Straus, Giroux, 1982.

Lord, Walter. _The Dawn's Early Light._ New York: W. W. Norton, 1972.

Lossing, Benson John. _The Pictorial Field-book of the War of 1812._ New York: Harper & Brothers, 1868.

Malone, Dumas. _Jefferson and His Time._ Boston: Little, Brown & Co. 6 vols., 1948-1981.

Mariana, John F. _The Dictionary of American Food and Drink._ New York: Hearst Books, 1994.

Mattern, David B., "Dolley Madison Has The Last Word: The Famous Letter." *Journal of the White House Historical Association*, Fall 1998, 38-41.

Mattern, David B., ed. *James Madison's "Advice to My Country."* Charlottesville: University of Virginia Press, 1997.

Mattern, David B. and Holly C. Shulman, eds. *The Selected Letters of Dolley Payne Madison*. Charlottesville: University of Virginia Press, 2003.

McCormick, John H. "The First Master of Ceremonies of the White House," *Records of the Columbia Historical Society*, VII, 1904.

McCoy, Drew R. *The Last of James Madison and the Republican Legacy*. New York: Cambridge University Press, 1989.

McCullough, David. *John Adams*. New York: Simon & Schuster, 2001.

Meade, Robert D. *Patrick Henry: Patriot in the Making*. Philadelphia: J.B. Lippincott Co., 1969.

Mecklenburg, Marion, and Justine S. Wimsatt. "The White House Full Length Portrait of George Washington by Gilbert Stuart: Conservation Treatment Report and Commentary, 1978." Unpublished. Office of the Curator, The White House.

Miller, Ann L. *Antebellum Orange: The Pre-Civil War Homes, Public Buildings and Historic Sites of Orange County, Virginia*. Orange, Virginia: Orange County Historical Society, 1988.

Miller, Ann L. *Historic Structure Report: Montpelier, Orange County, Virginia. Phase II: Documentary Evidence Regarding the Montpelier House, 1723-1983. Prepared for Montpelier, a Museum Property of the National Trust for Historic Preservation. July 1990*.

Miller, Ann L. *The Short Life and Strange Death of Ambrose Madison*. Orange, Virginia: Orange County Historical Society, 2001.

Miller, Ann L. *Pre-1900 Documentary Evidence of Major Exterior Elements on the Montpelier Mansion*. The Montpelier Foundation Architectural Research Department, May 2002.

Miller, John Chester. *The Wolf by the Ears: Thomas Jefferson and Slavery*. Charlottesville: University Press of Virginia, 1995.

Mills, W. Jay. *Historic Houses of New Jersey*. Philadelphia: J. B. Lippincott, 1902.

Mitchill, Samuel L. "Dr. Mitchill's Letters from Washington, 1801-1813." *Harper's New Monthly Magazine*, April 1879, 739-755.

Mitchell, Stewart, ed. *New Letters of Abigail Adams, 1788-1801*. Boston: Houghton Mifflin Co., 1947.

Mitnick, Barbara, and David Meschutt. *The Portraits and History Paintings of Alonzo Chappel*. Chadds Ford, Pennsylvania: Brandywine River Museum, 1992.

Monkman, Betty C. "The White House Collection: Reminders of 1814." *White House History*, Fall 1998, 33-37.

Moore, Virginia. *The Madisons: A Biography*. New York: McGraw-Hill Book Company, 1979.

Morison, Samuel Eliot. *The Life and Letters of Harrison Gray Otis, 1765-1848*. Boston and New York: Houghton Mifflin Co., 1913. 2 vols.

Murphy, Jim. *An American Plague: The True and Terrifying Story of the Yellow Fever Epidemic of 1793*. New York: Clarion Books, 2003.

𝒟. 𝒫. Madison

Pack, James. *The Man Who Burned the White House: Admiral Sir George Cockburn, 1772-1853.* Annapolis, Maryland: Naval Institute Press, 1987.

The Papers of James Madison, published by the University of Chicago Press (Congressional Series, volumes 1-10, 1962-1977) and the University of Virginia Press (all other volumes, 1977 to date).

Parmet, Herbert S., and Marie Hecht. *Aaron Burr: Portrait of an Ambitious Man.* New York: Macmillan Press, 1967.

Peacock, Virgina Tatnall. *Famous American Belles of the Nineteenth Century.* Philadelphia: J.B. Lippincott, 1901.

Peter, Grace Dunlop. "Unpublished Letters of Dolly Madison to Anthony Morris Relating to the Nourse Family of the Highlands." *Records of the Columbia Historical Society of Washington, D.C.,* 44-45 (1944): 219.

Phelps, Mary. "The Spoiled Son of Dolly Madison." *The Mentor,* July 1929, 15-16.

Pitch, Anthony S. "The Burning of Washington," *Journal of the White House Historical Association,* Fall, 1998, pp. 6-13.

Pitch, Anthony S. *The Burning of Washington: The British Invasion of 1814.* Annapolis, Maryland: Bluejacket Books / Naval Institute Press, 1998.

Powell, John Harvey. *Bring Out Your Dead: The Great Plague of Yellow Fever in Philadelphia in 1793.* Philadelphia: University of Philadelphia Press, 1949, reprinted 1965.

Prowell, George R. *The History of Camden County, New Jersey.* Philadelphia: L. J. Richards & Co., 1886.

Reeves, Matthew B. *Examining a Pre-Georgian Plantation Landscape in Piedmont Virginia. The Original Madison Family Plantation, 1726-1770. Presented to the 2003 Society for Historical Archaeology Conference, Providence, Rhode Island.* Orange County, Virginia: The Montpelier Foundation, 2003.

Roller, Robert Douglas. *Richardson-DePriest Family.* Charleston, West Virginia: privately published, 1905.

Russell, John H. *The Free Negro in Virginia, 1619-1865.* Baltimore: The Johns Hopkins Press, 1913.

Sale, Edith Tunis. *Interiors of Virginia Houses of Colonial Times.* Richmond, Virginia: William Byrd Press, 1927.

Seale, William. *The President's House: A History.* Washington: White House Historical Association, 1986. 2 vols.

Semmes, John E. *John H. B. Latrobe and His Times.* Baltimore: The Norman, Remington Co., 1917.

Smith, Margaret Bayard. "Mrs. Madison." *The National Portrait Gallery of Distinguished Americans.* New York: Herman Bancroft, 1836. III:1-10.

Smith, Margaret Bayard. *The First Forty Years of Washington Society, Portrayed by the Family Letters of Mrs. Samuel Harrison Smith* (Margaret Bayard). Gaillard Hunt, ed. New York: Charles Scribner's Sons, 1906.

Swick, Ray. *An Island Called Eden: The Story of Harman and Margaret Blennerhassett.* Parkersburg, West Virginia: Blennerhassett Island Historical State Park, 2000.

Syrett, Harold C., and Jean G. Cooke, eds. *Interview in Weehawken: The Burr-Hamilton Duel.* Middletown, Connecticut: Middletown University Press, 1960.

Taylor, Bayard. "The Quaker Widow." Edmund Clarence Stedman, ed., *An American Anthology, 1787-1900*. Boston: Houghton-Mifflin Co., 1900, #456.

Ticknor, George. *Life, Letters, and Journals of George Ticknor*. Boston: James R. Osgood, 1876. 2 vols.

Todd, Charles Burr. *The True Aaron Burr. A Biographical Sketch*. New York: A.S. Barnes & Co., 1902.

Upton, Harriet Tayloe. "The Family of James Madison." *The Wide Awake*. Boston, May 1888, 377-391.

Virginia: A Guide to the Old Dominion. Washington: Federal Writer's Project, 1941.

Virginia Historical Society. "The Payne Family of Goochland." *Virginia Magazine of History and Biography*, VI:313-316, 427-428, and VII:79-82, 200-201.

"Visit to Mr. Madison. From the correspondent of the Portland Avertiser [sic]. Orange Court House, Va. May 23, 1833." *Niles [Weekly] Register*, August 17, 1833.

Walters, Raymond Jr. *Albert Gallatin: Jeffersonian Financier and Diplomat*. New York: Macmillan Company, 1967.

Wandell, Samuel H., and Meade Minnegerode. *Aaron Burr*. New York and London: G.P. Putnam's Sons, 1925. 2 vols.

Weeks, Stephen Beauregard. *Southern Quakers and Slavery. A Study in Institutional History*. Baltimore: The Johns Hopkins Press, 1896.

Wenger, Mark R., and Myron O. Stachiw. *Montpelier Architectural Investigation 2001-2002*. Montpelier Station, Virginia: The Montpelier Foundation, February 11, 2003.

"The Will of Josias Payne." *Virginia Magazine of History and Biography*, VII:80-81.

Williams, S. "Leaves from an Autobiography." *The Ladies' Repository* (Cincinnati, Ohio), XIV (1854): 159.

Willis, Garry. *James Madison*. New York: Times Books / Henry Holt & Co., 2002.

Wilson, Robert H. *Philadelphia Quakers, 1681-1981*. Philadelphia: Philadelphia Yearly Meeting of the Religious Society of Friends, 1981.

Withey, Lynne. *Dearest Friend. A Life of Abigail Adams*. New York: Touchstone / Simon & Schuster, 2002.

Worrall, Jay Jr. *The Friendly Virginians: America's First Quakers*. Athens, Georgia: Iberia Publishing Co., 1994.

Young, James Sterling. *The Washington Community, 1800-1828*. New York: Columbia University Press, 1966.

Index

414

defeat of, 9
on his brother Jérôme's marriage, 240
Book of Common Prayer, 27
Booth, Mordecai, 302
Bordeaux, France, 257
Boston Globe, 251
Boston, Mass., 17, 29, 37, 73, 75, 151, 153, 167-168, 211, 283, 346
Brackenridge, Hugh Henry, 176
Bradford, Gamaliel, xiv-xv
Bradford, William, 176
Bradley, Abraham, 312
Brady, Matthew, 342, 361
Braintree, Mass., 211
Branson, Susan, 150
Brant, Irving, xvi
Brent, Richard, 166
Brick Church (Anglican), Orange Co., Va., 141
British newspapers, 8, 315
Brodeaux, Anna Maria. *See* Thornton, Anna Maria (Mrs. William)
Bronne, André de, 221
Brooke, Elizabeth, 84, 86
Brown, Miss, 307
Brussels, Belgium, 297
Burd, Edward, 104
Burgesses, House of. *See* Virginia House of Burgesses
Burr, Aaron, xv, 102-103, 106-107, 150-151, 176, 192, 195-196, 200, 207, 211, 222, 231-232, 235, 244-246, 262, 274, 313
duel with Hamilton, 233
introduces JM to Dolley, 108-109, 111
Burr-Hamilton duel, 233
Burr, Theodosia. *See* Alston, Theodosia Burr (Mrs. Joseph)
Burr, Theodosia Bartow Prevost (Mrs. Aaron), 102, 107
Bush Hill hospital (Philadelphia), 153
Byrd, William, 44

cabinet papers saved by DPM, 4-5
Calhoun, John C., 278

calomel pills, 101, 397n13
Campbell County, Va., 53
Canada, 9-10, 278, 287
Canons of Etiquette to be Observed by the Executive, 214, 220, 254, 258
Capitol, the, and Capitol Hill, 11, 205, 209, 219, 249, 253-254, 257, 277, 289, 309, 351
Carberry, Henry, 12, 294
Caroline County, Va., 139
Caroline Monthly Meeting (also known as Cedar Creek Monthly Meeting, Hanover Co., Va.), Va., 26, 29, 32, 53
Carpenter's Hall (Philadelphia), 75
Carraman, Mr., 328
Carroll, John, 239
Carroll, Charles, 296, 298-299, 301, 328
Carteret, Sir John, Earl of Granville, 34
Cary, Virginia Randolph (Mrs. Wilson Jefferson), 242
Cary, Wilson Jefferson, 242
Cary, Wilson Miles, 48
Catholics, 28, 239
Cathrall, Dr. Isaac, 96
Catlett, John, 140
Catlett, Rebecca. *See* Conway, Rebecca (Mrs. Francis)
Causten, Anna Payne (Mrs. James), companion of DPM after JM's death, 259, 343-344, 347-349, 354-357, 359-361
Causten, Dr. James H., Jr., 344, 359-361
Causten, Mary Payne. *See* Kunkel, Mary Causten (Mrs. John)
caustic soda, medicinal use of, 397n11
Cedar Creek Monthly Meeting, Hanover Co., Va., 23, 26, 29-33, 40, 43, 53-54, 59-60, 65-67, 69
Cedar Creek Preparatory Meeting, 67
Cedar Creek School, 55
Central America, 215
Charlemagne (Charles I, King of the Franks), 134
Charles I (King of England), 44

D. P. Madison

Dolley's life

Montpelier Foundation, 362
Montpellier plantation, Orange Co., Va.
  "within a squirrel's jump of
    heaven," 189, 393n25
  appearance, 362
  description of, 181-187
  DPM re-interred in family
    cemetery at, 1858, 360
  DPM sells plantation and slaves,
    352-354
  DPM's illness prevents planned
    post-nuptial visit to, 127
  entertainment at, 187-191, 332-334
  gardens and French gardener at, 193
  house built c. 1760, 141, 181
  JM departs from to marry DPM,
    119, 123
  JM dies and is buried at, 1836, 339
  John Payne Todd plays at, 238
  location of, 136-137
  Madisons bring furniture from to
    use at The Seven Buildings home,
    321
  Madisons move to while waiting
    for home in The Seven Buildings to
    be prepared, 1815, 319
  Madisons retire to, 1817, 325
  Madisons spend summers at, 208
  Marion duPont Scott wills
    property to National Trust for
    Historic Preservation, 1983, 361
  name origins and variant spellings
    of, 189, 389n9
  restoration to Madison-era
    slaves at, 144-145
  Walnut Grove, slave village at, 144,
    238
Montpensier, Duc de, 157
Moore, John, 140
Moore, Mr., 96
Moore, Mrs., 96
Moore, Rebecca Catlett Conway (Mrs.
  John), 134, 140
Moore, Thomas, 217
Moore, William, 177
Moorman, C., 56
Moors, 276

Morris, Anthony, 78, 89, 133, 358
Morris, Kitty, 84
Morris, Nancy, 56
Morse, Samuel F. B., 351-352
Mosby's Tavern, 45
mosquitoes, associated with yellow
  fever epidemic, 96, 102
Mother Amy (a slave of James and
  Dolley Madison), 35
Mount Airy, Va., 317
Mount Pleasant plantation, Orange Co.,
  Va., 136-142, 181
Mount Vernon plantation, 115, 174,
  179, 267
Moylan, Stephen, 148
*Mrs. James Madison: The Incompa-
  rable Dolley* (Arnett), xviii
muff (fur), 399n44
Mulberry Street (Philadelphia), 71
Murray, Judith Sargent, 150-152

Nantucket Island, Mass., Quakers
  from, 32
Napoléon. *See* Bonaparte, Napoléon
Napoleonic Wars, 277
Nassau Hall of the College of New
  Jersey, 176
National Gazetteer, 128
National Intelligencer, Washington
  newspaper, 6-7, 39, 199, 306, 318
*National Portrait Gallery of Distin-
  guished Americans*, xviii, 40, 343
National Trust for Historic Preserva-
  tion, 361-362
Native Americans, 20, 22, 33, 63, 150,
  229
  fear of attacks by, 278
Navy Department and Navy Yard, 6,
  273
Ned (a slave of Josias Payne and John
  Payne, Sr.), 24
Negroes. *See* slaves.
Negro-foot, Hanover County, Va., 145
Negrofoot post office, Hanover
  County, Va., 145
Negrohead Run, Hanover County, Va.,
  145

88, 90, 95-98, 100-103, 106-107,
116-117, 119, 121-124, 128-129,
131, 133, 145, 148-151, 153, 155-
158, 161, 163, 166, 169, 173-176,
179, 189-190, 196, 202, 207, 209-
210, 212-213, 215, 221, 223-226,
229, 240-243, 245, 254, 261, 264-
265, 273, 301, 314, 328-329, 344
Philadelphia Yearly Meeting, 60
Philpot, Mrs., 377n12
Physick, Dr. Philip Syng, 241-242
Pichon, Alexandrine-Emilie Brongniart
(Mrs. Louis-André), 248-249
Pichon, Louis-André, 215, 219, 248
Pickering, Thomas, 166
Pickering, Timothy, 167
Pig Point, Md., 286, 290
Pinckney, Charles Cotesworth, 195,
251
Pine Street Meeting, Philadelphia, 23,
80, 84-86, 88-89, 128
Pinkerton Alley (Trenton, N.J.), 59
Pittsburgh, Pa., 273
Pleasanton, Stephen, 298
Pocahontas, 20, 377n6
Polk, James K., 222, 341, 342, 356
"Polly" (DPM's macaw)
evacuated from White House by
Jean Pierre Sioussat, 300
lived at Montpellier, 326
Pompey (a slave of Joseph Hawkins),
138
Port Conway, Va., 140
Portland, Me., 187
Port Royal, Va., 134
Portugal and the Portuguese, 160
Potomac River, 83, 196, 204, 285, 307-
309, 315, 325
Presbyterians, 94, 141
"Presidentress," term used to describe
the First Lady, 261, 325
President's Furniture Fund, 262
President's House. *See* White House
Preston, Sally, 269
Preston, William Campbell, 269
Prevost, Frederick, 274
Prince George's County, Md., 1

Princeton University. *See* College of
New Jersey
Protestant Episcopal Church in
Virginia, 128, 356
Protestants, 161, 239
Proud, Robert, Quaker school for boys,
85
Prusia, Caty, 99
Public Friends. *See* Quakers
Publius (pen name for John Jay,
Alexander Hamilton, and JM,
authors of *The Federalist Papers*),
82
Puck magazine, 267
Puritans, 27, 49, 63
Pyne, Rev. Smith, 37, 356

Quadrille, a dance, 154
"Quaker shirt" (straitjacket), 47
Quakers (The Religious Society of
Friends), 3, 8, 15, 17, 19-24, 26
Book of Discipline, 55
certificates of good standing, 32
duties of the recorder of the
meeting, 35, 36-40
Inner Light of, 26, 50-51, 59, 27, 28
marriage rules, 29
N.C. Quarterly Meeting of, 31-33
Northern District Monthly
Meeting, Pa., 69-71, 73, 75, 77-81,
83-90, 94-96, 101, 107, 110,112,
116, 120-122, 125-129, 131-133,
141, 148, 150-151, 153-155, 170-
171, 174, 190, 202, 209, 242, 254,
258, 339, 356, 363
Philadelphia Yearly Meeting of, 60
reasons for disownment, 29-30
views on the American Revolution
and military service, 60-65, 68-69,
views on mental illness, 47, 49
views on slavery, 50, 63-64, 190
views on tavern-keeping, 56, 58-59
Queens of American Society, The (Ellet),
63
Quincy, Mass., 211

Ralph or Raph (a Madison slave), 144

D. P. Madison

Yrujo y Tácon), 168
Singleton, Angelica. *See* Van Buren,
    Angelica Singleton (Mrs. Abraham)
Singleton, Rebecca Coles (Mrs.
    Richard), 23
Singleton, Richard, 23
Sioussat, Jean Pierre ("French John"),
    12, 262, 295-297, 299-302, 319,
    326, 354
"Six Buildings, The" (Washington),
    207-208
Skinner, John S., 283, 285, 287
Slaney River, County Wexford, Ireland,
    21
slaves
    Ambrose Madison murdered by,
        137
    at Scotchtown plantation, 44-46
    cost of emancipation to John
        Payne, 69
    emancipation legalized in Virginia,
        68
    extreme punishment of, 144-145
    in Washington, 4
    JM leaves his slaves to DPM in
        will, 355
    JM's view on holding slaves, 336-
        337
    limited rights of, 150
    managed by DPM at
        Montpellier,189
    of JM Sr., 139, 142-144
    of JM's ancestors, 20
    of Payne family, 35
    owned and manumitted by John
        Payne, 64-66
    Paul Jennings, valet of JM,12
    punishment of, 18
    Quakers and manumission of, 63-65
    Quakers disown members for
        holding, 29
    Quakers support abolition of, 26
    whipped or executed,138
Smith, Harry, 304
Smith, James, 11
Smith, Margaret Bayard, (Mrs. Samuel
    Harrison), xvi, xviii, 36, 39-40, 186,
199, 201, 209, 217, 225, 254, 256,
    259, 270, 313
Smith, Samuel Harrison, 6, 39, 199,
    256, 270, 277, 318
Smith, Miss, 167
Society for the Propagation of the
    Gospel in Foreign Parts, 28
Somerset plantation, Orange Co., Va.,
    191
South Carolina, 28, 200, 245
Smith, Samuel Stanhope, 176
South River Meeting, Campbell Co.,
    Va., 53
South River, Va., 53,
Spain and the Spaniards, 160, 165, 168,
    200, 213, 215, 234, 245
Sparks, Jared, 346
Spotswood, Alexander, 21, 44, 377n11
Spruce Street (Philadelphia), 148
spyglass (telescope), 1, 2
Staffordshire ware (DPM's table
    service pattern), 261
Stanley, John, 59
Stanley, Thomas, 59
Stevenson, Andrew, 319
Stevenson, Sally A., 22, 335
Stevenson, Sally Coles (Mrs. Andrew),
    319
St. John's Protestant Episcopal Church
    (Washington), 37, 357
St. Louis, Mo., 227
St. Mary's College, 239
Stoddert's Bridge, Md., 291
St. Petersburg, Russia, 327, 344
Stuart, Gilbert, 160, 231-232, 266, 295,
    298
Stull, Capt. John J., 289
Sukey (a slave owned by JM), 295,
    299, 338
summer fever. *See* Yellow fever
Suter, Mrs. Barbara, 303
Syme, John, 22
Syme, Sarah Winston (Mrs. John). *See*
    Henry, Sarah Winston Syme (Mrs.
    John)

Talleyrand-Perigord, Charles Maurice

D. P. Madison